The Science of the Mind

The Science of the Mind

Owen Flanagan

second edition, revised and expanded

A Bradford Book
The MIT Press
Cambridge, Massachusetts
London, England

First MIT Press edition, 1984

Third printing, 1993

Printed and bound in the United States of America.

Library of Congress Cataloging-in-Publication Data

Flanagan, Owen J.
   The science of the mind/Owen Flanagan.—2nd ed., rev. and expanded.
     p.   cm.
   "A Bradford book."
   Includes bibliographical references and indexes.
   ISBN 0-262-06137-6 (hard).—ISBN 0-262-56056-9 (pbk.)
   1. Psychology—Philosophy—History. 2. Philosophy of mind—History. I. Title.
BF38.F58   1991
150′.1—dc20   90-42948
                                                     CIP

For Joyce, Ben, and Kate

Contents

Acknowledgments

I began writing this book during the academic year 1980–1981 while I was on leave from Wellesley College and a Visiting Scholar at Harvard University. Many people have helped me get from the first draft to the book you now have before you.

Roger Brown, Patricia Kitcher, Richard Lerner, John Macnamara, and James Moor read the earliest draft and gave valuable guidance.

David Pillemer, Jerry Samet, Kathryn Tolbert, and Ken Winkler gave sage advice on parts of later drafts.

Howard Gardner, Michel Grimaud, Robert Simon, Barbara Von Eckardt, Sheldon White, and Jeremy Wolfe read the next to penultimate version and made many helpful suggestions.

Jonathan Adler and Joyce Walworth provided constant support and thoughtful criticism. The two of them performed every service from helping me get my arguments in shape to reuniting split infinitives. I owe them my deepest thanks.

Karen Olson and Susan Sawyer helped with the bibliography, and Harry and Betty Stanton, my editors, helped make what was already an intellectually and personally exciting process even more so.

In addition to my gratitude to Wellesley College for supporting the leave during which the book was first conceived and to Harvard University for housing me during that year, I owe thanks to many colleagues at the Center for Advanced Study in the Behavioral Sciences at Stanford University, where I spent the summer of 1979 working out several of the ideas on the connection between moral philosophy and moral psychology which appear in this book. Thanks also to many colleagues who participated in Jerry Fodor's Institute on "Psychology and the Philosophy of Mind" at the University of Washington in Seattle during the summer of 1981 for helping shape my thinking on some of the philosophical issues in cognitive psychology and artificial intelligence. I am grateful to the Council for Philosophical Studies, the National Endowment for the Humanities, and the Mellon Foundation for various research grants which helped to support this project. Last but not least, thanks to my good friend and constant companion Wellesley's DEC-SYSTEM-20 for many thousands of conversations in EMACS, the language we both understand.

Wellesley, Massachusetts
July 1983

Preface to the Second Edition

I was very gratified by the reception to the first edition of *The Science of the Mind*. By the time of the fifth printing, it became clear that a second edition should be produced to keep readers abreast of some recent developments in mind science. The original discussion of AI was outdated because of new work in connectionism and parallel distributed processing. Chapter 6 has been substantially revised to reflect these exciting new developments, and minor revisions have been made in all the other chapters. The other major change involves the addition of the new chapter "Consciousness." This chapter reflects my most recent thinking about this the hardest problem in the science of the mind. I taught a seminar on consciousness in the spring of 1989 and had as visitors Dan Dennett, Mike Gazzaniga, Pat Kitcher, Carolyn Ristau, Georges Rey, David Rosenthal, and Bob Van Gulick. I am grateful to them for inspiring me to give the problem of consciousness a stab. Their ideas are reflected in the new chapter at many points. I am also grateful to the Sloan Foundation for making these visits possible. Two colleagues from Wellesley's psychology department and fellow members of our cognitive science group, Margery Lucas and Larry Rosenblum (now at the University of California at Riverside), and my colleague from philosophy, Ken Winkler, also participated in the seminar. I thank them and the wonderful group of students who shared in the excitement. This second edition is dedicated to the memory of my beloved brother Peter. He enriched my life and the lives of our entire family beyond description.

Wellesley, Massachusetts
May 1990

Introduction

Psychology, according to the standard fable, severed its connection with philosophy in 1879 and became a science. Armchair speculation was abandoned in favor of a rigorous empirical approach to the study of mind. Metaphysics and epistemology thus remained the harmless amusements of fundamentally unrealistic minds, while psychologists got on with studying the real thing.

Fortunately, the separation has not lasted. Thanks in part to the recent surge of interest in the cognitive sciences, as well as to a trend toward a more naturalistic style of philosophy, we are seeing the re-emergence of an exciting and fruitful alliance among philosophers, psychologists, and mind scientists generally. This book is intended as a contribution to this renewed alliance. In it I try to sort out the various ways in which philosophical assumptions appear in, affect, afflict, and illuminate the science of mind. Conversely, I examine the implications the science of mind has for traditional philosophical concerns.

Some of the philosophical issues I discuss have received their most vivid formulations and have taken their most surprising turns within psychological theories, such as the problem of self-knowledge in psychoanalysis and the problem of the unity of consciousness in cognitive psychology. Other traditional philosophical questions have been declared solved or dissolved by psychological theories, such as the problem of free will in behaviorism, the question of the incorrigibility of introspection in cognitive psychology, and the mind-body problem in artificial intelligence. My overall goal is to bring out the way philosophical concerns figure within psychology and to indicate the contribution psychology makes to the solutions of some reputedly unsolvable philosophical conundrums.

I think of science, especially the human sciences, as having a narrative structure. I mean this in two senses. First, individual theories of mind are often fruitfully read as stories about what the mind is or would be like if certain assumptions about it proved to be true. Second, the histories of psychology and philosophy of mind, taken together, comprise a series of chapters among which there is intelligible interplay between earlier and later chapters. Furthermore, the narrative, taken as a whole or in terms of its major episodes, involves all sorts of drama. There are the tragic theoretical flaws originating in unarticulated but seemingly noble philosophical assumptions; there are moments when theoretical single-mindedness born of shallow but honest commitment to a vision pays great dividends; there are the "reinventions of the wheel" born of forgetfulness, or commission of Santayana's sin of failing to attend to history; and there are the moments of unquestionably great insight by unquestionably great thinkers.

My views on the narrative structure of science and my abiding conviction that there is much to be learned from great thinkers, even if their theories are now considered wrong or outdated, help explain the structure of this book. I examine critically the ways in which important philosophical issues arise within several distinct theoretical traditions. I find it most useful to organize discussion around the views of some major figure, and have done so in all but three cases. Within the fields of cognitive science and Artificial Intelligence there are no agreed-upon single representatives. And no one has emerged to provide "the one true theory" of consciousness. Overall, the cast of characters includes René Descartes, William James, Sigmund Freud, B. F. Skinner, Jean Piaget, Lawrence Kohlberg, a mixed lot of philosophers of mind, cognitive psychologists and members of the artificial intelligentsia, and one evolutionary biologist, E. O. Wilson.

I will have succeeded by my own lights if I provide an account of the science of the mind that indicates just how philosophically rich its theories are and an account of the philosophy of mind that locates many of its main problems and concerns in the actual theorizing of mind scientists. For the reader, going through the book sequentially is the best strategy, but I have tried to make each chapter stand more or less on its own so that the book can be read in any order without a major loss to the overall project. In order to assist the uninitiated, I have listed several useful introductions to the material under discussion at the foot of the first page of each chapter, and I have included a list of suggested readings at the end of each chapter.

The Science of the Mind

Chapter 1

Minds and Bodies: René Descartes and the Possibility of a Science of the Mind

I begin with René Descartes, the father of modern philosophy, because Descartes raised, directly or indirectly, virtually all the significant issues related to the foundations of the science of the mind. His views remain—for friend and foe alike—the single most influential framework within which discussions of the philosophical assumptions and implications of psychology take place.

In 1663, thirteen years after his death, all of Descartes' works were put on the Index of the Roman Catholic Church, even though his writings contained two proofs for the existence of God as well as arguments for the incorporeality and immortality of the human soul. Descartes was a threat because he took the science of his day so seriously that he considered extending Galileo's mechanical conception of the physical universe to human behavior. Descartes' conclusion that the program of a *mechanics of the mind* could not in principle succeed was immaterial to the Church. Descartes had dared to think the unthinkable. He had taken the principles from his writings on meteors, optics, mathematics, and mechanics and considered their applicability to human phenomena. Descartes did this by developing the concept of the *reflex*, a unit of mechanical, predictable, deterministic action, and by examining the potential explanatory power of that concept.

Descartes' Philosophy of the Body: The Reflex Hypothesis

Descartes had a model close at hand that suggested the potential explanatory power of the concept of the reflex. The French Royal Gardens, a veritable seventeenth-century Disneyland, contained a small-scale society of hydraulically controlled robots, constructed so that once activated by an invisible water flow they moved, made sounds, and even played musical instruments.

The best introduction to Descartes' philosophy of mind is his *Discourse on Method*, Parts IV and V (1637), and his *Meditations*, I, II, VI (1641).

> You may have seen in the grottoes and fountains which are in our royal gardens that the simple force with which water moves in issuing from its source is sufficient to put into motion various machines and even to set various instruments playing or to make them pronounce words according to the varied disposition of the tubes which convey the water.

The water that flowed from under the ground into the robots' bodies was set in motion by the pressure visitors exerted on tiles as they walked along the garden paths.

> For in entering [strangers] necessarily tread on certain tiles or plates, which are so disposed that if they approach a bathing Diana, they cause her to hide in the rosebushes, and if they try to follow her, they cause Neptune to come forward to meet them threatening them with his trident.[1]

The robots in the Royal Gardens had three important characteristics: their physical structure was completely determined by their construction; their physical movements were completely determined by two variables, the tiles pressed and their physical structure; and they behaved like humans—they spoke, played musical instruments, and acted modestly and jealously.

Descartes was especially impressed by the fact that the automata in the Royal Gardens acted like humans but were mere machines. They appeared to be autonomous and self-moving. Their behavior seemed as if it was governed by rational motive and conscious choice. But this was not the case. The robots were moved by utterly inert and thoughtless external forces—forces that were invisible unless one looked beneath the surface, unless one literally turned over a few stones.

Descartes believed that there was a precise material analogy between the physical structure of the robots in the Royal Gardens and the internal physical structure of the human body. The tubes in the robots' bodies for channeling the water correspond to nerves in the human body. The springs and motors for controlling the movements of the robots' limbs correspond to muscles and tendons. The water carrying "information" to and fro corresponds to vaporous particles of blood, the so-called "animal spirits."

Descartes was also convinced that certain human responses, for example, knee jerks, pupil contractions, and the like, are just like the responses of the robots in the Royal Gardens. The application of an external stimulus causes stimulation of the nerve fibers, which causes the threads in the nerve marrow to be pulled. This pull causes an orifice in the brain to be opened.[2] This results in the vaporous spirits being released from the orifice and flowing into nerves that lead to the muscles and tendons, eventually causing, by inflation, the muscles and tendons to move. The entire episode consists of a totally mechanical and predictable information transfer from a stimulus that activates sensory receptors, to conductor nerves, to the brain, to effector nerves, and culminates in a completely determined response. The nature of the response, whether it is a knee jerk or a pupil contraction, for example, depends solely on the nature of the stimulus and the specific wiring diagram of the activated nerve fibers.

Except for the "animal spirits," which have been replaced by electrochemical processes, Descartes' conception of the mechanics of reflex action is remarkably close to the contemporary one. Once his analogy between the inorganic automata and the organic human body was drawn, the concept of the reflex arc was available. A *reflex arc* is a three-term causal sequence beginning with the application of an external stimulus, which gives rise to activity in the nervous system and terminates in a response. Theoretically, the terminal response can be internal or external—emotional, cognitive, or motor. Reflex arc routes are innate; they are wired into the physiology of the organism. Whether a specific reflex arc route is activated depends, however, on what happens in the external world. Thus we can say for a Cartesian automaton—the kind found in the French Royal Gardens—that the complete system of wired-in reflex arc routes exhausts its behavioral potential. What a particular automaton eventually does, how it in fact behaves, is the inevitable result of the interaction between the environment and the wired-in arcs. Such a system is deterministic in the sense that, barring mechanical failure, there is one and only one response for each stimulus. Or to put it another way: given any stimulus, it is impossible for the system to do other than it in fact does.

The attractiveness of the reflex arc model comes from the fact that there does not seem to be any theoretical limit to the behavioral potential of a reflex arc system. Notice, for example, that the Cartesian automata are already wired to play music. Suppose someone comes along and says, "OK, the robot can play Stravinsky but it can't play Mozart." The engineer's problem would then be to wire in all the necessary reflex arc routes so that the automata would have the potential to play Mozart—no simple task, but theoretically possible. Now suppose that an engineer were able to come up with just the right set of reflex arc routes to meet each objection of the form "but the robot can't do *x*." This would mean that it is not impossible (ignore for now the possibility that there might have to be an infinite number of routes) to construct a robot which can do everything a human can do.[3] And if it is logically possible to construct such automata, then it is also logically possible that we humans are already just such automata—that is, that we humans are just exotically complicated systems of reflex arc routes. And if we are merely exotic systems of reflex arc routes, then our behavior is the joint production of external stimuli and our reflex wiring—no more and no less. It was this possibility that tempted Descartes' mechanical imagination without ever fully capturing it.

Let us refer to any system whose behavior is, in principle, completely explainable in terms of reflex arcs (plus, of course, activating stimuli) as a mechanical system. And let us define *reflex mechanism* as any thesis of the form: a complete explanation in terms of reflex arcs exists for some system S. Thus reflex mechanism is true for the automata in the Royal Gardens. The question is, Is reflex mechanism true for humans?

Although Descartes was charmed enough with the reflex arc model to credit it with providing both an accurate description of the internal structure of the human body, of *res extensa*, and an adequate framework for explaining all animal behavior, his considered answer to this question was an unequivocal no.

Descartes' problems with the Church came from the fact that although he seriously underestimated the explanatory power of the concept of the reflex from the perspective of later thinkers like Ivan P. Pavlov and John B. Watson (for example, Descartes had no idea that there were learned, that is, conditioned reflexes that might be incorporated into some expanded conception of mechanism), he seriously over-estimated its power from the perspective of those institutions that saw all human action as lying outside of natural law and viewed experimental science as a threat to the epistemology of authority. It is important to remember that Galileo Galilei, a contemporary of Descartes, was called before the Papal Inquisition in Rome two different times in the first half of the seventeenth century. He was eventually silenced and placed under house arrest for life for bringing certain new mechanical concepts and experimental data to bear in his argument against the geocentric account of planetary motion. Galileo himself never even hinted, as Descartes did (for example, in *Treatise on Man* and *Passions of the Soul*), that mechanical concepts might have some applicability to the understanding of human nature.

From a modern perspective, however, it is hard to understand why the Church got so upset. Although Descartes insisted that a mechanical body was necessary for any action to take place, he rejected reflex mechanism for humans, that is, he denied that human action can be exhaustively analyzed in terms of reflex arcs. Most human action, he believed, is initiated at, so to speak, the center of the arcs—by the mind, by *res cogitans*. Descartes insisted that although all human behavior requires a body for its execution, not all behavior is initiated by other physical bodies. Some is initiated by an incorporeal mind.

Descartes' eventual rejection of reflex mechanism was based, in part, on his acknowledgment of the philosophical force of certain everyday intuitions. These intuitions surface in the following *Gedanken* experiment. Consider, for example, a knee jerk. It seemed obvious to Descartes that one's knee could jerk for either of two entirely different reasons. It could be made to jerk because an appropriate external stimulus is applied, or it could jerk because one decides to make it jerk. The first is a paradigm case of an involuntary action, the second is a paradigm case of a voluntary action. What the two entirely different kinds of events have in common is that they both require "animal spirits" to be released from the pineal gland in the brain and enter the knee. In this way both voluntary and involuntary actions require a body. What distinguishes the two events, however, is that the first admits of a mechanical, physicalistic, scientific explanation in terms of the reflex arc, while the second cannot be scientifically explained at all. The first event can be explained in terms of a chain, potentially infinite, of prior mechanical causes; the second event can only be explained in terms of a two-link causal chain, a chain whose first link is an entity of an utterly unique metaphysical kind, a kind not amenable to scientific scrutiny.

The reason Descartes believed that the first event can be mechanically explained and the second cannot deserves elaboration. A conceptual tool from recent philosophy of science will be helpful here. According to many contemporary philosophers, a typical causal explanation in science is an account where the event-to-be-explained, the *explanandum*, is shown to be a consequence of certain states of affairs described jointly by a general law about nature and a statement or set of statements depicting whatever relevant circumstances applied at the time the event-to-be-explained occurred. These latter statements describe "initial conditions" and, in conjunction with the statements describing general laws, constitute the *explanans* for the *explanandum*. Thus, for example, you have explained why the water is boiling (*explanandum*) when you tell me that all water boils at 100 degrees centigrade and that this water has a temperature of 100 degrees centigrade (*explanans*). This model of scientific explanation is called the *covering-law model*. Consider the following rough covering-law analyses of the two knee-jerk episodes described earlier:

1.

a. *Law*: If a knee is hit in the right spot with an external stimulus, it will jerk.

    b.   *Initial Condition*: This knee was hit by an external stimulus in the right spot.

    c.   *Explanandum*: This knee jerked (and a and b are the reason):

2.

    a.   *Law*: If a person decides to make his knee jerk, it will jerk.

    b.   *Initial Condition*: This person decided to make his knee jerk.

    c.   *Explanandum*: This knee jerked (and a and b are the reason).

Both 1 and 2 provide accounts of their respective *explanandum* by linking a statement describing a general law of nature with a statement describing some initial condition. Thus at the first level of analysis we can provide covering-law accounts for both reflexive and "willful" knee jerks.

One way of formulating Descartes' overall conjecture is as follows: at the first level of analysis one will indeed be able to generate a covering-law account for both involuntary and voluntary behavior. But if one tries to give a further and deeper account of one's first-order account—say, a second- or third-order account—if, that is, one tries to layer covering-law accounts (by, for example, taking the *explanans* from 1 or 2 and turning it into an *explanandum*), one will succeed in generating deeper causal accounts for involuntary actions, potentially ad infinitum: but one will fail utterly to produce deeper accounts for voluntary behavior.

For example, play the devil's advocate or, if you prefer, a Socratic gadfly, with any proponent of analyses such as 1 and 2. In particular, ask the proponent of these explanations for further information about the laws and initial conditions themselves. What you will notice after a while—at least this is the Cartesian bet—is that when you ask questions about the laws and initial conditions in 1, for example, Why do humans come wired with a knee-jerk reflex? What is the exact length of the reflex arc route? How come a stimulus of such and such strength produced a knee-jerk response of such and such strength? What caused the stimulus to strike with that force? you will get lots of detailed information from the biological and mechanical sciences. For example, you will hear: At the time we evolved, organisms with a knee-jerk reflex had greater genetic fitness than their counterparts who lacked the reflex and that's why almost all living humans have the reflex. The reflex route is 6.3 meters long. The intensity of the response is proportional to the intensity of the stimulus. The force of the stimulus is the product of its mass times its acceleration. And so on and so forth. You will be led, in effect, to more and more specific initial conditions and deeper and deeper covering laws.

When you ask for further information about the law and initial conditions cited in 2, however, you will be led to dead ends and explanatory circles. For example, you inquire Why do people do the things they decide to do? or Why did this person decide to make his knee jerk? or What is a decision made of? You will get answers like That is the nature of people. He just decided to do it. He decided to because he wanted to. (Why did he want to? Because he felt like it.) Decisions aren't made of anything. And so on. There will simply not be any deeper covering laws, any more informative things to be said about deciding-to-make-one's-knee-jerk than those things we have already said in 2—that, in effect, someone just decided to make his knee jerk.

When we ask questions about the knee-jerk reflex, we are led deeper and deeper into a world of utterly physical entities that obey utterly mechanical laws. When we ask questions about a "willful" knee jerk, however, we are led to some different kind of thing, some different kind of cause. What kind of cause? We are led, according to Descartes, to an agent that circumvents the hegemony of the mechanical-deterministic nexus by virtue of its immateriality and freedom. We are led to an agent whose behavior is governed by no other law than that which the agent himself creates. Descartes is explicit on this point. He says,

> But the will is so free in its nature, that it can never be constrained. . . . And the whole action of the soul consists in this, that solely because it desires something, it causes a little gland to which it is closely united to move in a way requisite to produce the effect which relates to this desire.[4]

On Descartes' view the mind performs some form of psychokinesis every time a voluntary action occurs. It deploys its immaterial powers to move the material body. The mind itself, however, is self-moved.

Descartes held not only that reflexes were involuntary, but in *Passions of the Soul* he tries to analyze all emotional states—from fear to love to remorse—as the passive physical outcomes of the way various animal spirits (the ancestors of hormones and neurotransmitters?) are induced to flow by external events.

Nonetheless, while Descartes argued that our physical passions create powerful dispositions to behave one way rather than another, for example, with lust rather than indifference, he insisted that our incorporeal soul can choose for or against the passions. Descartes concludes *Passions of the Soul* with the reminder that there is a simple way to avoid "suffering any inconvenience from the passions," namely, simply *will* not to be in a state receptive to the arousal of the disruptive passion. He says "our good and our harm depend mainly on the interior emotions which are only excited *in the soul by the soul itself*, in which respect they differ from its passions, which always depend on some movement of the [animal] spirits."[5]

This view of the mind-body relation explains why the covering laws used to make sense of voluntary behavior cannot be rooted more deeply in mechanical webs: what govern human actions are not, strictly speaking, laws of nature at all—human action is the straightforward result of autonomous agency, we are law unto ourselves. This, in turn, explains why accounts of voluntary action tend to locate the complete source of the action only one step back, in the agent himself, and it explains why such explanations resist further reductive analysis. Thus, although we can give explanations, even covering-law explanations, of voluntary human behavior, we should not also be understood to be putting forward scientific explanations, if by that we mean explanations in terms of natural law.

It is important to pause here and notice the two distinct philosophical moves Descartes makes. First, there is the rejection of reflex mechanism because of its incompatibility with actions like deciding-to-make-one's-knee-jerk—actions in which the motor response is caused by an internal volition and not by the application of an external stimulus to some sensory receptor as required by the reflex arc analysis. Second, there is the proposal that the essential element in actions like deciding-to-make-one's-knee-jerk is an incorporeal and free mind. The two moves are logically separable and making the first move does not automatically require making the second.

Part of the rationale for holding a position such as reflex mechanism comes from the fact that it coheres nicely with a commitment to metaphysical materialism, the thesis that everything there is, is material, and that everything that happens is the result of interactions between material things.[6] Reflex mechanism, however, is just one of an indefinite number of ways a materialist can give his abstract metaphysical commitment a semitangible, quasi-scientific form. One can, in fact, reject reflex mechanism and still be a card-carrying materialist. For example, one can argue, as many contemporary cognitive psychologists in fact do, that reflex mechanism is not, as it stands, rich enough to account for human behavior. The mechanical analysis of human action will need all sorts of complicated feedback loops, memory cores, and information processors to do the job. Then one tries to show that such an enriched conception of mechanism, call it information-processing mechanism, can handle cases like deciding-to-make-one's-knee-jerk without introducing any immaterial entities or forces. Or, one can argue, if one is a social learning theorist, that events like deciding-to-make-one's-knee-jerk are physical, presumably neural, events whose causes lie jointly in the nervous system and in the subtle, but utterly physical, conditioning mechanisms operating in the social environment. Both information-processing mechanism and social-learning mechanism are research programs committed to the proposition that so-called voluntary behavior will in fact yield to scientific analysis. In this way the two theories point up the fact that the *Gedanken* experiments we went through earlier are not by themselves sufficient to prove that all forms of mechanism are false, only that reflex mechanism is false. The moral is this: one is not logically required to embrace the view that our minds are incorporeal and free just because one finds some particular form of mechanism wanting, unless one has independent reason to think that materialism in general is false.

Descartes claimed to have precisely such independent reason for believing materialism, in any form, is false. This explains why he did not flinch as he made the logical leap from rejecting reflex mechanism to embracing a full-blown dualism. Descartes offered a set of arguments which, he believed, decisively and for all time establish that body and mind are entirely different kinds of things, the one material, the other immaterial, the one determined, the other free. To the degree that these arguments are effective they carry considerably more philosophical weight than our *Gedanken* experiments. They imply that every conceivable variety of materialism is false and that materialistic research programs such as information-processing mechanism and social-learning mechanism are destined to fail. I now turn to these arguments for mind-body dualism.

Descartes' Philosophy of Mind: Three Arguments for Dualism

Descartes' thesis that mind and body, *res cogitans* and *res extensa*, are completely different kinds of things rests on an intuition, which Descartes claims is universal, that our minds are somehow essential to our identity and to our existence in a way in which our bodies are not. Descartes gets to this deep-seated intuition by way of the primal universal intuition, *cogito ergo sum*, the intuition that while everything else can, in principle, be doubted, it is impossible for any person to doubt that he or she exists as a thinking thing. What is known first and best, according to Descartes, is that we exist as some sort of essentially mental entity.

In his *Meditations*, Descartes gets to this primal universal intuition by methodically doubting everything that he can find some logically possible grounds for doubting. Methodic doubt is designed to uncover what, if anything, is indubitable; it is designed, paradoxically, to save us from real doubt, from real and interminable skepticism.

Motivated by the ordinary confusions afforded by perceptual mistakes ("Hi, Joyce. Oh! Sorry, Amelie, I thought you were Joyce.") and dream states ("Was I really in China last night?"), Descartes discovers that it is logically possible that all ordinary commonsensical beliefs about the world, as well as all scientific propositions based on sense perception, might be completely false. If I can mistake Amelie for Joyce once, then I can mistake Amelie for Joyce all the time, and if I can do that then I just might be wrong about who my wife is. If it is logically possible that I have been wrong about such a basic thing as that, then it is also possible that I have the sun and the moon and protons and electrons all mixed up too. And if I can wonder whether I was in China last night, then it is possible that I was not asleep in this bed for the last eight hours, and if that is possible and I was in China, then all the theories about how long it takes to get from Massachusetts to China are false, if, that is, I was in Massachusetts in the first place, and so on and so forth. In this way common sense and science yield to Descartes' methodic doubt.

The mathematical sciences can also be thrown into radical doubt. Although mathematics is not perhaps based on sense perception, and although our dreams do not normally raise doubts about mathematics in the way they do about accepted truths of the physical and human sciences, it is logically possible that there is a grand deceiver—an Evil Genius—who causes everyone to feel certain that $2 + 2 = 4$ when in reality $2 + 2 = 17$. "Ah," you say, "but mathematics can't really be doubted. The truths of mathematics, after all, indirectly enter into the explanation of why the Golden Gate Bridge does not fall into San Francisco Bay, and why the bank and I agree about my checking-account balance, and how it was possible for Neil Armstrong to walk on the moon." To which you merely need to be reminded: neither evidence from common sense nor applied science can be used to protect mathematics from methodic doubt, because common sense and science have themselves already yielded to methodic doubt. There just might not really be a Golden Gate Bridge, or a Neil Armstrong, or a checking account.

It is even possible, Descartes discovers, to doubt that one has a body. The belief that one has a body is after all based on sense perceptions. We infer that we have a body. How do you know you have an aching knee? you feel it; how do you know you have a handsome face? you see it; how do you know you have a mole in the small of your back? you touch it; how do you know you have a deep voice? you hear it.[7] Since our inferences from sense perceptions are sometimes wrong, it is logically possible that they are always wrong, and that therefore we only seem to have a body.

As Descartes presses his doubt he eventually reaches a point at which his philosophical skepticism dissolves. Whereas he (remember the argument is supposed to apply to you as well) can doubt the claims of all the natural and social sciences, of mathematics, of theology, of common sense, and even the claim that he has a body, he cannot doubt that he exists as the kind of thing which is capable of engaging in cognitive processes. He cannot possibly doubt that he exists as a thinking thing. In the very process of wondering about his existence, in the very process of doubting all these other things, he affirms that he exists as a thinking thing. Descartes terminates his doubt when he says,

> But what then am I? A thing which thinks. What is a thing which thinks? It is a thing which doubts, understands, [conceives], affirms, denies, wills, refuses, which also imagines and feels.[8]

From the perspective of psychology and the philosophy of mind two important morals can be drawn from the process of methodic doubt: (1) that the very first thing known, and the thing most certainly known is that we are thinking things,[9] and (2) that without knowing anything whatsoever about the nature of physical things, including whether we even have a body, we are able to make an inventory of the functions of a thinking being. It is a being which doubts, understands, affirms, denies, wills, refuses, imagines, and feels.

One can easily see how these two consequences of Descartes' philosophy might lead from the view that because we can know about the mind without knowing anything about the body, our analyses of mental functioning will not be particularly illuminated or enhanced by referring to physical events, and therefore, no fruitful analyses of mental phenomena in physical, mechanical, or scientific terms exist. Descartes promotes precisely such a conclusion by way of his arguments for a mind-body dualism. Bodily, physical phenomena will be explained in accordance with mechanical principles, that is, in terms of reflex arcs. Mental, psychological phenomena will, strictly speaking, not be scientifically explained at all. This is because mental phenomena do not, strictly speaking, lie in causal networks. They initiate causal networks ex nihilo.

Descartes had three arguments which were meant to establish the metaphysical distinction between mind and body. In examining these arguments it is important to remember just what a strong conclusion Descartes intended to establish. He was trying to show not merely that a part of a person has the capacity for thinking, but that a person is actually made up of two utterly distinct substances: one substance, *res extensa*, consists of the physical reflex machinery, the second substance, *res cogitans*, consists of the nonphysical cognitive machinery.

The first argument for mind-body dualism follows directly from the idea that in the very process of methodically doubting everything which it is possible to doubt one affirms that one is, if nothing else, a thinking thing. The argument receives its most explicit formulation in Part IV of the *Discourse on Method* and can be put as follows:

> (1) I cannot possibly doubt that I exist as a thinking thing. (This was established as we tried to doubt our existence and found ourselves, therefore, affirming it.)
>
> (2) I can doubt, however, that I have a body, and thus that I exist as a physical thing.
>
> (3) Therefore, thinking is essential to what I am. My body is not. Furthermore, I know my mind more easily than I know my body. "From this I knew that I was a substance the whole essence or nature of which is to think, and that for its existence there is no need of any place, nor does it depend on any material thing; so that this 'me,' that is to say, the soul by which I am what I am, is entirely distinct from body, and is even more easy to know than is the latter; and even if body were not, the soul would not cease to be what it is."[10]

The argument is very seductive, in part, because the process of methodic doubt we just went through lends an air of indubitability to both premises—to the idea that our existence as thinkers is indubitable, while our physical existence is dubitable. Nonetheless, the conclusion does not follow from the premises unless we make a highly questionable assumption.[11] Call this assumption *Alpha*.

> *Alpha*: when an entity is known for certain to have property x, but not known for certain to have property y, then x is essential to the entity, and y is not.

If we make *Alpha* an explicit premise in the argument, then the conclusion that mentality is an essential and necessary property of humanity, while physicality is a contingent, accidental, unnecessary property of humanity does in fact follow.

However, *Alpha* is much too strong. Consider the case of a novice geometry student who knows beyond the shadow of a doubt that the trilateral figure drawn on the page, or defined by three pairs of Cartesian coordinates, is a triangle, but who sees no warrant whatsoever for the claim that the internal angles of the very same trilateral figure are equivalent to two right angles. Statements describing the student's epistemic situation in conjunction with *Alpha* permit, indeed require, the conclusion that triangularity is an essential property of the trilateral figure, while the property of having internal angles equivalent to two right angles is not essential. But this we know is false. Triangles necessarily have internal angles equivalent to 180 degrees.

Or consider your own epistemic situation right now as you read these very words on this page. Although you were not thinking about it, you probably harbor no doubt whatsoever that the entity before you is a rectangular piece of paper, a perfectly ordinary, everyday, rectangular piece of paper. But it is, I assume, easy for you to doubt that this piece of paper has molecular structure. (If you have trouble doubting that, you are just living proof of Bohr's thesis that "today's common sense is yesterday's science.") However, were you to conclude that rectangularity is an essential property of this page, while molecular structure is not, you would simply be wrong. *Alpha*, however, permits just this conclusion.

A defender of Cartesianism might try the following defense at this point. Indeed, *Alpha* is much too strong an assumption. Fortunately we do not need to assume it. We only need a much narrower assumption, one that isolates the unique and special epistemic relation a self has with itself, and with itself alone. Call this assumption *Beta*.

> *Beta*: when an agent knows for certain that *it* has property x, but does not know for certain that *it* has property y, then x is essential to the agent, and y is not.

The idea behind *Beta* is to restrict the applicability of any extra assumption required in the argument for dualism to cases where an agent or a self is reflexively assessing its own properties. In this way my counterexamples to *Alpha* which involve an agent assessing the properties of some external entity are defused.

However, *Beta* cannot save the argument. The only reason to allow *Beta* to take the place of *Alpha* would be if we had some very powerful reason to think that the kind of knowledge a self has *about itself* is privileged and incorrigible. But the idea that we have such special knowledge about ourselves is part of the conclusion of the very argument in question: "this 'me,' that is to say, the soul by which I am what I am, is entirely distinct from body, and is even more easy to know than is the latter." Therefore, on pain of circularity, it cannot be used to support the conclusion. *Beta*, in effect, is an unjustified assumption that is just as strong as required to generate the desired dualistic conclusion. In this way, the Cartesian begs the question—he tries to establish dualism by deploying a logic which makes dualism inevitable.

In a nutshell, the problem with the first argument for dualism is this: without an added assumption the argument fails to yield its conclusion; with either of two added assumptions the argument yields the desired conclusion, but one of these assumptions, *Alpha*, is false, and the other, *Beta*, is question-begging.

Descartes' second explicit argument for mind-body dualism occurs in the sixth of his Meditations.[12]

(1) If I conceive of two things and perceive with certainty that they are separate, different kinds of things, then they are separate, different kinds of things. If, for example, I see that one thing has property *A* and another thing has property *not A*, then I know that they are different kinds of things, because one and the same thing cannot have a property and its opposite.

(2) I perceive with certainty that I exist as a *thinking and unextended* thing.

(3) I perceive with (virtual) certainty that my body, or any body for that matter, is *unthinking and extended*.

(4) Therefore, mind and body are separate, different kinds of things. "This I (that is to say, my soul by which I am what I am), is entirely and absolutely distinct from my body, and can exist without it."

A technical philosophical distinction between *tokens* and *types* will be useful in discussing this argument (the token-type distinction will appear again and again throughout the book). A *type* or a *kind* can be defined, for now, as any class of things—physical objects, numbers, or whatever—organized in terms of some essential property shared by all members of the class. For example, the class of chairs is a type, defined (very roughly) as the class of artifacts that you can sit on. A *token* is an individual member of a type. Thus the chair you are now sitting on is a token of the type, chair. Tokens can differ dramatically in terms of their contingent properties, for example, an individual chair can have four legs or no legs, it can be brown or blue, short or tall, located in Tibet or in New Jersey, and so on. Tokens of a type, however, cannot differ in terms of their essential property(ies), that is, all individual chairs have to be the kind of thing you can sit on.

This relates to Descartes' second argument for dualism in the following way: Descartes wants to establish a *type-type dualism*. That is, he wants to establish that mind and body differ in some essential way. He wants to show that mind and body are different kinds of things, different in some ultimate metaphysical way.[13] The overall logic of Descartes' argument involves citing some token-token difference between his mind and his body (which is supposedly shared by your mind and your body) and claiming that the token-token difference is of the right sort to establish a type-type distinction. Thus in premises (2) and (3), Descartes claims that his mind possesses two essential properties which his body lacks, namely, thought and incorporeality. Indeed he claims that his body lacks these properties necessarily, since it possesses the exact opposite essential properties, thoughtlessness and corporeality. Insofar as there are two classical metaphysical types—"Spirit," the stuff of the gods, and "Matter," the stuff of granite and sand—whose respective essential properties are precisely these things, Descartes concludes that his mind and his body belong to two absolutely different metaphysical kinds.

This argument is supposed to be reproducible. Presumably, you and I and everyone else should be able to recapitulate the argument in our own case, and verify that the particular person we happen to be consists of two metaphysically distinct parts—a cognitive and immaterial part and a noncognitive and material part. This is where the argument runs into trouble. First, all materialists will deny premises (2) and (3) outright. They will deny knowing that their own body is unthinking; and they will deny that they possess any nonphysical parts. They will insist that individual persons are all tokens of the same type, the one and only type, that is, matter. Materialists will, in fact, deny that it is possible to have the sorts of intuitions Descartes claims to have regarding the essential nature of mind and body: an agent cannot know with certainty that he exists as a nonphysical thing, because there is no such thing as knowledge of nonphysical things; and an agent cannot know by clear intuition that bodies are unthinking, because the question of the nature of bodies is an experimental, not an intuitional, a priori issue. Second, even many people who are sympathetic with dualism will have trouble getting the powerful, clear, and distinct intuitions Descartes claims to have in premises (2) and (3). For example, what exactly is it like—or what would it be like—to perceive with certainty that one's essential self exists as an unextended thing?

The upshot is this: insofar as this argument for dualism stands or falls on its reproducibility as a *Gedanken* experiment, and insofar as many people do not share Descartes' intuitions, the argument will fail to persuade all those lacking conviction or needing conversion.

Descartes' third argument for dualism is in many respects his weakest. Nevertheless, the intuitions about personal identity to which the argument gives rise provide a very seductive reason for espousing some brand of dualism. This argument, like the previous one, appears in the sixth *Meditation*.[14]

(1) An entity cannot have a property and its opposite.

(2) My body is divisible, it has parts. Divisibility is part of what it means to be a body.

(3) My mind is indivisible. It has no parts. "For . . . when I consider the mind, that is to say, myself inasmuch as I am only a thinking thing, I cannot distinguish in myself any parts, but ap-

prehend myself to be clearly one and entire; and although the whole mind seems to be united to the whole body, yet if a foot, or an arm, or some other part, is separated from my body, I am aware that nothing has been taken away from my mind."

(4) Therefore, my mind and my body are different kinds of things.

Like its predecessor, this argument is an attempt to establish type-type dualism by isolating incompatible essential properties in a particular mind and body. The problem with this argument is that it openly begs the question of the divisibility, and hence the physicality, of the mind. Notice that it is not contradictory to deny premise (3) and assert that the mind is divisible. This means that (3) is not a necessary truth and that therefore it is logically possible that the mind is just the brain, and mental phenomena are just neural phenomena. And surely brains are as divisible as pies. Furthermore, if it is possible that the mind is the brain, then it is just not true as asserted in premise (3) that one's mind remains intact no matter what body part is removed.

What this means is that we need arguments to show us why premise (3) is more plausible than its denial. However, the support Descartes offers for this premise is thin and unconvincing. First, he claims that when he engages in introspection he discovers that his mind has no parts. As before, the evidence is *Gedanken*-experimental, and it is easy to imagine many people—especially if they have been influenced by Plato's or Freud's tripartite division of the mind or by recent cognitive psychology's idea of the modularity of the mind—claiming that they introspect all sorts of mental parts.[15] In fact, at one point in the argument Descartes admits that it is possible to introspect a variety of mental functions, a variety of mental faculties, for example, will, thought, emotion, and so on. But he claims that these are not, properly speaking, divisible parts; they are functions of one mind. However, by allowing that it is possible to introspect several mental functions, Descartes seems to lay his argument open to a serious materialistic objection, namely: we know that bodily functions, for example, walking and talking, are physical processes performed by physical parts, namely, legs and tongues. It would seem plausible, by analogy, to expect that the functions of the mind will turn out to be performed by similarly physical and divisible parts once the matter is experimentally studied.

The second major problem with Descartes' defense of (3) involves the claim that when he imagines an amputation, for example, of a foot or an arm, he fails to imagine that there would be any corresponding change in his mind.[16] But try imagining an amputation of both your arms and both your legs—notice any difference in your mind? If not, imagine getting rid of your spleen and your liver and your kidneys, and let's take out sections of your spinal cord—any difference? Still no difference? Let's get rid of your head and all the neural machinery it contains—any difference? Most people will be able to go only so far with Descartes' intuition—certainly as far as fingers and toes, but probably not as far as the heart or the brain. What exactly this proves about human nature I am not at all sure, but it does radically undermine the certainty Descartes attaches to the central premise of his argument. Because this third argument for dualism, like the second, relies on questionable or irreproducible intuitions, it fails to warrant its conclusion.

Its technical failure notwithstanding, Descartes is onto something very important in this argument. One's sense of self, one's feeling that one has a certain integrity, a consciousness which persists and has continuity over time, seem to depend very little, perhaps not at all, on the physical constancy of one's body. It is here that the mind-body problem connects with the problem of personal identity.

It is obvious to the naked eye that humans go through radical physical transformations on the way from birth to old age and death. What is not so obvious to the naked eye, although it helps explain these transformations, is that our bodies are continually cashing in old cells for new ones. Now suppose your average, everyday body cell has a life span of seven years (this is probably on the high side). If the average life of your average cell is seven years, and the average life span of a person is seventy years, then the average person has ten different bodies in a lifetime. The surprising thing is that you, like me, probably have no sense of having been displaced or replaced once, let alone several times. Somehow amidst numerous and radical physical transformations you and I have a sense that something essential is maintained and continues; we have a sense that we remain the same person from day to day. It is not implausible, therefore, to think that whatever it is that continues, whatever it is that makes an individual person who he or she is, whatever it is that accounts for personal identity occurs not because of the body but in spite of the body.

It is this sort of thinking that Descartes' third argument gives rise to, and that gives dualism some of its considerable plausibility, some of its great intuitive appeal. It is not decisive, however. In speaking of the average life of your average cell, I concealed two sets of facts that make the dualistic answer to the puzzle about personal identity less attractive. First, brain cells are atypical in that they can last a full lifetime, and those that die are not replaced. Second, all ordinary cells are replaced in accordance with each person's unique genetic program. This program, your genetic code, persists intact in each generation of cells; it passes from cell to cell in the same way the rules of a game, like Scrabble or Monopoly, are passed on with each newly manufactured package. It is possible, therefore, that either the persisting neurons in the brain, or the persisting genetic program in the DNA or both, provide a physical basis for explaining personal identity over time. Insofar as such a materialistic account is possible, the fact of continuous self-identity over time and amidst bodily decay does not establish dualism.

In the end, none of Descartes' arguments are sufficient to prove dualism. This does not mean that dualism is false, but only that we have been offered no overwhelming reasons to think that it is true. In criticizing Descartes' arguments I have shown that some variety of materialism, albeit probably not reflex mechanism, might be true. We are, it seems, at something of a metaphysical standoff, unable thus far to establish definitively, or to refute, either dualism or materialism.

Some philosophers, notably the American pragmatists, suggest that it is possible to make a rational decision concerning a metaphysical position even if one does not have a definitive argument for or against the position. They suggest examining the consequences, both positive and negative, of assuming a particular metaphysical position. See, for example, how assuming dualism as opposed to materialism fits with your other beliefs, examine how both positions on the mind-body problem make you conceive of human nature, and examine the consequences they have for how you think of the status and nature of a science of mind.

Conclusion

One of the main consequences, and what most people would think of as the main advantage, of Cartesian dualism is that it makes sense of the intuitive distinction between conscious, purposeful, and voluntary actions on the one hand, and mechanical, unintentional, and involuntary actions on the other. Behavior that results from the conscious direction of the bodily machine for the sake of achieving some purpose or end is a voluntary action. Behavior that results from the application of a stimulus to one's reflexive wiring is an involuntary happening. The first kind of thing *you do*. The second kind of thing is *done to you*. By making sense of the voluntary-involuntary distinction mind-body dualism makes sense of moral discourse.

When we speak morally, and almost all people in Western culture have done so, we employ an idiom which assumes certain things about human nature. At the most general level, the moral idiom assumes that people are capable of controlling their actions—it assumes that we are not mere reflex machines. When we call a person "good" or "bad," or an action "right" or "wrong" we make an assessment relative to certain attitudes we have about how people ought to act. But it seems silly to have any expectations about how people ought to act, if everything we do is the result of some inexorable causal chain which began millennia ago. "Ought," after all, seems to imply "can." Therefore, by employing a moral vocabulary filled with words like "ought" and "should" we assume that humans are capable of rising above the causal pressures presented by the material world, and in assuming this we appear to be operating with some conception of freedom, some notion of free will.

It is not only our scheme of moral expectations, our future-oriented conception of what ought to be the case that assumes free will, but our schemes of assessing actions and persons after the fact, our schemes for evaluating the past, seem to assume free will as well. When we blame or compliment a person for some action we assume that the person could have done otherwise, and that due to an act of will they chose the right or wrong path. If everything humans did was determined and inevitable in the same way the behavior of the robots in the French Royal Gardens was, then our schemes of attributing responsibility, of doling out rewards and punishments, would lose much of their sense.[17] Rewarding people for their altruism and philanthropy, or punishing them for their selfishness and mendacity would be as odd as rewarding or punishing people for their pulse rates or for the color of their eyes.

Cartesian dualism is attractive from the moral point of view because it takes as axiomatic that the mind is capable of rising above causal necessity and dominating the machinations of the bodily machine during the short time they are conjoined. Descartes spends the entire fourth *Meditation* providing a noble defense of metaphysical freedom of the will. On his view, error and evil are caused by the failure to exercise, or by an overexercise of, an autonomous human will. In one well-known passage in the sixth *Meditation,* Descartes tells us that the mind and the body are more intimately conjoined than are the sea captain and his ship, otherwise why would the mind *experience* such bodily states as hunger, thirst, and so on? My experience of my twisted ankle is far more intimate than the pilot's observation that his ship's rudder needs repair.

But it is important to stress that the passage does not altogether deny the analogy of pilot and vessel. Descartes writes, "I am not only lodged in my body as a pilot in a vessel, but that I am very closely united to it, and so to speak intermingled with it that I seem to compose with it one whole." [18] On one natural reading of this passage, I am lodged in my body as a pilot is in his vessel. It is just that I am *not only* lodged in my body in this way. In my capacity as patient to my own bodily states the analogy of pilot and vessel is inapposite. But in my capacity as a moral agent it is just right. In moral life it is possible for the vessel to dominate the pilot. But if this occurs, it is not due to natural necessity. It is not because the vessel overpowers the pilot. It is because the pilot allows himself to be weak. He fails to use the power he has.

Not surprisingly, many thinkers have wondered whether this Horatio Alger-like conception of human nature is worth preserving. Theorists as diverse as Freud, Skinner, Marx, and Mao have argued that it simply is not possible to pull oneself up by one's bootstraps, moral or otherwise, if the historical, social, genetic, and economic conditions in one's world are not just right. Other thinkers have tried to show that it is in fact possible to do justice to our intuitions about purpose, free choice, and moral responsibility within a mechanistic framework[19]. The Cartesian will respond that both approaches do far too much violence to certain inviolable assumptions of the moral point of view. Any form of mechanism, whether it be information-processing mechanism, social-learning mechanism, or economic-deterministic mechanism, will analyze the moral agency of persons in terms of causal chains leading back to the Big Bang, and in so doing will dissolve any semblance of genuine metaphysical freedom, any semblance of real autonomy, creativity, and agency.

One can be moral, of course, without being religious. (Nietzsche, in fact, went so far as to argue that one could not be moral if one was religious.) Nevertheless, religion has been attractive throughout the ages both as a system of answering ultimate questions about the past and the future, and as a way of justifying a particular moral conception. In the Judeo-Christian scheme of things, the answers to the ultimate questions and the particular moral conception link up in the following way: people who avoid temptation and choose the virtuous path on earth will be rewarded after physical death with everlasting life in heaven.

Descartes' mind-body dualism provides an elegant philosophical grounding for this portion of religious discourse which deals with personal immortality, with life after physical death. If humans are just exotic physical machines, as materialists believe, then the hypothesis that there is life after physical death is implausible since everything we know about bodies indicates that they die, decay, and disperse. If, however, our essence is nonphysical, then the possibility of immortality remains, since we have no evidence that nonphysical things die, decay, and disperse in the same way physical things do.

On the other hand, and this to many people's way of thinking is the main disadvantage of Cartesian dualism, we have no evidence whatsoever that there are any nonphysical things.[20] Furthermore, when we assume that there are nonphysical things we have to make some very implausible assumptions and give up some of our most cherished scientific principles, for example the principle, which Descartes espoused, that *ex nihilo nihil fit*, that something cannot come from nothing. Just such a principle holds a central place among modern scientific principles under the guise of the principle of conservation of energy.

Now, the principle of conservation of energy requires that the total amount of energy in the universe remain constant, even as it is continually transferred and transformed in and among the myriad systems of causal relations. If Descartes is right that a nonphysical mind can cause the body to move, for example, we decide to go to a concert and go, then physical energy must increase in and around our body, since we get up and go to the concert. In order, however, for physical energy to increase in any system, it has to have been transferred from some other physical system. But the mind, according to Descartes, is not a physical system and therefore it does not have any energy to transfer. The mind cannot account for the fact that our body ends up at the concert.

If we accept the principle of the conservation of energy we seem committed either to denying that the nonphysical mind exists, or to denying that it could cause anything to happen, or to making some very implausible ad hoc adjustments in our physics. For example, we could maintain that the principle of the conservation of energy holds, but that every time a mind introduces new energy into the world—thanks to some mysterious capacity it has—an equal amount of energy departs from the physical universe—thanks to some perfectly orchestrated mysterious capacity the universe has. Unfortunately, such an assumption is totally unwarranted except as a way of saving Cartesian dualism, and, therefore, utterly begs the question.[21]

Finally, and related to this, there are the consequences Cartesian dualism has for the very possibility of a science of the mind, for the very possibility of a scientific psychology. Three such consequences stand out. First, if the human mind is nonphysical, then it lacks one of the main properties in terms of which modern science conceptualizes the objects in studies. Second, if the human mind is capable of initiating causal chains while itself remaining above mechanical necessity, then the mind-body relation violates the lawfulness (for example, the conservation principles) which modern science expects of the systems it studies.[22] Third, if the human mind is known first and best by the agent himself—if, in fact, the only sort of reliable epistemic access to a human mind is the sort of access a person has to his own mind—then psychological knowledge is not subject to the broad intersubjective tests characteristic of scientific method. If, therefore, science is construed as the activity of providing lawful analyses of physical systems by way of tests which warrant intersubjective agreement, then mental phenomena, as characterized by Descartes, systematically escape the purview of science.

It might be possible to adjust certain tenets of Cartesian dualism so that it is less at odds with the idea of a scientific psychology. For example, we might play down the nonphysicality of the mind and play up that which is certainly true, namely, that it is exceedingly difficult for a community of scientists to observe what goes on in a human mind. If we trade in the nonphysicality of the mind for its non-observability, for its opacity, then dualism is not necessarily incompatible with a psychological science. For example, we might reconceptualize the mind-body distinction along the lines of the electron-table distinction. We have indirect access to the former and direct access to the latter, but both electrons and tables are physical. We could, in effect, trade in metaphysical dualism for a less problematic epistemological dualism: mind and body are not different in kind, but simply differ in terms of accessibility. Mental phenomena, on such an analysis, are simply hard to get at in a way some (other) bodily phenomena are not.

Whether such a case for scientific psychology can be made, and some of the profound intuitions behind Cartesian dualism simultaneously maintained, remains to be seen. Regardless, therefore, of the ultimate validity of Descartes' line of argument, he deserves the greatest intellectual respect for setting a sincere and profound challenge to both the philosopher of the mind and the scientist of the mind. To the scientist he offers the challenge of generating a theory of human nature which does not deny the purposeful, cognitive, deliberative, willful, and free aspects of human cognition and human action. To the philosopher he delivers the conundrum of explaining whether and how this can be done, whether and how, that is, that our sense of ourselves and our sense of scientific explanation can be meshed without doing radical violence to either.

Suggested Readings

Primary Sources

Descartes (1634), *Traité de l'Homme.*
Descartes (1637), *Discourse on Method.*
Descartes (1641), *Meditations.*
Descartes (1649), *Passions of the Soul.*

Three Excellent Studies on Descartes

Kenny, Anthony (1968), *Descartes: A Study of His Philosophy.*
Williams, Bernard (1978), *Descartes: The Project of Pure Enquiry.*
Wilson, Margaret (1978), *Descartes.*

The Most Recent Contemporary Defense of Dualism

Popper, K., and Eccles, J. (1977), *The Self and Its Brain.*

Chapter 2

Naturalizing The Mind: The Philosophical Psychology of William James

Naturally there was an enormous amount of discussion of the status and principles of the science of mind between Descartes' dismal seventeeth-century prognosis and William James's 1890 masterpiece, *The Principles of Psychology*. The leap to James is justified for three reasons, however. First, James writes at the most critical juncture in the history of psychology: in the very first generation in which a generally recognized scientific psychology existed; in the first years in which the higher mental processes that Descartes claimed were not amenable to scientific study were in fact being analyzed by scientific methods.[1]

The second reason for passing directly to James is that by his time both of the hypotheses made available by Descartes (on the one hand the hypothesis that people were just elaborate reflex machines, and on the other the hypothesis that people were thinking things not governed by natural law) had been fairly well worked out. And both hypotheses had been found wanting. Reflex mechanism seemed scientific but far too simplistic to stand a chance of providing an adequate theory of mind, while dualism had the requisite complexity without the slightest semblance of science. James writes in response to the failure of both programs to provide an adequate theory of the mind.

Third, James writes in the immediate aftermath of Darwin. The Darwinian revolution in biology had profound consequences for all the human sciences, and James was only too happy to avail himself of evolutionary thinking. Thanks to Darwin's theory he was able to understand mentality as a product of natural selection, and was thereby able to situate the origin and function of mental life in the natural world. Furthermore, he was able to do so without accepting the simplistic suggestion that the human animal is a mere bundle of reflexes.

My overall line of argument is this: James's work is the first for-

---

The best introduction to James's philosophy of mind and psychology is his *Psychology: The Briefer Course* (1892).

mulation of the naturalistic position in the philosophy of mind. On the naturalist view, mentality has no metaphysically odd properties (although as we shall see James has trouble in not endowing our minds with free will). The naturalist sees the world as comprised of physical objects, their properties, and their relations. The naturalist departs from traditional materialism however, by denying that mental phenomena, naturalistically interpreted, require a simple mechanical analysis, for example, a reflex analysis. The naturalist parts company with the reflex mechanist because he reads evolutionary theory as pointing not merely to increased complexity of biological organization but also as pointing to the need for increasing complexity at the level of explanation as we ascend the phylogenic scale: reflexes require reflex analyses; full-blown mental phenomena require mentalistic analyses. Naturalism, you might say, is what you get when you take classical (say, Cartesian or Newtonian) materialism and reconstitute it with evolutionary concepts, in particular with the concept of different levels of biological organization and the concept of organisms as functional systems which continually change by interacting with other functional systems.[2]

In this chapter I first examine James's conception of the subject matter and appropriate methods of a science of the mind. Second, I sketch out James's general theory of conscious mental life, his descriptive, broadly phenomenological theory of the topmost level of mind. Here I also indicate the way evolutionary ideas inspired James's answer to the question of the function of conscious mental life, and show how some of the main tenets of his pragmatic philosophy, much of which was developed after 1890, can be seen to follow from the theory of conscious mental life he proposed in the *Principles*.[3] Third, I examine James's surprisingly modern discussion of the mind-brain relation. Most of the candidates that James considers for the solution to the mind-body problem still have their proponents among contemporary philosophers, cognitive scientists, and neurophysiologists. In fact, most contemporary naturalists still favor James's general stance that mental life, as we experience it, is a causally effective functional feature of the incredibly complex interaction(s) that humans, considered as biological organisms, have with the natural and social environment. Last, I discuss James's views on the problem of free will and determinism. By and large, James is able to accommodate our ordinary commonsense conception of humans within his naturalism. But he balks on free will, seeing no way to make consistent our ordinary view of humans as moral agents with the point of view assumed by a science of mind. I try to indicate the way around this impasse, and suggest how a naturalist can handle the free will problem.

William James: Mentality and Introspection

James's two-volume *Principles of Psychology* is an exhaustive compendium of the state of American and European psychology at the end of the nineteenth century, interspersed with James's philosophical reflections on the mind-body problem, the nature of consciousness, free will and determinism, and the appropriate methods and subject matter of psychology. James's philosophical sensitivity, unfortunately, is not always matched by the rigor of his arguments. This is partly because James is a master of phenomenological description and therefore is able to have his philosophical points occasionally emerge from his rich and suggestive portraits of ordinary human experience rather than from persuasive logical arguments. Then there is the fact that James moves, as one commentator puts it, "at a trotting pace." In those places where James produces more vigor than rigor (and there are many such places) I try to supply the implicit or missing argument. My interpretive emphasis will be to read James as a committed naturalist whenever I can.

James's *Principles* begins with the announcement that "Psychology is the Science of Mental Life, both its phenomena and of their conditions."[4] Psychology in effect has two jobs: it must accurately describe mental phenomena, and it must explain the causal conditions that give rise to these phenomena.

James often writes as if mentality is synonymous with consciousness or with conscious mental life. In fact, James's continual emphasis on the methodological primacy of introspection (*"Introspective Observation is what we have to rely on first and foremost and always"*)[5] is implicitly supported by the (widely shared) assumption that we are systems in which *all or most mental life is actually conscious or capable of becoming conscious.*

The assumption, however, that introspection—"the looking into our own minds and reporting what we there discover"—can give us a remotely complete picture of mentality, looks exceedingly suspect from the perspective of contemporary cognitive psychology. Consider the following well-known experiment by James Lackner and Merrill Garrett.[6] Subjects were instructed to attend to just one channel in a set of earphones. In the attended channel subjects heard the ambiguous sentence, "The officer *put out* the lantern to signal the attack." In the unattended channel the first group heard sentences which, if understood, would provide an unambiguous interpretation of the sentence heard in the attended channel ("He *extinguished* the lantern"), while the second group heard irrelevant sentences ("The Red Sox are playing a double-header tonight"). Both groups could report with great accuracy what they had heard in the attended channel but neither group could report what they had heard in the unattended channel. Nevertheless, the first group favored the suggested reading of the ambiguous sentence more than did the second group. This indicates that the sentence in the unattended channel was understood, even though it could not be consciously reported by the subjects. The sentence was not only acoustically processed, but semantically processed as well.

Lackner and Garrett's experiment raises two sorts of worries about James's view. First, it may well turn out to be the case that much, even most, of our mental life is not accessible to consciousness. The amount accessible by "looking into our minds and reporting what we there discover" may be only the tip of the iceberg. In this case, the prominence of conscious mental life is a poor indicator of its importance in an explanatory psychology: its prominence is an artifact of the accident that the features of mental life of which we are aware coincide with the class of features we take (not surprisingly) to be significant in our psychological economy. If, however, much of our mental life operates unbeknownst to us, then introspective evidence is a most unpromising basis on which to construct a psychology. The second worry is this: if we are required to override the authority of conscious introspection even occasionally, then it simply cannot be right that we have to rely on introspection "*first, foremost and always.*"

On the whole, James is not nearly as perceptive about methodology as he is about metaphysics. He is generally impatient with those who fall prey to excessive worries about the epistemological status of introspection. He says "*introspection is difficult and fallible . . .* [but] *the difficulty is simply that of all observation of whatever kind.*"[7]

The admission of the fallibility of introspection is characteristic of James's pragmatism; it indicates that he is not totally naive about introspection and not guilty of a Cartesian-like faith in the incorrigibility of careful self-observation. On the other hand, James is largely insensitive to concerns about the extent to which mental life is conscious, as well as to questions about when introspective evidence can be overridden (as in the Lackner and Garrett experiment) and when it is simply useless (as for example in trying to give a description of mentality at the neural level).[8] To be sure, James's acknowledgment of the fallibility of introspection involves an implicit acceptance of the idea that introspective reports will sometimes have to be overridden, but he shows no anticipation of the modern view which sees introspection as—at most—a part of a methodological check-and-balance system whose authority can be, and often is, vetoed.

Toward a Theory of Conscious Mental Life

Even though James certainly underestimates the extent to which mental life is unconscious, he is no doubt correct that however psychology ultimately turns out we will require that it include a theory of conscious mental life (CML). That is, we will want a theory of the topmost level of mind, even if that level turns out to be just the tip of the iceberg. I want to read James's contribution as an attempt to lay the groundwork for such a theory.

James's attempt to provide a naturalistic theory of CML looks all the more brave a century later. Dennett correctly observes that

> one of philosophy's favorite facets of mentality has received scant attention from cognitive psychologists, and that is consciousness itself: full-blown, introspective, inner-world phenomenological consciousness. In fact if one looks in the obvious places . . . one finds not so much a lack of interest as a deliberate and adroit avoidance of the issue. I think I know why. Consciousness appears to be the last bastion of occult properties, epiphenomena, and immeasurable subjective states—in short, the one area of mind best left to the philosophers, who are welcome to it. Let them make fools of themselves trying to corral the quicksilver of "phenomenology" into a respectable theory.[9]

My proposal is that James's major concern in the *Principles* is precisely "to corral the quicksilver of 'phenomenology' into a respectable theory."

There are several questions such a theory will need to answer the following: (1) What is CML like? (2) What is CML for? That is, what is the function of CML in the overall economy of the systems which possess it? (3) How is CML realized? That is, how (and where, if anywhere) is CML realized in the nervous system? Here I want to sketch out James's answers to the first two questions and suggest the ways in which his answers connect with his philosophical pragmatism (the third question will be discussed later).

What Is CML Like?

The question "what is CML like?" openly asks for a phenomenological answer, for an answer primarily in terms of the features of mentality accessible to introspection. As I read James he sees CML as marked off from the rest of nature by the constellation of seven essential features: *purposefulness, intentionality, consciousness* itself, *personality, personal change, personal continuity,* and *selectivity.*

CML is purposeful and willful.   James is emphatic that *"The pursuance of future ends and the choice of means for their attainment are thus the mark and criterion of the presence of mentality in a phenomenon."*[10] Elsewhere in the *Principles* he says, *"no actions but such as are done for an end, and show a choice of means, can be called indubitable expressions of Mind.*"[11]

Purposefulness, in James's view, is the property of behaving instrumentally, of mentally representing some goal, choosing the means to reach it, and doing so. Purposeful behavior, as has been noticed since at least the time of Aristotle, requires teleological explanation. That is, citation of the goals or ends which an organism represents to itself will need to figure prominently in the explanation of the organism's behavior. For example, if you know that it is my goal to make spaghetti sauce for dinner tonight, then you will understand why I am chopping garlic. Furthermore, your accurate understanding of my goal will enable you to rule out other possible explanations that are compatible with my behavior, for example, that I am trying to make my eyes water, or that I am trying to make garlic soup. Because it is my purpose to make spaghetti sauce, I have represented this goal to myself and my current behavior is a means to that end. My internally represented purpose then explains, or is relevant to the explanation of, my current behavior.[12]

Notice that this first characteristic is not, strictly speaking, a feature of CML alone (nor is it fully accessible to introspection). We represent means and ends to ourselves mentally, but such representing is truly purposeful or willful only if it results in action. The assumption here is simply that we deliberate about our goals, calculate the means-ends relations most appropriate to reach those goals, then decide to act, and do so. The assumption is simply that purposeful cognitive processes interact with (the rest of) our bodily system to produce purposeful action.

CML has intentionality.   The concept of intentionality is a medieval notion with philosophical roots in Aristotle and etymological roots in the Latin verb *intendo*, meaning "to aim at" or "point toward." The concept of intentionality was resurrected and clarified by James's contemporary Franz Brentano. The thesis that intentionality is the ineliminable mark of the mental is therefore commonly referred to as "Brentano's thesis." Strictly speaking, the principle has nothing to do with *intending* as such, even though *intending* is intentional in Brentano's sense. Intending in its usual sense is already captured by the first feature of CML; intentionality is a much more general notion.

Brentano distinguished between mental acts and mental contents. My belief that today is Monday has two components. There is my act of believing and there is the content of my belief, namely, that today is Monday. We can represent the two components with the following general schema which neatly displays what Brentano called the property of "intentional inexistence," the content literally exists *in* the act: *Act[Content]*.

My belief that today is Monday is identical from an act point of view with my belief that no one can explain how the primordial stuff involved in the Big Bang got there in the first place, because these are both beliefs. The two beliefs differ radically, however, in content. This is obvious if we substitute in our bracketing schema: Belief[today is Monday] ≠ Belief[no one can explain how the primordial stuff involved in the Big Bang got there in the first place].

Beliefs are not alone in having meaningful intentional content—desires, hopes, expectations, memories, loves, and hates have intentional content too. Language wears this fact on its sleeve. We say that people desire that [_____], hope that [_____], expect that [_____], perceive that [_____], and so on, where whatever fills in the blank is the intentional content of the mental act.[13] Intentionality, then, refers to the widespread fact that mental acts have meaningful content.

In the *Principles*, James makes clear his great admiration for Brentano's views on consciousness and emphasizes that intentionality is an essential feature of mentality. James says, "*The psychologist's attitude towards cognition . . . is a thoroughgoing dualism*. It supposes two elements, mind knowing and thing known, and treats them as irreducible."[14] The dualism James is referring to here is not mind-body dualism, not metaphysical dualism, but an epistemic dualism: the dualism whereby there is both consciousness and its contents. It is a mark of mentality that it always takes a meaningful object.

Mental phenomena, in James's and Brentano's view, have intentionality, nonmental phenomena do not. We have beliefs about what it's like on the top of Mt. Everest, but the top of Mt. Everest isn't about anything. We have hopes about the quality of our dinner wine, but our dinner wine isn't about anything. We may have hopes or expectations about our Christmas presents but our Christmas presents are not about anything (unless of course our presents include books, but books are only derivatively about something: *Anna Karenina* is about Anna Karenina only because we attach meaning to ink marks on paper). We can think of or about unicorns that they are beautiful, but unicorns are not of or about anything, and so on.

In fact, and this turns out to be an important feature of intentional states, unicorns don't even exist. The fact that we are capable of having beliefs, desires, or opinions about nonexisting things secures the thesis that the contents of mental states are *mental representations*, not the things themselves—since in the case of unicorns, ghosts, devils, and our plans for the future there simply are no real things to be the contents of our mental states! On this interpretation, James is an advocate of what Jerry Fodor calls the *representational theory of mind*.

Although Brentano himself was no materialist, his thesis that intentionality is the ineliminable mark of the mental suggests the possibility of a criterion of demarcation between the mental and the nonmental which has no essential connection to Descartes' metaphysical dualism. Mental phenomena, on such a view, could turn out to be as physical as tables and chairs, or at least as metaphysically unproblematic as walking and talking and breathing. What will always distinguish them, however, their physicality or lack thereof notwithstanding, is the fact that mental phenomena have content, they have an "aboutness" that tables and chairs lack.

CML is conscious.   The reason for marking off consciousness in addition to purposefulness and intentionality, is to make clear that mere purposeful-looking behavior and merely being in an information-bearing state are not to count as sufficient for ascribing CML to an organism. After all, much of the inanimate world can be analyzed, metaphorically at least, in purposeful and intentional terms, but it fails to meet the criteria for CML.

Take a rain cloud, for example. One might argue that rain clouds behave purposefully—they rain for the sake of getting rid of the moisture that is causing their oversaturation; and they contain meaningful information about their level of oversaturation in the form of weight relative to volume. (Analogously, the summit of Mt. Everest contains information about weather patterns over the centuries, my dinner wine contains information about its age, thermostats contain information about mean molecular kinetic energy, and so on.) James's view is simply the commonsensical one that clouds don't rain on purpose, even if raining serves all kinds of purposes; and clouds are not aware of the information encoded in their water weight. The water content of a cloud is the cloud's physical content, to be sure, but it is only informative intentional content to us. Consciousness, in James's view, is the simple epistemic feature of sentience or awareness. It is hard to say much more about it except that it is all around us, more familiar than anything else and less well understood than anything else. It is, as Dennett aptly puts it, the "quicksilver" of the philosophy of mind.[15]

One might question whether these first three features—purposefulness, intentionality, and consciousness—are really essential features of CML. There seem to be particular mental states which lack one of the latter three features (the same argument will hold for each of the four remaining features of CML), and, therefore, the coexistence of these features cannot be essential to each and every mental state. Certain emotions, for example, seem to lack the property of purposefulness—they seem just to happen. Other states such as pain are arguably non-intentional—what, after all, is the object which "intentionally inexists" in a pain state? And then there are unconscious mental states and processes, for example, the processes whereby this very second you are semantically and syntactically processing this sentence. Consciousness, of course, cannot be a requirement for a bona fide top-level state if there is unconscious mental life operating at the topmost level.

It seems to me that there is one reasonable move for the Jamesian to make in response to this credible objection. He must argue that indeed purposefulness, intentionality, and consciousness are not required properties of every particular (*token*) mental state which will fall under a theory of CML, but that these properties must figure prominently in any (*type* of) biological system if we are to reasonably attribute a CML to that system.

CML is personal, private, uniquely one's own.   This feature of CML is, according to James, an "immediate datum." Thoughts, feelings, and the like do not sit around disembodied. All thoughts and feelings are "owned," that is, all thoughts and feelings occur to someone.

> In this room—this lecture room, say—there are a multitude of thoughts, yours and mine, some of which cohere mutually, and some not. . . . My thought belongs with *my* other thoughts, and your thought with *your* other thoughts. Whether anywhere in the room there be a *mere* thought, which is nobody's thought, we have no means of ascertaining, for we have no experience of its like. The only states of consciousness that we naturally deal with are found in particular consciousnesses, minds, selves, concrete particular I's and you's.[16]

This, of course, is not to deny that one's mental life can be understood by and shared with one's fellow humans. James's pragmatism keeps him from worrying that the fact that we all occupy a unique point of view generates some inescapable and horrifying version of the problem of knowledge of other minds. The point is simply that all normal humans experience, indeed possess, integrity and identity as persons. We are each the location of a mental life—a personality. There is, as Thomas Nagel puts it, "something it is like" to be each particular one of us.[17]

Nor is it particularly surprising that evolution should have equipped us with a sense of identity, a unified consciousness. John Dewey puts it bluntly: given that "consciousness exists at all, there is no mystery in its being connected with what it is connected with."[18]

CML is always changing, in flux.   This feature can be introspected as well as supported by an elegant logical argument. I will leave the introspection to you; the logical argument runs as follows: it is impossible for a human to have the same thought or feeling, the same intentional state, more than once because no event can ever recur identically. To do so it would have to have all the same properties it had the first time around, and to do this it would have to have the same spatio-temporal properties of the first thought or feeling. But every thought or feeling takes place either before or after every other thought or feeling, and every thought or feeling takes place in a mind, an intentional system, modified by previous experience. Because every mental event takes place in a different space and time from every other mental event and in an experientially reconstituted system, every mental event is different from every other mental event.

Because mental life is in flux, human personality, as well as the experiential quality of mental life is never fixed, permanent, or stationary. It is therefore an untenable idea that in addition to our biological selves there exists an unchanging and indestructible *self*.

CML is sensibly continuous, it flows like a stream.   The metaphor of the stream of consciousness is rich and seductive. James's thesis that consciousness wends its way in an uninterrupted flow helps temper the previous thesis. James distinguishes between transitive and substantive states of consciousness. Traditional psychology and epistemology, as well as ordinary discourse, tend to focus on the substantive states, the places where the mind finds rest in some stable configuration, such as in the perception of a room, the image of a beautiful day, the snapshot memory of great-grandfather's face. We focus on states that represent objects and events we consider important. What we talk less about are the states that take us from one of these states to the next. Ralph Barton Perry, James's student, puts it this way: "The practically habituated mind flies from perch to perch, and is aware of the perch rather than of the passage."[19] This feature of CML in conjunction with the two previous ones has an important consequence for the philosophical problem of personal identity.

The problem of personal identity often receives an all-or-none answer. Many rationalists follow Descartes and claim that amidst radical physical changes to one's body one remains exactly the same person. The irresistible conclusion is that something immutable, and therefore non-physical, must account for our persistent identity over time. On the other hand, many empiricists, following Hume, are unable to find any empirical warrant for the belief in a *self* which has a unified consciousness and integrity and sameness over time. After all, all the empirical evidence points to the persistent changeability of everything. What we call the self or the person on this view is at best a "mere bundle of perceptions and ideas"—at worst, a vaporous wish.

James's coalition of evolutionary thinking with the twin theses that CML is in flux and that it has continuity provides a way around the all-or-none impasse of traditional formulations of the problem of personal identity. Against the rationalist we bring the phenomenological data that we do not in fact experience ourself as exactly the same person over time. In this way we get rid of the idea that there is some immutable *self* that needs to be accounted for. Against the empiricist's skepticism we bring the phenomenological data of continuity, and we locate the naturalistic ground of this continuity in our biological integrity.

The fact that we experience CML as having continuity implies, if anything, that it is very much like all other natural phenomena, which under normal circumstances change gradually and in coherent and patterned ways. We are organisms, after all, actual biological systems that satisfy all reasonable criteria for sameness over time.

The naturalist's position is simply that our particular kind of biological organization, our unique kind of nervous system, provides a physical basis for memory and the feelings of self-connectedness and prospectiveness that generate the problem of personal identity in the first place. Our bodies, in effect, provide a basis for the solution to the problem of personal identity. The very system that generates the conundrum about personal identity *is* the answer: personal identity is experienced in the phenomenologically real data of our continuousness, and this continuousness can in turn be exhaustively grounded in our biological continuousness.[20]

CML is selective, attentive, and interested; it is excited by some features of the world, not by others. "It is interested in some parts of these objects to the exclusion of others, and welcomes or rejects—*chooses* from among them, in a word—all the while."[21] This point can be brought out nicely by reflecting on James's well-known conjecture that the perceptual world of the newborn is all noise and chaos. According to James, "Infants must go through a long education of the eye and ear before they can perceive the realities which adults perceive. *Every perception is an acquired perception.*"[22] The way humans reduce the original noise and chaos and come to move about in an orderly and comprehensible universe is by selective attention, by moving some of the world to figure and leaving the rest as ground.

Selective attention, of course, (and James discusses this at length in his important chapter on "Habit") can be carried out consciously and for special cases, or it can be carried out unconsciously and habitually.

I, for example, have to make great conscious mental effort to concentrate on a philosophy text if there is choral music playing, whereas I have no trouble tuning out orchestral music, the sounds of radiators, airplanes overhead, passing cars, and the like. I do the latter habitually. My young son meanwhile is forever announcing the cause—"Plane, Daddy"—of things I hardly even notice.

For John Dewey, as for James, one of the most conspicuous aspects of mentality is its selectivity, its interestedness. Dewey says, "natural beings exhibit *preference* and *centeredness*."[23] Given the interested nature of CML, it follows that it is a mistake to think that stimuli can be identified independently of an interpretive human response, for example, in the language physicists use to describe physical objects and events. Dewey uses Baldwin's analysis of cognitive processing in terms of a reflex model to make this point. Baldwin describes the process of a person responding to a sound as follows: the noise occurs—sensory receptors in the ear are activated—attention is directed toward the noise—a motor response results from the attended-to sound.

Dewey points out that hearing a sound is itself an intentional act, not a mere happening as is a reflex response. We do not merely hear sounds. We hear sounds as significant. "If one is reading a book, if one is hunting, if one is waiting in a dark place on a lonely night, if one is performing a chemical experiment, in each case, the noise has a very different psychical value; it is a different experience."[24] The selective nature of CML helps secure two important philosophical points, one epistemological, the other ethical. First, the acknowledgment that CML is selective and interested requires the rejection of all naive brands of traditional empiricist epistemology, especially as they are embodied in the attempts of some psychologists to apply a reflex arc model to higher cognitive processes. In particular, any model that depicts the typical psychological causal chain as proceeding unidirectionally from sense impression to cognition to volition must be rejected. The objection to such a model is simply that it fails to take into account how interested and how selective mental life is. Our mental life is such that volitional and cognitional acts are already taking place at the receiving stage. We never, as reflex arc theorists would have it, experience the world as such, and then think about it, and then act toward it. We experience a world as we, in some sense, choose to experience it, one that we have already constituted in accordance with our personal aims, interests, and expectations. The second—ethical—implication of the selective, interested nature of CML is this: because each person's mental life is uniquely constituted by the particular experiences he or she has, and the particular constellation of interests and expectations he or she brings to those experiences, it follows that the universe of human thought and action is a pluralistic one. A psychology that promotes the view that everything is experienced differently by every person supports, therefore, a social philosophy that takes individuality seriously, and treats it respectfully.

To recapitulate the analysis thus far, our kind of CML has seven essential features: purposefulness, intentionality, consciousness, personality, personal change, personal continuity, and selectivity. Taken together, suitably entwined, and described in greater detail, these seven features provide the phenomenological, largely descriptive portion of a theory of CML. They answer the question "what is CML like?" The question remains, "what is our kind of CML for?" That is, "what function does it serve?" This is the second question a theory of CML must answer.

What Is CML for?
James's answer to this second question facing any theory of CML comes less from introspection than from evolutionary biology. Part of the attraction of evolutionary theory comes from the fact that it provides a naturalistic way of accounting for the origin and function of CML that does not also try to explain its features away—as, say, mere side effects of more interesting and metaphysically basic processes.

Before Darwin the "what is mental life for?" question might have been given a theological answer—"Only God knows what conscious mental life is for" or alternatively, "Conscious mental life serves the function of satisfying God's desire that we be created in His image."

Darwinian theory, however, requires a naturalistic answer to the functional question. Our kind of mental life must have appeared initially as a biological accident (due to a mutation or a novel hereditary combination), and subsequently became a species characteristic because it conferred a survival advantage, and therefore a reproductive advantage, on those individuals who possessed it.

But what kind of survival advantage could our particular kind of CML confer? What advantage that would not be just as well conferred if we were unconscious automata governed wholly by reflexes and instincts? It is in answering this question that the phenomenological features of the topmost level of the mind begin to make sense.

Briefly, and very roughly, CML gives organisms that possess it the ability to adapt quickly to novel states of affairs (quicker, that is, than organisms that must go through a long conditioning process or, even worse, actual evolutionary change). To be specific, intentionality involves the ability to represent past, present, and future states of affairs to ourselves and this means that we can know, remember, and plan. But knowing, remembering, and planning are only adaptive in a system that can map out means-ends relationships and then actively pursue its satisfactions. And such a purposeful system is only adaptive if in fact it can accurately identify its ends as *its ends*, that is, only if it has a sense of continuing identity or personality over time. Finally, the capacity for selective attention, for picking out salient features in a novel situation, is an exceedingly economical way of accommodating new states of affairs, given that the world has an enormous number of regular features—far more economical, for example, than exhaustively trying to understand all (the infinite number of) properties of the objects in one's sensory environment. The seven main features of the topmost level of mind then form a logically related package that gives us certain advantages in reaching an adaptive functional relationship with the changing natural and social environment.

This conception of humans as organisms who are intelligently (and often happily) struggling, changing, and adapting to, and because of, a changing natural and social world is an idea James appropriates directly from Darwin. However, the attractiveness of the Darwinian point of view could only have been reinforced, and therefore recolored, by James's own participation in a turn-of-the-century American *Zeitgeist* which emphasized human energy, ingenuity, and creativity as tools for mastering nature.

An important philosophical thesis emerges from James's evolutionary answer to the question "what is CML for?" The psychological thesis that mental life seeks the most functional, adaptive fit with the environment supports, and is supported by, the view that truth—or as James should have said, the ultimate test of the truth of a system of beliefs—lies in its functionalness, in its adaptiveness, in its predictive power.

James is often attacked for his theory of truth by critics who read him as suggesting that what is true is what satisfies or pleases us. For example, if astrology pleases me it's true, and if believing in personal immortality satisfies me, it's true, and if believing that I am a world-class tennis or chess player pleases me, it's true, and so on. Without entering into a full-scale defense of James's often confusing remarks on truth, let me say this much. There are two main philosophical questions about truth: What is it? and How do we test for it? that is, what are the conditions under which we say of a sentence or a theory that it is true?

A theory of truth as usually conceived is an attempt to answer the first question; the second question comes under a theory of verification. From a modern perspective, and thanks mostly to Alfred Tarski, the consensus is that the answer to the first question is: truth is a property of sentences. In particular, a sentence is true just in case it corresponds to the state of affairs it depicts.

James can be read as having two sorts of disagreements with such a view. First, it seems to smuggle in both *metaphysical realism*, the view that there is some one way the world out there is really carved up (say, from the God's-eye view), and *epistemological representationalism*, the view that the epistemic project is simply to bring our conceptual scheme into line with the way the world is really carved up. James is emphatic that there is no one way the world really is, nor are our minds what Richard Rorty calls "mirrors of nature." The world is carved up in accordance with human values and interests.[25]

James's second objection to the idea of truth as correspondence is that we do not in fact test the truth of individual sentences by looking for a one-to-one match between them and the world. Instead we bring a whole view of reality, a whole way of "attending," to experience. We then modify our system of beliefs by acting on them and receiving feedback from nature about their quality. What we call "true" then is simply the set of beliefs that works best in the long run, the set of beliefs that has predictive adequacy, that is verified in action more often than not.

Israel Scheffler puts James's considered view this way: "The satisfactory character of a true belief consists in its *predictive adequacy*. If a given belief is true, then, and only then, if you act on this belief, forming your expectations in accordance with it, experience will *satisfy these expectations or predictions*, it being irrelevant whether or not *you are satisfied also*."[26]

So put, this is exactly the sort of conception of true belief one would expect to get from a naturalist like James. Just as biological traits are differentially selected for if, ceteris paribus, they lead to increased reproductive success of the organisms which possess them, so too feedback from nature helps us to select the beliefs that yield predictive success from those that do not. To the former we ascribe truth and to the latter falsity.

A sophisticated correspondence theorist might respond to the latter set of pragmatic complaints by insisting that a genuine theory of truth, namely his, smuggles in no metaphysical or epistemic claims whatsoever. That is, it renders no opinion on the question of whether the world is carved up independently of human interests, nor on the question of the representational adequacy of our conceptual scheme(s). The correspondence theorist, on this view, is simply analyzing what "true" means. "True" means "corresponds to reality" even if no sentence uttered thus far has in fact done so!

The correspondence theorist might then accept James's functionalist account as a theory of verification, as a theory about the conditions under which we in fact ascribe the predicate "is true" to sentences. On such a view James would be taken as answering the "conditions of verification" question, and therefore as not really proposing a theory of truth at all. This way of looking at the conflict, and thereby defusing it, has some merit. But I suspect that James would respond by insisting that a theory of truth which analyzes truth independently of our actual functioning in the world is a theory which does no work; it is a theory nobody needs.

Mind and Brain: How Is Conscious Mental Life Realized?

According to my analysis thus far, James is able to find a happy accommodation between his commitment to evolutionary explanation, his naturalism, his desire to protect the phenomenological validity of introspective reports, and his pragmatic philosophy. Tensions begin to surface, however, as James tries to answer the third question facing a theory of CML: How, and where if anywhere, is CML realized? Or to put the question in Kantian terms: How is CML possible? This question, of course, is simply one of many ways of pointedly raising the mind-body problem.

James's discussion of the mind-body problem is remarkably modern, if a bit disorganized and distracting in its conflation of several logically distinct positions. James wends his way through a wide number of candidates for a solution before he offers a glimmer of his own preferred position, which I call *naturalistic functionalism*. The plausibility of this position emerges from the deficiencies of the four other main contenders for *the* solution to the mind-body problem.

Epiphenomenalism. This is the theory that CML is a causally inconsequential byproduct, or side effect, of physical processes in our brains. James quotes Huxley's startling version of epiphenomenalism:

> The consciousness of brutes would appear to be related to the mechanism of their body simply as a collateral product of its working, and to be completely without any power of modifying that working, as the steam-whistle which accompanies the work of a locomotive engine is without influence upon its machinery. Their volition, if they have any, is an emotion *indicative* of physical changes, not a *cause* of such changes. . . . The soul stands to the body as the bell of a clock to the works, and consciousness answers to the sound which the bell gives out when it is struck . . . to the best of my judgment, the argumentation which applies to brutes holds equally good of men. . . . We are conscious automata.[27]

James aptly refers to the epiphenomenalist position as the "inert spectator" view of the mind or the "conscious automaton" theory.

The attraction of the theory, as far as I can tell, could only be to someone who felt compelled to admit the existence of CML, but who had definite suspicions about its physicality. In particular, only if one thinks of CML in Cartesian terms, that is, as nonphysical stuff, and only if one is convinced that causal interaction between the physical and nonphysical realms is impossible, does it make sense to take an epiphenomenalistic stance and thereby deny CML causal efficacy.

In the end, however, the epiphenomenalist's position is either incoherent or implausible. First, even if we conceive of CML in Cartesian terms, epiphenomenalism undermines its own rationale, which is to keep distinct metaphysical kinds from interacting, by allowing causal interaction between body and mind in one direction. On the epiphenomenalistic view, CML is a causal outcome of certain physical processes—the terminal side effects of biological processes. The epiphenomenalist, however, provides no intelligible reason as to why causality in the body-mind direction is any less worrisome than in the mind-body direction.

Alternatively, if we really take the locomotive engine steam-whistle analogy seriously we have no reason to think of the mind in Cartesian terms in the first place. A steam whistle's "hoot" is, after all, an utterly physical process. But it we are under no pressure to think of CML in nonphysical terms, then we have no interaction problem to worry about, and epiphenomenalism loses its initial appeal.

Furthermore, as soon as we take a materialist stance on CML, the epiphenomenalist position loses its status as a distinctive solution to the mind-body problem and becomes instead simply a particular theoretical position on the relative causal efficacy of the different physical components and processes that make up a person. On this interpretation, epiphenomenalism is simply the thesis that CML has the same incidental relation to the whole person as the steam whistle has to the locomotive engine.

To James such a view seems highly implausible on empirical grounds. All the data point to CML as more analogous to the steam engine which powers the locomotive and produces the steam, than to the quaint but terminal hoot. James insists that epiphenomenalism is an *"unwarrantable impertinence in the present state of psychology."*[28]

Against the epiphenomenalist, James musters the commonsensical evidence that we often bring about what we in fact mentally intend. He then joins this evidence to evolutionary theory, arguing that it is "inconceivable that consciousness should have *nothing to do* with a business which it so faithfully attends."[29] After all, species-specific characteristics normally are selected for because they confer some survival advantage on the organisms that possess them. But CML cannot enhance an individual's survival advantage "without being in some way efficacious and influencing the course of his bodily history."[30]

Parallelism. This theory has its classical advocates in Leibniz and Malebranche and is an attempt to maintain dualism without having to accept either the interaction between two distinct metaphysical kinds Cartesianism requires, or the epiphenomenalists' deflationary stance on mental activity. James quotes Clifford, an articulate proponent of parallelism: "The two things are on utterly different platforms—the physical facts go along by themselves, and the mental facts go along by themselves. There is parallelism between them, but there is no interference of one with the other."[31]

As with all positions on the mind-body problem, James acknowledges that this view cannot be straightforwardly proved or disproved. But parallelism has several worrisome features. First, there is the unyielding puzzle as to why there are these two utterly independent but parallel chains of events—a metaphysically odd state of affairs. No less odd, after all, than if the two metaphysically distinct kinds interacted. Second, there is the puzzle as to how the two chains keep their perfect symmetry. The only answer to this question ever proposed in the philosophical literature has been theological: God flawlessly orchestrates the parallel symmetry. Third, parallelism has the implausible and unparsimonious consequence that

> If we knew thoroughly the nervous system of Shakespeare, and as thoroughly all his environing conditions, we should be able to show why at a certain period of his life his hand came to trace on certain sheets of paper those crabbed little black marks which we for shortness' sake call the manuscript of *Hamlet*. We should understand . . . all this without in the slightest degree acknowledging the existence of thoughts in Shakespeare's mind. [B]ut, on the other hand, nothing in all this could prevent us from giving an equally complete account of . . . Shakespeare's spiritual history, an account in which gleam of thought and emotion should find its place. The mind history would run alongside the body-history of each man, and each point in the one would correspond to, but not react upon, a point in the other.[32]

The idea that there might be two such utterly distinct stories about Shakespeare's writing of *Hamlet* does remind us of the widely shared—and to my mind, reasonable—suspicion that any analysis of a significant human act framed totally in the languages of physics and neuroscience will fail to capture certain essential facts related to the meaning and significance of that act. Surely from a physical point of view this play called *Hamlet* is just a series of ink marks on paper, but to Shakespeare and to us it is a story, a meaningful intentional object. At the very least it is an important insight fostered by the parallelist position, that a full-blown science of mind may indeed require different levels of description, some intentional, some not, in order to answer different explanatory questions.

But on the whole the parallelist view is too extreme. Its fundamental flaw is the same as the epiphenomenalist's: namely, the evidence for interaction is overwhelming. It is simply too implausible to assume that Shakespeare's decision to write a play was not causally related to his taking pen in hand, but rather that the two events, the decision to write a play and the movements of his hand over paper just happened to coincide!

Mind-Stuff Theory.   This theory comes in two slightly different versions, both of which are intended as challenges to Cartesian dualism. The central contention of both versions is that the mind as a whole is the straightforward sum of its parts. According to James, mind-stuff theory attempts to *"explain the constitution* of higher mental states by viewing them as *identical with lower ones* summed together."[33] One version of the mind-stuff theory says that CML is identical to the sum of physical particles comprising our brains. The other version, classically identified with Hume, says that CML as a whole is the simple sum of a large number of impressions and ideas—a mere "bundle" of impressions and ideas.

But James worries: if the mind is simply a bundle of impressions and ideas, *who* or *what* notices that? The answer that suggests itself is that it is consciousness that does the noticing. But if that is right, then mind-stuff cannot be a theory about what elements make up CML, since in order to make sense of the position we need to assume that CML exists in addition to the elements which supposedly make it up.

In a thought experiment befitting a modern cognitive scientist, James dares us to "take a sentence of a dozen words, and take twelve men and tell to each one word. Then stand the men in a row or jam them in a bunch, and let each think of his word as intently as he will; nowhere will there be consciousness of the whole sentence."[34]

According to James, the basic problem with the mind-stuff theory is that *"All the 'combinations' which we actually know are EFFECTS, wrought by the units said to be 'combined,' UPON SOME ENTITY OTHER THAN THEMSELVES* . . . no possible number of entities (call them as you like, whether forces, material particles, or mental elements) can sum *them-*

selves together. Each remains in a sum, what it always was; and the sum itself exists only for a *bystander* who happens to overlook the units and to apprehend the sum as such."[35]

Thus the mind cannot be identical to the sum of its parts because we need the mind to do the summing and to acknowledge the addition. But one and the same entity cannot be one of the elements being added and the adder![36] The mind-stuff theory, in effect, begs for a Master Homunculus.

Master Homunculus Theory.   This theory comes in two varieties: a materialist version and a spiritualist version. The materialist who admires the anti-Cartesian motivation of the mind-stuff theory, but who is sensitive to the latter objections can suggest the following thesis. "Every brain-cell has its own individual consciousness, which no other cell knows anything about. . . . There is, however, among the cells one central or pontifical one to which our consciousness is attached."[37]

James, however, objects to this brazen materialistic tactic of claiming the existence of a physical location for our mental masterworks on the grounds that there is absolutely no physical evidence that there is any one such place in the brain (not even Descartes' pineal gland!). "There is no cell or group of cells in the brain of such anatomical or functional preeminence as to appear to be the keystone or centre of gravity of the whole system."[38]

Waiting in the wings of course is our old friend the Cartesian who holds what James calls the "spiritual monad theory." He holds that every remotely plausible theory of the mind requires the existence of a Master Homunculus who comprehends and orchestrates the goings-on of the cognitive system. The Cartesian insists that because there is no evidence that this Master Homunculus is located in the two and one-half pounds of gray matter between our ears, we are logically compelled to assume that it exists nonphysically—as an immaterial *soul* or *thinking-substance.*

Just as James objects to the materialist version of the Master Homunculus theory on the materialist's own grounds (namely, the localization evidence is missing), he challenges the Cartesian on his. The basic problem is this: it is analytic that the Cartesian can produce no direct empirical evidence for his immaterialist hypothesis. Therefore, his theory must have either strong intuitive, introspective, and phenomenological warrant or it must have logic and parsimony on its side. But James insists it does not have the former since we do not ever introspect a Cartesian *soul,* a *pure immutable ego.* Rather we introspect our ordinary everyday self thinking. So, Cartesianism fails the introspective test one would expect to be its primary warrant. What about its warrant on grounds of logic and parsimony? James waffles here. He brushes away standard worries about interaction between two metaphysically different kinds of substances on grounds, *pace* Hume, that all causality is completely mysterious.[39] Still, it is hard to see how Cartesianism could be viewed as the most parsimonious solution to the problem at hand since it requires two metaphysical kinds, while the naturalist is aiming at one.

Furthermore, all Master Homunculus theories, materialist or spiritualist, cause themselves a deadly logical problem. (James would have saved himself a lot of trouble, and not in the end been so tempted by the belief in free will if he had been fully aware of this problem.) The raison d'être for the Master Homunculus is the concern that the very idea of CML presupposes a "comprehender," what James calls a "by-stander," who exists in addition to the elements of the system. But if we always need a comprehender who must exist in addition to, and outside of, what is being comprehended, then we have an infinite regress on our hands.

This is easy to see: suppose I assert that the Master Homunculus is located in area *Omega* of my left cerebral hemisphere, or alternatively that it is located in my *soul*. I can now be asked how I comprehend or am conscious of either of these facts. But according to the logic that gave rise to the postulation of a Master Homunculus in the first place I cannot say that I comprehend that area *Omega* is the seat of CML *with* area *Omega*, or that I comprehend that my CML is realized in my *soul with* my *soul*, because then there is no comprehender or bystander outside the system. The infinite regress is then generated by the requirement that we need a new bystander for each higher-level act of self-comprehension.

The alternative is to give up the requirement that there must always be an outside comprehender or bystander, and endow some part of, or the whole of, the brain or the soul with reflexive powers, with the ability to loop around itself. If the only way to stop the infinite regress is to allow the reflexivity we obviously possess at some point, then why not allow it a place in the cognitive system from the very start? My own view is that this is precisely the direction in which a naturalist must move.

Naturalistic Functionalism. Within the two lengthy volumes of the *Principles*, James expresses attraction to the charms of virtually every conceivable solution to the mind-body problem, including the position that, fortunately, the psychologist is probably better off not worrying about it! I think, however, that his underlying naturalism, as evidenced by his unwavering commitment to evolutionary theory points clearly to a preferred solution, a clearly favored answer, to the question, "how is CML realized?"

If I am right, the tactic that tempted James, without ever fully delivering him from the charms of traditional metaphysical solutions, was to move in the direction of upping the ante on the amount of interaction between cerebral components from that proposed by the mind-stuff theory, and then against master-homunculi theories to endow the entire system with reflexive, self-looping powers from the start.

James's commitment to Darwin's theory of evolution constrained him in two ways. First, he had to provide a theory of the function of CML that saw it as an adaptive, causally efficacious trait. Second, he had to view the initial appearance of CML as an orderly, lawlike outcome of natural selection, rather than as, say, an extra added attraction conferred by God. James says, "We ought therefore ourselves sincerely to try every possible mode of conceiving of consciousness so that it may *not* appear equivalent to the irruption into the universe of a new nature non-existent to then."[40]

Let us define two kinds of emergentism to get a grip on what James might have in mind here. Call *Naturalistic Emergentism* (NE) the view that the world consists of natural objects, natural events, and natural processes, as well as all their properties and relations. According to NE all novel features of the universe must emerge in lawlike ways from the complex interactions of natural objects, events, and processes. The universe is "closed," according to NE, in the sense that natural (that is, physical), stuff cannot give rise to nonnatural, for example, immaterial stuff. NE, however, is a holistic, not a reductionistic view: novel states of affairs can arise from the complex interactions between existing things.

Call *Metaphysical Emergentism* (ME) the thesis that novelty may appear in nonlawlike ways, for example, miraculously. ME is the thesis that the universe is "open" in the sense that nonnatural stuff might (conceivably) emerge from natural stuff. Neither NE or ME, let me say at the start, can be proven one way or the other. They are, respectively, the regulative ideals of two distinct world views.

NE, however, is the attitude of the evolutionary biologist, and that of the scientist in general, and it is the view to which James the psychologist is committed. According to NE, the birth of an utterly new, genetically distinct mammal is the lawlike outcome of the combination of a sperm and an ovum, neither of which on its own is that mammal; the emergence of water is the lawlike outcome of the bonding of two hydrogen atoms and one oxygen atom—none of which are wet on their own; the emergence of a new species with all its attendant morphological and behavioral traits and abilities is the lawlike outcome of natural selection, and so on. If one is to hold NE consistently then CML must also be viewed as a feature that has emerged via natural selection in creatures with our particular kind of biological organization.

The clue NE provides to the question "how is CML realized?" is by leading us to focus on those features of our biological organization that distinguish us from creatures without CML, such as amoeba, or from creatures with (apparently) less rich CML than us, such as dogs. The distinguishing feature, of course, is the complexity of our nervous system as a whole, and our brain in particular.

So why are we not led straight back to the mind-stuff theory, to the view that CML is simply the brain; or to the materialist version of the Master Homunculus theory, the view that CML is simply one part of the brain? The underlying problem with these particular forms of naturalism is that they imply that CML is a *thing*.

In a paper written in 1904, "Does 'Consciousness' Exist?", James admits that for over twenty years, and therefore before the writing of the *Principles*, he had "mistrusted 'consciousness' as an entity."[41] What could this mean? James answers, "I mean only to deny that the word stands for an entity, but to insist most emphatically that it stands for a function."[42]

James's remarks suggest two things. First, they suggest that we conceive of CML as analogous to walking or breathing. Surely, walking and breathing are not things or entities in any ordinary sense of those terms. Walking and breathing are functions of our bodies. The fact that they are functional phenomena rather than things explains why questions like "what is the function of breathing or walking?" or "what is the breathing or walking done by?" are much more coherent and answerable than the localization question "where is the breathing or walking?" Notice further that the difficulty of answering the last question does not evoke any great fears about the metaphysical status of breathing and walking. We harbor no worries that breathing and walking might be occult, nonnatural phenomena.[43]

On this analysis, the snag with traditional formulations of the mind-body problem is the tendency to think that we must frame a solution in which CML is analyzed as *a thing*, preferably as *The Thing*. It is not at all surprising that this never works. Mental states are functional states and functional properties of the complex commerce we have with the outside world.

James's phenomenological description of CML as a "stream of thought" is, as I understand it, a clear attempt to dislodge this expectation that if CML is to be a respectable feature of the natural world it must turn out to be a thing.

The second thing James's functionalist stance suggests, especially in light of his evolutionary sympathies, is that we answer the question "what is consciousness done by?" in the same sort of way we answer the question "what is breathing done by?" by citing some complex interaction with the world of some major body part: (mostly) the brain in the first instance, and (mostly) the lungs in the second.

James is careful to insist that although "a higher state *is* not a lot of lower states; *it is itself*. When, however, a lot of lower states have come together, or when certain brain-conditions occur together . . . we have not for a moment pretended that a higher state may not emerge. In fact it does emerge under those conditions. . . . But such emergence is that of a new psychic entity, and is *toto coelo* different from such an 'integration' of the lower states as the mind-stuff theory affirms."[44]

As I read James here, his suggestion is that because CML is a functional outcome of brain-world interaction, it is not simply identical to the brain—"*it is itself*." Just as the naturalist explains the species origin of CML as a function of gene-brain-world interactions which have taken place over the phylogenic long haul, he explains its current nature, in you and in me, as a function of brain-world interactions taking place over the ontogenic short haul.

Or, to make the point in a way that will bring out the important methodological lesson of the functionalist view of mind: just as a full description of a breath will have to talk about much more than just the lungs, and just as even the most complete physiological description of my legs will not suffice for an analysis of a stroll across the room, so too we will need to analyze CML in its own functional terms. Talking about bundles of neurons or bundles of impressions and ideas will simply not do the job. Dewey puts it best:

> Breathing is an affair of the air as truly as of the lungs; digesting an affair of the food as truly as of the tissues of the stomach. Seeing involves light just as certainly as it does the eye and optic nerve. Walking implicates the ground as well as the legs; speech demands physical air and human companionship as well as vocal organs.[45]

The philosophy of mind and the science of mind converge here. The functionalist solution to the philosophical mind-body problem indicates why reductionist strategies typically fail: they tend to underestimate the complexity, the robustness, and the functionally emergent properties of the phenomenon under study.

Naturalism and Free Will

We now come to the snag, the single but overwhelming reservation

James has about the naturalistic direction of his own thought, with the very conception of a science of the mind. Namely, what happens to *free will*, to the feeling that we make autonomous choices, that we are masters of our own fate, and not mere cogs in some Cosmic Machine born at the Big Bang?

Near the very end of the almost thirteen hundred pages which comprise the *Principles*, James is overwhelmed with worries that in the end the challenge to the philosopher to show how a scientific conception of the mind is compatible with our ordinary conception of human nature may be insoluble, just as Descartes thought. According to James, our ordinary sense of ourselves, the one we need to make our existence not seem absurd, to make life worth living, may, at the limit, be incommensurable with the theory of human nature a psychological science must assume. When push comes to shove it seems as if philosophy, moral philosophy in particular, will simply not allow psychology. Harking back to the theme of an earlier paper, "The Dilemma of Determinism," James announces in the last pages of the *Principles* that,

> the most that any argument can do for determinism is to make it a clear and seductive conception, which a man is foolish not to espouse, so long as he stands by the great scientific postulate that the world must be an unbroken fact, and that prediction of all things without exception must be ideally, even if not actually, possible. It is a *moral* postulate about the Universe, the postulate that *what ought to be can be, and that bad acts cannot be fated, but that good ones must be possible in their place*, which would lead to the contrary view.[46]

In the "Epilogue" to his *Psychology: The Briefer Course*, written two years after the *Principles*, James tips his hand even more clearly,

> Let psychology frankly admit that *for her scientific purposes* determinism can be *claimed*, and no one can find fault. If, then, it turn out later that the claim has only a relative purpose, and may be crossed by counter-claims, the readjustment can be made. Now ethics makes a counter-claim; and the present writer, for one, has no hesitation in regarding her claim as the stronger, and in assuming that our wills are "free." For him, then, the deterministic assumption of psychology is merely provisional and methodological.[47]

James's point is this. A psychologist looking for the laws that govern human action is behaving sensibly only if he assumes that human action does, in fact, behave in a causally regular manner: in a manner such that any time an effect occurs, there exists a cause or set of causes sufficient to produce the effect, that is, such that the effect was inevitable.

The assumption that human action is lawful in this sense regulates the actual search for psychological laws. On the other hand, all the ordinary modes of human interaction and discourse, all the rewarding, and criticizing, cajoling, admiring, and goading we engage in with each other and ourselves seem to require the assumption that we are *free*, that we are, in some metaphysically significant sense, self-governing and self-creating. It requires that, with regard to voluntary action, any effect that we bring about might have been otherwise, had we chosen it to be otherwise.

The problem, as James sees it, is that the belief in determinism seems to fit best with the scientific vision of things, while the belief in free will seems to cohere best with our social, moral, political, and legal practices. Given this conflict, James the pragmatist leans toward the assumption he takes to underlie the most comprehensive, widely shared life form, our social one. Thus he bets on free will.

My suggestion is that there is a way out of this bind. In fact I am convinced that James's naturalistic theory of CML provides a model for conceiving of the mind that allows for the beliefs: that actions can be done on purpose; that action can be rational; that deliberation can result in free choice; that such choices can go against very powerful desires and inclinations; that we can think of humans as responsible—all this without the paradoxical requirement that some actions, namely those of our free will, be totally uncaused.

The position I advocate is known as *compatibilism*, its classical advocates are Locke, Hume, and Mill.[48] James himself disparagingly referred to this view as *soft determinism*. The soft determinist differs from the hard determinist in the following way: the hard determinist thinks that so long as our behavior is caused at all, there is no sense in which our actions are free; the soft determinist thinks that the question of free action depends on the *type(s)* of cause(s) our behavior has. In particular, if our actions have as their proximate cause, processing by a system such as CML, they can count as free, rational, voluntary, purposive actions.

First, let me indicate why the belief in the Cartesian notion of *free will*, the one James is tempted by, is incoherent; this will make it easier to see why naturalism should not be abandoned. According to the Cartesian, the human mind consists of a faculty of Understanding which is limited, and a Will which is unlimited and unconstrained: "the will is so free in its nature, that it can never be constrained." The Understanding supplies a scenario of possible action or belief options, and the Will chooses among them. So if I go to my favorite restaurant and look at the menu, it is my Understanding that represents to me the five luncheon options I have. Then my Will chooses among them in a totally unconstrained way.

But what could "unconstrained" mean here? One thing it could mean is that my willing is totally random, a chance event. On this interpretation, my telling the waiter "Toasted cheese and tomato on rye, please" is metaphysically comparable to a coin toss. Unfortunately, if we interpret "unconstrained" to mean random, then we lose exactly what the concept of *free will* is meant to do, namely, provide an analysis of our actions as not random or arbitrary, but rather as fully in our control. The Cartesian therefore cannot really mean that our voluntary actions are unconstrained.

Perhaps he means that voluntary actions are only constrained by our preferences. On this interpretation, once my Understanding represented the menu options, I willed in accordance with my preference for toasted cheese and tomato on rye. But on this view my Will is constrained by my preferences, so it is not in the strict sense free or unconstrained. Furthermore, it is a natural question to ask: What is my preference for toasted cheese and tomato on rye based on? One answer is that it is based on my current biochemistry, my views about a sound diet, my memory of what I ate yesterday, my plans for dinner tonight, and so on.

In this case, we have a situation where my Will is constrained by my preferences, and my preferences are constrained by all these other things, and these things in turn by still other things, and so on, presumably ad infinitum. But this is exactly the way the soft determinist wants things to turn out, so it cannot be what the Cartesian intends. The Cartesian's only option is to argue that the preference that constrains the Will is itself unconstrained, utterly freely chosen in a prior unconstrained act of the Will. But then we are back to the view that the act originates in a random event, which is of no help at all to the Cartesian.

Under no interpretation, therefore, can the Cartesian get his concept of *free will* to do the job he wants: either he has our voluntary actions originating in random events, or he has them embedded in systems of prior constraints ad infinitum.

James should have seen that the concept of *free will* to which he was attracted would cause him exactly the same problem that its metaphysical companion the "Spiritual Monad" solution to the mind-body problem causes; it requires an utterly mysterious agent to exist outside the system. The alternative is to bite the naturalistic bullet as, for example, James's disciple John Dewey did after reading James's *Principles*.

In 1894, in a paper "The Ego as a Cause," Dewey argues that the main question facing the science of mind is whether in discussing human action we can "carry back our analysis to scientific conditions, or must we stop at a given point because we have come upon a force of an entirely different order—an independent ego as an entity in itself.''[49] Dewey argues that reference to a *free will* which initiates causal chains ex nihilo is merely an excuse for our ignorance of the determining conditions of the state of the person. It is a way of stopping inquiry in a manner compatible with our hubris, but it does not give an adequate rendering of the causal facts.

When James himself surveyed proposed solutions to the mind-body problem, he rejected any view that cast doubt on the overwhelming evidence that CML is causally efficacious, that it gets things done. It's obvious that if I consciously decide to go to the ball game, I go.

Now on the traditional view, one of the most important things *free will* does is boss the body around. For example, it gets my body to the ball game. Viewed from one perspective, therefore, CML and *free will* serve the same explanatory function. Both, so to speak, explain how my body gets to the ball game.

But if CML and *free will* can do the same explanatory work, then given a sufficiently rich description of CML as a natural, functional representational system, one has no need for the additional and ultimately incoherent concept of *free will* in order to explain how our wishes, desires, and choices materialize in action. Let me explain what I mean.

Our particular kind of CML, according to James, is a functional system that has evolved naturally. Its most salient features include the ability to (self-) consciously represent past, present, and possible future states of affairs, and to choose means to bring about the ones considered most desirable. Furthermore, the system changes over time: it is responsive to feedback from the natural and social environment, and is thereby continually updating the information it contains, as well as adjusting the interests and expectations it has.

Such a system is all the soft determinist needs. First, actions can be done on purpose by such a system since the system can represent desired goals and choose the means to reach these goals. Second, so long as the chosen goals are the desired goals, actions are "free" in the sense that they are performed in accordance with the agent's preferences. Third, there is nothing mysterious about CML having the causal power (which is probably more of the information-exchange variety than of the brute force variety) to boss the (rest of the) body around, since on the naturalist's view, both are parts of the larger integrated system comprising one person. Fourth, actions (can) involve rationality and deliberation for such a system. The entire evolutionary advantage of having evolved a representational, information-processing system, rests, after all, on the causal efficacy of thinking about things and weighing options before acting. Fifth, it is easy to explain how it is possible for such a system to make choices that go against powerful desires and inclinations: the system is extremely sensitive to informational feedback from the natural world. In this way the system can learn that it will have to override strong inclinations because although their satisfaction may powerfully please the agent, others do not feel the same.

Sixth, there remains an essential place for the notion of responsibility, although it has to be stripped of all its Cartesian appendages. CML, on the naturalist's view, is a deterministic system, albeit an informationally sensitive system, embedded in an environment in which it interacts with myriad other deterministic systems. If, therefore, one is looking for a concept of responsibility which will justify punishing and blaming people for past deeds on grounds that they could have acted other than they in fact did, then one will be disappointed. The only theory which can supply such a notion is the Cartesian theory of *free will*, and that theory is incoherent.

But if we conceive of morality in the naturalistic manner of Dewey we can preserve a concept of responsibility very nicely. Dewey insists that "morals has to do with acts still within our control, acts still to be performed . . . the moral issue concerns the future. . . . The moral problem is that of modifying the factors which now influence future results."[50]

What this suggests is that we think of humans as responsible for their actions in the following way: CML is an incredibly plastic, informationally sensitive representational system. Any individual CML is capable therefore of responding to enormously varied features of the environment, in enormously complex ways. Our modes of social interaction, our ways of passing information about our attitudes toward the actions of others—from hugs and frowns to moral philosophizing, imprisonment, and canonization—are thus ways of taking advantage of the plasticity and information-processing capacity of CML, and enabling others to become able to respond, in moral and nonmoral situations, in ways which they cannot, and do not, at present.

The soft determinist views as meaningless the idea that people are responsible for past actions in the sense that they could have done other than they in fact did. But the idea of promoting a sense of responsibility is utterly intelligible, since it is prospective. It involves the acquisition of knowledge, information, and motivation so that we have the ability to respond differently than we now do.

In the end, then, James's theory of CML, naturalistically interpreted, needs no help from the concept of *free will* in order to give an account of purposeful, rational, and free action. All this is good for the naturalist and the pragmatist, and it is not ultimately surprising. As Dewey perceptively notes, what humans "have esteemed and fought for in the name of liberty is varied and complex—but certainly it has never been metaphysical freedom of will."[51]

Conclusion

I can now summarize my views on William James.

(1) James offers a rich phenomenological description of conscious mental life (CML) in terms of seven essential features: purposefulness, intentionality, consciousness itself, personality, personal change, personal continuity, and selectivity. This phenomenological theory constitutes the descriptive portion of a science of mind. It constrains the explanatory portion of psychology by requiring a theory of the origin and function of a system with these features, which does not, thereby, fall into the trap of explaining them away.

(2) Thanks to the influence of evolutionary biology, James is committed to a naturalistic explanation of the origin and present function of CML. CML presumably emerged by way of natural selection because it gave our species certain survival, and therefore reproductive, advantages. On such a naturalistic view, we must assume that CML causally interacts with (the rest of the) body. It is simply too implausible to think that such a powerful representational system might have evolved with no causal power relative to the overall system it is part of!

(3) James's naturalism takes him in the direction of a functionalist solution to the mind-body problem—toward the view that CML is a causally effective feature of brain-world interactions, rather than a thing. In this way, he avoids the Scylla of metaphysical dualism and the Charybdis of a simplistic materialism.

(4) Unfortunately, James cannot quite take his naturalism to the limit. He sees no way to make consistent the view of persons as moral agents with the deterministic assumption of a science of mind. I argued that a consistent naturalist should deal with the free will problem by taking a soft determinist stance. This is the only stance, as far as I can see, that simultaneously allows a science of mind, does the least amount of damage to our ordinary conception of persons, and does not require an epiphenomenalistic account of the phenomenological features of CML.

In the next chapter I turn to Sigmund Freud's attempt to provide a theory of mind in which unconscious mental life is featured prominently. Freud serves as a perfect counterpoint to James. While Freud paints unconscious mental life with the same purposeful, willful, and intentional strokes James uses on conscious mental life, he resurrects the concern that no matter how completely we fill out James's theory of conscious mental life we may have only described the tip of the iceberg.

Suggested Readings

General Primary Sources

James (1890), *The Principles of Psychology.*
James (1892), *Psychology: The Briefer Course.*

On Free Will

James (1884), "The Dilemma of Determinism."
Dennett (1978c), "Free Will and Personhood," in Dennett, *Brainstorms.*
Dennett (1984), *Elbow Room: The Varieties of Free Will Worth Wanting.*
Dewey (1894), "The Ego as a Cause."
Dewey (1922), *Human Nature and Conduct: An Introduction to Social Psychology.*

On Consciousness

James (1904), "Does Consciousness Exist?"
Dennett (1978e), "Toward a Cognitive Theory of Consciousness."
Rorty (1982b), "Contemporary Philosophy of Mind."

On Intentionality

Dennett and Haugeland (1987), "Intentionality."

On Introspection

Lyons, William (1986), *The Disappearance of Introspection.*

Four Good Commentaries

Flower, E. and Murphy, M. (1977), *A History of Philosophy in America,* especially vol. 2 chapter 11.
Myers, Gerald E. (1986), *William James: His Life and Thought.*
Perry, R. B. (1938), *In the Spirit of William James.*
Scheffler, I. (1974), *Four Pragmatists: A Critical Introduction to Pierce, James, Mead, and Dewey.*

Philosophical Implications of Pragmatism

Rorty, R. (1982a), *Consequences of Pragmatism.*

Chapter 3

Science and the Secret Self: The Case of Sigmund Freud

The philosophical implications of Sigmund Freud's psychoanalytical theory are so varied and so numerous that one cannot begin to do justice to them in one chapter. Freud revolutionized as much as Nietzsche—and in part because of Nietzsche—our philosophical conception of human nature.[1] He created an epistemological crisis by questioning the degree to which human motives are known and knowable. He painted the selfish, aggressive, and sexual quality of human motivation more vividly than any previous thinker. He saw accidents as intentional, and dreams, not rational discourse, as reflecting our real hopes, desires, and wishes. He viewed religion as an illusion, morality as a social invention, and culture itself as the compromise that makes social life possible by keeping us busy with tasks which keep our mind off what we would really like to be doing.

The very formulation of Freud's theory and the evidence on which he based it provoke serious reflection on methodological issues, on issues in the philosophy of science. Are Freud's autobiographical data, or his clinical data based on inferences about what his patients were often *not* saying, good evidence for psychoanalytic theory? Does the logic behind Freudian theory protect the theory from any possible refutation? Are a theoretician's motives, while doing science, any less likely to be infiltrated by unconscious wishes than his or her motives while doing more ordinary things?

Here my focus is on a small subset of these questions. First I discuss Freud's views on the mind-body problem and on the nature of psychological language. Then I discuss the implications of Freudian theory for the problem of self-knowledge, and for introspection as a method for gaining personal or psychological knowledge. Finally, I discuss the problem of verifying or falsifying psychoanalytic theory.

First, one general comment is in order about the national character

---

The best introduction to Freud's thought is his own *Introductory Lectures on Psychoanalysis* (1917).

of psychological theory. In 1927, when speaking of Edward L. Thorn-dike's and Wolfgang Köhler's recent primate research in America and Germany respectively, Bertrand Russell noted with amusement that

> One may say broadly that all the animals that have been carefully observed have behaved so as to confirm the philosophy in which the observer believed before his observations began. Nay, more, they have all displayed the national characteristics of the observer. Animals studied by Americans rush about frantically, with an incredible display of hustle and pep, and at last achieve the desired result by chance. Animals observed by Germans sit still and think, and at last evolve the solution out of their inner consciousness. To the plain man such as the present writer, this situation is discouraging.[2]

Russell's witty remark contains more than a grain of truth about psychological theorizing. Freudian theory is dramatically different from mainstream American psychology. Until very recently the major focus of American psychology was on action taking place in the external world, that is, behavior. The focus of Freudian theory is on action taking place in the deep recesses of the mind. Furthermore, American psychology traditionally has shared with the British philosophical and psychological tradition a view of human action motivated by rewards and punishments doled out in the social environment.

Although Freud's discussions of the pleasure principle might seem to be compatible with such a conception, there are important differences. In particular, the character of the Freudian pleasure principle is such that it seeks satisfaction by fantasies of revenge, sexual relations with one's parents, and other seamy things. The pleasures and pains of traditional American psychology, on the other hand, are simple utility, and pragmatic gains and losses. Freud, in fact, denies that our deep-seated, repetitive, and unconsciously motivated dispositions can be altered by manipulating ordinary rewards and punishments.

Adolf Grünbaum puts Freud's doubt concerning the susceptibility of behavior to manipulation by pleasant or unpleasant consequences this way: "(unconscious) yearnings repeatedly give rise to behavior which is largely insensitive to ensuing unhappiness or happiness, and oblivious to errors of judgement. Hence there is little scope for learning from experience, change, or growth; instead, there is considerable enslavement to unconscious dictates."[3] In the Freudian scheme of things, it is possible, although certainly not inevitable, that insight into one's unconscious motivation can lead to emotional and behavioral changes which no amount of satisfying or dissatisfying consequences will ever bring about.

In 1920 Freud finally called attention to the distinction between the two kinds of hedonism in *Beyond the Pleasure Principle*. But the differences between Anglo-American motives and Austro-Germanic motives—between utilitarian and "depth psychological" thinking—had been vividly portrayed years before by Nietzsche in *Beyond Good and Evil* (1881) and *The Genealogy of Morals* (1887). I shall only comment that the issue of the national character of theory is worth watching out for. One would think, especially if one is operating with standard conceptions of scientific truth and with the expectation that psychology contains such truths, that psychological theory should not turn out to be culturally relative.

Freud on the Mind-Body Problem and Psychological Explanation

By Freud's time the mind-body problem had become the mind-brain problem. Descartes had located the single point of commerce between *res cogitans* and *res extensa* in the brain, and neurophysiological and physiological research in the eighteenth and nineteenth centuries had come to locate the center of most interesting nervous system activity in the cerebral cortex. So common was the assumption of the brain's centrality by the beginning of the twentieth century that the great Russian psychologist Pavlov unreflectively subtitled his famous book *Conditioned Reflexes*, "An Investigation of the Physiological Activity of the Cortex," even though he worked almost exclusively on intact animals and studied only their overt behavior.[4]

During the 1870s Freud was trained as a neurologist, within a medical tradition committed to the universality and adequacy of a materialistic account of human behavior. Hermann von Helmholtz and Ernst Brücke, the latter Freud's mentor and the former Brücke's mentor, were committed to a model of mind in which all the elements were physical, and in which all the causal relations between the elements were governed by mechanical principles, similar, for example, to the hydraulic principles that governed the behavior of Cartesian automata.

As late as 1895, when he wrote *The Project for a Scientific Psychology*, Freud was still under the sway of this mental model. In the *Project* Freud espoused a *type-type identity* position on the mind-body problem. Type-type identity theory is the theory that each kind of mental event, described in its own everyday mentalistic way, is actually identical to a neurological kind, described in a precise materialistic way. Thus, for example, Freud hypothesized that the class of events we ordinarily refer to as "perception" (constituted by all your individual perceptions and mine) is identical to the neurological class constituted by the activity of *phi* neurons; the class of events we call "memory" is identical to activity of the neurological class *psi* neurons; and the class of events we call "consciousness" is identical to the activity of the neurological class *omega* neurons.

Freud's confidence that an exhaustive list of mind-brain identity statements could be spelled out was underwritten by his commitment to metaphysical materialism. Nevertheless, the isolation of all the mind-brain identity statements—in itself an enormous project—was to be only the first step in the overall project of creating a science of mind on an epistemological par with medicine, and with as useful applications as medicine.

The second step was eliminative *reductionism*. Freud says the "intention is to furnish a psychology that shall be a natural science: that is *to represent* psychical processes as quantitatively determinate states of specifiable material particles, thus making these processes perspicuous and free from contradiction."[5] The idea behind reductionism is this: once all the mind-brain identity statements get mapped out, reformulate all your psychological laws by trading in the old-fashioned mentalistic vocabulary for the newfangled neurological vocabulary.

Suppose, for example, that the identity theorist discovers that what we call "love" is just a complex set of neuron firings in the lower left-hand corner of the right cerebral hemisphere, designated scientifically as "qrxt-firings at velocity v and rate r in sector 1704." If this identity statement were true, then we could rewrite our ordinary psychological generalization "when people fall in love they have trouble getting their work done" as "when people are in the state of having qrxt-firings at velocity v and rate r in sector 1704 they have trouble getting their work done."

It is essential to point out, however, that materialism does not necessitate reductionism. If type-type identity theory turned out to be true then it would follow that reductionism is possible. But reductionism would not be required. Thus, for example, I might refuse to trade in love-talk for qrxt-talk on all sorts of pragmatic grounds: I'm not used to qrxt-talk; all my nonscientific loved ones will not understand my expressions of affection; it's easy to tell when a person is in love even if one does not have access to his or her brain states; the two ways of talking have different connotations (even though they have the same denotation) and these connotations are worth preserving, and so on.[6] I could display this sort of resistance to the reductionist move, to the move to replace my ordinary way of talking with some explicitly materialistic vocabulary and still claim to be a card-carrying materialist. All I need do is profess my faith in the materiality of all mental phenomena. Materialism is primarily a metaphysical attitude, while reductionism is primarily an epistemological or methodological strategy.

And although they usually go together like a horse and carriage, you can have one without the other.[7]

Actually, not even all versions of identity theory entail the possibility of reductionism. *Token-token* identity theory does not. *Types* refer to classes of entities, events, or processes, and *tokens* refer to individual members of a type. For example, "chair" is a type and the one you are sitting on is a token of the type. For reductionism to be possible, the *types* of psychology must map neatly onto the *types* of neuroscience. But that may be too much to expect. Consider the following analogy (from Dan Dennett): a clock is the *type* of thing that tells the time. OK, but notice "type of thing that tells the time" is not a very materialistic way of putting things; it describes clocks in functional terms. So, let's try to define "clock" in terms of a type—a mode of classification—available in physics. You will soon notice that there is no clear-cut set of physical features that defines the class of clocks. There is, in effect, no one *type* of physical thing by virtue of which all *token* clocks belong to the *type* clock. Some clocks run on springs and motors, some are digital, some have batteries, some are big, some are small, some contain sand, and so on. All clocks, of course, are physical. So token-token identity theory is true of clocks; each and every clock is a physical thing. But type-type identity theory is false of clocks; there is no physical vocabulary that can do the job our functional way of talking about clocks does.

The bet of the so-called "token-physicalist" is that the types of psychology will turn out to be just as impossible to map onto neuroscientific types as the type "clock" is impossible to map onto a type from physics. This way of thinking is typical of the modern functionalist solution to the mind-body problem which I see Freud anticipating. The attractiveness of the functionalist position is that it allows one to believe in materialism without reductionism.

But let's suppose for the time being that type-type identity theory is true, and thus that the reduction of psychology to neuroscience will someday be possible. We still need some justification for engaging in the tiresome project of replacing our psychological vocabulary with its neurological equivalent. After all, if two languages have the same conceptual resources, that is, if they are capable of saying all the same things, then why isn't the choice of language an inconsequential matter of what a particular scientist is comfortable with?

The justification Freud recommends in the *Project* for urging reduction in the direction of neuroscience is that by representing psychical processes in terms of specific material particles, we will make these processes "perspicuous and free from contradiction." His rationale for reductionism is that ordinary psychological vocabulary is vague and imprecise, and this imprecision limits our understanding of the psychological phenomena. This sort of view achieved its most articulate form and found its most sympathetic audience in the 1920s and 1930s when the operationists and logical positivists promoted the view that all legitimate scientific discourse should be framed in an explicitly materialistic vocabulary.

The remarkable thing from the perspective of the philosophy of mind and the philosophy and history of science is that Freud no sooner announced the program of materialism with reductionism than he abandoned it. In 1895, the very year of the *Project*, Freud stated that it was a "pointless masquerade to try to account for psychical processes physiologically." He came to say of the search for biological correlates of neurotic thoughts that "there are either no observable changes in the anatomical organ of the mind to correspond to them, or changes which throw no light upon them."[8] And he proposed in 1917 that "psychoanalysis must keep itself free from any hypothesis that is alien to it, whether of an anatomical, chemical, or physiological kind, and must operate with purely psychological auxiliary ideas."[9]

Statements such as these and almost all of Freud's work after 1895 support, and are supported by, what I call the *Thesis of the Autonomy of Psychological Explanation* (*Autonomy Thesis*, for short), the thesis that the science of the mind should proceed to frame its laws and principles in terms of its own specialized vocabulary without trying to force translations into the vocabulary of any already existing natural science. The *Autonomy Thesis* involves the wholesale rejection of the reductionist program. Whether it should also be seen as involving the rejection of materialism is harder to tell.

I will return to the question of Freud's ultimate attitude toward materialism. But first it will be useful to examine some of the reasons that might have led him to abandon the reductionist program of the *Project* in favor of the *Autonomy Thesis*. In examining these reasons I am more concerned with offering a plausible philosophical reconstruction of the sorts of considerations that might lead to a rejection of reductionism than I am in telling the precise historical story behind Freud's rejection of reductionism. Nevertheless, there is plenty of evidence that the story I am about to tell is historically credible.

Broadly speaking, two sets of facts seem particularly relevant to Freud's rejection of reductionism. First, there are facts having to do with the state of the art. Second, there are facts having to do with intentionality. The state-of-the-art problem is simple and straightforward. In order to carry out a program of reducing one science to another, the modes of classifying things, the typologies, in both sciences have to be clearly and completely worked out. The reason is obvious: a necessary condition of a scientific reduction involves having your type-type identity statements in place (philosophers of science call these "bridge laws"). But you cannot possibly have your type-type identity statements in place if you do not have the typologies of both the science to be reduced and the reducing science down pat. For example, if you have not clearly worked out, within your psychology, what love is, and if you have not clearly worked out, within your neuroscience, what qrxt-firings are, then you don't stand a chance of credibly asserting that love is a qrxt-firing.

This, however, is precisely our scientific plight: neither psychology nor neuroscience is in a sufficiently conceptually rigorous state to warrant more than the fantasy of a reduction. One might still hold onto reductionism as some sort of regulative ideal for the science of the next millennium. But for now the project of "operating with purely psychological auxiliary ideas" and getting psychology itself in shape is a perfectly appropriate and respectable enterprise. The state of science makes any more ambitious program a "pointless masquerade."

The second set of considerations that make the *Autonomy Thesis* attractive has to do with intentionality. Intentionality is the feature that allegedly distinguishes mental phenomena from physical phenomena; it is the feature whereby mental states have semantic content. Many (some say most or all) mental events—for example, beliefs, desires, hopes, loves, wonderings, expectings, and so on—are about something; they take an object. But the object they take is no ordinary physical object. It is a semantic object. For example, my belief that Santa Claus is coming to town does not imply that there is a fat bearded man accompanied by reindeer and presents jaunting around inside my cranium. It is just that when it comes to that nonexistent entity, Santa Claus, I represent things to myself in ways that you perhaps do not. That Santa Claus is coming to town is just, in some mysterious way, the content, the object, of one of my beliefs.

Whatever the exact nature of this representing relation turns out to be, it seems clear that beliefs, desires, and so on, are essentially related to their contents. You have not told me anything about your beliefs until you tell me about their content. The content of your beliefs is their essence. Now if the content of a mental state is its essence, it would seem to follow that talking about semantic or intentional content will be required by any theory that wants to account for psychological phenomena. For example, in order to understand why I put out cookies and milk on Christmas Eve and your other adult acquaintances do not, you will need to talk about the content of our respective Yuletide beliefs.

Because of considerations such as these, the philosopher Franz Brentano (from whom Freud took three and one-half years of elective courses while in medical school) argued that intentionality was the ineliminable mark of the mental. This view, which has come to be known as "Brentano's thesis," implies that no language that lacks the conceptual resources to capture the meaningful content of mental states, such as the language of physics or neuroscience, can ever adequately capture the salient facts about psychological phenomena. (What is it about your qrxt-firing, for example, that makes it love of Adrienne as opposed to love of modern art?) If intentional content is ineliminable, then psychology is, and must remain, a science with its own unique vocabulary, and the *Autonomy Thesis* is won outright.

Not only is it safe to assume that Freud was influenced by Brentano's views on intentionality, but there is also reason to think that the sorts of psychological phenomena Freud came across during the 1880s, the decade following his initial exposure to Brentano's ideas, would have reinforced these ideas. I have in mind Freud's exposure to the case of Anna O. and the hypnotic techniques of Jean Baptiste Charcot and Hippolyte Bernheim.

Between 1880 and 1882 Freud collaborated with Josef Breuer on the case of "Anna O." Anna O. was twenty-one years old when she came to Breuer suffering from a host of maladies, including paralysis and loss of feeling on her right side, impaired speech and vision, and an aversion to food. Breuer's startling discovery was that if, under hypnosis, Anna expressed "forgotten" memories and feelings associated with a time several years earlier when she nursed her dying father, her symptoms would disappear. Anna herself dubbed the discovery the "talking cure."

In France, Charcot and Bernheim further advanced hypnotic technique and theory. Charcot, whom Freud visited for five months in 1885–86, made two important discoveries: under hypnosis, paralysis or amnesia can be induced in otherwise normal people by "suggestion"; and induced paralysis often involves loss of feeling and movement in a portion of the body that the average person thinks of as a unit, but is not a unit from a neuroscientific point of view. The neurologist, for example, might know that if one of your arms is really paralyzed, you should also have no feeling in the vicinity of the corresponding shoulder blade. Induced paralysis, however, frequently fails to cooperate with the neurological facts.

Meanwhile, Bernheim, whom Freud visited in 1889, was replicating the Anna O. results systematically: under hypnosis people remember all sorts of things they sincerely claim not to remember in the normal conscious state. Bernheim also made important discoveries regarding "posthypnotic suggestion": if, under hypnosis, a subject is instructed to touch (upon awakening) the tip of his nose every time any food-related word is uttered, he will do so, but he will not remember a thing about the original suggestion.

This relates to the *Autonomy Thesis* in the following way: in all these cases the surprising psychological phenomena are best explained by reference to some meaningful mental content. Anna O.'s cure is the result of talking about the content of some specific memories related to her father's death, and some feelings she had about him. The specific form of Charcot's patients' paralysis is best explained in terms of the ideas the patients had about what constitutes a paralyzable body-unit. And Bernheim's posthypnotic suggestion is only explicable in terms of the effect of some specific semantic content; if we fail to mention the content of the suggestion it is impossible to explain why we have a nose-toucher as opposed to an ear-twitcher. What is probably most exciting about all these results is that they show that unconscious mental content is as capable of being causally effective as is conscious mental content.

The moral I want to extract (and attribute to Freud) is simply this: intentional content must figure essentially in psychological explanation. A purely psychological language, consisting of the vocabulary of (conscious or unconscious) belief, memory, desire, wish, and so on, can provide a framework in which intentional content figures essentially, while the languages of chemistry, physics, and neuroscience, at present at least, cannot. For reasons such as these the *Thesis of the Autonomy of Psychological Explanation* was an unquestioned assumption of Freud's theorizing from 1895 onward.

I now return to the question of Freud's considered position on the mind-body problem. Some people have interpreted Freud's anti-reductionism, as evidenced by his advocacy of the *Autonomy Thesis*, as implying antimaterialism. For example, his student and biographer Ernest Jones claims that "Freud held that not only was the essential nature of both mind and matter quite unknown, but they were so *intrinsically different in kind* as to make it a logical error to translate a description of processes in the one into terms of the other."[10] The view that Jones attributes to Freud is a kind of metaphysical dualism—mind and body are intrinsically different in kind.

In particular, Jones calls Freud an "adherent of psychological parallelism." According to parallelism, every mental event is correlated with some physical event, but mental events are neither identical to, nor causally related to, physical events. The advantage of this position, which goes back to the seventeenth-century philosopher Leibniz, is that it allows one to do psychology without giving up dualism and without countenancing all the problems associated with Cartesian mind-body interaction. On the parallelist view, mental events and physical events both obey strict causal laws. They just happen to hum along on utterly distinct, but perfectly correlated, causal paths.

What this view makes problematic, without ever resolving, is how and why the lovely symmetry between mental and physical—psychological and neural—events is maintained. The philosopher Malebranche when faced with this problem saw fit to introduce God's continual intervention to make the two causal networks keep their perfect correlation. Leibniz, on the other hand, required God to set a "preestablished harmony." To have to introduce God to explain the workings of the mind, however, is to introduce a big Spirit in order to get rid of the perplexities of a world of little spirits, and to magnify the complications one presumably set out to reduce.

Fortunately, it is unnecessary and implausible to read Freud as an advocate of any kind of metaphysical dualism. First of all, he was certainly not a Cartesian dualist, since he denied the existence of free will. Freud insisted that the expectation of strict causal necessity among all events was an essential part of the scientific *Weltanschauung*. Like William James, but without any of the reticence, Freud viewed determinism as the assumption that makes sense of doing scientific psychology. Second, dualism of the parallelist variety—the kind Jones attributes to Freud—is incompatible with the existence of certain psychological phemonena which Freudian theory openly accepts, for example, psychosomatic illnesses, and physical accidents caused by mental wishes. Recall that the parallelist solution avoids the problem of the causal peculiarities of Cartesian interactionism—violation of conservation principles, and the like—by denying that there is any interaction between *res cogitans* and *res extensa*. But if the two fail to have commerce it is hard to see how phenomena like psychosomatic illness can be explained, unless we invoke Malebranche's God, so that self-punitive thoughts happen to occur just as bleeding ulcers do.

There are two ways to understand Freud's position on the mind-body problem that fit much more coherently with his overall view on psychological explanation. (I favor the second interpretation, but both are credible.) First, we can read the post-1895 Freud as committed to neutrality on the question of the nature of mental events. This is compatible with Jones's remark that "Freud held that . . . the essential nature of both mind and matter is quite unknown," and it is compatible with Freud's advocacy of the *Autonomy Thesis*. The advantage of the neutrality approach is that it allows one to proceed to study mental phenomena in whatever vocabulary seems most likely to capture their important features, while letting the metaphysical chips fall where they may.

The fact that Freud might have set aside or claimed neutrality on the mind-body question contains an important philosophical lesson, namely, there are ways to proceed with a psychological science without committing oneself to a position one way or another on this central philosophical question. Nevertheless, one can avoid taking a stance on the mind-brain question and do psychology only if one is willing to take other equally foundational, and unproved, philosophical stances. For example, presumably one would have to assume that mental phenomena, whatever they turn out to be made of, obey laws. So, one can be parsimonious about one's metaphysical commitments, but one cannot avoid them altogether.

The second interpretation requires utilizing my earlier analysis of materialism without reductionism, and reading Freud as a materialist who recognized the folly of thinking that any single scientific vocabulary could adequately describe, let alone explain, all facets of the material world. One look at the languages of all the different sciences reveals that they are designed for different jobs. Physics, for example, is not designed to talk about feelings of sexual pleasure even though feelings of sexual pleasure may well be utterly physical phenomena.

On this reading, Freud was something of a Spinozist: he conceived of the world as being comprised of one sort of stuff which obeys strict causal laws; but he realized that there were myriad aspects of that one world and that no one way of sizing it up could possibly do justice to all its aspects.

I find this interpretation of the metaphysical foundations of psychoanalysis the most convincing. It is the only one that fits both my argument that Freud espoused the *Autonomy Thesis* and the persuasive case made in the recent scholarly literature that Freud was firmly committed, throughout his entire life, to the materialistic metaphysic of the science of his day.[11]

The picture of psychological explanation that emerges is this: (1) Psychological research is regulated by an a priori metaphysical commitment to a view of human behavior as governed by scientific law; this commitment is most sensibly supported (although it need not be) by an a priori commitment to materialism. (2) Nevertheless, psychology requires its own proprietary vocabulary; it will appropriate neither the language of physics, chemistry, or neurology, nor will it seek the eventual reduction of its laws to the laws of these sciences. (3) In particular, the language of psychology must be essentially intentional in order to pick out the salient features of mental life; psychological laws, therefore, will be framed in terms of a language of belief, wish, desire, motive, and so on. (4) However, the intentional content of the laws of a mature psychological science will consist not only of ordinary conscious content, but, as often as not, unconscious content.

Two difficulties arise at this point. First, what evidence is there that unconscious mental content must figure in the explanation of human thought and action? Second, what method shall we use to get at unconscious mental content? I now turn to these problems.

Psychoanalysis and Self-Knowledge

Descartes claimed that "there is nothing which is easier for me.to know than my mind." Descartes seems to have meant something like this: each person knows for sure that he has a mind, that he is a cognitive sort of entity. Whether Descartes himself thought that the primacy and the infallibility which characterize our knowledge that we have a mind extend to the contents of our mind is an unanswerable question, since Descartes simply does not have much to say on the matter. Nevertheless, there is an important psychological and philosophical tradition, which I will refer to as Cartesianism; it does take the added step: each person is in an epistemically privileged position with respect to the contents of his or her own mind; of all the things one can possibly know, the self is known first and best.

The entire thrust of Freud's thinking is meant as a challenge to Cartesianism so construed.[12] This is not to say that Freud thought that self-knowledge was impossible, while his opponents thought that self-knowledge was infallible. Philosophical discussions of self-knowledge and introspection often cast the debate in terms of these extremes, but that is unfair to both sides. Freud's entire therapeutic theory, in fact, is based on the premise that self-knowledge is possible, indeed necessary, if neurotics are to regain their psychological health. Furthermore, almost no one holds (at least not any more) that self-knowledge is infallible, only that it is the most reliable method for gaining information about psychological states.

Freud was led to worry about the human capacity for self-knowledge, about the opacity of one's own mind to oneself, not by reflections on the inability of severe neurotics or psychotics to make accurate self-assessments, but by his observations of the way, in ordinary everyday life, people hide their real wishes, intentions, and motives from themselves. In a series of books written at the turn of the century—*The Interpretation of Dreams* (1900), *The Psychopathology of Everyday Life* (1901), and *Jokes and Their Relation to the Unconscious* (1905)—Freud argued that many perfectly mundane and pedestrian human actions are the result of motives of which we are unaware, and which we would, in fact, deny having were they attributed to us.

Freud's challenge to the Cartesian thesis on self-knowledge is important, not only for substantive psychological theory, but for psychological methodology. If, as a Cartesian would have it, a person's own reports of his mental states are eyewitness accounts, and therefore to be trusted in a way that, for example, your inferences about my mental states are not, then introspection is not only a reliable method for gaining psychological knowledge, it is the very best method. It has epistemological primacy.

If, on the other hand, introspection is highly inferential (if, that is, we are in no more of an eyewitness position with respect to our own minds than we are with respect to other minds), or, alternatively, if introspection is noninferential but unreliable (imagine that the mind's eye has the same degree of accuracy as the real eyes of a person who has defective vision), then first-person psychological reports have no special status.

If the latter point of view is correct, then there is an illuminating analogy to be drawn between the mind and subatomic particles, for example, electrons or muons. There is no way at present (and probably, in principle) to observe an electron or a muon directly. All the information physicists claim to possess about electrons and muons (including that they exist) comes indirectly, from tracking them and observing their paths in cloud chambers.

If we have only indirect access to our own minds, or, alternatively, if we have direct but highly unreliable access, then both an individual seeking self-knowledge and the psychologist seeking the laws governing the mind are in the same predicament—they are both just following tracks.

In any case, Freud's unique formulation of the problem of self-knowledge came from his masterful observations of some heretofore unnoticed properties of *parapraxes* (literally, "faulty acts," but popularly known as "Freudian slips") and dreams.[13] It was in analyzing these ordinary phenomena that Freud provided a new vocabulary with which to describe and explain human actions.

Consider the fact that we all spend a considerable amount of our life sleeping and a considerable amount of our sleeping time dreaming. We dream about things that we couldn't possibly do within normal physical laws, for example, flying self-propelled to China and back before daybreak, and things we couldn't possibly do and get away with in normal moral law, for example, murdering our boss, or having sexual relations with relatives. We also dream about much that seems perfectly nonsensical. Moreover, in our waking lives we all occasionally slip up and make mistakes of a particularly embarrassing variety—"Thank you, Jeff, I'd lust to come to dinner on Thursday"; "Susan, your cubist paintings are remarkable, they remind me of Pinocchio's"; "I take great pleasure in giving this award to my distinguished colleague, Professor,

uh . . . Professor . . . to my extinguished colleague, Professor Smith."
All of us have probably at some time or another said the exact opposite
of what we intended, heard the exact opposite of what entered our
auditory canal, forgotten or misplaced something obvious and important,
and so on.

The medical model available in Freud's day explained dreams and
parapraxes in terms of random neural firings caused by somatic stimuli.
According to this model, parapraxes are simple mistakes caused by the
somatic interference of exhaustion, excitement, or disinterest. Dreams,
on the other hand, are odd neural states caused by the combined effects
of the random aftershocks of the day's stimulation, the so-called "day's
residue," and the disturbances caused by somatic stimulation occurring
during sleep, for example, a full bladder, sexual arousal, street noise.
The nonsensical character of dreams is then easily explained by the
fact that there is no rhyme or reason to the patterns of either the neural
aftershocks or the somatic stimuli that occur during sleep.

Freud challenged this account on three grounds. First, it fails to explain
the form dreams or parapraxes take. Some dreams, everyone will admit,
make sense and it is hard to see how this could be so if we are dealing
with random neural firings, with "unmusical fingers wandering over
the keys of a piano." Parapraxes, in fact, commonly take the form
exactly opposite of the one intended, thus their embarrassing quality.
It is hard to see how this could be random, or accounted for merely
by exhaustion, excitement, or distinterest. Second, dreams are optical
while none of the somatic stimulation occurring during sleep is optical.
Third, in analysis, neurotic patients often talk about their dreams and
view them as being just as important as many occurrences of ordinary
conscious life.

These observations led Freud away from the traditional view and
back to a more Hellenistic view of dreams and parapraxes. Dreams
and odd utterances, he came to think, are meaningful, nonrandom
occurrences. They are rich in revealing intentional content. The source
of their meaning and content, however, lies outside the realm of ordinary
rationality. For the Greeks (and other ancient peoples) this realm was
with the gods. Dreams are messages humans get when in special com-
munion with the deities on Mount Olympus. For Freud the unobservable
realm was in the person himself, in the deep recesses of his unconscious.
The Hellenistic observation that dreams seem to come from somewhere
else, from an alien source, is explained by the fact that our unconscious
self is, in fact, a stranger to our conscious self.[14]

Parapraxes, then, are mistakes whose form and meaning are caused
by the conflicting intentions of our conscious, polite, well-socialized
self, and our unconscious or subconscious, impolite, unsocialized self.

The fact that slips sometimes take even the person himself by surprise is explained by the fact that unconscious wishes are usually unknown to the person himself.

According to Freud, dreams are even more thorough representations of our unconscious than parapraxes are. This is because slips sometimes express subconscious or preconscious wishes, that is, wishes whose content the person is aware of, but trying to suppress. For example, you were probably partially aware of your feelings toward Susan's art when you accidentally compared it to Pinocchio's instead of Picasso's.

Dreams, on the other hand, because they occur in utterly nonsocial circumstances, are more likely places for deep, socially unacceptable thoughts to surface. Freud called dreams the "royal road to the unconscious activities of the mind" and he said of his theory of dreams, "Insight such as this falls to one's lot but once in a lifetime."[15] The view on the nature of dreams to which Freud's clinical data ultimately led him (although as we shall see there is considerable controversy about which did the leading, Freud or the data) can be summarized by the following five logically ordered theses:

1. Dreams have meaning; they are phenomena with intentional content.

2. The meaning of dreams, except in the important case of children, however, is not usually obvious. What we remember is itself a representation of the "manifest" (the plot) content; and the "manifest" content is already a "substitute" for the "latent" content, that is, what our unconscious really intended the plot to mean.

3. The real meaning of dreams is concealed from the person himself because the unconscious content of dreams expresses socially unacceptable wishes—for example, incestuous or murderous wishes, which would shock even one's own superego (the private depository of shared moral and social rules which individuals start to learn very early). During sleep the superego is "resting" enough to let the unconscious surface, but is not so off guard that it will let any disturbance through.

4. Dreams, therefore, occur in a code (thanks to the "dream work" that translates our unconscious wishes into a metaphorical language). This code allows for the "hallucinatory" satisfaction of our unconscious wishes. Were we not to get this sort of satisfaction the burden of repression required in waking life would become too great and we would burst forth with neurotic and psychotic habits. We would, in effect, bring our nonsense into the waking world.

5. Since dreams are in a code that even the dreamer does not consciously understand, we need special techniques to get at their meaning. "Free association," that is, letting the person say whatever comes to mind, is the best method because it allows the dreamer to call up new

substitutes for the "manifest" content which is itself already a substitute for the "latent" content, and may eventually take us to the real meaning. We know we are at the real meaning when either the freely associated thoughts begin to tell a coherent story (by being permeated with symbols with "fixed," publicly accessible meaning),[16] or when the dreamer recognizes that he has hit on the meaning, or when the dreamer shows irrational "resistance" to a set of his own associations or to the dream interpreter's interpretation of the story his free associations tell.

The important thing is not the truth of the details of this account— some of the details, such as the thesis that all dreams express wishes, or that there are dream symbols with "fixed" meanings—are almost certainly false. What is important is the fact that Freud's views on dreams contain the central theoretical intuition behind all his thinking. Dreams are not atypical in being governed by unconscious processes, in being opaque to the dreamer himself. They are typical, or so Freud thought, of much mental life in this respect. A considerable amount of what we think and say, whom we choose to think and say it with, what we choose as a career, how we work, and how we play, is governed by an unconscious that is continually attempting to achieve a modicum of libidinal satisfaction in a variety of socially acceptable disguises— in codes which the conscious mind cannot crack.

Freud developed this conception of the mind throughout his long career. In *Civilization and Its Discontents*, which he wrote in 1930, he reemphasized his conviction that his psychoanalytic theory applies equally to normal people and to neurotics and psychotics. All humans come into the world governed by the pleasure principle, seeking to satisfy all their innate biological desires (which include sex and aggression) on demand. Unfortunately reality does not, and cannot, cooperate. Both natural and social necessity, which together make up what Freud calls the "reality principle," require compromise. We are all called upon to make adjustments to our scheme of natural desires, and to find ways to protect ourselves from the ensuing discontent. This is the work of the defense mechanisms. At one extreme we can make our compromise by simply repressing our natural desires; at the other extreme we can rechannel our natural desires into things like sports, art, or science. The first way of making the compromise, repression, is one of the primary causes of mental illness, since, according to Freud's hydraulic conception of mental energy, repressed material is almost inevitably bound to seep out, if not burst forth, from some unexpected place in one's personality. Sublimation is a much better way of making the compromise, because, like dreams, it permits the disguised release of our unacceptable wishes and desires.

It is important, from a philosophical perspective, to notice that, according to the latter analysis, it is not (necessarily) the amount of self-knowledge that separates normal, well-adjusted people from neurotic or psychotic people, but rather the sorts of defensive tools they deploy. This is easy to see. Freud sometimes characterized mental health in terms of the ability to love and work. Suppose you come across a happily married philosopher who is faithful to her husband, devoted to her children, and who loves to teach and write philosophy, when, that is, she is not playing sports. And suppose that this person's life continues in this way until her death. It is easy to imagine such a life. But it is also easy to imagine this person being utterly in the dark as to why she is so happy with monogamous marriage, why she loves philosophy and sports so much—and it is especially easy to imagine her denying that her love and work are in any way related to deep-seated sexual and aggressive wishes.

From a Freudian perspective, therefore, the difference between a sublimator, like this philosopher, and a repressed neurotic does not turn on the amount of self-knowledge about ultimate motives the individual possesses. It turns on whether the multitude of primitive wishes, hopes, and desires comprising the pleasure principle get indirectly satisfied or not. The moral is simply this: self-knowledge is a genuine problem, and there is no reason to think that it is any less of a problem for a well-adjusted person than for a poorly adjusted person.

This brings us back to the philosophical thick of things. For the Cartesian, there is no problem of self-knowledge. Each person is uniquely and certainly aware of himself as a thinking, willing, feeling, and desiring thing. By focusing the mind's eye reflexively, the Socratic charge to "know thyself" can be met—the specific content of one's thoughts, feelings, and desires can be revealed. Introspective knowledge is easily accessible, and largely self-verifying.

There is, however, a serious problem of other minds implied by Cartesianism. The other side of Descartes' belief that one is in a uniquely privileged epistemological situation with respect to one's own mind is that all our knowledge of bodies, including our own, is inferential, based on sense data, and therefore fallible. Now consider: how is it, on such an account, that we come to know what another person has on his or her mind? How is it that we come to know what another persons thinks, feels, and believes?

Because Cartesian dualism allows mental events to cause physical ones, and because one's own mind's eye cannot directly observe another person's mental state, it must be that we infer mental states in others on the basis of their physical behavior—on the basis, so to speak, of what their bodies do. This means that our beliefs about other people's minds are inferences about inferences, and are, therefore, highly corrigible knowledge claims. On this account, other minds are just like electrons: they are known only through the evidence their tracks leave.

A Cartesian might try to narrow the chasm between self-knowledge and knowledge of other minds by pointing out that some of our inferences about another person's psychological state are based on inferences from introspective reports the person makes about himself. For example, suppose you tell me that you are happy or sad because you have won or lost a fellowship; or that you do philosophy in order to sublimate some sexual feelings you have toward your opposite-sex parent; or that you are telling me so much about yourself because you like and trust me. These reports, a Cartesian might argue, are highly reliable because you are giving eyewitness testimony. And because you are giving eyewitness testimony my claim that you are in these psychological states (with these particular causes) is strongly warranted.

Unfortunately, whereas Cartesianism does seem to imply that introspective knowledge that a person has, so to speak, with himself and about himself is extremely trustworthy, it gives no reason whatsoever for thinking that the reports people give to others accurately reflect that knowledge.[17] To show this would require showing that people do not lie or misrepresent themselves, and that is impossible. Thus, in its own way, even Cartesianism fails to make a case for the reliability of inferences about other minds on the basis of introspective reports. Such reports are behavioral, and all inferences from behavior to what lies behind it are radically underdetermined by the evidence.

Freud complicates matters even further, by undermining the Cartesian confidence about self-knowledge. What the mind's eye claims to be our real thoughts, motives, and wishes are not even probably, let alone necessarily, our real thoughts, motives, and wishes. This is because the mind's eye is the rational, conscious, language-using part of the self and it lacks the desire, as well as the ability, to observe the irrational, unconscious, nonlinguistic part of the self.

In this way, Freud collapses the problem of self-knowledge and the problem of other minds. One is, by and large, in the same epistemological situation with one's own self as one is in with others, namely, the situation of making inferences from behavior, or from (reports of) conscious thoughts, to what lies behind them. The strong possibility of self-deception exacerbates the problem on the home front in the same way distance does on the foreign front.

The consequences for psychological methodology are enormous. The Cartesian philosophy of mind provides a relatively clear-cut (albeit not unproblematic) procedure for weighing psychological data: namely, measure third-person psychological observations against the epistemically superior data provided by first-person reports. Freud's philosophy of mind, on the other hand, implies that all our ordinary, first- and third-person methods for gathering psychological data are about equally likely to yield truth or falsity. But if all our ordinary psychological methods are equally chancy, then there is no obvious epistemological reason to give any one type of evidence greater weight than any other. And if there is no procedure to decide how to weigh psychological data, then we haven't a prayer of understanding psychological phenomena.

Given this epistemological predicament, it is fair to wonder whether personal and psychological knowledge is possible at all. And if it is possible, how is it possible? What method should we use to stay on the right track? What method should we use to weigh all the different data we get? Paradoxically, just as Freud paints us into this epistemological corner, he offers us a way out: deploy the psychoanalytic method in tracking the mind—use the interpretive techniques of psychoanalytic theory to weigh confusing or conflicting psychological data.

The overall idea is this: there is no simple or completely reliable way to gain psychological knowledge about oneself or about others. Nevertheless, you can have a scientifically valid conception of the mind if you know what to look for, if you have a procedure for distinguishing between relevant and irrelevant evidence. The proper procedure for weighing data is the method of psychoanalytic interpretation. Although this method cannot be described algorithmically, it is something a person rigorously trained in psychoanalytic theory can learn to apply in order to achieve veridical psychological knowledge. Think, for example, of the difference, in old Westerns, between a good Indian tracker and an average cavalry officer—the Indian always knew where to find the nearest water hole because he had the right theory about the way birds and deer and raccoons move about in relation to water. In the end, then, our psychoanalytically motivated worries about how to weigh psychological data reliably are to be placated by the promise of psychoanalytic theory itself: a scientifically valid analysis of the mind will emerge when psychological data are evaluated in the light of the known truths of psychoanalytic theory.

An example will help. According to Freud, the importance of having a correct interpretation of psychological phenomena is especially important in dealing with neurotics. Although both normal and neurotic people tend to lack self-knowledge systematically, an accurate self-assessment is essential if a neurotic person is to get out of his neurotic rut. Suppose, for example, that a certain man has a chronic problem establishing good romantic relations with women, and suppose he spends several years in analysis talking about this problem as well as about everything else under the sun. A trained analyst will have to interpret and weigh all this verbal data in order to transform it into a narrative that makes possible a coherent and manageable diagnosis of the patient's problem. The analyst might, for example, interpret the multifarious clinical data in light of Freud's theory about the universality of the Oedipus complex, and judge that this man's problem is caused by an unresolved oedipal attachment to his mother. His inability to get romantically involved with appropriate females is caused by his inability to give up the (unconscious) idea that he is already involved with his mother. According to psychoanalytic theory, this man will be able to free himself from his neurotic behavior only if and when he understands and accepts that his strong unconscious attachment to his mother is, in fact, the cause of his problem.[18]

For reasons which this hypothetical example bring up, Freud's recommendation that we organize and interpret psychological data in light of psychoanalytic theory has met with resistance from many philosophers and psychologists. Although most contemporary thinkers are sympathetic to the idea that theory is always required to give form to data, many think that Freud asks us to make far too great a leap of faith, or that he bullies his theory onto the data. For example, what independent evidence (that is, what evidence besides Freudian theory itself) could make us think that some adult's romantic problems were caused by an unresolved and unconscious attachment to his mother? Concerns such as these have to do with the scientific status of Freudian theory, to which I now turn.

Is Psychoanalysis Scientific?

Freudian theory has been accused of a multitude of methodological sins—sins that some critics claim irrevocably taint its claim to be good science and other critics claim so darken its soul that it cannot be considered science at all. The critics who claim that psychoanalysis is not science do not intend merely to suggest that it is more like literature, art, and music than like physics or chemistry; they mean to suggest that it is intellectual gobbledygook—pure, unadulterated, but undeniably seductive nonsense. Because psychoanalysis, unlike literature, art, and music, is put forward as science, and is not, it is intellectually disreputable pseudoscience. One of the main promoters of this line of criticism is the philosopher of science Karl Popper. Popper ungenerously compares psychoanalysis to astrology.

It turns out that it is much more difficult than Popper and others once thought to draw a line of demarcation between genuine science and pseudoscience. The last fifty years of work in the philosophy of science seems to show that a clear and complete account of what exactly makes a theory a scientific one, or what exactly distinguishes good science from bad science, is not possible. Nevertheless, there is some consensus as to what sorts of considerations are relevant to accepting a theory as scientific. Two widely accepted rules of thumb regarding scientific acceptability can be framed as follows (call the first rule the falsifiability condition, and the second rule the corroboration condition):[19]

1. *Falsifiability Condition*: a theory that purports to be scientific is worth serious consideration only if there are conceivable empirical outcomes that would count against it.

2. *Corroboration Condition*: a theory that satisfies (1) is credible to the degree that it has been tested and not refuted.

The idea behind the first condition is that we want there to be a way of discovering if a theory is false, if indeed it is false. For example, the proposition that God exists is often put forward in an unfalsifiable manner—for many true believers there is no conceivable state of affairs that would count against the proposition. It is a useful habit, whenever one hears a scientific hypothesis put forward, to think of what would count against it, rather than what would count for it. If you can think of some test result that would count against the hypothesis, then it meets the falsifiability condition.

The idea behind the second condition is that we want to know how much probability to assign to any theory we are seriously entertaining. We assign fairly high probability to the hypothesis that cigarette smoking causes lung cancer because the potentially falsifying prediction that cigarette smokers will have a higher incidence of lung cancer than nonsmokers is continually corroborated in a wide array of carefully controlled experiments.

How does psychoanalysis measure up against these two conditions? Is psychoanalysis falsifiable, and, if it is, how much credibility should we assign to it, that is, how many tests has it passed where it might have been falsified, but was not? But first a word of caution about "it." Psychoanalytic theory is really a large set of theories. There is a theory about the sexual basis of neurosis, a theory about male-female sex differences, a theory about developmental stages (oral, anal, and so on), a theory about fixed symbols in dreams, a theory about the nature of morality, a theory about homosexuality, a therapeutic theory, and so on. The general thesis that unconscious mental processes are essential causal forces binds all these different subtheories and makes them psychoanalytic. Freud's overall theory is held together by the general theory of the unconscious in much the same way Newton's physics is held together by the theory of universal gravitation, and Darwin's biology is held together by the theory of natural selection.

Nevertheless, even though the general theory of the unconscious provides a unifying thread to the entire theory, it is entirely possible that some of the subtheories will fare well and some will fare badly on our scale of scientific acceptability. Many critics of psychoanalysis act as if the theory is a logically neat and tidy body of homogeneous doctrine, and thus as if the discovery of one serious problem with any part of the theory will set off a "domino effect" which will bring down the entire theoretical edifice. But the logical relations among the different parts of Freudian theory (this is equally true of Darwinian, Newtonian, and Einsteinian theory) are simply too complex and multifaceted for any one set of results to make or break the entire theory (the one important exception is noted later).

It is probably a wise idea at this point to spend a moment forestalling two common lines of argument relating to the scientific status of psychoanalysis, one pro and one con. Many Freudians claim that various psychoanalytic hypotheses are subjected to tests all the time in psychoanalytic therapy. They argue that, insofar as therapy is successful, the psychoanalytic hypotheses deployed therein are scientifically vindicated.

This argument is notoriously problematic. First, it is not clear what the logical relations are between psychoanalytic theory and psychoanalytic therapy, and thus it is not clear that the theory gets tested in therapy. For example, the piece of psychoanalytic theory that says that punishment of early sex play causes sexual difficulties later on does not logically imply the therapeutic theory that it is necessary to talk about the original causes of one's sexual problems in order to get over them. In fact, it is logically possible that the exactly opposite therapeutic prescription might be true, that is, that people will only get over the sexual problems caused by early punishment of sex play if they do not talk about their problems and only if they forget about the original causes. Second, and this is the other side of the coin, even if patients do get better in therapy it is not obvious that their improvement has to do with the validity of the theory. It might have to do with the color of the therapist's eyes, or with suggestibility, or with hormones, or with the passing of time. Third, it is not clear from the available evidence that psychoanalytic therapy is effective, or that it is any more effective than therapies aligned with nonpsychoanalytic theories. Evidence of therapeutic effectiveness is simply too slippery—logically and empirically—to count significantly toward the scientific acceptability of psychoanalytic theory.

Meanwhile, some critics argue that psychoanalysis is hopelessly unscientific because Freud discovered many of its central principles and subtheories, for example, the Oedipus complex, by analyzing himself.

This method of theory construction is unacceptable, the critics say, for two reasons: first, it is inconsistent with the theory itself, since one of the cardinal tenets of psychoanalysis is that we all systematically lack self-knowledge; second, it violates the scientific canons which require intersubjective tests.

This objection rests on a "genetic fallacy." The manner in which a belief arises or a theory is generated does not, in and of itself, determine its epistemological status. I, for example, learned that water is H_2O in a joke when I was seven. But the theory that water is H_2O is no joke. Isaac Newton, according to an amusing fable, discovered the theory of universal gravitation when an apple fell on his head. The theory of universal gravitation, of course, is a terrific theory, but the fact that Newton was hit on the head by an apple is not the reason. Like Newtonian physics, psychoanalysis might be able to pass tests of scientific acceptability even though the context of its initial discovery does not provide the grounds for its acceptability.

Let us now take a closer look at the scientific acceptability of three different psychoanalytical hypotheses: (1) the general hypothesis that unconscious mental processes are (often) an important causal element in what we feel and think, and how we act; (2) the hypothesis that dreams (often) express unconscious sexual wishes; and (3) the hypothesis that paranoia has a homosexual basis. My remarks are by no means meant to constitute a definitive analysis of the scientific status of these hypotheses, let alone of psychoanalysis as a whole. I merely want to provide a preliminary evaluation of these three hypotheses, and to give a sense of how an in-depth assessment of the scientific status of psychoanalysis would have to proceed.

(1) The *unconscious hypothesis*: Insofar as this hypothesis provides the glue that binds the entire theory, its scientific acceptability is a necessary condition for assigning credibility to almost any psychoanalytic subtheory. In this way, psychoanalytic theory as a whole turns on the credibility of this hypothesis. Were we to discover that the unconscious hypothesis was false, we would have good reason for thinking that most of Freud's subsidiary hypotheses were false as well.

It seems to me that the unconscious hypothesis can meet the falsifiability condition. We might, for example, test people under hypnosis, just as Bernheim did, and see if we could generate unconscious memories, beliefs, and so on, which were causally efficacious in a posthypnotic state. For example, I might hypnotize a group of people and tell each of them that I want them, once they come out of their trance, to say something about their mother whenever they hear the word "philosophy" uttered (and to forget this instruction). It would count against the unconscious hypothesis if the subjects in such an experiment did not display the appropriate posthypnotic behavior.

If this is a good experiment (it might be questioned on grounds that it assumes that hypnotic and ordinary phenomena are alike, but I will avoid that very important question here) then the unconscious hypothesis also meets the corroboration condition (meeting the corroboration condition is, of course, always a matter of degree). Many people, I am told, from Bernheim to the present, have tested for posthypnotic suggestion and obtained results that could have, but did not, refute the hypothesis. Such results, therefore, corroborate the hypothesis that some actions are caused by unconscious memories. The stronger claim that unconscious phenomena are often causally effective would require more wide-ranging tests.

Now it is tempting to say something like this: the unconscious hypothesis passes all tests of scientific acceptability because it is immensely useful in explaining human behavior. The problem with this view is that it is not at all obvious that people who take such a stance ever put the hypothesis to a genuine, possibly falsifying, test. They may see confirmations everywhere because they already, a priori, view the world through psychoanalytically tinted glasses. Karl Popper put the problem this way:

> Freudian analysts emphasized that their theories were constantly verified by their "clinical observations". . . . It was precisely this fact—that they always fitted, that they were always confirmed— which in the eyes of their admirers constituted the strongest argument in favour of these [both Freud's and Marx's] theories. It began to dawn on me that this apparent strength was in fact their weakness. . . . It is easy to obtain confirmations or verifications, for nearly every theory—if we look for confirmation.[20]

The problem, then, is this: it is easy to beg the question of the scientific acceptability of a hypothesis simply by unreflectively accepting the hypothesis and interpreting data in terms of it. To the extent that any Freudian holds the unconscious hypothesis as an a priori tenet, to that extent he or she has no philosophically legitimate basis for believing that the hypothesis has scientific merit. Nevertheless, there are ways (for example, the hypnosis experiment I envisage) to test the unconscious hypothesis. To the extent that it passes or has passed such tests it is, in fact, scientifically acceptable.

(2) The *dream hypothesis*: The discussion of the previous hypothesis points to the fact that a particular hypothesis or theory may have scientific merit even though an exponent of the hypothesis or theory might protect it from all tests, and in this way keep it from showing

that merit. The hypothesis that dreams (often) express unconscious sexual wishes is interesting in this regard. Freud's own work is full of impatience with questions and challenges to his theory. At one point Freud uses the metaphor of the "judge" to describe the psychoanalyst and the "defendant" to describe anyone who doubts a psychoanalytic interpretation.[21] Suppose one were to ask Freud, or some Freudian who thought this way, what possible empirical outcome would count against the dream hypothesis? An orthodox Freudian might propose the following: give a group of trained psychoanalysts the text of a dream and ask them to interpret it. If these experts come up with roughly similar interpretations which cite unconscious sexual wishes then the dream hypothesis satisfies both the falsifiability condition and the corroboration condition. If on the other hand their interpretations are wildly askew, never mention sex, and so on, that would count against the dream hypothesis.

Something has clearly gone wrong. We know that any group of analysts who have mastered Freud's dictionary of dream symbols will pass this test with flying colors. But we cannot take their success as a reliable indication of the scientific worth of the dream hypothesis because the mastery of the dictionary of dream symbols presupposes the dream hypothesis, and therefore predestines the test result. The fact that psychoanalysts find the dream hypothesis necessary in offering psychoanalytic interpretations of dreams is guaranteed a priori.

The scenario I have just sketched is not meant as a caricature. Freud's advocacy of the hypothesis that dreams often express deep-seated sexual wishes depends almost exclusively on his own intuitive satisfaction with his dream interpretations. When offered experimental evidence for some of his hypotheses, Freud once wrote, "I cannot put much value on these confirmations because the wealth of reliable observations on which these assertions rest make them independent of experimental verification. Still it can do no harm."[22] As Freud presents matters, therefore, the dream hypothesis does not satisfy either the falsifiability or the corroboration condition. I leave it to the reader to think up a possible set of experiments that might actually test the dream hypothesis without begging the question of its validity so overtly. Discussion of the next hypothesis might help provoke the imagination in this regard.

(3) The *paranoia hypothesis*: One can see how the problem we had with the dream hypothesis might arise here as well. That is, an orthodox Freudian might suggest that it would count against his hypothesis that paranoia (in males) has a basis in unconscious homosexual wishes, if a group of psychoanalytic judges failed to ascribe latent homosexual wishes to paranoid psychotics. Barbara Von Eckardt discusses an imag-

inative experiment of H. S. Zamansky's that provides a way around such a viciously circular proposal.[23]

The experiment goes as follows: take a group of paranoids and a group of schizophrenics and show them a series of pairs of photographs consisting of various combinations of male and female figures. Ask the subjects which picture they prefer and which picture has greater overall surface area. The prediction is that (if the paranoia hypothesis is correct) the paranoids will express greater preference for pictures with females in them than for pictures with males in them (since they will want to deny their attraction to males) but they will spend more time looking at the pictures of males when asked about the relative surface areas.

This experiment puts Freud's paranoia hypothesis in falsifiable form. It would count against the hypothesis if the predicted outcome failed to materialize. Since the prediction did in fact materialize—that is, the paranoids expressed greater preference for the pictures of females, but looked longer at the pictures of males than did the schizophrenics—the hypothesis achieves some amount of corroboration; it could have lost credibility, but did not. This is not to say that the hypothesis is true, or even remotely true, but only that it is not impoverished relative to our scale of scientifically acceptable hypotheses. It is not pseudoscience.

If we wanted to test the scientific merits of the paranoia hypothesis further we would have to think of new experiments to help us choose between Freud's hypothesis and the alternative hypothesis that most paranoids are heterosexuals through and through, but given that they are paranoids, they are scared of strangeness and prefer familiar, un-threatening contexts. This hypothesis, it seems to me, implies the same experimental outcome as Zamansky's: if a paranoid perceives that he is being asked about his sexual preference he will answer truthfully—perhaps because he is terrified of the consequences of telling a lie—that is, he will choose the pictures of females; but if he is asked something utterly mundane (for example, about surface area) his extreme preference for unthreatening as opposed to threatening interpersonal situations will surface—that is, he will look longer at the pictures containing members of his own, familiar sex, than at pictures containing members of the opposite, unfamiliar sex.

The moral is simply this: it is undoubtedly true that Freud and many Freudians display an annoying insensitivity to the need to frame psychoanalytic hypotheses in falsifiable form. Nevertheless, my brief analysis of three of Freud's subtheories should make it clear that it is possible, if one is imaginative enough, to think up tests that permit the possible falsification of portions of psychoanalytic theory. To the degree that the various portions of the theory pass these tests, they stand vindicated—for the time being. A theory that passes a wide array of tests that have the potential for falsifying it, and that are designed to force choices between it and alternative hypotheses, has relatively high scientific merit. There is no a priori reason to think that psychoanalysis might not turn out to contain many acceptable hypotheses if it is tested in this manner, even if it has not been so tested thus far.

Conclusion

I can now summarize my overall evaluation of Freudian theory:

(1) Freud makes a strong case for the ineliminability of intentional vocabulary in psychology, for the essential explanatory use of a vocabulary that cites the meaningful content of mental states. Psychology will be an autonomous science; it will deploy a theoretical framework that cannot be reduced to physics or chemistry or neuroscience. Psychology's autonomy follows from epistemological considerations, that is, from facts about what needs explaining rather than from any metaphysical assumptions about the duality of mind and body. The autonomy of psychological explanation is compatible with metaphysical materialism.

(2) Freud makes an equally convincing case for the thesis that at least some of the important contents of mental states are unconscious.

(3) By establishing (2) Freud establishes that there are deep epistemological problems related to self-knowledge.

(4) By establishing (3) Freud raises profound doubts regarding the veridicality of introspective reports of psychological states.

(5) By establishing (3) and (4) Freud points to the need for a new procedure for weighing psychological data. (3) and (4), after all, imply that no traditional method for gathering psychological information is incorrigible or privileged.

(6) Freud puts psychoanalytic theory itself forward as the required new procedure for weighing and interpreting psychological data. But he puts the theory forward less cautiously than its merits recommend. Freud relies too heavily on his sense that psychoanalytic theory fits the facts. What Freud did not understand is that there are always indefinitely many theories which fit any set of facts. We need, therefore, to see all the psychoanalytic subtheories undergo, and pass, a wide array of potentially falsifying tests that distinguish between them and their rivals before we will have reason to accept them as true.

(7) It could turn out (I suspect it probably will) that the theses about intentionality, self-knowledge, and the causal efficacy of unconscious processes are true, while many of the subtheories about the specific nature and content of unconscious processes are false or in need of modification.

The exciting, and somewhat surprising, thing from my perspective is that those Freudian theses which I expect to see vindicated—intentionality, the anti-Cartesianism about self-knowledge, and the causal efficacy of unconscious processes—have just resurfaced, in thoroughly transformed guise, in some recent models in the related fields of cognitive psychology, cognitive science, and Artificial Intelligence.

As we shall now see, however, B. F. Skinner made a valiant effort, in the years between Freud and the rise of modern cognitive psychology, to construct a scientific psychology which sidesteps mentioning the psyche. Skinner suggests the paradoxical possibility of a complete science of human behavior that avoids the epistemological difficulties of providing an account of mentality itself. Skinner's work can be read, therefore, as an explicit challenge to the view, shared by Freud and modern cognitive theorists, that psychological explanation must be intentional, that an adequate psychology must make essential reference to the meaningful contents of (conscious or unconscious) mental states.

Suggested Readings

Two Best Primary Sources for an Overview of Freud's Thought

Freud, S. (1917), *Introductory Lectures on Psychoanalysis*.
Freud, S. (1933), *New Introductory Lectures on Psychoanalysis*.

Collected Works

Freud, S. (1953–1974), *The Standard Edition of the Complete Psychological Works of Sigmund Freud*, J. Strachey, ed.

Three Important Intellectual Biographies

Gay, Peter (1988), *Freud: A Life for Our Time*.
Jones, E. (1953), *The Life and Work of Sigmund Freud*, two volumes.
Sulloway, F. (1979), *Freud: Biologist of the Mind*.

On the Scientific Status of Psychoanalysis

Cummins, R. (1983), *Psychological Explanation*. See the chapter on Freud.
Grünbaum, A. (1979), "Is Freudian Psychoanalytic Theory Pseudo-Scientific by Karl Popper's Criterion of Demarcation?"
Grünbaum, A. (1980), "Epistemological Liabilities in the Clinical Appraisal of Psychoanalytic Theory."
Grünbaum, A. (1984), *The Foundations of Psychoanalysis: A Philosophical Critique*.
Grünbaum, A. (1986), Précis of *The Foundations of Psychoanalysis with Peer Commentary*.
Von Eckardt, B. (1983), "The Scientific Status of Psychoanalysis."

General Philosophical Essays on Freud

Wollheim, R. (1974), *Freud: A Collection of Critical Essays*.
Wollheim, R., and Hopkins, J. (1982), *Philosophical Essays on Freud*.

Chapter 4

The Science of Behavior, Antimentalism, and the Good Life: The Philosophical Psychology of B. F. Skinner

B. F. Skinner is without doubt America's most influential psychologist ever, yet he remains an enigma. On the one hand, he is a champion of a new form of epistemological and metaphysical puritanism, fighting tooth and nail for a psychology free of loosely defined concepts and against the weight of philosophical theories that refer to entities like self, mind, consciousness, and free will. On the other hand, Skinner often waxes philosophical. He has referred to behaviorism as "a philosophy of science,"[1] and he has proposed the necessity of a philosophical "critique of the methods, data, and the concepts of a science of behavior."[2] Furthermore, Skinner has persistently argued that the eighteenth-century Enlightenment ideal of a society in which people are free, rational, creative, and happy can be most effectively achieved by the application of the principles of behavioristic psychology—a psychology that simultaneously denies that people are really free and rational in the Cartesian sense of having free will and the capacity to reason without the constraints of strict causal necessity.

Skinnerian psychology, therefore, is full of philosophical assumptions and paradoxes, full of epistemological, metaphysical, and political commitments even though Skinner correctly portrays himself as rejecting traditional philosophical conceptions of the nature of mind, the proper subject matter, and the proper methods of psychology. Here I examine five central tenets of Skinner's system and attempt to reconstruct and critically evaluate their supporting arguments.

First, I examine Skinner's criticisms of two different kinds of mentalistic psychology, Cartesianism and Freudianism. Skinner thinks that any psychology supported by either theoretical framework will have deadly methodological and substantive deficiencies.

Second, I examine Skinner's argument—which Carl Hempel made

The best introductions to Skinner's thought are *Science and Human Behavior* (1953) and *About Behaviorism* (1976).

famous as the "theoretician's dilemma"—that "Brentano's thesis" is false. Psychology, according to this argument, can avoid the use of terms that refer to both meaningful internal states and their contents— to beliefs, thoughts, motives, and so on—as well as to nonmeaningful neural states, and still give complete coverage to its domain of inquiry. If this argument is correct, then psychology can offer a complete account of human behavior without mentioning internal states at all. Psychology need go neither intentional nor neurophysiological.

Third, I examine Skinner's views on the problem of self-knowledge and on the use of introspective methods in psychology. We shall see that part of Skinner's antipathy to mentalistic psychology comes from his belief that the way humans learn language weighs decisively against giving any gold stars for reliability to first-person psychological reports. Whereas the problem of self-knowledge heightened Freud's interest in the mind as such, it points Skinner in the exactly opposite direction.

Fourth, I discuss the central substantive notion of Skinnerian psychology: the concept of operant behavior. In particular I focus on the question of whether, and if so how, the concept of operant behavior solves the twin problems of behavioral novelty and purpose, the problems of how anything truly new and truly goal-directed can occur in a fundamentally mechanistic system. Skinner claims that his operant psychology is an advance over the classical behaviorism of John B. Watson and Ivan P. Pavlov precisely because it provides a solution to philosophical conundrums about novelty and purpose.

Finally, I examine the relation between Skinner's philosophy of mind and his political philosophy. The two inquiries are obviously connected. An adequate philosophy of mind will contain a theory of the most general and basic human aims, interests, and aspirations, and the mechanisms whereby these aims, interests, and aspirations can be satisfied. An adequate political philosophy will contain a theory of how best to maximize, systematically and collectively, the satisfaction of human aims, interests, and aspirations. Of course, whether Skinner's particular conception of the "ideal" society is the right one depends, among other things, on whether his basic psychological theory is correct, on the specific logical relations between his psychology and his politics, and on whether, as he seems to assume, the psychological fact that we desire or aim at something proves anything about whether what we desire and aim at is really valuable and worthwhile.

My overall assessment of Skinner's psychology runs along the following lines. Skinner's behaviorism is not, as I have heard some philosophers and psychologists assert, simply false. In fact, Skinner is certainly right that there are epistemological pitfalls to mentalistic psychology, and he is right that humans are (to some extent) operantly conditionable. He is even right that the concept of operant behavior sheds some interesting light on how psychology might deal with the conundrums about novelty and purpose. Furthermore, he has many interesting and important things to say about schedules of reinforcement and the differential effects of positive reinforcement and punishment. Nevertheless, Skinner's conception of psychology is limited, and he almost invariably gets himself into philosophical trouble whenever he makes global proclamations about metaphysics, epistemology, politics, or the nature of psychological explanation. Thus, whereas Skinner is right to be concerned about the metaphysical and methodological foundations of psychology he tends to throw the baby out with the bathwater and make psychology epistemologically safe at the price of making it epistemologically impoverished (for example, by removing cognitive processes from psychology's domain of inquiry). If we were to accept Skinner's conception of psychological explanation as legislative, both methodologically and substantively, of explanation in all branches of the field we would simply never know what we want to know, and psychology would never be about all that we want it to be about. We would never have a true and complete science of mind. On the other hand, I am not sure if we would now know with such confidence that psychological explanation must be intentional and cognitive had we not met with Skinner's bold programmatic claims to the contrary.

Skinner's Critique of Two Kinds of Mentalism

In the very act of construing psychology as the science of behavior rather than as the science of mind or of consciousness or even, as many texts now say, the science of mind and behavior, Skinner emphasizes that he follows the tradition of psychologists who, since John B. Watson, worry about psychology's slow growth and locate the obstruction in certain archaic but pervasive metaphysical and epistemological attitudes.

The great metaphysical offender is the Cartesian type of dualism that implies that the human mind is unobservable, except to the person himself, nonphysical and free, which thereby makes a psychological science impossible. The epistemological offenders are psychologies that, whatever their stance on the physicality and lawfulness of what Skinner prefers to call "covert" or "private" events, fail to exercise sufficient caution in the tales they make up about the workings of and the relations between the events that take place in our heads. The first kind of psychology talks openly of fictions, whereas the second kind, of which psychoanalysis is Skinner's favorite example, exaggerates the mysterious quality of the laws of human action.

A bit of history is in order here. Skinner began his career in the

1930s at a time of growing international epistemological conservatism. Due, among other things, to the sudden appearance of paradoxes and controversies in mathematics and physics, and to the ideological excesses of political theories that promoted nationalism on biological grounds, many philosophers and scientists, especially in Vienna and Berlin, argued for rigid criteria of publicity and testability for the mere utterance of any statement that purported to be scientific. The honest hope of these self-proclaimed operationists and logical positivists was that public definitions and public tests of all scientific statements would allow the resolution of the paradoxes and controversies in the sciences, and prevent future ideological misuses in the name of science.

Many psychologists, Skinner's teacher E. G. Boring and his fellow graduate student S. S. Stevens being among the most prominent, promoted operationistic and positivistic procedures in psychology. In fact, the operationistic attitude was so dominant during the 1930s that Skinner tried to avoid writing an experimental dissertation by suggesting to Boring that he do a thesis in which he would try to construct operational definitions for classical psychological concepts like "belief," "motive," and "desire."[3]

The fundamental idea behind operationism was that the meaning of a concept is exhausted by the tangible physical operations used to decide whether or not to apply the concept. For example, we might operationally define the concept "belief" in the following way: "X believes that p" just in case when X is asked "p?" X says "yes" or nods. Because the meaning of a concept is equivalent to the tangible physical operations used to decide whether to apply it, we can substitute the words "means that" for the words "just in case" in this definition so we get "X believes that p" means that when X is asked "p?" X says "yes" or nods. This analysis, then, exhausts the meaning of "X believes that p."

But, you might object, this analysis is surely wrong: it confuses procedures for deciding when to apply a particular concept with the question of the meaning of that concept. Even though we might verify "X believes that p" operationally, we intend "belief" to refer to more than the procedures used to decide whether to apply the term "belief." We intend "belief" to refer to some psychological state or disposition in X. This objection, however, will not wash with the operationist. The objection tries to smuggle the connotative, "surplus meaning" of concepts back into science, and that is exactly what the operationists thought should be given up. From the operationistic perspective of the young Skinner, then, the failure to ground traditional psychological concepts exhaustively in physically observable phenomena and operations would mean that they were scientifically unacceptable nonsense.

It should be obvious, without going into detail, why the latter form of empiricism preordains the behaviorist's antipathy to Cartesianism. *Res cogitans*, after all, has, by definition, no publicly observable properties whatsoever. All statements about *res cogitans* therefore are unscientific gobbledygook.

One has to be careful, of course, that in rejecting Cartesianism one does not also make psychology barren, a science able to talk only about overt behavior. In his early days Skinner seems to have done just that. In reflecting recently on his own attitudes during the 1930s Skinner says "I preferred the position of *radical behaviorism*, in which the existence of subjective entities is denied."[4] The radical behaviorist's position makes the problem of the surplus meaning of intentional psychological terms simply dissolve. An operational definition of "belief," after all, only seems to leave something out if you think that "there are subjective entities or dispositions inside people called beliefs. But since there are no such "subjective entities" inside people's heads, there simply is nothing that needs talking about that we cannot talk about in fully operationistic terms.

By the end of the second world war Skinner's views had changed somewhat. He says then, in speaking of his operationist mentor E. G. Boring, "The irony is that while Boring must confine himself to an account of my external behavior, I am still interested in Boring-from-within."[5] Skinner seems to have realized that a psychology that simply refused to admit the reality of any subjective, cognitive and affective, phenomena was just too incredible to satisfy the minimal plausibility constraints on an adequate psychology.

Since 1945 Skinner's publicly announced strategy for trying to maintain psychology's richness without Cartesian assumptions has been to take a materialistic stance on the mind-body problem. According to Skinner, those mental events that truly exist (and not all of the historically accepted ones do) are made of the same (physical) stuff and obey the same sorts of laws, generally the laws of operant and respondent conditioning, as overt behavioral events. Thoughts, for example, are not the immaterial predecessors of material actions, they are actions themselves. Behavior is both overt and covert, public and private. The difference between mental phenomena and physical phenomena is not a metaphysical one, it is an epistemological one. Private mental events are simply less accessible than public events.

This materialistic metaphysical stance serves a regulative function in the Skinnerian scheme of things. It gives the behaviorist permission to study existing mental phenomena without worrying about these phenomena having any peculiar Cartesian-like metaphysical features. Interestingly, however, Skinner's materialism has never taken him in the direction of attempting to make psychology epistemologically safe by reducing it to neurophysiology. There are three basic reasons for Skinner's resistance to going neurophysiological.

First, he considers reductionism impractical. We can at present observe human behavior more or less directly and more or less continuously with our normal sensory apparatus. But we have at present no generally available technologies, for example, cerebroscopes, with which to peer into each other's brains.

Second, and this is related to the first, Skinner recognizes that even if type-type mind-brain identity theory is true we will need a very careful description at the level of behavior before we know what the actual identities are. Thus even if we all carried cerebroscopes around, it is not clear that we would have the faintest idea what we were looking for in all that gray matter inside each other's cranial cavities. For example, in order to search for the brain state identical to the psychological state of "being in love," a psychologist will need to be sure even before he starts to search for the neural correlate that he has a bona fide case of "being in love" on his hands. Description and understanding at the psychological or behavioral level, therefore, will have to precede (temporally if not logically) description and understanding at the neural level.

Third, Skinner, I think, believes—and this, surprisingly, is something he shares (up to a point) with William James and many phenomenologists—that even if identity theory is true, we will always be better off describing and analyzing human experience and behavior in its own molar terms rather than in the molecular terms of physics or neuroscience. Thus even though the book I now see to my immediate right is just a collection of physical particles, it is best described, if you are interested in its stimulus value to me, as a physical hunk, as a nice big fat book. And although my going to see Bogart and Hepburn in *The African Queen* last night might be describable in terms of the physical trajectories governing my bodily movements on the way to the movie theatre, and in terms of the multitudinous optical, auditory, and neural events my body underwent once I got there, it is best described, if you are interested in its features as part of my experience, as my going to the movies to see Bogart and Hepburn in *The African Queen*.

Skinner calls his sort of molar behavioral analysis a "functional analysis." And at least in terms of the argument I have just set forth, Skinner's rationale for "functional analysis" shares some common themes with Freud's argument for the *Thesis of the Autonomy of Psychological Explanation* as well as with the arguments of some contemporary philosophical functionalists who also promote materialism without reductionism. On the other hand, Freud and modern functionalists tend to think of describing experience "in its own terms" as describing it intentionally, in terms of the structure and content of our mental states. Skinner, as we shall see shortly, believes in the autonomy of psychological science, but he has a certain allergy to a full-blown "intentional stance."[6]

In any case, Skinner's metaphysical commitment to the view that overt and covert behavioral phenomena are made of the same (material) stuff, and obey the same sorts of laws, implies that potentially discoverable lawlike generalizations exist for all genuine psychological phenomena. But it is important to notice that this commitment is programmatic, not empirical. It is not as if Skinner can show us, at this time, how exactly to analyze private psychological phenomena (although he sometimes talks as if he can). Skinner's post-1945 metaphysical stance is utterly promissory. It is really only an expression of his confidence that materialism is an adequate world view and that, therefore, a complete science of human behavior is possible. That confidence will be vindicated, of course, to the extent that a coherent system of psychological laws governing overt and covert phenomena is discovered.

On the other hand, a materialistic metaphysical stance cannot be what makes Skinner's behaviorism behavioristic. Materialism is simply not sufficient to give behaviorism its unique flavor as an approach to psychological explanation. This becomes obvious as soon as one is reminded that a similar metaphysical position is held by nonbehavioristic thinkers such as Freud as well as by many contemporary cognitive psychologists.

Traditional behavioristic theories got their special behavioristic flavor by doing one of two things: denying that private events exist, or admitting that private events exist but demanding operational definitions of them. According to the story I have just told, Skinner once advocated the first tactic, but has rejected it since 1945. With regard to the second, Skinner remarked in 1964, speaking of the lack of success of operationism in physics, "Applied to psychological problems operationism has been no more successful."[7]

Skinner's mature psychology, then, is not behavioristic in either of the traditional ways. What makes his theory behavioristic is really only an attitude; it consists of a certain epistemological conservatism that remains from his early operationistic and positivistic days. Unfortunately this attitude keeps Skinner from fully deploying his regulative materialistic metaphysic to propose an in-depth analysis of the rich terrain of cognitive processes, of human emotion, of thought and belief, and, in general, of the organism-from-within. Thus although Skinner says that "Science often talks about things it cannot see or measure,"[8] and although he gives behaviorists permission to talk about private events—

"the radical behaviorist may in some cases consider private events (inferentially perhaps, but nonetheless meaningfully)"[9]—his theory continually seems to be biting its own tongue. Thus even though Skinner's materialistic metaphysic gives him license to analyze the world within, he persistently displays the attitude that reference to private phenomena—even if these phenomena are construed as physiological events or behavioral processes—is, by and large, more trouble than it is worth, and is to be avoided whenever possible.[10]

It is this tendency which explains the widespread feeling that even Skinner's mature psychology is somehow constitutionally incapable of yielding the rich promised account of the events, and the relations among the events, which take place between our ears. I can illuminate this point best by discussing Skinner's objections to Freud's mentalism.

Whereas Skinner thinks that Cartesian mentalism makes psychology impossible, he thinks that Freudian mentalism, for all its determinism, underemphasizes the most important causes of behavior. Skinner's overall critique can be framed as follows. Suppose, as most people assume, that much of what we think, feel, wish, and believe has environmental determinants, and that much of how we overtly behave is determined by these thoughts, beliefs, wishes, and feelings. If this is the case then we can simplistically schematize the typical psychological causal chain in terms of three links, environmental events (E) cause mental changes (M) which cause overt behavioral changes (R):

$$E \longrightarrow M \longrightarrow R$$

As things stood at Freud's time and as they stand now, we are in a relatively good position to observe environmental and overt behavioral events and to describe the causal relations between them. We are, however, in a poor position to observe the intervening mental events.

According to Skinner, what Freud did was to make masterful observations about, for example, the way early childhood punishment of sex play makes people act peculiarly later on. Such observations and the causal generalizations based on them are of the form $E \longrightarrow R$. What Freud then proceeded to do, however, was to infer the character of the middle link in such causal chains. This caused three sorts of trouble.

First, since the middle link is generally unobserved, inferences about it are always underdetermined by the evidence and therefore are poorly understood. This is evidenced by the degree to which the language of Freudian psychology is metaphorical. Think, for example, of the largely analogical quality of almost all the main theoretical terms of Freudian psychology: "libido," "id," "repression," "sublimation," and so on. Almost all these terms can be illuminatingly analyzed in hydraulic terms, in terms of irrepressible geysers, deep dark oceans, and bursting sewer systems. And that, according to Skinner, shows just how little we really understand what we are talking about.

Second, speculative stories about the mysteries of the mind are so enthralling, regardless of their truth value, that they steal the show from the more mundane environmental and behavioral facts. Consider, for example, the Freudian hypothesis to the effect that paranoia is caused by latent homosexual wishes. Even supposing that this hypothesis is true, it fails to provide any clue whatsoever as to what causes latent homosexual wishes. But because the story is so exotic we do not even think to ask the obvious question. Skinner puts the worry this way: "Early punishment of sexual behavior is an observable fact which undoubtedly leaves behind a changed organism. But when this change is represented as a state of conscious or unconscious anxiety or guilt, specific details of the punishment are lost."[11]

Third, and this follows from the second, when we lose sight of environmental particulars we lose sight of what we need to know if we are going to change both the behavior and the mental events that precede or accompany behavior. As Skinner's argument goes, if we are going to be able to treat sexual dysfunction and its accompanying anxiety, it will be by careful observation of the environmental situations in which sexually dysfunctional behavior decreases. If we are going to be able to teach parents how not to create sexually dysfunctional adults it will be on the basis of careful observations of actual child-rearing practices.

Overall, then, Skinner's complaints against mentalistic types of psychologies can be summarized as follows. Some mentalistic psychologies, for example, Cartesianism, make flagrant use of "explanatory fictions." Explanatory fictions are mental terms that have no reference at all. According to Skinner's metaphysic, notions like an incorporeal mind, res cogitans, a free self, and the like, are the stuff of philosophical fantasy. They simply fail to refer to existing entities or processes. So when we say things like "I did that of my own free will," we are simply speaking Cartesian-inspired nonsense. There just is no such thing as free will.

Explanatory fictions even show up with surprising frequency in places outside of the speculative musings of philosophers. Consider the following two everyday psychological explanations: (1) "John keeps vandalizing school property because he is a juvenile delinquent"; (2) "Mary keeps acting nuts because she is crazy." The temptation here, according to Skinner, is first to think that there is some mental entity inside John called "juvenile delinquency" and inside Mary called "craziness," and second to think that this mental entity explains behavior. But, Skinner argues, there simply are no such mental entities as juvenile delinquency or craziness, and deferring to them does no explanatory work whatsoever (if you doubt this, reread the examples several times).

Other types of mentalistic psychology, for example, Freudianism (but also most types of cognitive psychology and neurophysiology) are more respectable, since they do not openly use explanatory fictions in formulating their laws and hypotheses. Nevertheless, they tend to offer unsatisfactory explanations by focusing too much attention on "mental way stations." Mental way stations differ from explanatory fictions in that they do, in fact, have a psychologically real referent, albeit usually a metaphorical one. Unfortunately, when mental way stations start to figure prominently in psychological explanations they tend to make us lose sight of the more visible and manipulatable environmental determinants of behavior or of the behavior itself.

Suppose, for example, that I tell you that "John is vandalizing school property because he often feels frustrated" or that "Mary is acting nuts because she feels extremely guilty." Even if we allow the psychological reality of feelings of frustration and guilt, we still have no explanation of the prior causes (assumed to be environmental) of the feelings of frustration and guilt. So here we have lost sight of the environment. Alternatively, if I tell you that "John feels frustrated because his teachers tell him he has no talent" or that "Mary feels extremely guilty because she accidentally tipped over a canoe and caused her younger brother to drown" I have failed to mention the behavioral effects of John's and Mary's respective environmental histories and mental states. So here we have lost sight of the overt behavioral consequences. Talk of mental way stations, according to Skinner, is simply too seductive to be trusted. If a mental way station fails to lure us away from the first salient link in a psychological causal chain, it will lure us away from the last link. In either case we will remain stuck in the middle, in the most obscure place of all.

In sum, Skinner thinks that one variety of mentalism, Cartesianism, speaks openly of "fictions;" the other variety of mentalism, Freudianism (and contemporary cognitive psychology), tends to get stuck in explanatory quicksand. In this manner Skinner tries to shift the burden of proof of scientific respectability to the mentalist because on Skinner's assessment of past performance the mentalist is either speaking nonsense or filibustering.

But, of course, the arguments I have just presented are far from decisive, especially as regards the second kind of mentalism. First, it is not at all obvious why a mentalist could not resolve to avoid getting stuck at the middle link in three-term causal chains. Even if Skinner is right that there is a strong temptation to get stuck there, scientists

have historically shown great strength in the face of explanatory temptation once it is pointed out to them, for example, in avoiding the
powerful temptation to infer causality from simple correlations, or to
impute statistical significance to indecisive, but prima facie convincing,
data. I see no reason whatsoever to think that psychologists could not
be equally convinced of the wisdom of framing psychological generalizations, whenever possible, in terms of environmental, mental, and
overt behavioral processes. Second, and this follows from the first, it
seems obvious that leaving out any salient link in a psychological causal
chain will result in an incomplete psychology. If psychology were to
ignore mental causes of behavior or the mental effects of the environment it would be no less impoverished than if it ignored environmental
inputs and behavioral outputs. The thing we want psychology to do
is link the environment to behavior through mentality.

The Theoretician's Dilemma

Skinner, nevertheless, is tenacious about his epistemological scruples.
He comes prepared to fortify his state-of-the-art criticisms of mentalistic
psychology with a purely logical argument against what he calls "theories." This argument has come to be known as the "Theoretician's
Dilemma." A theory in Skinner's positivistic sense refers not, as it
normally does, to a systematic collection of generalizations and principles but to any explanation that refers to unobservables.[12] Skinner's
arguments against theories apply equally, therefore, to mentalistic speculations and to neurophysiological speculations. Skinner puts his purely
logical argument against theories this way:

> The objection to inner states is not that they do not exist, but they
> are not relevant in a functional analysis. We cannot account for
> the behavior of any system while staying wholly inside it; even-
> tually we must turn to forces operating on the organism from
> without. Unless there is a weak spot in our causal chain so that
> the second link is not lawfully determined by the first, or the third
> by the second, then the first and third links must be lawfully
> related.[13]

The argument can be restated as follows: Suppose once again that E
is some set of historical and/or contemporary environmental conditions,
and M is some set of internal mental or neurophysiological states, and
R is some set of overt behavioral responses. If we assume that determinism is true and that environmental determinants normally precede
mental changes that normally precede behavioral changes, then the
typical psychological causal chain is of the form E $\longrightarrow$ M $\longrightarrow$ R.

If such chains are the rule so that some set of environmental events lawfully brings about some set of mental events, and these mental events in turn lawfully bring about an overt behavioral response, then it follows transitively that the environmental events bring about the overt behavioral response. That is, if E $\longrightarrow$ M $\longrightarrow$ R, then E $\longrightarrow$ R. This being so, if we are merely interested in explaining the occurrence of the overt behavioral responses we can do so without any mention whatsoever of mental events. References to internal mental or neurophysiological states, therefore, are not logically necessary for a psychological science that seeks to explain overt behavior. Psychology can do its job without deploying a neurophysiological or an intentional vocabulary. The alleged dilemma the theoretician faces is this: either mental events lawfully link environmental events and behavior, in which case we don't need to talk about them, or mental events do not lawfully link environmental events and behavior, in which case we shouldn't talk about them.

The first thing to notice about this argument is that it is utterly neutral, Skinner's bias notwithstanding, with respect to the question of whether we eliminate references to mental events or references to environmental events from our explanations. This is due to the fact that on the purely logical presumption of transitivity, mental events explain overt behavioral events just as well as environmental events explain them. That is, if it is true that E $\longrightarrow$ M $\longrightarrow$ B, then both E $\longrightarrow$ B and M $\longrightarrow$ B.

On purely logical grounds, therefore, references to environmental events are just as unnecesary as references to mental events. The logic of explanation requires only that we cite some necessary cause of the effect in question, and on the assumption of three-term causal chains either environmental or mental events fit that bill. If we wish to explain overt behavioral responses (and the whole argument assumes that these are the *explananda* we are aiming at) we need to mention one or the other, but Skinner's argument gives us no reason on its own for preferring explanations of behavior in terms of environmental events over explanations in terms of mental or neural events.

Not surprisingly, Skinner tries to promote the preference for non-mentalistic explanations by running the latter, purely logical, argument against "theories" together with his pragmatic objections to mentalism. That is, references to unobservables are epistemologically more problematic than references to observables, and references to the middle links in three-term causal chains are not useful for prediction and control. The fully fortified version of the argument, then, runs as follows: because references to mental events are logically eliminable and because such references are epistemically problematic and practically useless, we ought to avoid referring to mental events whenever possible. Still, the argument does not work. In part, it fails because Skinner openly begs the central questions about the nature of psychological explanation.

First, there is the view that the purpose of science is prediction and control and that references to mental states do not advance these goals. There is, of course, nothing necessary about this view of science. It is the view of the alchemist or the engineer. It is not, however, the view of many cognitive psychologists. One can quite reasonably take the opposing view that the purpose of psychology is to provide a purely explanatory account of psychological states. Or one can even accept Skinner's conception of the purpose of science but argue that references to intentional mental states are, in fact, useful in prediction. Knowledge of the next president's beliefs, for example, seems as reasonable a basis as any for predicting what policies he will try to implement.

Second, there is the assumption—not to mention the assumption of determinism itself—that typical causal chains are three-term chains that start in the environment. This is by no means certain. It begs the entire nature-nurture question. Some behavior is undoubtedly tied in with biological schedules (for example, the increased interest in sex at puberty). Many psychologists claim that similar connections to biology hold for many of our logical, cognitive, and linguistic competencies. To whatever extent this is true, to that extent we are dealing with two-term causal chains, or with three-term chains where the illuminating action takes place at the second link, within the psychological economy of the organism.

Third, Skinner operates here with a restrictive conception of "explanation." Skinner seems to think that to cite *any* cause of an event is to provide a satisfactory explanation of that event. So if I say "she died of a gunshot wound to her head" I have explained her death; and if I say "she died of a ruptured artery in the brain" I have explained her death; and if I say "he was making a fast getaway from the bank at which she worked, she screamed, he shot her in the head, the bullet ruptured an artery and that's why she died" I have explained her death. But it should be obvious from this example that not all true explanations are equally good. The citation of some cause is logically necessary, but it is not sufficient for adequate scientific explanation. Among the class of logically acceptable explanations some are much richer and more complete than others. Skinner's arguments against "theories" fail to speak to this point.

Because Skinner's three assumptions—first, that the purpose of science is prediction and control, second, that the true causes of behavior are environmental, third, that the citation of any cause of an effect is sufficient for an adequate explanation—are questionable, and because the purely logical argument for avoiding references to internal states is not decisive, Skinner's prescription for an epistemologically secure psychology has no overriding philosophical justification. There is no reason, therefore, to abandon our intuitions regarding "Brentano's Thesis," that is, our intuitions that psychology must make essential reference to intentional mental states if it is going to do the job we want it to do.

One might be tempted to suggest a compromise at this point or at least a compromise interpretation of Skinner's considered position. Once again let *explanandum* refer to that which stands in need of psychological explanation, and let *explanans* refer to that which does the explaining. Skinner's position might be construed to be that one should avoid using intentional concepts in one's *explanans* at all costs, whereas they can appear in one's *explanandum*. Such a proposal gains its philosophical attractiveness from considerations having to do with the logical peculiarities of intentional idioms,[14] their underdetermination by observation, the problems of other-minds and self-knowledge—all of which make intentional states and processes seem unfit to bear the bulk of the explanatory weight in psychological explanation.

On such a view it would be permissible to explain my knowledge of the Pythagorean theorem (a private intentional state) in terms of my geometry professor's verbal behavior and the manner in which he reinforced my elegant proofs (both nonintentional events), but it would not be permissible to explain my behavior of following sports—religiously reading the sports section of the newspaper, watching sports on TV—in terms of my great fondness for sports, my belief that physical fitness is an important value, and my need for nonacademic diversions.

Unfortunately even this compromise strategy will not work. Intentional states need to be smuggled in on the *explanans* side of things if sense is to be made of Skinner's most Spartan experimental setups. Consider the following simple experiment. Take a pigeon or a rat at 80 percent of normal weight, put it in a "Skinner box," and give it the task of learning to peck or paw a disc in return for food pellets delivered on some stipulated schedule of reinforcement. After a time one will be in a position to say something like this: The animal pecks or paws at rate x in the presence of stimuli s because it is on schedule r. One ends up, or so it seems, with an explanation characterized in utterly nonintentional terms. However, there is a trick. The true behavioral laws Skinner comes up with in situations such as these make sense precisely because there are true mentalistic laws which underlie them. That the animal pecks or paws at rate x in the presence of stimuli s on schedule r makes sense because we know that any organism at 80 percent of normal weight is hungry and desires food. Dennett puts it this way:

> Skinner's experimental design is supposed to eliminate the intentional, but it merely masks it. Skinner's nonintentional predictions work to the extent they do, not because Skinner has truly found nonintentional behavioral laws, but because the highly reliable intentional predictions underlying his experimental situations (the rat desires food and believes it will get food by pressing the bar—something for which it has been given good evidence—so it will press the bar) are disguised by leaving virtually no room in the environment for more than one bodily motion to be the appropriate action and by leaving virtually no room in the environment for discrepancy to arise between the subject's beliefs and the reality.[15]

Furthermore, it seems patently clear, especially if we move from pigeons and rats to people, that intentional ascriptions often surface in illuminating ways in our *explanans*. For example, if you ask why Professor Smith is spending the entire summer working in the library and are told that he wants to finish writing his book before classes start in the fall, you have been given a perfectly respectable explanation by almost everyone's lights, and an intentional, mentalistic ascription figures in it in an essential way.

Thus the strategy of making psychology epistemologically secure by not allowing mental terms to occupy places in one's *explanans* seems doomed to failure. In highly artificial experimental situations intentional categories are assumed, and in nonartificial ones involving humans they are likely to shed some explanatory light.

I trust that the foregoing analysis makes clear the knotty character of the unresolved tension between Skinner's bold materialistic metaphysic on the one hand, and his epistemological conservatism on the other. Skinner's materialism would seem to provide the green light to proceed to talk about both public and private, intentional and nonintentional events, with the confidence that one is never referring to some shadowy Cartesian substance. Paradoxically, Skinner's epistemology continually seems to refuse his own metaphysical permission to go ahead and enter the realm of mentality and intentionality.

For the last thirty-five years, Skinner has been stressing the importance of taking the problem of privacy seriously, while at the same time trying to show how we can (and should) avoid reference to mental events. If we evaluate Skinner less in terms of what he says and more in terms of what he does—as any good behaviorist would, I assume, want to be judged—then the evidence is overwhelming that the latter bias, and not the former, is the heart of the behaviorist position. In fact, as far as I can tell, there is no known behavioristically inspired psychology that allows itself the conceptual resources needed to talk about all the elusive phenomena in psychology's domain of inquiry.

This, of course, is not to deny that Skinner has many interesting things to say about the links between the environment and behavior, nor to deny that his criticisms of Cartesianism and Freudianism are in many respects right on target. It only suggests that the list of all true generalizations linking the environment and behavior will not satisfy the demands of those who want a bona fide science of mind. I suppose Skinner would reply that the conception of psychology I have in mind is unnecessary, epistemologically too risky, philosophically misconceived, or impossible. But I have examined all his arguments to that effect and found them wanting.

Skinner on Self-Knowledge

In at least one respect there is more substance to Skinner's reluctance to talk about mental phenomena than initially meets the eye. This comes out nicely in his discussions of the problem of self-knowledge. Like Freud, Skinner thinks that it is difficult to know oneself. But his reasons for thinking this are different from Freud's. For Freud, self-knowledge is one casualty of our inability to face up to the aggressive, sexual, generally seamy content of our unconscious. For Skinner, on the other hand, the problem of self-knowledge arises from the way we learn language.

The nature of the connection between language learning and self-knowledge is an old philosophical puzzle. There are those who believe that knowledge is, strictly speaking, linguistic.[16] On this view, a child sees dogs but does not know what dogs are until he knows how to use the predicate "is a dog"; a child experiences pain but does not know that he experiences pain until he has the words to describe pain; a child sees a red thing but does not know that it is a red thing he sees until he possesses color words, and so on.

As I understand this point of view one does not violate its spirit if one acknowledges that although the link between knowing and saying is very strong, it is not logically necessary. For example, when my son was fourteen months old he would call the husky next door "dog." He even greeted her with "Hi dog," whereas he greeted me with a very distinct "Hi da." However, Ben also called birds and infants "dog," albeit less frequently than he called the dog next door "dog." So, did Ben know the difference between dogs and birds and infants? Can't we just presume he saw that dogs, birds, and infants are different natural kinds, even though these distinctions did not show up clearly in his language?

It is conceivable that Ben knew these things even though he was not able to put them into the right words. Nevertheless, the plausibility of the view linking knowing and saying is, I think, what lies behind the fact that most of us probably would feel that we couldn't be sure that Ben had these distinctions right until he used the words correctly. One's inclination is to acknowledge only that Ben was on the way to knowing these things.

Others deny that there is any unusual epistemic significance to language and believe, therefore, that there is nonlinguistic knowledge: for example, the sort that children and lower animals have of pain and pleasure, or the kind that Zen monks or poets or moralists have of truth, beauty, and goodness. This kind of knowledge, if it exists, is ineffable—that it exists is as much as we can say.

This does not mean, however, that the believer in nonlinguistic knowledge believes in occult properties, nor that there can be no intersubjective evidence for such knowledge. For example, one can imagine all sorts of ingenious psychological experiments that might test to see if Ben, or some animal for that matter, was able to discriminate dogs from birds despite the lack of linguistic ability.

If one thinks that knowledge is fundamentally linguistic, then the problems of knowing something and describing it more or less collapse into one another. If you really know what color magenta is, you ought to be able (barring emotional blocks and the like) to point to it on the color spectrum and tell me "that's magenta." If you really know the Pythagorean theorem you ought to be able to prove it on a blackboard. If, on the other hand, one believes that there is nonlinguistic knowledge, then the problems of knowing and describing are separate. It is entirely possible that I know the Pythagorean theorem but can't put it into words, or that I knew what pain was before I knew any language, or that I know what is right but can't describe it, and so on.

Skinner tends toward the view that knowledge is intimately connected to language. This orientation affects his position on self-knowledge in two important ways. First, the powerful link between knowing and saying implies that one knows one's private, and public, self to the degree to which one possesses and unambiguous vocabulary which one is facile at using in describing oneself—in the same way one knows geometry to the degree that one can do proofs in geometrical language. Second, and this follows from the first, whenever we hear a person struggle with a self-description and end by saying "Well, I know what I mean about what I'm feeling, but I just can't find the words for it, I just can't describe it correctly" that the person actually does not know what he or she means, actually does not know what is going on inside him or her.

Given the frequency with which such situations of failure to self-describe occur, we can legitimately wonder what could cause them to be so common. Skinner's answer to this question rests on his observations of some differences in the way we learn the language of private states and events from the way we learn the language or public objects and events. All words, to start in the simplest place, are acquired on the basis of the "law of effect"—by the rewarding, ignoring, shaping, and correcting of novices by mature language users. Children, thanks perhaps to some sort of imitative or babbling instinct, make an appropriate noise, for example, "ma," in the appropriate situation, that is, in the presence of mother, and are rewarded. Thanks to the way humans are wired to learn, and to subsequent reinforcement and shaping, a child comes to identify unmistakably its unique mother with a word such as "mom." Such an account of language learning is paradigmatic for Skinner.

According to Skinner, however, the situation of the community in teaching a child words like "mother," or "red," or "bike," or "ball" is very different from its situation in teaching the child words like "toothache," or "happy," or "sad," or "pain." In teaching a child the word for mother or red, the community is in the advantageous position of being able to check directly the accuracy of the verbal response it reinforces. If a child calls "ma" to its father or calls a green ball "red" we are certain that he has made a mistake and can respond accordingly. Of course, we do not correct children's verbal mistakes in the sense of commenting on the rightness or wrongness of every response; normally we allow children to start with overgeneralizations, for example, using the term "ma" to refer to both mother and father, and then gradually shape the response in the direction of the right referent. The important point for Skinner is that with regard to words like "ma," and "bike," and "red," we all know exactly what the right referent is. We are totally confident about teaching such words because reliable public evidence exists by which we can tell whether or not a child's verbal identifications are correct.

But how would we teach the word for red if either the individual or the community were color-blind? The simple answer is that we would not and could not teach it. Certainly we can teach a color-blind individual to use the word "red" correctly in certain circumstances, for example, to say things like "you better slow down, the traffic light up ahead is red." But here he doesn't have clue as to what "red" really means, he just uses it to refer to the top illuminated bulb in a traffic light.

Skinner provocatively argues that, with respect to the problem of teaching words for private events, we are in a situation similar to that of trying to teach color words and color discriminations in a world of partially, and unpredictably, color-blind people. Whereas most of us are not color-blind, however, we are all naturally—at least partially—other-mind blind.

This blindness is caused by the fact that "a small but important part of the universe is enclosed within the skin of each individual."[17] Other-mind blindness puts us at a disadvantage in teaching others words that refer to private events in *them*. This is because we are in no position to check that they are in the state we think they are in—for example, pain as opposed to mere discomfort, happiness as opposed to elation, jealousy as opposed to envy—when we try to teach them to make private references. Skinner says that a "characteristic result of these defective contingencies is that responses are often controlled by a mixture of stimuli the nature of which is *not clear to the community or listener or to the speaker himself.*"[18] He goes on to bemoan the fact that even "in the careful practices of the psychological laboratory, it is doubtful whether terms descriptive of, for example, emotional states are under precisely the same stimulus control from speaker to speaker."[19]

Furthermore, since *ex hypothesi*, knowing the words that refer to private events is a necessary condition for knowing the private events, it follows that we are also in a poor position to equip others with the tools required for self-knowledge. Skinner says, "It is social reinforcement which leads the individual to know himself. It is only through the gradual growth of a verbal community that the individual becomes 'conscious'. He comes to see himself only as others see him, or at least only as others insist that he see himself."[20] In this roundabout way, then, the problem of other-minds causes the problem of knowledge of one's own mind.

Of course, there are ways to circumvent our other-mind blindness. We teach a child the word for pain by inferring that he is in pain because he is receiving stimulation, for example, dental drilling, that would cause pain in us, or because he is responding in ways we respond when we are in pain, for example, by crying. The nice thing about the pain example, however, is that for biological reasons most of us seem to have evolved to have roughly similar private pain reactions to many of the same sorts of things. Nevertheless, whenever we infer that someone else is in pain we are making an inference of a whole different order from the one required to know that the ball we are playing catch with is red.

But if pain seems relatively unproblematic, consider words like "happy," "sad," "amused," "bemused," "pensive," "depressed," "manic," "bucolic," "overstimulated," "melancholic," "jealous," "envious," and "elated." How do we make reliable inferences about the presence or absence of these states in novices when we teach them these words in the first place? How do we know that different linguistically competent individuals mean the same things we do when they employ these terms?

Skinner's answer to the first question is that we stake the reliability of our inferences about private events on public behavior and public stimulation. Skinner emphasizes that "the public origin of subjective terms must not be forgotten."[21] We infer that our child is sad if he is crying or has just fallen down. But we could be very wrong; our child may just be engaging in a private conspiracy to gain our attention. And there is, in principle, no certain way to get at the truth of the matter.

Skinner's answer to the second question is that we simply cannot be sure that people use the language of private events to mean the same things. In fact, given the poor position the verbal community is in as it tries to teach others how to make subtle discriminations of private events, it seems unlikely that the language of private events has great uniformity. The highly metaphorical character of the language of private events would seem to support the thesis that its range is ambiguous and its reference imprecise.

Overall, Skinner's views on language learning reinforce his extremely mixed feelings about references to mental events within a psychological science. Because the language we use to describe private events is imprecise and metaphorical, and because the methods we use to isolate private events are irreducibly inferential, we are generally better off without this language.

I have already discussed some problems with this view of scientific explanation, but two new objections are worth pointing out. First, many scientific terms from our very best science are also irreducibly inferential. For example, we infer the existence of electrons because of the tracks they leave in cloud chambers, and because of the explanatory richness this inference adds to our overall ability to understand and predict the nature of physical reality. The fact that mental terms are theoretical terms in psychology provides no more epistemological warrant, in and of itself, for excluding them from psychology than the theoretical status of terms like "electron" and "gluon" provides warrant for excluding them from physics. Second, and this is related to the first, Skinner underemphasizes the ways in which the language acquisition story he tells might actually lead to greater optimism regarding our ability to communicate about privacy.

Many philosophers inspired by Wittgenstein would completely agree with Skinner's reminder that "the public origin of subjective terms must not be forgotten." But they would use this reminder to explain how it is that we can, and sometimes do, come to communicate so very well with "subjective terms." We introduce these terms in very rich and informative contexts. For example, we introduce the term "pain" to a novice in rich stimulatory (he has a scraped knee) and behavioral (he is screaming at the top of his lungs) settings.

Mature language users come armed with a well-developed theory of the logical and conceptual relations that hold between the stimulatory and behavioral indicators of pain and actual pain states. Novices are introduced to the term "pain" in myriad contexts which fit the theory according to the lights of the mature language users, and eventually the novices come to share the same theory, the same linguistic practice, the same language game, the same form of life with the mature language users.[22] Overall, the process by which a novice comes to learn how to correctly use the mental term "pain" from his parents and playmates is not so different from the way a physics student learns how to use the theoretical term "electron" from his physics professor. In both cases learning the correct usage admits of degree, but learning the correct usage is entirely possible.

Once again, therefore, the epistemological conclusion Skinner draws from a series of perceptive insights goes too far. What does seem to follow fairly straightforwardly, however, is that if Skinner is even approximately right about the relation between acquiring a language and acquiring knowledge of—inner and outer—reality, then Cartesian views about self-knowledge are just plain wrong.[23] Self-knowledge is not simply there for the asking. The contents of our minds do not sit there neatly laid out in their proper a priori categories merely awaiting the attentive perusal by each person's mind's eye—every person's mind's eye being equally capable of its own sort of 20/20 vision.

For Skinner, self-knowledge, when and where it exists, is a social product. How we categorize mental events, and how well we do so depends on the breadth, depth, and intricacy of the language we have learned, and on the contexts in which that language is introduced and subsequently utilized. These things, of course, will vary from individual to individual, from linguistic community to linguistic community, and from time to time.

Some of the implications Skinner draws from his argument are extreme, but the overall thrust of this part of his analysis strikes me as being close to the mark. If it is true that competence in a language of private events is in some important sense a necessary condition for knowledge of one's own private events, then we have reason to doubt that everyone has extensive self-knowledge or that anyone is in incorrigible touch with all his own private states. This doubt in turn provides grounds for some wariness toward even the most sincere introspective reports. Furthermore, if Freud is right that humans are powerfully inclined to resist self-knowledge for reasons that have nothing to do with the language acquisition process (and this is not necessarily inconsistent with what Skinner says), then we have two sets of reasons to take the problem of self-knowledge seriously. Finally, if contemporary cognitive scientists are right that even if we had all the linguistic concepts in the world, we would still not have a clue as to how to describe how we do such very simple things as counting or remembering faces, then we have three sets of reasons to abandon any residual Cartesian confidence about self-knowledge.

The Concept of the "Operant": Selection by Consequences

Even in the days when a science of mind was still just a gleam in someone's eye, thinkers like Descartes, William James, and John Dewey clearly understood that a successful psychology must overcome two intimately related obstacles. The first obstacle is the problem of novelty; the second is the problem of purpose. The problem of novelty is the problem of how it is possible to do anything which is truly new, creative, and imaginative if our behavior is the mechanical result of past conditioning. The problem of purpose is the problem of how it is possible to be motivated by future goals, to be forward-looking planners, to be teleologically oriented, if our current state is a straightforward product of this same past conditioning. Why do we care so deeply about the future if we are just products of the past?

These two problems looked insuperable to Descartes, because, on the one hand, he thought that the evidence was overwhelming that humans do, in fact, perform novel and purposeful acts and, because, on the other hand, all bona fide science, as he understood it, assumes that the systems it studies are mechanical systems, and mechanical systems simply do not behave creatively or purposefully. Think, for example, of a simple mechanical system like a child's windup toy. The toy performs a small number of determinate motions that are strictly dependent on the number of times the gears are turned. The toy, however, does nothing creative and nothing purposeful. It might do something unpredictable—it might break. But breaking is caused by outside forces and is no longer unpredictable once we take these outside forces into account. We buy the toy for the sake of giving pleasure to our children, but it's not the mechanical toy that behaves for the sake of giving pleasure to our children, it's us. There thus seems to be some sort of essential difference between a human system and a mechanical system. I can sharpen the force of this worry by briefly reviewing the approved style of psychological explanation within the behavioristic camp around 1920.

A certain portion of human behavior is like the behavior of Cartesian automata or the windup toy. That is, certain responses are elicited by prior stimuli in a (virtually) all-or-none fashion. Think, for example, of responses like the knee-jerk response to a tap on the knee, pupil contractions to light, and salivation to food in the mouth. Responses such as these comprise the class of *unconditioned reflexes*. Unconditioned reflexes, as far as we know, come with the biological wiring.

If we let uS = unconditioned stimulus, and let uR = unconditioned response, we can write the general law governing unconditioned reflexes as follows:

Law 1:   For all uS and uR, $uS \longrightarrow uR$, where Probability (uR, given uS) = ~1

Another portion of human behavior involves building on these unconditioned reflexes and actually acquiring new stimulus-response links. The acquisition process is called *classical* or *Pavlovian conditioning* and the acquired behaviors are called *conditioned reflexes*. The acquisition proceeds in the following way: Take an unconditioned reflex like salivation (uR) to food-in-the-mouth (uS), and take a new stimulus (preferably one not linked to any other unconditioned reflex), for example, a gently ringing bell, and pair this new stimulus with the uS. Call this new stimulus the conditioned stimulus (cS). The first stage of the conditioning process then looks like this:

(a): uS (food-in-mouth) + cS (bell) $\longrightarrow uR$ (salivation)

After we have paired the food-in-the-mouth and the bell a number of times, we can take the food away and the bell alone will elicit a very similar, but not quite identical, salivation response. (The new response might, for example, contain a slightly smaller amount of saliva than the original uR.) Because this response is not quite identical in form to the unconditioned response and because it is in response to a new stimulus we call it the conditioned response, cR. Thus at the second stage we find that

(b): cS (bell) $\longrightarrow cR$ (salivation)

We can write the general law governing classical conditioning then as:

Law 2:   For all uS, uR, cS, and cR, if $uS \longrightarrow uR$, and uS is paired with cS, then (after a time) $cS \longrightarrow cR$, where uR and cR are very similar responses, and where Probability (cR, given cS) > 0, but varies depending on the strength of the initial link, the number of times cS has been presented without uS, and so on.

I will refer to any psychology that analyzes human behavior in terms of unconditioned and conditioned reflexes, in terms of Law 1 and Law 2, as a stimulus-response psychology, "S-R psychology," for short.[24] The fundamental theoretical assumption of S-R psychology is that all human behavior can be analyzed in terms of antecedent eliciting stimuli. From the perspective of experimentalists like John B. Watson and Ivan P. Pavlov this assumption was a matter of irrefutable behavioristic dogma; it secured behaviorism's place in the mechanical sciences.

Skinner is frequently called an S-R psychologist, but he is not. Basically, Skinner's disagreement with the S-R psychology of Watson and Pavlov has to do with its inability to solve the twin problems of novelty and purpose.

Take the problem of novelty first. Law 2, the law governing conditioned reflexes, looks prima facie as though it might be able to make the problem of novelty yield, since classical conditioning explicitly involves the acquisition of new stimulus-response connections. Unfortunately the novelty that results from classical conditioning occurs in the wrong place. What is new is always the eliciting stimulus, never the response. This is easy to see. Essentially, Law 2 involves straightforward stimulus substitution. Thus we can get an organism to salivate to a bell, to the sight of food, to a light, to a plate, or to the sound of the word "escargot," by substituting these things for the original unconditioned stimulus of food-in-the-mouth. But in every case the response is a very close approximation of the original unconditioned response.

However, the problem of novelty is really the problem of response novelty. How did I come to write the previous sentence, a sentence that I probably have never written before? How did Julius Erving make that incredible reverse slam-dunk? How did Bach come to write his captivating, ethereal motets? The only answer to these questions available to the S-R theorist is preposterous. He must maintain that a response like uttering a novel sentence, or slam-dunking a basketball in a new way, or composing a motet, can be broken down into a series of very small response units, all of which exist originally as unconditioned responses, but which are now being elicited in an exotic and coherent pattern by an equally exotic and coherent chain of unconditioned and conditioned stimuli.

S-R psychology fares no better when it comes to the problem of purpose. Suppose an exchange student had just arrived on planet Earth from Mars and inquired what humans were doing when they engaged in the practice we know as "jogging." We would probably tell him something like "They are running in order to keep fit and trim." Supposing the Martian understood the concept of running, the concepts of fitness and trimness, and the concept of doing one thing in order to achieve something else, this would suffice. Notice, however, that our explanation is framed in utterly teleological terms. People jog in order to achieve certain ends, they jog for the sake of certain future goals. In fact, it is not clear how we could ever describe, let alone explain, a practice like "jogging" without referring to the goals of the practice.

Unfortunately the S-R theorist is ill-equipped to talk about the goals, ends, and consequences of behavior. His analytic framework, as depicted in Law 1 and Law 2, is limited to antecedent eliciting stimuli and the resultant behavior. There is no place in his framework for descriptions of the consequences of behavior.[25] But the suspicion is irresistible that even the richest account of the set of stimuli antecedent to a jog around the lake will never satisfactorily explain what the jogger is doing and why.[26] In the end then, S-R psychology fails to provide a framework for analyzing human behavior that can coexist with a commitment to the psychological reality of novel and purposeful behavior.

Skinner thinks that we can get a purchase on these two problems without giving up our hopes for a scientific psychology by availing ourselves of an enriched conception of behavior and and a more biological, less mechanical model of explanation. The category we must add to the S-R account is the category of *operant behavior*. Operant behavior is behavior governed by the "law of effect"; that is, behavior acquired, shaped, and maintained by stimuli following responses rather than by stimuli preceding them. Skinner claims that operant behavior is really just one instance of the familiar process of "selection by consequences."[27]

The process Skinner has in mind figures most prominently in analyses of biological evolution. Suppose we notice that the male members of a certain species of pheasant have developed significantly longer tail feathers over several generations, and we wonder why. A standard evolutionary analysis might proceed as follows: when the biological trait of longer than average tail feathers on the males first appeared it was found attractive by the females and led to greater reproductive success for the males with long tail feathers than for those with short or average ones; furthermore, since reproductive success involves passing on one's genes, the greater reproductive success of the pheasants with the long tail feathers led, in turn, to a relative increase in the frequency of the long tail feather trait.

This is a typical sort of evolutionary explanation and has the following general form: if some biological trait leads to an increase in the reproductive success of organisms that possess the trait, then the trait will increase in frequency in subsequent generations.

The analysis of operant behavior at the individual level is strictly analogous to this evolutionary one at the species level. Operant conditioning is meant to explain the ontogenesis of new responses in the same way the theory of natural selection is meant to explain the phylogenesis of new biological traits. In both theories the environment does not so much push and pull as it selects. The basic principle of operant conditioning is this: if a response is emitted, and is followed by reinforcement, then that (sort of) response will become more probable in the future. We can schematize this principle in a way that will show its distinctiveness from the S-R model. I'll call this schematization Law 3 so as to make it clear that Skinner understands this law to apply in addition to the laws of classical conditioning discussed above.

> Law 3:   For any response R, and for any reinforcing stimulus rS, if R is emitted, and R is followed by rS, then probability (R) increases.[28]

Strictly speaking, an operant is a class concept and is defined in terms of the characteristic functional relation which holds between "(1) the occasion upon which a response occurs, (2) the response itself, and (3) the reinforcing consequences."[29] An operant, then, is a class of functionally equivalent responses, that is, a class of responses that (in similar situations) lead to similar consequences. Thus we should read "probability (R) increases" in Law 3 to mean "the probability of a response of a certain kind increases," where the kind is determined by the typical context(s) in which the response occurs and by its characteristic consequence(s).

Skinner's central substantive claim is that most interesting human behavior—brushing one's teeth, jogging, slam-dunking a basketball, composing a choral piece, speaking one's native language—is operant behavior that is acquired, shaped, and maintained by consequential stimuli, and therefore is not amenable to analysis in terms of antecedent stimuli as required by S-R psychology. In fact, Skinner says that operant conditioning is only possible because we have evolved to possess "a susceptibility to reinforcement by certain kinds of consequences and a supply of behavior less specifically committed to eliciting or releasing stimuli. (Most operants are selected from behavior which has little or no relation to such stimuli.)"[30]

The question is, how does the operant conditioning model overcome the problems of novelty and purpose when the classical conditioning model fails to do so? Take the problem of novelty first. Operant conditioning involves a conception of humans as creatures disposed to try out all sorts of novel, motor, cognitive, and verbal responses. Although the initial causes of these novel behavioral attempts lie, no doubt, in the multifarious intricacies of our genetic, neural, and anatomical selves, they are not usefully analyzed as arising from specific eliciting stimuli. Nevertheless, once a new response occurs and is reinforced, future responses of the same sort become more likely. (Notice the parallel with the evolutionary argument: new biological traits can occur for a wide variety of reasons—genetic drift, changes in the environment, or accidental genetic mutation; if, however, a new trait arises (for whatever reason) and leads to higher than average reproductive success for organisms which possess the trait, then the trait will become more common in the population.)

Thus, according to an operant analysis, when I wrote and revised this novel sentence that you are now reading, I was engaging in trying something similar to operant responses for which I was reinforced in the past, for example, trying to write grammatically correct English, trying to say something that follows from what I said in the previous sentence, trying not to repeat myself, and so on. When Julius Erving makes a basketball shot he has never made before, he is elaborating on a repertoire that is itself an operantly shaped elaboration of certain natural skills he possesses. Similarly when Bach composed a motet he was both elaborating on the choral conventions of his time and responding to the feedback provided by his own uniquely musical ear. The feedback system in Bach's ear was, I assume, partly the result of operant conditioning and partly innate. The important thing is that a musical system that gives one feedback about one's compositional tries is a reinforcement system—compositional responses that sound right become part of the final score, those that do not sound right drop out.

If this way of making room for novelty fails to convince, the operant psychologist can try shifting the burden of proof by the following rhetorical tactic: if you think that the theory of evolution explains how novel biological traits evolve but reject the theory of operant conditioning as an explanation for behavioral novelty, you are being inconsistent. Both theories address the problem with an identical explanatory principle, the principle of selection by consequences. Therefore, either the theory of evolution and the theory of operant conditioning can both explain novelty or neither theory can. Since you accept that the theory of evolution does explain biological novelty, you should also accept that the theory of operant conditioning can explain behavioral novelty.[31]

There are, of course, two obvious ways to diminish the force of this seeming dilemma: (1) give up evolutionary theory, or (2) accept evolutionary theory and accept that if humans were operantly conditionable then the problem of behavioral novelty would yield, but deny that there is any evidence that people are operantly conditionable. To my mind, giving the operant model credit for giving at least the beginning of a solution to the problem of novelty is far more sensible than is either of these ways of denying it that success.

With respect to the problem of purpose it is fairly easy to see how the concept of operant behavior can give us some leverage. Recall that two operant responses are members of the same class if they have the same functional relation to the same contingencies of reinforcement. Thus, to borrow an example of Ned Block's, suppose you see someone moving about frenetically, flailing his arms and legs, and you wonder what the person is doing. You hypothesize that he is either trying to get a bumblebee out of his clothes or doing the latest dance.[32] Presumably you would decide between these two hypotheses by coming to understand the context in which the behavior was taking place—is there music playing? are there other people around doing the same thing? is there a beehive nearby?—and by trying to understand the goal of the action—does he stop shaking if a bee falls from his trousers? does he stop shaking when the music stops? and so on.

Now this everyday project of coming to understand purposeful actions in terms of the contexts in which they arise and the goals they seek to achieve is very much the same project as identifying an operant response in terms of the three-term contingency consisting of the stimulus situation in which the response is emitted, the response itself, and its characteristic reinforcer. S-R psychology has trouble with purposeful behavior because of its inability to talk about the goals, the ends, and the consequences of behavior.

An operant analysis, on the other hand, requires that we talk about these things. The perhaps unexpected moral is simply this: in order to adequately capture the purposefulness of human behavior we must provide some sort of teleological analysis, an analysis in terms of ends and goals and the like. An operant analysis, unlike an S-R analysis, recognizes this, and allows the required teleological reference in the place in its laws (see Law 3) held for reinforcers. Skinner is so confident about his brand of behaviorism's ability to solve this problem that he has proclaimed "that operant behavior is the very field of purpose. . . . By its nature it is directed toward the future: a person acts *in order that* it will happen, and the order is temporal."[33]

But, you say, there is a trick: Skinner's reinforcers simply are not the same as the purposes described in ordinary teleological discourse. For Skinner, reinforcers occur outside the organism and must be exhaustively defined in terms of observables. Ordinary purposes, on the other hand, are intentional objects in Brentano's sense—if it is my goal to become president of the United States then it is my goal regardless of whether I ever succeed and regardless of whether I ever tell anyone of my desire—becoming president is simply a private conscious aim of mine. Because my goal does not exist outside me, it cannot be exhaustively defined in terms of publicly observable events, and thus a Skinnerian analysis cannot really solve the problem of purpose.

This sort of objection is an obvious one and takes us back to our earlier worries about Skinner's methodological views and his overall allergy to intentionality. I have already remarked on Skinner's confusing, shifting, and somewhat inconsistent views on matters mental, but this objection raises a point worth emphasizing. The substantive psychological view that human behavior is, at least in part, operantly conditionable has, as far as I can tell, no logical affinity—although admittedly it has a historical one—with any particular epistemological position on the admissibility, or lack thereof, of talk of privacy, mentality, intentionality, and the like. There are no nonmethodological reasons, therefore, why operant responses and their reinforcers cannot be construed as utterly mental phenomena. If this is right, then a cognitive psychologist could accept, as many do, that operant conditioning is a psychologically real process.

Nevertheless, it is possible that the operant model is capable of accommodating philosophical worries about novelty and purpose in the ways I have been suggesting only if its powers of expression are not gagged by the sort of methodological puritanism to which Skinner is prone.

My sense is that this conjecture is right, and that Skinner may, as a matter of fact, be kept from allowing his important insights about operant behavior to yield the solutions we have been seeking within the theory he has presented. But if this is right, the failure is not the fault of the substantive notion of operant behavior governed by the "law of effect"; it is the fault of Skinner's excessively restrictive epistemology.

One final point on the issue of operant behavior: my suggestion that the concept of operant behavior makes the philosophical problems of novelty and purpose yield does not logically entail that any human behavior actually is operant behavior governed by the "law of effect"—although I certainly think that some of it is. It is logically conceivable, although utterly unlikely, that all human behavior is the straightforward result of our genetic program. This would mean that all our behavior is the result of pure biological selection, and thus that ontogenic development occurs independently of environmental conditioning. But such an analysis would still give us leverage on the problems of novelty and purpose, since natural selection allows for novel biological traits, and is teleological in the sense that it analyzes changes in the frequency of biological traits in terms of their reproductive consequences.

I emphasize this point for the following reason. Skinner sometimes acts as if the fact that the operant model solves some philosophical problems associated with S-R psychology implies the soundness of an environmentalist solution to the nature-nurture controversy. That does not follow. Certain kinds of nativism can avail themselves of similar solutions to the problems of novelty and purpose. What is true is that the nature-nurture question can be framed as the question of how much behavior is the result of operant selection (and any other acquisition process operating in an individual's lifetime), and how much is the result of natural selection? This only shows that we have an elegant way of formulating the question; we have a long way to go before we know the answer.

Psychology and the Good Life

Skinner stands in a long line of thinkers—Plato, Machiavelli, Bacon, and Hobbes are among the most famous—who see a connection between psychology and politics. Insofar as psychology provides us with laws of human behavior it identifies the causal forces that make individuals tick. This in turn enables us to predict how individuals will act and enables us to shape and control their actions if we so desire, and if we are able to control the causal forces that make them tick.

This line of thinking, thoroughly and self-consciously Baconian, has led Skinner to talk often throughout his career of "behavioral engineering," and the "design of cultures." He has even offered two similar blueprints for the sort of society he has in mind in *Walden Two* and *Beyond Freedom and Dignity*.[34]

The usual way of quibbling with Skinner involves characterizing his utopian schemes as instances of Aldous Huxley's *Brave New World* or Anthony Burgess's *Clockwork Orange*, and then claiming Skinner is a fascist and a megalomaniac. I am not going to do this. Skinner's conception of the good life is not at all like the fictional worlds depicted by Huxley and Burgess. Skinner's utopia is fashioned after the liberal view spawned in the Enlightenment. His ideal society is a lightly governed, economically and socially egalitarian one in which people behave rationally, morally, and creatively, and in which they freely choose how, and when, and with whom they live and work.

All the fuss is caused by the fact that Skinner's liberal society is to be created by the consistent and self-conscious application of the principles of his operant learning theory, that is, positively reinforcing people for desirable behavior, stopping the use of punishment, and so on. Skinner's response to those who object to his means but not his ends is by arguing that human behavior is controlled—always has been and always will be—at all times and in all places. Thus, he claims not to be promoting new methods of psychological control but merely suggesting more rational and effective applications of the ones that are already operative in nature.

Skinner is almost certainly correct that his methods of behavioral engineering are neither novel nor morally objectionable per se, if human behavior is in fact governed by deterministic natural laws. What Skinner is guilty of, however, is an excessive confidence about the legitimacy of his conception of ends, and that is what I intend to criticize.

Skinner thinks of science much more in terms of prediction and control than in terms of explanation. There is nothing necessary about this view of science. Skinner, however, speaks as if there is, and much of his urgency about cultural design depends on this incorrect view. For example, he has argued against his critics that those "who reject the scientific conception of man must, to be logical, oppose the methods of science as well."[35]

It is clear from the context in which Skinner makes this remark that he thinks the opponents of cultural engineering are people who, because of archaic philosophical commitments, for example, to free will, *res cogitans*, and the like, reject out of hand the possibility of scientific psychology. Having rejected this possibility, they are logically committed to rejecting the application of scientific principles to the control of human behavior.

Skinner tries to reduce such a position to absurdity by arguing that because it is silly to doubt the possibility of scientific psychology, it is also silly to "oppose the methods of science." The argument fails, however, because Skinner assumes that prediction and control are part of scientific method, and this, as my earlier argument showed, is partly false and partly question-begging. Whereas it may be true that people who think scientific psychology is impossible are logically committed to the impossibility of successful psychological engineering, it is highly implausible to think that all those who reject the idea of psychological engineering do so because they reject the possibility of scientific psychology.

A proponent of scientific psychology, say Skinner's brand, may also be required to espouse the hypothetico-deductive, experimental scientific method. But there is nothing odd about espousing this method, and rejecting prediction and control as a goal of one's theorizing. This is because prediction and control are not a necessary part of scientific method.[36] They are a part of post-seventeenth-century cultural ideology that has been added to an older conception of science as explanation and understanding. Skinner, therefore, is certainly wrong that we are logically restrained from opposing the application of the principles of scientific psychology if we do not oppose scientific psychology itself.

My second concern has to do with the fact that the credibility of the program of designing an ideal culture rests on the credibility of the program of stipulating the desirable ends of culture, and on the credibility of controlling the causal factors that govern human action. Since Skinner is an avid environmentalist, he assumes that the project of manipulating the causal factors that control human behavior is not problematic. If, however, the pervasive suspicion that Skinner has underestimated the relative role of innate biological determinants of behavior is right, then it is unreasonable to expect operant conditioning practices located in the environment to give us wide-ranging powers of control over human behavior. There is nothing in the least incoherent about a conception of human nature as utterly subject to scientific law, but not particularly malleable. Even if we set this important issue aside there is one very important reason to resist confidence in the program of stipulating a set of uncontroversial cultural goals, even on Skinner's own grounds.

The reason is this: any stipulation of the ideal ends of a society must be framed in terms of the reinforcers of some individuals in the society, that is, in terms of things that give some of the people pleasure. However, according to Skinner, the fact that some set of ends produces pleasure for some set of people is due to the fact that they have found achieving those ends pleasure-producing in the past. But the fact that some set of people has found some set of actions pleasure-producing in the past proves neither that these things are inherently good, nor good for everyone, nor that they will continue to be thought so highly of, nor continue to be so pleasure-producing in the future. Because, therefore, reinforcers differ from individual to individual, social group to social group, and because there is no special reason to think that the ends desired by the majority, or by the most powerful or articulate are actually the best, or even if they are, that they will continue to be the best in the future, there is no reason to have much confidence in any scheme which stipulates *the* desirable ends for a culture and tries to engineer them into existence.

Skinner has responded to arguments such as mine with two sorts of counterarguments. Sometimes he suggests the following simple criterion for deciding on worthwhile ends: "What is good for the culture is whatever promotes its ultimate survival."[37] The basic idea is that we should look at the features that account for the differential success of culture A over culture B (for example, the United States over the Roman Empire), and promote these features. Although there is something to this method, it is not sufficient to yield philosophically secure decisions about ends. First, what promotes the survival of a culture may not be good for many individual members of that culture. The issue of the relative rights of the individual and the collective is one of the overwhelming questions in political theory, but it does not figure at all in Skinner's criterion. Second, it is conceivable that a culture could have features that led to its "ultimate survival" but that were considered morally reprehensible by almost everyone's lights. For example, suppose one cultural group immunized themselves and then introduced a deadly biological agent into the atmosphere. This would greatly enhance this group's possibilities for "ultimate survival" relative to the now-extinct cultures with which it used to share the earth, but no one, I presume, would want to call this culture's diabolical and paranoid imagination "good."

At other times Skinner impatiently insists that it is not so hard to define the good life—let people be rational, creative, happy, and well-behaved. But by this tactic he conceals the crucial point—whose kind of rationality? His, which equates scientific understanding with scientific control, or a Buddhist's? Whose kind of creativity? Andy Warhol's or Michelangelo's? Whose kind of happiness? Mine or yours? Whose kind of 'good behavior'? Saint Paul's or Bertrand Russell's or Sartre's or Mao's?

The point is that once we try to get beneath utopian sloganeering we will have to get specific about ends, and this is where we will confront radical differences of opinion. When Skinner gets specific, he talks as if liberal enlightenment values are universal and uncontroversial. This, of course, is false and utterly begs the question.

I do not mean to suggest that some ends are not better than others or that all moral and political views are equal or that we should do nothing active to improve the human condition, but in a pluralistic world many views may be equally good and adaptive. If this is so, then we are all much better off allowing many views of the good life to coexist, and occasionally conflict, than we are trying to engineer any one end-state philosophy.[38] One can accept Skinner's substantive psychology without accepting either his general view that psychology should be used for practical purposes, or his specific views on the ideal society and the relationship between psychology and political philosophy.[39] Indeed one might argue that his psychology itself provides reasons for being wary of accepting either. Reinforcers, after all, are selective, but they are not choosy.

Conclusion

I can now summarize my overall evaluation of Skinner's theory.

(1) Skinner correctly points out that there are some pitfalls to mentalistic psychology. Mentalistic psychologies which share Cartesian-like assumptions about the nature of mind are metaphysically unwieldy, while mentalistic psychologies that share the Freudian intrigue with the inner workings of the psyche and a lack of methodological caution are prone to a variety of epistemic difficulties.

(2) Skinner also correctly points out that there are aspects of the language acquisition process that militate against excessive confidence both in the amount and clarity of our self-knowledge and in our ability to share with others whatever self-knowledge we do possess.

(3) But Skinner takes (1) and (2) too far. He proposes that psychology take the philosophically safest route by avoiding mentalistic formulations altogether, by largely avoiding talking about private events, by simply refusing to take the intentional turn promoted by Brentano and others. And he argues provocatively that there is nothing to be lost in terms of either the richness or completeness of the science by so doing. But here he is simply wrong. First, Skinner's purely logical argument for avoiding talk of mental events fails. Second, Skinner himself has to smuggle in mentalistic assumptions in order to make sense of his simplest animal experiments. Third, human psychology would simply not be explanatorily complete were it not to provide a theory of reasoning, of cognitive processing, of the emotions, and so on. Overall, Skinner promotes a psychology with a tendency to bite its own tongue whenever the inclination to discuss mentality surfaces.

(4) Nevertheless, Skinner's substantive notion of operant behavior governed by the "law of effect" has considerable more philosophical power than it is often given credit for. The concept of operant behavior suggests a way to mesh the possibility of a scientific psychology with an acknowledgment of the fact that humans do novel and purposeful things. On the other hand, Skinner may overestimate the extent to which human behavior is, in fact, operantly conditionable as opposed to the extent to which it is determined by more biological factors. Skinner sometimes talks as if any person can learn almost anything, and that is probably wrong.

(5) Skinner's political philosophy assumes the latter sort of environmentalism which his operant analysis makes tempting. Whether and how much of a problem this is depends on which side of center we ultimately come down on in the nature-nurture controversy. But the main problem with Skinner's attempt to wed psychology and political theory arises from his naive assurance that the reinforcing value of

some behavior, or stimulus, or practice bespeaks the behavior's, or stimulus's, or practice's moral or political goodness. Such assurance is notoriously problematic.

In the end, then, Skinner's prescriptions for a methodologically secure psychology are too confining to be worth the security. On the other hand, I would bet that many of Skinner's substantive observations regarding the process of learning are sure to be vindicated. In the next chapter, I examine the cognitive-developmental psychologies of Jean Piaget and Lawrence Kohlberg. These theories incorporate both the negative and positive lessons which our examination of Skinner's theory point up, namely, that psychology must in some essential way be cognitive, intentional, and mentalistic, and it must provide an account of learning, of change, and of development.

Suggested Readings

General Introductions

Skinner, B. F. (1953), *Science and Human Behavior*.
Skinner, B. F. (1976), *About Behaviorism*.

Central Philosophical Works

Skinner, B. F. (1964), "Behaviorism at 50."
Skinner, B. F. (1972b), "Are Theories of Learning Necessary?"
Skinner, B. F. (1972d), "A Critique of Psychoanalytic Theories and Concepts."
Skinner, B. F. (1972f), "The Operational Analysis of Psychological Terms."
Skinner, B. F. (1981), "Selection by Consequences."

Psychology and Political Philosophy

Skinner, B. F. (1948), *Walden Two*.
Skinner, B. F. (1971), *Beyond Freedom and Dignity*.

Important Criticisms

Chomsky, N. (1959), "Review of Skinner's *Verbal Behavior*."
Dennett, D. (1978d), "Skinner Skinned."

Philosophical Foundations

Smith, Lawrence D. (1986), *Behaviorism and Logical Positivism*.

Philosophical Work in the Behaviorist Mold

Quine, W. V. (1960), *Word and Object*.
Ryle, G. (1949), *The Concept of Mind*.

Chapter 5

The Case for Cognitive-Developmental Psychology: Piaget and Kohlberg

Jean Piaget's theory of cognitive development and Lawrence Kohlberg's theory of moral development beg for philosophical attention. Probably no other psychologists in history have expressed such pride and confidence in the connections between their psychological theories and traditional philosophical concerns. Indeed, both have proclaimed that their theories have very specific normative implications, Piaget's for epistemology and Kohlberg's for ethics.

Piaget, for example, would like to be read as providing psychological grounds for rejecting epistemological relativism and solipsism—the intimately related views that all knowledge claims are equally valid and that all knowledge is to be judged solely from one's own perspective. Piaget claims to be able to show that some ways of thinking, such as the ways logicians and scientists think, are superior to others and that these superior ways presuppose the rejection of the egocentrism needed to get relativism and solipsism off the ground. Piaget actually prefers to call his theory "genetic epistemology" rather than psychology.

In a similar vein, Kohlberg, whose elaborate psychology of moral development takes its inspiration from Piaget's *The Moral Judgment of the Child* (1932), claims to be able to show that egoism and relativism are ethically inadequate ways of making moral judgments.[1] In fact, he goes so far as to argue that his psychological data resolve the seemingly interminable philosophical debate between Kantians, who promote strict adherence to an absolute, universalizable, categorical imperative, and Mill's followers, who promote adherence to the hypothetical imperatives of happiness-maximizing utilitarianism. Kant wins!

Here I examine in some detail Piaget's and Kohlberg's respective attempts to chart their way between the Scylla of naive empiricism

Three excellent introductions to Piaget's thought are Herbert Ginsburg and Sylvia Opper, *Piaget's Theory of Intellectual Development* (1969); Howard Gardner, *The Quest for Mind: Piaget, Lévi-Strauss, and the Structuralist Tradition* (1973); and Margaret Boden, *Jean Piaget* (1979). The best introduction to Kohlberg's theory is his *Essays on Moral Development*, volume 1, *The Philosophy of Moral Development* (1981a), and volume 2, *The Psychology of Moral Development* (1984).

and the Charybdis of extreme nativism and arrive at some empirically and philosophically safe port.

First, I try to give a preliminary sense of the overall thrust of cognitive developmental psychology by discussing the standard objections Piaget and Kohlberg make to traditional empiricist and nativist philosophies of mind.

Second, I examine Piaget's central theoretical constructs—cognitive structures and cognitive stages—and discuss several epistemologically motivated objections to his structuralist model of the mind.

Third, I look at the relation between Piaget's theory of cognitive development and biological and cybernetic models as a way of shedding further light on the question of the overall status of his stage theory.

Fourth, I discuss the puzzling question—pressed with a vengeance by Jerry Fodor—of whether Piaget is actually able to give a nonnativistic account of cognitive development within the constraints of his biologically and cybernetically inspired psychology.

Fifth, I examine Piaget's adequacy thesis, the thesis that—in terms of spatial, temporal, causal, and logical development—each stage of psychological development is epistemologically more adequate than its predecessor, that is, each stage a child goes through involves a more adaptive and correct view of reality than its predecessor. I argue that because both nativistically inspired and empiricistically inspired psychological theories imply some version of the adequacy thesis, its appearance in Piaget's theory does not in itself warrant a preference for his theory over any of these others.

Sixth, I raise some objections to Kohlberg's claim that his stages of moral development actually fit the stage-criteria specified by Piaget.

Finally, I criticize Kohlberg's courageous extension of Piaget's adequacy thesis to the moral sphere. Kohlberg claims that each successive stage of moral development is ethically superior to its predecessor in the same way each stage of spatial or temporal or logical development is epistemically superior to its predecessor. I offer some grounds for skepticism regarding Kohlberg's version of the adequacy thesis.

Cognitive Development, Empiricism, and Nativism

Taken together, Piaget and Kohlberg actually put forward a wide array of theories. There are Piaget's theories about the development of the concepts of self, object, space, time, and causality; his theories about the acquisition of principles like associativity, transitivity, and conservation; his theory of the four-stage development of intelligence from the sensory-motor intelligence of the infant to the formal-logical intelligence of the adolescent; and finally there is Kohlberg's moral stage theory. What binds all these different theories and gives them their unique theoretical flavor is the commitment to the cognitive as well as the developmental nature of the phenomena in question.

In particular, what make Piaget's and Kohlberg's theories "cognitive" is the commitment to the necessity of talking about intentional mental phenomena—about thoughts, beliefs, wishes, internal representations, cognitive structures, mental processes, reasoning procedures, and the like—without any of the reticence characteristic of behaviorism. What makes their theories "developmental" is the belief that the ways in which we process experience—be it physical, mathematical, or moral experience—normally change in an orderly, increasingly adaptive, species-specific fashion.

According to Piaget and Kohlberg, the cognitive and developmental emphases of their theories are necessitated, respectively, by the short-comings of empiricist psychologies which overemphasize the external determinants of behavior and knowledge and view the human mind as a *tabula rasa*, and nativist psychologies which overemphasize the degree to which human nature is fixed by heredity.

The objection to empiricism is simply this: if the mind is a blank slate, then whatever way stimulation is received is the way it must be processed, represented, and expressed. If, as Locke put it, the mind is just a "storehouse of ideas"—if, that is, there is nothing of consequence between our ears—then sensory inputs and cognitive and behavioral outputs must be identical. Thus if we go for a walk in the park, all that can possibly be represented in the mind are discrete and dis-organized impressions of the things in the park (notice that even this and the subsequent examples assume that our minds have some minimal representational structure, the structure of, say, a camera or a tape recorder). If we see John and Mary walking hand in hand ten different times, then all that can possibly be represented by the mind are ten different impressions of this connected thing: John and Mary. If we hear or see the novel sentence "Titan, the largest moon of Saturn, has an atmosphere more conducive to organic life than Saturn itself," all that could be represented in our minds is a series of meaningless sounds or marks.

Experience, of course, falsifies this view of the mind. We do much more than merely make Xerox-like copies of physical objects. We notice that the tulips in the park are in bloom and take pleasure in the fact; we organize the ducks and the people and the flowers and the trees into their appropriate natural kinds. We conjecture that John and Mary are in love and we speculate about the prospects for their romance. And we generate and understand sentences we have never heard be-fore—we possess the wondrous capacity to give meaningful semantic interpretations to the essentially meaningless scratches and sounds which come before our eyes and ears. Experience does not, so to speak, go in one ear and out the other. The equipment between our ears transforms sense impressions, it does not merely copy them.

Actually, even the British empiricists, the philosophers historically most identified with the copy theory of mind, recognized that the mind does not simply mirror nature. What Locke, Berkeley, and Hume did attempt, however, was to construct the most parsimonious model possible by which to explain the mental transformations of sense inputs. According to Hume, for example, the mind is equipped at birth with three structural principles, resemblance, contiguity, and cause and effect. Thanks to these "laws of association" we group together things that look alike, occur together, and are causes and effects of each other.

The mind, therefore, is not a true *tabula rasa*, not a completely blank slate. It has a structure. It comes wired to process experience in certain ways. It is a *tabula rasa*, however, at least from the perspective of the empiricists, in the sense that its structure is minimal and unchanging. It is a storehouse after all, not a computer.[2]

In much the same spirit as Kant's challenge to what he took to be Hume's excessively sparse description of mental terrain, Piaget and Kohlberg challenge this view of the mind—what Karl Popper calls the "empty bucket" theory. Piaget, for example, believes that as a result of the combination of the rich innate structure of our mind, normal biological maturation, the processing of experience, and the tendency of biological systems to seek a maximally adaptive fit with the environment, the mind continually builds more and more elaborate systems of rules, more and more elaborate structures with which to organize experience and adapt to reality.[3] An illuminating account of human psychology will, therefore, need to talk much more about internal mental structures than many empiricists would like.[4]

The cognitive-developmental objection to nativism—what Piaget calls "preformationism"—rests on three fairly uncontroversial observations. (1) We change over time. (2) We change in an environmentally sensitive way. That is, our thinking about everything from the nature of the physical world to morals is extremely responsive to features of the actual natural and social world with which we happen to find ourselves interacting. (3) The changes we undergo involve not only the specific content of our thoughts but our mode of thinking as well. For example, the thinking of an intelligent eighteen-year-old differs from the thinking of an intelligent one-year-old not only in content—for example, in thinking about sex, music, and geometry as opposed to blocks, the sandbox, and her mother's breast—but in form as well. The eighteen-year-old is able to represent things to herself linguistically, to rotate geometrical figures mentally, to deploy deductive proof procedures, to make reliable inductive inferences, and to utilize unconsciously and unerringly the principles of conservation and transitivity; the one-year-old, on the other hand, shows no evidence that she is capable of organizing experience is any of these ways.

The formal or structural features that distinguish the thinking of the eighteen-year-old from the one-year-old are not properly thought of as explicitly present at birth. Of course the genome—the complete informational content of the genes—contains the program which specifies all possible behavioral and cognitive abilities. Nevertheless, in addition to a certain kind of genome, the development of more sophisticated modes of thought requires bodily maturation, motor, perceptual, and cognitive experience with the environment, development of certain neural paths, and so on.

There is, of course, a certain amount of caricature in the way cognitive-developmental psychologists like Piaget and Kohlberg describe empiricism and nativism. Many if not most psychologists would deny holding either position in the forms just discussed. On the other hand, the extreme empiricist and nativist philosophies of mind do in fact have several influential and widely respected proponents; Skinner comes to mind on the empiricist side, and in some tendentious moments, Jerry Fodor comes to mind on the nativist side.

In sum then, Piaget and Kohlberg believe that the need for psychology to go cognitive, to take a firm "intentional stance," is necessitated by certain characteristic shortcomings of empiricism.[5] The need for psychology to go developmental is necessitated by certain characteristic shortcomings of nativism. By examining Piaget's stage theory we can become clearer as to just what such an alternative theory will look like, as well as get a sense of some of the problems and prospects it faces.

Stages and Structures

Imagine the following situation: Smith is observing a computer which so far has been observed to output 1 when the input was 1, 2 for 2, 3 for 3, 4 for 4, and 5 for 5. Smith names the computer *In One Ear and Out the Other*. Jones comes along and asks Smith to explain the way *In One Ear* "thinks." Smith explains that given 1, *In One Ear* says 1, given 2 it says 2, and so on. Jones explains that he does not want a list, an enumeration, of *In One Ear*'s responses but the rule in accordance with which *In One Ear* responds. Smith responds that the rule *In One Ear* uses is "If n, then n" where $n = \{$positive integers$\}$.

Smith now feeds *In One Ear* 6 and gets the output 126. Smith is surprised and suggests that *In One Ear* has made a mistake. Jones suggests that it is Smith who has made the mistake and that the rule the poor misnamed computer actually uses is "If n, then $(n - 1)(n - 2)$ $(n - 3)(n - 4)(n - 5) + n$." Smith and Jones now test with 7 and 8, and so on, and find that this seems to be the right rule.

White, the programmer, now comes along and explains that the rule *In One Ear* actually uses is "If n, then $(n - 1)(n - 2)(n - 3)(n - 4)$ $(n - 5) + (2n - n)$." Jones continues to claim victory for his hypothesis on the ground that the rule he used to describe *In One Ear*'s program is logically equivalent to White's rule, and thus it is one correct description of the structure of *In One Ear*'s thought. To which White the programmer objects that Jones's rule is not, as a matter of fact, the rule the computer uses, since the computer closes each computation with the frivolous $+2n - n$ maneuver, not with the logically and functionally equivalent $+n$ routine cited by Jones.

I want to extract several morals from this example. First, in one classical sense, citing the logical or mathematical rule (or one equivalent to it) that a computer uses in getting from input to output is identifying the underlying functional structure of the computer's transformational procedures.

Second, if we are not the programmer of the computer—this is just the age-old problem of other-minds applied to computers—we are in the position of Smith and Jones having to inductively tease out the structure of the computer's inner workings from its overt behavior.

Third, not all logically equivalent descriptions of the structure of a computer's inner workings provide equally accurate descriptions or explanations, although they may well yield equivalent behavioral predictions. Notice, for example, that although both Jones's rule and White, the programmer's, rule will predict equally well all possible outputs of *In One Ear* (assume that there are no measurable differences in computational time), Jones's description of how *In One Ear* "thinks" is, strictly speaking, empirically wrong since the computer actually goes through its unparsimonious $+2n - n$ routine. Furthermore, if we require a true explanation to refer to empirically real, and not merely predictive, processes, then Jones's rule does not truly explain *In One Ear*'s behavior either. On the other hand—at least this is my intuition—this last is probably too strong a requirement on explanation. For both principled and pragmatic reasons we should probably allow all functionally equivalent descriptions of a computer program compatible with the evidence to count as a bona fide explanation of the computer's behavior.

In One Ear's story relates to Piaget's work in several important ways. Piaget and his colleagues begin by assuming that humans process experience in accordance with the cognitive structures and categories they possess, and that, therefore, these cognitive structures and categories lie in explanatory relation to behavior. For example, take the difference between a five-year-old and an eight-year-old on the following conservation task: a child is given two balls of clay and asked to make sure that they are the same size. Once the child is satisfied that the two mounds are equal, the experimenter rolls one of them into a long sausage and asks "Does this one have more, less, or the same amount of clay as the ball?" Only a rare five-year-old will answer "the same" whereas most eight-year-olds know the answer, and find the question silly.

Piaget wants to say two things about this situation. First, the eight-year-old possesses a mental competence that the five-year-old lacks; he understands and operates with an abstract conservation principle and he possesses the category of reversible operations, that is, he understands that the sausage could easily be reconstituted as a ball. Second, these cognitive structures and categories causally explain the eight-year-old's behavior on the conservation task.[6] The eight-year-old produces the solution because he in fact frames and operates on the problem with the mental structures he possesses.[7]

Furthermore, as the example makes clear, Piaget's cognitive structures are very much like the one that explains *In One Ear*'s behavior: *In One Ear* accepts input that fits the category of number, plugs it into his transformation rule, and gives the appropriate numerical output. Similarly a human mind can be conceptualized, very roughly, as a system of complex mental structures that perform operations and transformations on experiential input. Margaret Boden puts the point this way:

> According to Piagetian theory, the child gradually develops increasingly well-articulated and inter-related *schemata*, or representations. It is in terms of these intentional models that the psychological subject constructs and interprets the world (and all possible worlds), and it is through their active mediation that thinking and motor action are generated.[8]

The research program of Piaget and his colleagues consists in the attempt to identify the entire system of cognitive structures and categories that figure in the organization of experience, and to plot their interrelations and patterns of development.

The Piagetian, however, is in much the same situation as Smith and Jones are in the *In One Ear* example, only worse. Piaget's only option is to infer hidden mental structures, like conservation principles, from behavior. But as we saw from Jones's case with *In One Ear*, such inferences can fit all possible observable evidence and still be wrong. Furthermore, in the human case, unlike the computer case, there is no original programmer with whom to check the validity of one's inferences, nor in most cases is there introspective access to one's mental structures. For example, the eight-year-old in the conservation experiment cannot introspect the abstract reversible operations schema he supposedly deploys in coming up with the solution (although the child's report that the reason the sausage contains the same amount of clay as the ball is "because you could make it into a ball again" counts as evidence that such a schema is operating behind the scenes). As we shall see, it is easy to allow these facts about our collective epistemic predicament with respect to other-minds to generate a sort of perverse and, I think, ultimately unhealthy skepticism.

From a Piagetian perspective the main difference between the computer case (*In One Ear*'s case anyway) and the human case is that *In One Ear*'s computational structure is fixed the day he is programmed. The mental structures with which humans process experience change dramatically and in an orderly fashion from infancy to adolescence.

The orderly changes in groups of mental structures—in ways of viewing the world—are best conceptualized, according to Piaget, in terms of a stage progression. For Piaget, a stage usually refers to a relatively stable constellation of a wide array of logically homogeneous cognitive structures (although sometimes Piaget talks about the stages in the development of a particular concept or structure). Piaget claims that there are four stages in the development of intelligence: the sensory-motor stage (0 to 2 years), the preoperational stage (2 years to 7 years), the concrete operational stage (7 to 11 years), and the formal operations stage (11 years on).[9]

The first stage is given over to getting a sense of things—one's body and the objects in the world, the second stage to learning how to represent this continually developing sense in the form of words and mental images, the third stage to mentally manipulating those representations in sophisticated and counterfactual ways—for example, by being able to represent to oneself that the process that made the ball of clay into a sausage of clay is reversible, and the fourth stage to becoming proficient at manipulating representations of representations (you, for example, unlike many bright children, immediately understood the solution to the conservation task without actually seeing the physical transformation of the ball of clay into a sausage of clay—you, an adult, can perform mental operations on purely linguistic objects).

Piaget makes five important claims about the development of children's sense of the external world. First, he claims that the stage sequence is universal in two respects: all the stages are found in all cultures, and all normal individuals reach the highest stage. Second, he claims that all children move through the stages in exactly the same sequence. Third, he claims that each stage integrates the competencies acquired in the previous stage. Fourth, he claims that, barring physiological damage, the sequence is irreversible. If a child reaches stage $n + 1$, she will not later regress to stage n or $n - 1$. Fifth, he claims that each stage is logically more complex than its predecessor(s) and constitutes a more adequate conceptualization of reality than its predecessor(s).

For reasons that will become clear, I want to postpone explicit discussion of Piaget's adequacy thesis and discuss first the relative merits of conceiving of cognitive change as a sequence of orderly, universal, integrative, and irreversible changes in systems of mental structures. This assessment is best begun by briefly discussing several possible challenges to Piaget's way of looking at things.

(1) The Unfalsifiability Objection.   This is always a good opening gambit; the requirement that a theory be potentially falsifiable is generally viewed as a sort of minimal requirement for taking it at all seriously. If a theory is unfalsifiable we can dismiss it out of hand.

However, the unfalsifiability charge will not work against Piaget. First of all, the theses of cultural universality, irreversibility, and invariant sequence which form the core of Piaget's theory entail risky predictions that could easily turn out to be false. Second, the specific claims about the chronological emergence of cognitive structures also lead to potentially falsifiable predictions. For example, it would count against the theory if eight-year-olds typically failed on conservation tasks, or if a significant number of three-year-olds succeeded on tasks requiring formal logical skills.

One might persist, however, and try to use the case of *In One Ear* to make an unfalsifiability argument argument motivated by skepticism about knowledge of other-minds. This argument would run as follows: The Piagetian is always inferring cognitive structures from behavior. But inferences from behavior to what lies behind it are always radically underdetermined by the evidence. Remember that Jones's inference about *In One Ear* fitted all the conceivable facts but didn't quite hit the mark. Furthermore, there never would have been a way to know that Jones was wrong if it had not been for the existence of White the programmer. But in the human case there is no programmer around to identify our incorrect conjectures, and thus there is no definitive way to show that a conjecture about a mental structure is false, if indeed it is false. So Piaget's theory really is unfalsifiable.

This argument is overstated. The case of Jones with *In One Ear* does nothing to undermine the possibility of subjecting incompatible empirical hypotheses about mental structures to potentially falsifying tests. For example, it is compatible with an eight-year-old's success on the clay conservation task that she operates with a general principle of conservation of mass, or that she has memorized the correct answer. But it is easy to think of all sorts of tests that would lead to a choice between these two hypotheses.

All the case of Jones with *In One Ear* shows is that it is conceivable that there might be no empirical evidence forcing a choice between a number (potentially infinite) of logically equivalent descriptions of a mental structure. For example, suppose that all the potentially falsifying empirical evidence supports the conjecture that the eight-year-old operates with a principle of conservation as opposed to a memorized fact. The case of Jones simply shows that we might not be able to choose between certain logically equivalent abstract descriptions of this conservation principle. But it does nothing to undermine the potential falsifiability of the empirical thesis that a principle of conservation and not a memorized fact is operating behind the scenes. Furthermore, the latter is the only sort of falsifiability we expect of our scientific theories. In fact, if we were to be overcome by skeptical doubts about logically equivalent hypotheses and the radical underdetermination of theory by observation, we would have to give up subatomic physics, molecular biology, and astronomy, to name a few, along with cognitive psychology![10]

(2) The "Bad Experiments" Objection. Several philosophers and psychologists have objected to Piaget's experimental paradigm on grounds that in testing for the possession of a certain cognitive structure, such as conservation, children of different ages are given exactly the same problem to solve. The objection is to the underlying assumption of this experimental paradigm: it assumes that the task is understood in the same way by a young child and by an older child (that is, they possess identical information-processing abilities), and that only their solution strategies differ. This assumption permits the conclusion that the young child's inability to solve the problem and the older child's ability to solve it are caused by the operation of different underlying cognitive structures. There is, however, some reason to believe that some of the Piagetian tasks are inherently misleading; their very design will throw a young child off the scent of a solution. For example, the fact that the experimenter tells the child to pay attention as he rolls out the ball of clay may naturally incline the younger child to think that the solution to the problem involves figuring out the significance of what the experimenter is doing (as in a magic trick). But success on the task actually demands that the child discount the significance of exactly what he or she is asked to attend to, namely, the experimenter's action.[11]

This suspicion that the failure of young children on certain Piagetian tasks may be due less to the lack of certain overarching cognitive structures than to certain naive expectations about their social relations with experimental psychologists (namely, that the child trusts the experimenter), or to simple conceptual confusions, or to lower information-processing capacities, has been recently vindicated by evidence that when the tasks are modified, or more care is taken in making sure children understand the nature of the problem to be solved, they show far less egocentrism and far greater competence on conservation, causality, class inclusion, and quantitative tasks at younger ages than Piagetian stages predict.[12]

These new results are important, but it is not clear that they should be read as seriously undermining Piaget's stage theory so much as empirically and methodologically refining it. This new research may well require that we change the age-riders on the different stages, and change our views about the rate of developmental change, but, by itself, it does no logical damage to Piaget's overall model.

On the other hand, there is now overwhelming evidence for the existence of *décalage*, that is, different levels of achievement on problems requiring the same mental operations. For example, children typically understand conservation of substance well before they understand conservation of weight, and they understand conservation of weight before they understand conservation of volume. If décalage turns out to be the rule rather than the exception, then Piaget's claim that there are homogeneous stages of cognitive development will be undermined. We may still be able to plot the development of task- and domain-specific mental structures, but not the development of logically homogeneous stages.

(3) The Description versus Explanation Objection.   Suppose, to borrow and modify an example I have used previously, I tell you that "Mary is acting nuts because she is going through a crazy stage." Have I explained Mary's behavior? It seems to me that the answer is no. All I have really done is describe one fact twice, or at most elaborated on what needs to be explained—Mary is acting nuts and she's acting nuts a lot lately—but I have not explained Mary's peculiar behavior.

Assuming your intuitions run with mine so far, we will add a complication to the example. Suppose that Mary is 16 years old and that psychologists have discovered that every person acts peculiarly between the ages of 14 and 17 and have designated that period as the "crazy stage." Is "Mary is acting nuts because she is going through the crazy stage" explanatory on such assumptions? One is tempted to say yes. But one has to be exceedingly careful here. What is no doubt true is that if one knows that a certain person is between 14 and 17, one can predict with high reliability that that person will act peculiarly. Such predictive ability can provide an almost irresistible temptation to think that one knows more than one knows—to think, for example, that one has hold of a genuine causal explanation and not just a useful descriptive generalization.

But it is easy to imagine circumstances in which the claim to possess an explanation is simply wrong. Suppose, for example, that the scientist who first discovered the "crazy stage" says something like this: "The 'crazy stage' is just a shorthand name I gave to a certain set of behavioral regularities that occur between the years 14 and 17. It merely describes a certain pattern in nature. I do not, however, mean it to refer to any entity, or process, or set of cognitive structures inside certain teenagers." To which one might object, "But look, there has to be something going on inside the 14- to 17-year-olds that explains the peculiar ways they respond to the world." To which the honest and cautious discoverer of the "crazy stage" might well respond, "There may or may not be such internal processes. But I haven't a clue as to what those internal processes are or if indeed there really are any lawlike internal processes lying behind the phenomena in question. I'm just describing a behavioral pattern—to claim that the 'crazy stage' really explains the behavioral peculiarities would just be hand-waving on my part."

Piaget is sometimes accused of offering a descriptive theory as if it were an explanatory theory—of putting forward a theory like the "crazy stage" theory and claiming for it not merely predictive but explanatory power as well.[13] Although Piaget is no doubt guilty of lapses in this regard, I think that overall he can be defended against this charge.

Piaget certainly sees himself as promoting an explanatory theory. Thus the sentence "Most eight-year-olds get the conservation task with the clay right because they are in the concrete operations stage" is meant by him to be explanatory. The sentence is not to be read as merely equivalent to one describing the observation that eight-year-olds usually get the conservation problem right; it is to be taken as referring to certain cognitive structures that are shared by eight-year-olds (but not by three-year-olds) and that account for their success on the task. Strictly speaking, of course, the concrete operations stage explains success on the conservation task only indirectly. Because a stage is the name for a lawfully related system of cognitive structures only some of which explain the success on the conservation task, the explanation can and should be refined as follows: "Most eight-year-olds get the conservation task with the clay right because they understand the principle of identity and possess a mental transformation rule, a cognitive structure, called 'reversible operations.' "

What vindicates Piaget's claim to be putting forward an explanatory theory as opposed to a merely descriptive one is the way he proceeds experimentally. Piaget begins with the plausible assumption that what accounts for the transformations of experiential input into behavioral output are cognitive processes. Next he observes children in problem-solving situations, and notices similarities in the task-specific response patterns of children of similar ages. He then conjectures on what mental structures might account for these behavioral response patterns and tests his conjectures in a wide variety of experimental situations. These inferences are then refined in accordance with general methodological criteria like simplicity and consistency, and are adjusted in accordance with the feedback from the experiments designed to test their plausibility. Eventually the empirical, logical, and chronological relations among all the different inferred age- and task-specific mental structures that have withstood experimental analysis are examined. Finally, to the extent that these structures are found to constitute temporally persistent, sequentially produced, and logically related interactive systems, we infer the existence of cognitive stages.[14]

It is conceivable, of course, that all of Piaget's specific empirical claims are false, and it is no doubt true that Piaget is often guilty of methodological lapses. Nevertheless, the procedure just outlined is the one Piaget claims to follow, and it is exactly the way to proceed if one wishes to explain behavioral regularities in terms of hidden cognitive regularities. In fact, the hypothetico-deductive procedures that Piaget deploys are precisely the same ones that legitimize physicists' right to claim explanatory power for hidden entities and processes like electrons, muons, gluons, and electromagnetic fields.[15]

(4) The "No Empirical Meat on the Bone" Objection.   R. S. Peters motivates this objection nicely when he says that Piaget sometimes offers "logical truths dressed up in psychological guise, such as that learning must proceed from the simple to the complex, or that concrete operations with objects must precede abstract thoughts about them."[16] Flavell and Wohlwill put a similar objection this way:

> Providing one accepts Piaget's characterization of what these [concrete and formal] operations consist of, it is logically possible for the child to be capable of the former and incapable of the latter, but not conversely. Formal operations are supposed to take products of concrete operations as their objects, and hence presuppose the capability to exercise these operations. . . . the ability to multiply or coordinate two relations presupposes the ability to apprehend the two relations individually; the representation of class hierarchies implies the ability to represent a single class; and so on and on.[17]

The strong form of the objection is this: the claims about cultural universality, invariant sequence, and the logically integrative quality of successive stages look like interesting empirical claims but are not. It is logically inconceivable that the sequence in the development of intelligence could turn out any other way. If an organism is capable of manipulating representations of representations it follows logically that it is capable of manipulating representations, and if an organism is capable of manipulating representations it follows that it possesses representations (words, ideas, and the like), and if it possesses representations, it follows that it uses these representations to represent, from which it follows that it comprehends the entities and processes to which the representations refer. Piaget's stage theory, therefore, is not an empirical theory at all; it consists of trivially true "logical truths dressed up in psychological guise."

It seems to me that it is easy to defend Piaget against this charge. First, the latter argument unfolds from an empirical observation, namely, that (some) adult humans are capable of abstract mental operations.[18] Of course this need not have been the case. We might have had the cognitive abilities of unicellular bacteria. Because, therefore, the conclusion of the argument originates from an empirical fact it has empirical content.

Second, the charge that it is inconceivable that the stage sequence and the logical relations between the stages could have turned out any other way involves a failure of imagination and a conflation of logical priority with temporal priority. The fact that some mental competency A logically presupposes, and thus integrates, competency B does not mean that B necessarily must be learned before A. It is conceivable that A could be learned outright and all at once, without learning B first. Alternatively it is conceivable that human intelligence might not undergo any development whatsoever or that human intelligence might proceed through Piagetian stages in reverse order. It is possible, after all, that we might have burst forth from our mother's womb as physically adept as a ballet dancer, and with a full-blown (Lamarckian) memory of the things in the universe (with names attached), and a fully operative system of abstract logical abilities. And it is conceivable that these exotic inborn cognitive abilities might be stable from birth to death; or alternatively that they might come undone in an orderly manner so that our inborn cognitive sophistication yielded to a complete inability to abstract and only a vague sense of things by the time we were twelve!

The moral is simply this: the claim that Piaget's theory is empirically empty or trivially true is wrong. It simply is not true, as Brainerd, for example, says, that "it is rarely possible to imagine predicted sequences turning out any other way."[19] As our *Gedanken* experiments amply testify, the age-related series of stages Piaget claims to have uncovered could have been otherwise—the facts about human intelligence could have turned out very differently. But if there are other possible ways that human intelligence might have turned out, then Piaget's analysis cannot be necessary, and if it is not necessary then it is not logically true, and if the theory is not logically true, then (if it is true at all) it is empirically true.

I do not intend my defense of Piaget against the latter set of objections to be taken to imply that I think his theory is without problems; in fact, several shortcomings and suspicions come immediately to mind. First, Piaget's theory cannot be viewed as a complete psychology because, for example, there is no well-developed theory of language, motivation, or emotion. Second, and this is related to the first, Piaget tends to concentrate "too much on the psychological significance of abstract logical structure while tending to ignore the effect of concrete content and context."[20] Third, there is the suspicion about the unity and generality of Piaget's stages. Piaget's stages of cognitive development tend to integrate all of a child's abilities into one neat interdependent package. Piaget, for example, views "language to be *all of a piece* with acquisitions made at the level of sensorimotor intelligence."[21] This view, which emphasizes the unity, generality, and interdependency of cognitive structures, may well turn out to be seriously overstated if décalage turns out to be common, or if the view (shared by Noam Chomsky and Jerry Fodor as well as by some neuroscientists and workers in Artificial Intelligence) that the mind is a collection of many independent modules, say one for language, one for face-recognition, one for auditory-processing, one for logic, and so on, is vindicated.

Putting these very important worries aside there is still the crucial question of how Piaget explains the acquisition of increasingly powerful cognitive structures and stages. It is in answering this question that the combined cybernetic-biological model that supports Piaget's conception of cognitive development surfaces. Several philosophers, psychologists, and biologists have argued that the information-processing and biological underpinnings of Piaget's theory do not provide the conceptual apparatus needed to explain satisfactorily how cognitive development takes place.

Assimilation, Accommodation, and Autoregulation

Piaget begins his major theoretical work, *Biology and Knowledge*, with the proclamation that "Life is essentially autoregulation."[22] The basic idea is this: all biological systems, from plants to fruit flies to humans continually work at achieving an adaptive fit with the environment and this work is carried out by systems, sometimes armies of systems, that are relatively self-contained and self-regulating.[23]

Actually there are good examples of such systems outside of biology. Take the thermostatically controlled water-heating system in your home. A thermostat is a heat-sensitive device; it registers information about the mean molecular kinetic energy in its immediate vicinity. A standard thermostatically controlled water-heating system functions as follows: the thermostat is on the surface of the water tank; when the temperature on the surface of the tank goes below a certain temperature the thermostat sends an electrical signal that starts the heater; when the temperature reaches the proper level, the thermostat sends an electrical signal that turns the heater off. The system's job is to keep the water temperature constant; it does so by having the thermostat respond to information about the temperature in its immediate environment and by then regulating the behavior of the heater by sending it feedback about the information it is receiving. Such a system is a simple example of a cybernetic system, an information-processing system, the kind of system that, suitably jazzed-up, has captured the imagination of contemporary workers in Artificial Intelligence. (Notice, by the way, that Cartesian automata are not really autoregulating systems in even the low-level sense the water-heating system is.)

Piaget makes it clear again and again in *Biology and Knowledge* that he views biological systems, and by implication cognitive systems, as paradigm cases of cybernetic systems. Our bodies keep a temperature of 98.6° in roughly the same way the water-heating system keeps the water temperature in the tank constant. Piaget says that cybernetic models are the only ones which throw any "light on the nature of autoregulatory mechanisms . . . they all bring some sort of logic into play."[24]

According to Piaget, the logic cybernetic systems deploy is the logic of assimilation and accommodation. Consider the water-heating system again. The system starts in the assimilative mode. It passively accepts all temperature inputs, say, between 160° and 180° without batting a metaphorical eyelash. Then a disruptive input ("disruptive" relative to the system's design) is received—for example, the water in the tank cools down to 159°. The system then switches into its accommodative mode and acts to get rid of the disruption, that is, it starts heating the water. Once the water is heated sufficiently the system reverts to its assimilative mode until the next disruption occurs, and so on.

The trouble with the mechanical and even the biological thermostat examples is that although the systems in question are self-regulating feedback systems they never do anything new—except eventually break down. But if the story Piaget tells about cognitive development is right, he needs to explain how the mind builds richer and richer systems of cognitive structures. Unlike the water-heating system "cognitive equilibration is . . . 'accretive' . . . the disequilibria do not lead back to the previous form of equilibrium, but to a better form."[25]

Piaget calls his theory constructivist precisely because it purports to explain (not merely describe) this "accretive" quality of cognitive development. He says "autoregulation is eminently constructivist (and dialectical) by its very nature."[26] Of course it is not really true that autoregulating systems are essentially or necessarily constructivist systems, since a water-heating system is an autoregulating system but it does not have the potential to construct new and better modes of operation.

Let us distinguish then between two kinds of autoregulating systems: nonconstructivist autoregulating systems like the water-heating system and constructivist autoregulating systems like a human cognitive system. What accounts for the difference between these two kinds of systems? What, in particular, accounts for the constructivity in the second kind of self-regulating system? What accounts for the fact that humans come to organize experience with a series of increasingly powerful and adaptive systems of cognitive structures?

Piaget often speaks as if the processes of assimilation and accommodation are sufficient to explain constructivity. The following sort of story is standard: cognitive development occurs through a process of assimilation and accommodation. First, there is assimilation. For example, the newborn takes in the mother's nipple in a manner determined by how she has come wired to suck. Almost immediately, there will be need for accommodation; the child will have to adjust the way she purses her lips and refine the manner in which she sucks in accordance with the shape of her mother's nipple and in accordance with her nutritional needs. In general, as soon as the infant starts to suck, move, and play she will begin to have experiences which conflict with her original ways of structuring reality (compare Freud's story of the pleasure principle meeting the reality principle). This will result in adjustments in her sensory-motor and cognitive structures. These new structures will then meet the world assimilatively, require further accommodation, and so on, until structures are arrived at that require no further or only minimal adjustment. The mind, on this analysis, does not simply read the right answers off the world outside (where are the answers written anyway?), nor does it confront the world with permanently fixed structures. It actively and dialectically engages the world and constructs a system of rules that are increasingly adaptive.

Strictly speaking, however, it cannot be quite right that assimilation and accommodation explain the difference between autoregulating systems that are constructive and those that are not, since stomachs, hearts, and water-heating systems assimilate and accommodate, but they don't construct new, increasingly adaptive modes of assimilation and accommodation.

As I understand Piaget—to the extent that he is sensitive to this issue at all—he introduces a concept of *equilibration*, distinct from the concept of *equilibrium*, to account for constructivity. In both *Biology and Knowledge* and his later work, *Adaptation and Intelligence*, Piaget implies that the difference between autoregulating systems like the water-heating system, and the constructive system of human intelligence is that the former system operates only with an equilibrium principle whereas the latter system operates with an additional principle—the principle of equilibration.[27]

The difference is this: the principle of equilibrium is the principle whereby a system seeks harmony with its environment, whereby it seeks to minimize disequilibrium; the principle of equilibration, on the other hand, is the principle whereby a system strives for maximal control over the environment.

Piaget construes the principle of equilibration as a drive, located presumably in the biological economy of the organism, that promotes *"a continual search for a better equilibrium."*[28] An autoregulating system, then, that operates with a principle of equilibration is an assimilation-accommodation system with a twist. It seeks not mere harmony with the environment but the best fit possible.

The principle of equilibration is really designed to do two intimately related jobs for Piaget. First, it is to solve the problem of explaining what distinguishes constructive autoregulating systems, such as the cognitive system, from nonconstructive systems. "Equilibration in its various forms appears to constitute *the fundamental factor of cognitive development.*"[29] Second, it is to explain how it is possible for humans to construct new and increasingly powerful systems of cognitive structures. This is, of course, our old friend, the problem of novelty, which in Piaget's case is the problem of how it is possible for the child to construct a richer system of cognitive structures from a weaker one. Let us see whether the principle of equilibration can satisfactorily solve these two problems and by so doing account for stage transition.

Does the principle of equilibration—the principle that governs systems that seek to optimize, not merely harmonize, their fit with the environment—explain the difference between a constructive autoregulating system and a nonconstructive one? There is reason to be suspicious.

First, Piaget places a good deal of emphasis on the biological support for an equilibration drive.[30] But several evolutionary and molecular biologists have expressed skepticism over the wide-ranging and imprecise explanatory use Piaget makes of the principle of equilibration.[31]

Second, the principle is vague at best. It is hard to tell, for example, what distinguishes the drive to optimize, which Piaget calls the equilibration principle, from the drive to harmonize, the equilibrium principle. Economists, for example, often state that humans seek to maximize profits and minimize losses. Assuming the economists are right about human nature, is this evidence of a distinct drive to optimize, or is it just a way of describing the particular way humans seek to harmonize with the environment?

Third, if the suspicion that the principle of equilibration is really more descriptive than explanatory turns out to be right, then it cannot possibly explain the difference between constructive and nonconstructive autoregulating systems because all it really does in that case is describe the fact that such differences exist. Invoking the principle in an explanatory manner, then, is like explaining the difference between people and rocks by invoking a "principle of aliveness."

Finally, there is a worry about circularity. If the principle of equilibration is going to explain cognitive development we will need to postulate that there is an actual rule of the form "continue to search for better equilibrium between your cognitive structures and the environment," as well as procedures for so doing, programmed into (and thus represented in) the cognitive system from the start (the claim is that the water heater is governed by no analogous "improve-thyself" principle). Piaget sometimes speaks as if just such a principle is encoded into some conscious sector of the mind and applied consciously. For example, in *Biology and Knowledge* he speaks of conscious (or barely subconscious) "reflective abstraction" as the essential feature in human cognitive equilibration.[32] But this raises the specter of circularity. The task is to explain the development of intelligence, but Piaget seems to do so—once we uncover what he means by equilibration—by citing intelligence itself.[33]

None of these worries about the psychological reality and explanatory power of the equilibration drive are decisive, but they do show that we will need to know much more about the principle of equilibration before we can be assured that it can explain, not merely describe, the differences between constructive and nonconstructive autoregulating systems.

The Constructivist's Fallacy

Let us assume for the time being that Piaget is right, that our cognitive system is governed by an equilibration drive. Assume also that this optimizing drive is somehow suitably encoded in the brain, but not that it need be consciously represented.[34] Can this drive, together with the interaction the mind has with the world, explain how we construct more and more powerful mental structures? Jerry Fodor leads a pack of critics who think the answer is an unqualified no.

Many philosophers and psychologists consider Fodor's argument— which I will refer to here as the argument for the *constructivist's fallacy*— an esoteric curiosity, a side issue in the whole development versus preformation debate. It is nevertheless essential for us to deal with this argument because Fodor is convinced that it proves that Piaget's research program (and all psychological research programs, for that matter) requires the extreme nativism—the preformationism—that Piaget is confident he can avoid. Let me sketch how Piaget thinks his equilibration account explains the production of new and richer cognitive structures, and then explain why Fodor, and his colleague Noam Chomsky, think Piaget's story does not—in fact cannot—work.

The Piagetian story of stage transition goes roughly as follows: Take a child who does not understand conservation at age five and who does at age eight. What happened? At age five the child operated with mental structures that made long-and-thin a more salient variable for judging the amount of some substance than short-and-fat. By age eight the child understood that a short-and-fat hunk of clay could be molded into a long-and-thin sausage of clay and that the long-and-thin sausage could then be reconstituted as a short-and-fat hunk of exactly the same size as the original. The eight-year-old's mental structures are richer in that they contain the concept of reversible operations which the same child lacked at age five. What happened in between was that the equilibration drive caused the child to persist in trying to construct structures that optimally fit the environmental feedback she received.

The theory as thus framed avoids extreme nativism. The child does not come wired to understand reversible operations—she constructs the concept. And the theory avoids naive empiricism. The environment merely provides feedback about the quality of the mental structures the child constructs and projects; it does not simply imprint the right structure on the mind.

For Fodor all this talk about the child constructing new and richer structures is talk of a logical impossibility. He says, "it is *never* possible to learn a richer logic on the basis of a weaker logic, if what you mean by learning is hypothesis formation and confirmation."[35] Fodor's argument assumes only that in order to test a hypothesis it must be intentionally represented, that is, meaningfully represented, in the cognitive system.

In a nutshell Fodor's argument is this: Piaget's standard story is one of hypothesis formation and confirmation (the hypotheses and the confirmations or disconfirmations need not, of course, be consciously represented). The five-year-old child projects (that is, tries out) a mental structure without the concept of reversible operations, while the eight-year-old projects a mental structure with the concept of reversible operations. The eight-year-old's hypothesis ends by being confirmed in a way that the five-year-old's does not.[36] But if the child is testing a hypothesis with the concept of reversible operations in it, then she is not learning the concept of reversible operations, she is just testing to see if the concept of reversible operations which she already "knows" applies.[37] The question then arises: how did she come to have the ability to represent the hypothesis containing the concept of reversible operations in the first place? Piaget's answer is that she constructed it, goaded only by feedback from experience and the equilibration drive. But from what materials did she construct the richer hypothesis? It is inconceivable that she could have constructed it from a representationally weaker cognitive system. You simply cannot build the concept of "reversible operations" out of a conceptual system that contains only the concepts "fat" and "thin," "tall" and "short"; it just does not have the requisite expressive power. Therefore, Piaget's story does not really explain how new and richer hypotheses are constructed (no one, according to Fodor, can do that). Piaget tells interesting little stories about hypothesis testing but he doesn't provide a clue as to where the hypotheses come from in the first place.

Fodor insists that the only answer to that question, the question of where the richer hypotheses come from, must be nativistic. In order to test a hypothesis about a cognitive structure one must be able to represent all the concepts (and in that sense "know" all the concepts) that make up the hypothesis. But if one must know a hypothesis in order to test it, and if richer hypotheses cannot be constructed from weaker ones, then all conceivable hypotheses must be available for formulation because of innate (or maturational) features of the representational system. At best, then, Piaget's equilibration drive vaguely describes the procedure the cognitive system uses to track down richer, more adaptive hypotheses from the innately available stockpile.[38]

Fodor's argument does not prove as much as he would like, but it does point to some weaknesses in Piaget's equilibration account of stage transition. Fodor, it seems to me, is right that Piaget's theory is a theory of hypothesis formation and confirmation. Furthermore, Fodor is certainly right—and this is all the constructivist's fallacy really comes to—that one cannot build new and richer hypotheses out of less rich conceptual resources *simpliciter*. Piaget often talks, however, as if this is precisely what the child does. The child constructs hypotheses that involve entirely new ways of conceptualizing reality out of old and less effective conceptual materials.

Fodor's point is that if Piaget's psychology is to be even conceivably true Piaget will have to acknowledge that this way of talking should be taken metaphorically, not literally. In particular, Piaget will have to admit that however a child goes about representing a hypothesis she does so with the representational tools available to the cognitive system at the time she tests a particular hypothesis; the child does not construct richer hypotheses out of weaker ones. Fodor thinks that as soon as Piaget admits this much, he will have no choice but to accept the nativist view that all mental structures that can be tested against experience are available for testing, thanks to the innate or maturationally emergent representational powers of the cognitive system. They are not learned and they are not constructed.

The question is: can Piaget accept that whenever a child goes about representing a hypothesis she does so with the representational tools already available to the cognitive system without acceding to the nativism Fodor wants to ascribe to him? I think he can.

There are several conceivable theories concerning how mental structures become available to the representational system and how particular ones from among all those available are selected for testing, that do not require subscribing to the sort of nativism Piaget finds objectionable. Consider the following logically possible positions which seem to me to run the gamut from a fairly conventional nativism to views more consonant with the constructivist style of thinking Piaget advocates:

(1) Preformation without Plasticity. A representational system that allows the formulation of all possible hypotheses is present at birth and the equilibration mechanism causes the cognitive system to search through the potentially infinite list of hypotheses in a rigidly determined, environmentally insensitive order until it finds one that is confirmed by experience. For example, the system might come wired to find and formulate the available hypotheses in serial order from simplest to most complex until one is strongly confirmed.

(2) Preformation with Plasticity. A representational system that allows the formulation of all possible hypotheses is present at birth and the equilibration mechanism causes the cognitive system to search through the list of all possible hypotheses is an environmentally sensitive way. For example, the system might be wired to start by conjecturing the simplest hypothesis applicable in a given situation, but then be programmed to skip around depending on how it understood the nature

of the disconfirming feedback (again this representational ability, this plasticity, would have to come with the cognitive machinery).

(3) Some Preformation–Some Maturational Emergence with or without Plasticity. Some representational capacity is present at birth, the rest becomes available to the cognitive system in accordance with the genetic program governing biological maturation. The cognitive system in this case might formulate and test hypotheses as they become available to the representational system, and it could do so in either an environmentally sensitive way or an environmentally insensitive way.

(4) Some Preformation–Some Interactive Emergence with or without Plasticity. Some representational capacity is present at birth, the rest becomes available as the result of the interaction between the organism and the environment. On this view new representational possibilities emerge in the system in the same way that the powerful representational medium, DNA, emerged eons ago from the primeval "soup of life." Such a system would, by definition, be environmentally sensitive in one obvious sense. Nevertheless, it is conceivable that it might utilize its emergent representational powers in either an environmentally sensitive manner or an environmentally insensitive manner.

Environmental sensitivity or the lack thereof is of course always a matter of degree. But what I have in mind in distinguishing an environmentally sensitive, that is, plastic, hypothesis-generating system from an environmentally insensitive one can be brought out by a zany example. Suppose that humans are born with an explicit representation of *Webster's New International Dictionary* (second edition) in their brains and are wired to try to figure out word meanings. Now suppose that such a human shows up at a zoo and meets a zebra. How is he going to figure out what to call it? (Suppose also that all the explicit feedback the person gets is "yes" or "no.") One way the system might do this is by projecting hypotheses in alphabetical order: It's an *a*, an *aa*, an *aalii*, an *aam*, an *Aani*, an *aardvark*, and so on, until finally (2,979 pages later, to be exact) it conjectures *zebra* and receives confirmation. Alternatively the system might be wired to be sensitive to natural kinds, like "animal," so that it would start by conjecturing *aardvark*, then *aardwolf*, skip over *anesthesia* and *antithesis*, try *bear* and *boar* but not *bucolic*, and so on. The first system is environmentally insensitive compared to the second. Now a system that operates like (4) is environmentally sensitive in an additional sense: its representational capacities actually increase because of sensory and motor contact with the environment.

In any case, the theories mentioned above by no means exhaust the logically possible ways in which representationally rich hypothesis-generating cognitive systems might work. We could, for example, mix elements of (3) and (4) and have part of the representational system preformed, part of it emerging according to the maturational program, and part of it emerging from interactions of the organism with the environment. But all the theories sketched, as well as all possible mixed theories, satisfy Fodor's requirement that the cognitive system must have all the necessary representational resources at the time it projects a hypothesis (although it need not always have possessed them).

Furthermore, none of the theories above makes the mistake of having a richer representational system emerge solely from a weaker one. If there are maturationally emergent representational powers, their emergence is orchestrated by the already representationally rich genetic program; and if there are representational powers that emerge from interactions with the environment, these are the joint production of the complete biological endowment of the organism and its multifarious commerce with the world. That new representational powers might emerge in the brain as a result of this rich interaction is no less possible than that DNA was cooked out of a steaming cauldron consisting mostly of nitrogen, water, ammonia, carbon dioxide, and electricity. Even Fodor grudgingly admits this possibility, although he insists on calling any environmentally caused change in an organism's representational capacity a "trauma"![39]

The moral is simply this: the constructivist's fallacy can be avoided in a number of ways, some of which, at least in spirit, are compatible with the sort of mental model Piaget tries to promote. It is simply not true that the fallacy can only be avoided by embracing a position committed to the preformation of the entire representational system. Furthermore, even if the entire representational system is preformed this does not preordain the environmental insensitivity of the system. As evidenced by theory (2), a preformed representational system could be environmentally sensitive.[40]

This is all good for Piaget since the only sort of preformationism he really needs to object to is one committed to preformation of the representational system plus environmental insensitivity. As I understand Piaget (assuming he would be willing to concede the point about the impossibility of testing a hypothesis about a mental structure with a representational system lacking the power to represent that hypothesis) he would want to be read as promoting a theory like the mixed theory I just mentioned, in which the representational system is only partially preformed, the rest of its expressive powers emerging through maturation and mostly through active engagement with the environment, and in which the cognitive machinery is environmentally very sensitive.

That is, the cognitive system selects from the available stock of hypotheses the hypothesis which seems most probable given the nature of the environmental feedback. The essential point is that it is possible to be a constructivist in this sense and avoid committing the constructivist's fallacy.

Unfortunately, Piaget's preference for such a model of the mind cannot be secured at this time. First, as many critics have noticed, the stage sequence data Piaget presents is compatible with several of the hypotheses sketched above. For example, the data supporting gradual stage development and the chronological persistence of the stages, look prima facie more compatible with theories along the lines of (1) and (3), that is, theories that see the mechanism governing hypothesis generation and testing as environmentally insensitive and maturationally highly constrained.[41] Second, Piaget depends on the equilibration principle to explain stage change in constructive autoregulating systems, but it is not obvious that the principle does much more than describe the fact that humans test and reject lots of hypotheses before they settle on ones they can live with. The question still remains: what exactly is the nature of the (equilibration) program that governs which hypotheses are chosen for testing and when, and what is the relative role of maturation and experience in fixing systems of cognitive structures?[42]

Before we can settle on a particular model of the mind we need to know much more about the actual cognitive mechanisms governing hypothesis selection and stage transition, as well as whether the entire representational capacity of the mind is, in fact, set at birth or whether it changes over time, and, if it changes over time, how it does so. If equilibration really explained stage transition then one would expect there to be some precise way of formulating the relevant equilibration laws, similar, for example, to the way the laws governing embryonic development are formulated or to the way Skinner's laws about the relative effects of different schedules of reinforcement are formulated. But it should be clear from what has been said that Piaget does not offer any precisely stated equilibration laws.

Thus Piaget's use of biological and cybernetic metaphors to erect a model of a constructive autoregulating system does not also give rise to a clear, empirically vindicated explanation of stage transition. On the other hand, questions about the precise nature of cognitive mechanisms are only starting to be asked, and no one really knows when answers to questions of the sort we have been asking will be forthcoming, nor what exactly they will look like. In the meantime there is nothing philosophically disreputable about betting on one model of that mechanism over others.

To summarize the last two sections: Piaget postulates the existence of an equilibration drive that goads the human cognitive system to greater and greater heights. In Piaget's theory the equilibration drive is the drive to find an optimal fit between one's cognitive structures and one's environment. The equilibration drive is designed to explain two things: the difference between constructive and nonconstructive autoregulating systems; and how and why the child continually constructs new and richer hypotheses about mental structures. Overall, the equilibration drive is intended to explain stage development. We discovered, however, that the hypothesized equilibration drive is simply too vague, too descriptive a theoretical construct, to do either job satisfactorily. We also discovered that in one important sense, the story Piaget tells about the construction of new and richer cognitive structures has to be taken metaphorically; if taken literally it gives rise to the constructivist's fallacy.

On the other hand, this inability to account for the transition from stage to stage or structure to structure does not show that Piaget's theory is false or misguided. Even if the décalage data holds up, requiring us to give up the view that there are logically homogeneous stages in favor of the view that there are changes in specific cognitive structures which are highly domain- and task-specific, we will still have patterns of development to explain. The fact that Piaget's theory does not adequately explain the circumstances and mechanisms under which such change occurs just means that there is lots of interesting work to do. Furthermore, Piaget's theory is at present full of hints as to what lies behind cognitive change: it has partly to do with sensory-motor experience, partly to do with the amount and type of confirming and disconfirming feedback we get from the world, partly to do with the way we are programmed biologically, partly to do with maturation, and so on.

Piaget's Adequacy Thesis

Setting aside worries about what causes stage transition or transition between mental structures, I want to examine briefly Piaget's adequacy thesis, the thesis that the psychologically most advanced stage of development is also the epistemologically most adequate.[43] The overall idea is this. The infant's view of reality, her metaphysic, is (allegedly) initially phenomenalistic. The infant sees the world as populated by objects which come in and out of view and which, therefore, from her egocentric perspective, come in and out of existence. Epistemically the infant's world is utterly solipsistic: objects exist only if they are in view. This is evidenced, according to Piaget, by the fact that children under six months do not search for objects removed from sight. For example, they will not search for a treasured rattle if it is placed under a handkerchief. At this stage the infant lacks the concept of object permanency. In fact, at first the child shows no understanding of the distinction between the perceiver and the object of perception, between the knower and the known. Gradually all this changes. The child comes to understand that objects are permanent and that there is a distinction between the self and the world. The phenomenalistic metaphysic and solipsistic epistemology of the sensory-motor child yield to the more advanced view of the preoperational and operational child. Still, the child under eight behaves something like a metaphysical idealist and epistemological relativist, frequently mistaking appearance for reality and her relative perspective for *the* perspective. Thus the sausage of clay that looks bigger than the ball of clay is bigger; the railroad tracks that appear to intersect in the distance do intersect; the time that seemed to go so quickly during the game of catch did in fact go quickly, and so on. Eventually, the child achieves the highest stage of cognitive development in which relativism and idealism yield to absolutism and realism, to the view that there is a world-out-there, and the way it is is independent of how it appears to her. At this highest stage, the child has certain abstract mental models of the way the world works in full operation, and thus moves about as if the cognitive system had Euclid's understanding of geometry, Newton's (actually it is probably more like Aristotle's) understanding of space, time, and causality, and Kant's understanding of logic. Because this last stage of cognitive development involves a more accurate understanding of the external world and one's relation to it than the earlier stages, it is also epistemologically superior to the earlier stages.[44]

It seems to me that there is something quite right in Piaget's view that the last stage of cognitive development is also epistemologically more adequate than its predecessors. But it is important to defend Piaget against the charge that his argument for the adequacy thesis is based on a variety of genetic fallacy, the fallacy of locating the justification of a belief in the fact that it is the most recent or latest belief. Fortunately, Piaget does not make the mistake of arguing that the last stage of cognitive development is the most adequate epistemologically just because it is the last stage. Nor does he argue that it is the most adequate because once having reached the highest stage children never regress. The adequacy thesis has support quite independent of these facts.

First, there is the fact that almost everyone except the most tendentious philosophical skeptics, idealists, relativists, and egoists will agree, for principled reasons, on the superiority of the last stage as described above. The warrant for claiming epistemic superiority for the structures comprising the last stage comes the way most epistemic justification comes, from verification in practice and from predictive success. The mental structures comprising the earlier stages produce more errors and are simply not as well suited for safe and successful negotiation of reality as those comprising the last stage. Second, there is the integrative quality of the last stage; it integrates the competencies of the earlier stages and then goes beyond them. The overall idea behind integration is that each successive reasoning procedure does all the good things done in the earlier procedures and then improves on them.[45]

The question arises: Does the fact that Piaget's highest stage of cognitive development is also the most adequate stage from an epistemological point of view increase the credibility of his overall theory? In particular, does the convergence of his empirical psychology with normative epistemology provide additional support for choosing his constructivist model over more traditional empiricist and nativist models?

It seems to me that although Piaget talks a much better epistemological game than most psychologists, both his stage data and the thesis of the adequacy of the highest stage can be accommodated by empiricist and nativist models as well by his more hybrid model.

Assume for the time being that all of Piaget's data supporting the universality, irreversibility, and invariant sequence of the cognitive stages are in good order, and that the argument for the adequacy thesis has been spelled out in all the necessary detail. It seems to me that if one leans toward a sophisticated empiricist, learning theoretical philosophy of mind, then one could claim that universality, invariance of sequence, and irreversibility of the stages are caused by the fact that all children in all cultures are exposed to a roughly identical world, in terms of its spatial, temporal, causal, and logical structure. The gradual unfolding of the stage sequence is explained by the fact that learning something as complex as the nature of the spatial, temporal, and causal world takes time—about the same amount of time for all biologically intact humans. The fact that children do not give up their more advanced conceptions for less advanced ones is due to the fact that they are more reinforced by nature for deploying the more advanced conceptions. The later conceptions are epistemologically more adequate than the earlier ones because they more accurately reflect the way the world is. Finally, the reason all children in all cultures eventually fix on more or less identical conceptions of space, time, causality, and logic is that the nature of space, time, causality, and the logical structure of reality are invariant across the earth.

Alternatively, one might try to give a nativistic interpretation of Piaget's stage data and a purely evolutionary explanation of the epistemological superiority of the highest stage. The nativist's story might run as follows. The universality and invariance of sequence of cognitive stages is not due to experience. It is due to the fact that humans are wired to mature in certain ways. Although all our cognitive structures are not in operation at birth, they gradually come into operation thanks to the way we are programmed, similar, for example, to the way puberty is biologically preprogrammed but takes twelve or thirteen years to become explicit. On this view, experience merely facilitates cognitive development in the same way nutrition facilitates sexual development. The fact that all children in all cultures ultimately fix on identical conceptions of space, time, causality, and logic is explained in terms of some sort of species-specific evolutionary adaptation. The highest stages of cognitive development are the most adequate because, as on the first account, they most adequately reflect the way the world is (and has been since the biological adaptations in question first evolved). The difference is that whereas on the learning theoretical account we gradually come to learn the way the world is, on the second account our genes gradually make the way the world is known to us.

The moral is simply this: Theories of cognitive development naturally raise epistemological issues about the relative adequacy of different ways of viewing the world. Piaget has many illuminating things to say about the way in which the world view, certain parts of it anyway, of the average 12-year-old roughly converges with scientific and logical theories which have only recently been articulated, and which in most people's eyes, seem approximately to describe the way the world is. However, the fact that the 12-year-old's world view is more adequate epistemologically in this sense does not in itself increase the credibility of Piaget's preferred constructivist philosophy of mind. Traditional empiricist and nativist theories can also account for the epistemological convergence between the child's mind and the way the world is.

On the other hand, there may well be independent reasons of a more general kind for preferring Piaget's sort of model to these others, and there may well be epistemological features of certain kinds of knowledge that ultimately might make the empiricist or nativist concede defeat. For example, the empiricist model, it seems to me, will have trouble explaining why $2 + 2 = 4$ is logically necessary and not just highly probable. After all, "the sun will rise tomorrow" has the same degree of past confirmation (100 percent) as $2 + 2 = 4$, but no one would say that the sun's rising is necessary. The extreme nativist, on the other hand, will have trouble explaining the development of knowledge that could not conceivably have been encoded in the genes, for example, the development of quantum physics. I will leave it to the reader to speculate about the ways various epistemic facts might be used to increase or decrease the relative credibility of various models of the mind. My suspicion is that some sort of Piagetian-style model (probably with structures but without stages) will begin to look better than the traditional empiricist and nativist competition, and will gain more precision, once a careful inventory is done of all the epistemic facts which need explaining.

Conclusion

I can summarize my evaluation of Piaget as follows.

(1) Piaget makes a convincing case for the theoretical assumption that active mental structures, active systems of intentional mental representations, causally mediate the human organism's interactions with the world and its actions in the world.

(2) Although these mental structures cannot be directly observed, Piaget typically shows the sort of methodological caution required by a theory which gives unobservable processes a central explanatory role. First, his theory is falsifiable; it does not consist of "logical truths dressed up in psychological guise." Second, the claim that cognitive structures and stages lie in explanatory relations to behavior and are not merely descriptive is consistent with the intuitively acceptable background assumptions of Piaget's philosophy of mind, and it is supported by his experimental data. Piaget does, however, show a certain insensitivity to the possibility that factors besides cognitive structural ones, such as differences in expectation, attention, information-processing capacity, or linguistic ability, might account for differences in the performance of young and older children. Some recent research indicates that such factors are often influential, and thus it is likely that the age-riders on Piagetian stages will have to be adjusted. There is also evidence that children's performance on cognitive problems is more task- and content-specific than Piaget's model of general-purpose stages would lead one to believe. This may eventually require that we give up the belief in the existence of general logically homogeneous stages and instead talk about the development of specific cognitive structures. It may even require that we give up the expectation that cognitive structures can be differentiated in terms of their underlying logic for the view that a cognitive structure differs from its predecessors primarily in its information content.

(3) Whereas Piaget can make a plausible case that his cognitive structures lie in explanatory relations to behavior, he cannot claim to have told us what causally explains structural change itself. Piaget's deference to an equilibration drive and to biological and cybernetic models il-

luminates more by way of analogy than by way of precise explanation. We possess, at present, only a series of hints as to the sorts of processes that account for cognitive change.

(4) Nevertheless, Piaget's failure to tell an adequate story of stage or structural transition does not mean that he has no grounds for rejecting the views that the entire representational system is present at birth and that the cognitive system is environmentally insensitive. There are all sorts of possible models of cognitive systems which develop new representational capacities and are environmentally very sensitive. Thus there is nothing intellectually disreputable about betting that humans are one such system even if one cannot yet prove it, especially in light of the fact that all the observable evidence supports such a view.

(5) Piaget's adequacy thesis, the thesis that the highest stage of cognitive development is also the most adequate epistemologically relative to the spatial, temporal, causal, and logical structure of our world, can be vindicated. The highest stage of cognitive development involves a descriptively more adequate representation of the world than its predecessors, and thus its deployment makes for more error-free and safer navigation. On the other hand, we might muster some humility in the face of the psychological facts by noting that with regard to the physical and logical structure of reality, the world view of physicists and logicians is more adequate still (in terms of match with the way the world actually is) than is the world view of an average, cognitively competent person.

Lawrence Kohlberg: Duties, Dilemmas, and Moral Stages

One can read the history of moral philosophy as a history of a wide variety of defenses for a wide variety of moral conceptions. The fact that no defense of any particular moral conception has ever won over an entire community, philosophical or otherwise, for any length of time, is often attributed to the fact that moral issues and moral conceptions are culturally relative in a way that arithmetic issues and arithmetic conceptions, for example, are not; or to the fact that ethics is not like mathematics or science. Logical or empirical tests cannot decide the facts of the matter, in part because there are no facts of the matter. Nonrelativists, on the other hand, typically attribute moral disagreement to the fact that ethics is a special kind of wisdom which only some people have—philosopher-kings, priests, or gurus, for example.

Lawrence Kohlberg has bravely confronted this central issue of moral philosophy, that is, whether moral knowledge or wisdom exists, and if so in what guise. Kohlberg argues that the conjunction of his empirical data on moral development with a certain class of widely respected ethical theories adds up to an argument for the view that there is an objective moral "good" and that humans can know this "good." Philosophically, Kohlberg aligns with Plato, Kant, and Rawls. With Plato he claims that the "good" is one, not many; with Kant he claims that true morality is formal, universal, and exceptionless; and with Rawls, he claims true morality is, by and large, simply a theory of perfect reciprocal justice.[46]

Taking his cue from Piaget, Kohlberg claims that there are five or six (depending on the state of his scoring manual) stages of moral development that define the progression from moral immaturity to moral maturity. In general, humans proceed from egocentric orientations in which simple pleasure and pain are the main considerations, to contractual, altruistic, and principled orientations. At stages 1 and 2 the fact that an action typically gets rewarded or punished is the best reason for considering doing it or refraining from doing it. Eventually (stage 3) most children become motivated to be "good" boys or "good" girls, and they have a concrete, internalized conception of what "good" means. This stage sometimes is transformed into a more sophisticated moral conception (stage 4) in which the individual sees himself as obligated to a less concrete system of relations and institutions, and bound to the implicit as well as the explicit conventions of the social contract of his particular social group. Often this stage yields to a transitional substage (41/2) in which the person, motivated in part by a recognition of the conventional basis of morality in the previous stages, starts seriously to doubt the objectivity of morals and begins to think that choice is completely subjective and relative. Sometimes a person who has passed through this substage reaches a view which recaptures morality from the snares of relativism. Morality is then seen as having a higher source than either social conventions or individual preferences, for example, a source in the "greatest good for the greatest number"—if one is a stage 5 utilitarian—or in the obligation to promote "universal justice"—if one is a stage 6 Kantian-Rawlsian. Kohlberg calls stages 1 and 2 preconventional, stages 3 and 4 conventional, stages 5 and 6 postconventional.[47]

Like Piaget, Kohlberg claims that his stages are structured wholes that are universal, follow an invariant, irreversible, and increasingly integrative sequence, and that the last stage of moral development is also the most adequate ethically. In this way Kohlberg claims to have resolved the interminable controversy about the best moral conception. Stage 6 is the best—Kant and Rawls were right. Aristotle, Hume, Bentham, and Mill were wrong.

Following Piaget further, Kohlberg claims that moral stage transition results from a constructive process. Individuals seek to meet moral problems with a maximally adaptive and coherent system of mental structures. When problems are confronted that cannot be assimilated into one's standard mode of moral thinking, accommodation takes place. If the accommodative mode solves moral problems more adequately than the previous mode, it will be selected until it meets problems it can't solve, and so on. From this it follows that people cannot simply be told how best to think about moral matters; they have to actively experience conflicts between their current ways of thinking and the situation at hand before they can find better ways to process moral problems. Kohlberg claims to reject the view shared by utilitarian philosophers and behaviorist psychologists that a person's moral philosophy is the simple product of the reward-punishment conventions in his social context, and the view of some Kantians that the proper moral theory is naturally available to any rational person. On the other hand, Kohlberg's constructivist theory keeps strains from both sorts of theories: the social environment provides the feedback that confirms or disconfirms our schemes of moral reasoning, and the best moral philosophy is the one most rationally adapted to reality.

With the overall structure of Kohlberg's theory clear, I want to examine the main claims Kohlberg makes by considering two broad objections to his theory. The objections voice a mixture of methodological, logical, and empirical concerns. Later I will examine Kohlberg's specific argument for the adequacy thesis, the thesis that the last stage of moral development is ethically superior to the earlier stages.

The Bad Experimental Paradigm Objection
This objection, or set of objections, is quite important, though difficult to state without a clear idea of Kohlberg's basic experimental procedure. Kohlberg's basic strategy for tracking down a subject's moral stage is by confronting him with hypothetical moral dilemmas. For example, an individual is told a story about a man named Heinz whose dying wife needs a drug which Heinz cannot afford because the inventor of the drug will sell it only at an exorbitant price. The subject is told that Heinz stole the drug and is then asked whether he should have done so. Alternatively, the subject is asked what Heinz ought to do, given the bind he is in. Other standard Kohlbergian dilemmas involve military suicide missions and overcrowded lifeboats. Kohlberg listens to what the subject says about what Heinz or the military officer or the captain of the ship ought to do, and infers his stage of moral development from what he says.

There are, it seems to me, three potentially serious problems with this paradigm. The first has to do with certain naive presuppositions it makes about what the subject's verbal behavior means in response to a hypothetical dilemma—naive presuppositions, that is, about which underlying cognitive processes the verbal behavior points to. The second has to do with the failure of the paradigm to link moral thinking to moral action. The third has to do with the lack of comprehensiveness of the underlying conception of morality—with the fact that there are many kinds of moral issues besides dilemmas of justice or fairness.

(1) The first major problem concerns the issue of what exactly is being tested. The essence of a Kohlbergian experimental task involves asking the subject to give a verbal report about how some hypothetical third party should resolve a moral dilemma. The question that worries me is: what should the subject's verbal report be taken to indicate? what competence is it designed to test for? Kohlberg speaks, again and again, as if these hypothetical moral dilemmas are designed to test for the subject's own underlying moral philosophy.

There are several problems with this view. It presupposes that the subject is putting himself in the place of the third party in the moral dilemma and, in some important sense, describing how he thinks he should act if he were in the same situation, or predicting how he thinks he would act if he were in the same situation. Without this presupposition there is no reason to think that we are getting at the subject's own moral philosophy, the one the subject actually deploys in thinking about the moral issues he confronts.

But this seems a lot to presuppose. The degree to which such projection takes place might well vary dramatically among individuals. Common sense, in fact, indicates that people have all sorts of ideas about how others ought to behave which diverge substantially from how they think they should act and even more substantially from how they would act.

Perhaps it would be better simply to ask people straight out what they would do if they were faced with a certain moral problem. But would this help? We would still be asking the person to deal with counterfactuals (things which might happen but have not), and counterfactuals are notoriously hard for most people to reason about. And we would still be counting on the fact that the subject has the self-knowlege necessary to report accurately on his underlying moral philosophy and to predict correctly the behavior that his philosophy would give rise to.

A related concern has to do with the completely verbal nature of Kohlbergian tasks. The concern rests on the suspicion that, in some important sense, talk is cheap. Suppose for the time being that we were to accept that the subject is, in fact, telling us about what he takes to be his genuine beliefs when he talks about some moral dilemma. The question then arises: is he offering us his theory about what he would do or what he should do? These are crucially different. Furthermore, why should we think that the subject really knows what he thinks about how he should act, or that he correctly predicts how he would act?

Such worries are not idle. There is good experimental evidence, thanks to a classic study by Hartshorne and May, that points to a significant gap between what people say about moral issues and how they behave when faced with moral temptation.[48] Furthermore, there is a growing consensus among cognitive psychologists that people are not very good at predicting or explaining their own behavior or describing the mental structures which underlie their behavior.[49] Add to this data Freudian-type worries about lack of self-knowledge and the possibility that armies of defense mechanisms are activated when we are confronted with morally loaded dilemmas, and we have all sorts of reasons to be suspicious about taking subjects' verbal reports uncritically as evidence for their actual moral philosophy.

Kohlberg is strangely silent about methodological issues such as these. But his silence leaves his experimental paradigm, the source of all his data, in an extremely vulnerable position. It is exceedingly unclear exactly what sort of underlying competence, if any, is represented by a subject's verbal behavior in response to Kohlbergian moral dilemmas.

(2) The second major problem for Kohlberg's experimental paradigm is related to the first and is provoked by the suspicion that actions speak, if not louder than, at least as loud as words. Since Kohlberg's data consist exclusively of narratives produced by his subjects, we might wonder whether his data are sufficient to support a theory of moral development in the fullest sense of morality.

Piaget claims that his stages describe systems of cognitive structures which mediate the child's actual behavior when confronted with spatial, causal, and logical problems in the world. The child who understands object permanency looks for the missing rattle under the handkerchief; the child who understands conservation is not upset when her drink is poured from the long tall glass into the short fat one. She understands that her juice ration has not thereby been decreased.

Kohlberg's moral stages, on the other hand, describe systems of mental structures which mediate the subject's verbal behavior when confronted with a hypothetical moral dilemma. The purely verbal nature of the evidence on which the inference to underlying moral structures is based does not warrant any particular view about how the subject will actually behave when confronted with moral problems. Kohlberg's standard experimental paradigm does not generate any data about actual, that is, nonverbal, behavior. The whole theory, so to speak, stays indoors.

This means that Kohlberg's theory is much weaker than Piaget's theory on which it is modeled. Although Piaget is sometimes guilty of overestimating children's verbal responses, his experimental paradigm provides a potentially exhaustive procedure for telling whether or not a child possesses some underlying cognitive competence, such as conservation. We simply see whether the child actually solves correctly all the verbal and nonverbal conservation problems we give her. What more could we expect of someone who understands conservation?

Kohlberg's experimental paradigm, on the other hand, provides no similar exhaustive test for underlying moral competence. This is because moral competence is not simply a matter of saying the right things; it is a matter of doing them as well. Unfortunately, Kohlberg's experimental procedures yield no data on actions.

If one's intuitions run in the direction of thinking that moral action is the essential component of morality, then this is a fairly serious shortcoming of his experimental paradigm. And even if one does not think that way, it seems obvious that an adequate theory of moral development will have to provide a theory of moral behavior, as well as a theory of the relation between what people say about moral issues and how they act. Unfortunately, Kohlberg's experimental paradigm is ill equipped to do either.

There is one line of defense Kohlberg might make to this objection. In one paper he says, "What I am ready to predict is not that people in a moral situation will do what they said they should do outside that situation but that maturity of moral thought should predict to maturity of moral action."[50] Kohlberg goes on to point to several studies which bear out this prediction. In fact his confidence grows so quickly from this handful of correlational studies that he goes on to espouse the view, which he calls Socratic, that at least for the higher stage individual, "He who knows the good chooses the good."[51] This view turns out to be somewhat overstated. In the very same paper Kohlberg asserts, agreeing with Hartshorne and May, that "Almost everyone cheats some of the time. Cheating is distributed in bell-curve fashion around a level of moderate cheating."[52] In any case, the strategy of expanding the data base to include actual behavioral observation and predicting that there will be a correlation between moral stages and type and degree of moral action is a good one. It will increase the generality of Kohlberg's theory and increase its potential falsifiability.

The question, however, will still arise: what will we say if we find—as the Hartshorne and May data predict we will—that there is at least some cleavage between the moral stage assigned on the basis of what someone says and how he acts? It seems to me that we could say one of three things (leaving out mixed possibilities). First, we might try to get rid of the gap between cognitive stage and behavior by questioning our behavioral observations, for example, by claiming that what first looked like cheating really was just a misunderstanding. Second, we might try to get rid of the gap by revising our original inference from verbal behavior to the underlying moral stage, for example, by arguing that someone who is dishonest simply cannot be at stage 6; he or she simply fooled us by talking a good stage 6 game. Third, we might accept the gap and revise our views on the extent to which the underlying moral structures causally influence behavior—for example, by claiming that there are all sorts of other motivational factors at work in addition to one's underlying moral philosophy. Which way one goes will depend in part on one's underlying convictions about whether or not actions do in fact speak louder than words. If I am right about Kohlberg's fairly naive faith in verbal reports I would expect him to prefer the first or third routes once the discrepant data come in, but I could be wrong.

In any case, the fact remains that on the basis of the data Kohlberg has generated thus far we are not warranted in claiming that the moral structures he describes causally mediate nonverbal moral behavior. There simply is not much data on action, nor could there be, given the prevailing experimental paradigm.

(3) The third major objection to Kohlberg's experimental paradigm follows in part from the first two. It has to do with the comprehensiveness of the underlying conception of morality. Kohlberg sometimes talks as if he has a theory of moral development as a whole, as if he is in possession of *the* moral psychology. But it is inconceivable that his experimental procedure as it currently exists could yield such a general theory. First, as we have already seen, there is no way the current data base can yield a theory about the mental structures which mediate moral or immoral action, because the experiments do not study actions in the real world. Second, the sorts of problems Kohlberg has his subjects talk about are all of a very specific sort and constitute only a portion of the set of ethical issues humans confront. The problems are all dilemmas; thus there is always a small determinate number of possible options (usually two, but not always, therefore the name "dilemma" is slightly misleading), and all the problems are problems of justice or fairness. They all have to do with adjudicating between competing, incommensurable claims over property rights, the right to life, obligations to keep contracts, and the like. Needless to say, many moral issues are far more open-ended (how can I be a good and loyal friend?) and have nothing to do with justice or fairness (parents' moral re-

sponsibility to help their children become autonomous, self-controlling agents, and to protect them from physical or psychological harm).

The issue of sex bias comes into question at this point. Kohlberg's theory is based on data drawn from an all-male sample—originally eighty-four males, now around fifty—whom he has been testing and retesting since the late 1950s. Several critics have argued that this sampling bias, plus the narrow conception of morality presupposed by his use of hypothetical dilemmas in which all the problems are problems of justice and in which almost all the chief actors are males empowered to make life-and-death decisions for others, has produced a narrow and skewed picture of moral psychology. Carol Gilligan, for example, has argued persuasively that females conceive of morality "in a different voice" than males.[53] This, of course, is bad news for Kohlberg because, as we have seen, for him the voice is everything.

In any case, because Kohlberg tests subjects with a limited kind of moral problem, we cannot be sure, even if we allow that the subjects' verbal behavior is a good indication of the actual underlying moral structures he or she uses in dealing with problems of justice, that these structures are similar to the cognitive structures they use in dealing with moral issues which have more to do with friendship, caring, responsibility, and the good life.

In sum then, Kohlberg's experimental paradigm has three major weaknesses: First, it presupposes that the subject is normally talking about his internalized moral philosophy when he talks about what some third party should do in the face of a moral dilemma; it presupposes certain naive views about the accuracy of self-descriptive verbal reports; and it pays insufficient attention to the distinction between reports of what one thinks one should do and predictions of what one thinks one would do in a morally difficult situation.[54] Second, Kohlberg, unlike Piaget, provides no theory (nor can he, given his current data base) of the mental structures which mediate moral and immoral actions. Third, Kohlberg only studies subjects' responses to a limited kind of moral problem and thus cannot claim a comprehensive theory of the development of even moral cognition, until, at a minimum, he studies what subjects say about other kinds of moral problems.

None of these deficiencies is fatal. They could all be overcome, it seems to me, by expanding the experimental paradigm, showing more sensitivity to the problems surrounding self-descriptive verbal reports, compensating for the sex bias of the original sample, and increasing the comprehensiveness of the underlying conceptions of morality and moral competence. My guess, however, is that all these methodologically wise moves would yield data that would make a coherent stage theory of moral development harder rather than easier to defend.

The Failure to Satisfy Piaget's Stage Criteria Objection
This objection concerns the question of whether Kohlberg's theory should actually be classified as a developmental stage theory. The objection is motivated by some doubts about whether the evidence warrants viewing the development of moral thinking in terms of logically homogeneous systems of mental structures which follow an invariant and irreversible sequence of increasing adequacy. The objection is that Kohlberg's stages do not satisfy Piaget's stage criteria. Let's look at these criteria in turn:

(1) *Universality*. Piaget claims that his cognitive stages are universal in two respects: all the stages are found in all cultures; and all (biologically normal) children go through all the stages at approximately the same ages and eventually reach the formal-operations stage.

Usually, Kohlberg claims universality for his stages only in the first respect; all the moral stages are found in all cultures. He does not claim, however, that all individuals reach the last stage of moral development. In fact, his data indicate that most people get stuck at the middle stages.[55] Furthermore, Kohlberg's stages differ from Piaget's in that they have no neat and tidy age-riders. There are fifty-year-olds who have the moral sensibilities of Hitler and twenty-year-olds who speak like the most saintly moral philosophers. Finally, Kohlberg himself has recently admitted that there is no empirical evidence that his highest stage is found in all cultures. Kohlberg's stages, then, are not universal in either of the ways Piaget's stages allegedly are.

(2) *Structured Wholes*. The basic idea is this: a bona fide stage consists of a logically homogeneous and coherent set of concepts and structures. It seems to me that, as they are described, Kohlberg's stages can meet this version of the structured wholes criterion. Basically each Kohlbergian stage is a neatly packaged, internally consistent, moral philosophy. Stage 6, for example, sounds like Kant's moral philosophy. A typical stage 6 subject will talk of universal ethical principles and the obligation never to treat another as a means to an end but always an end in himself. Stage 5 subjects, on the other hand, sound a good deal like descendents of John Stuart Mill: we hear talk of promoting the greatest amount of happiness for the greatest number, respecting different value systems, and the like. From a purely logical point of view both Kant and Mill developed conceptually coherent systems, that is, their moral theories follow from their basic assumptions. The case can, I think, be made that each of Kohlberg's stages, sympathetically interpreted, reflects a conceptually tidy moral philosophy and thus that each stage has the sort of logical coherence required by the structured wholes criterion.

But it might be argued that in order to qualify as a developmental stage theory one must satisfy a stronger form of the structured wholes criterion. Not only must each stage be described as a conceptually coherent system, but individuals must actually occupy the stages so described. This seems a sensible demand, otherwise we have a stage theory that doesn't apply to real people. Kohlberg, in fact, states the structured wholes requirement in the stronger form. He says that one "implication of the Piagetian stage model is that stage structures are *structured wholes.* That is, individuals are consistent in their stage of moral reasoning regardless of the kind of dilemma presented to them, regardless of the moral issue on which the subject must take a stand."[56]

It is not obvious, however, that Kohlberg's theory can satisfy this stronger form of the requirement, that subjects' verbal behavior consistently reflects that they are actually in one of the conceptually coherent stages (allowing for individuals in transition between stages).

Kohlberg asserts with confidence that, according to his longitudinal data, "on the average two-thirds of an individual's thinking was assignable to a single modal stage."[57] The question is: if the average person can be scored in one stage two-thirds of the time is that enough response consistency to meet the structured wholes criteria? The answer to this question depends in part on the nature of the other third of his responses. If the other third was simply too ambiguous to score, or was scored one stage up or down from the predominant stage, we might pass the theory on the structured wholes requirement.

There are some worrisome data, however. Some recent research indicates lower rates of response consistency than Kohlberg's two-thirds, and lots of scattered responses. In fact, depending on the problem, a significant number of adults endorse moral positions which can be scored in as many as four or five different stages.[58] Until researchers replicate Kohlberg's data claiming two-thirds response consistency and little scatter, we will not be sure whether the theory does in fact meet the stronger form of the structured wholes requirement.

(3) *Invariant Sequence.* To count as a stage theory in the Piagetian sense, it is also required that there is no stage skipping, that is, no subject should move from stage 1 to stage 6 without passing though stages 2, 3, 4, and 5. Kohlberg insists that "no cases of stage skipping were found in the longitudinal data."[59] Assuming Kohlberg's data are right this is a highly significant result. It could easily have turned out otherwise. In fact, I would have bet against invariant sequence. I think, for example, of stories of great moral transformations like those of Saint Augustine and Mary Magdalene—people who seem to leap over several stages at once. But perhaps these are just the exceptions that prove the rule. Or perhaps such individuals just changed how they acted, not how they reasoned. Ultimately, however, whether or not Kohlberg's

theory really meets the invariant sequence criteria depends on replication of his data on response consistency. The invariant sequence claim presupposes that at any given time we know what stage a person is in, otherwise we would have no grounds for claiming that some individual had moved from stage 2 in 1980 to stage 3 in 1983. But if independent experimenters continue to find much response scatter then it will be hard to justify the claim for invariant sequence because it will be hard to justify the claim that at any given time a given individual is really in a particular stage. Thus we will have to wait for data to firm up the conviction that the theory meets the structured wholes criteria before we can be sure that it meets the invariant sequence criteria.

(4) *No Regression.* Not only is it required that the stages proceed in an invariant sequence, but it is required that the sequence be nonregressive; that is, if a person reaches stage 3 we should not discover at some later time that he has regressed to stage 2. In general, if an individual has reached stage n he should not at some later time be found to be at stage $n-1$. Kohlberg has trouble satisfying this criterion. Gilligan and Murphy, two of Kohlberg's colleagues, put the problem this way: "There has been a persistent finding of late adolescent regression from the highly logical Stage 5 to mixed (4/5) or conventional (Stage 4 or 3) scores in adulthood. . . . This finding led Kohlberg to undertake the complete revision of his scoring system . . . rescoring of his own data by his revised system has virtually eliminated regression, it has also eliminated Stage 6 and drastically reduced the incidence of Stage 5."[60]

The sort of regression referred to is of an intuitively familiar kind: the wide-ranging idealism of late adolescence gives way to more relativistic, self-centered, pragmatic attitudes after college. Rather than accept the regression evidence, Kohlberg decided that his scoring manual needed revising and this in turn required a highly significant change in his theory. He has recently said, "Continuing empirical work with our longitudinal sample in the United States and Middle East has not allowed us to confirm the existence of, or define, a sixth stage."[61] In dropping stage 6, however, we see the disappearance of the stage that Kohlberg has been telling us all along is the ethically most adequate! The important question now is: why not just accept the intuitively plausible regression evidence and give up the no-regression claim? Kohlberg, as far as I can tell, obstinately refuses to consider this possibility. But he does so without any convincing argument. Meanwhile, some of his colleagues, like Gilligan and Murphy, are arguing that the more realistic adult moral orientation should not in the first place have been seen as a regression toward stage 4 1/2 relativism but rather as a progression beyond the excessively abstract fifth and sixth stages to an even higher stage of "contextual relativism." Needless to say the theory is in a mess with regard to the no-regression requirement.

(5) *Integration.* Each stage in a bona fide stage sequence should logically integrate the competencies of the earlier stages. Thus, for example, in Piaget's theory the child who understands conservation does so by integrating the concept of object permanency that he acquired at an earlier stage with the concept of reversible operations that he has just acquired. The basic idea is that the higher-level competence presupposes the lower-level one: you couldn't possibly know that the amount of water stays the same when it is poured from a tall thin glass into a short fat one unless you understood that substances can be permanent under various transformations.

The best way to test whether a stage sequence is integrative is to see if earlier stages are logically contained by later ones. Take Kohlberg's stage 6, for example: does stage 6 logically contain stage 5? It all depends on how we describe stage 6. Kohlberg sometimes describes stage 6 as Kantian and stage 5 as Millian. So one way of asking the integration question is to ask: does Kant's moral philosophy logically contain Mill's moral philosophy? Put this way, it seems to me that the answer is no, and the reason is obvious. Mill's moral theory is concerned with promoting the greatest amount of happiness for the greatest number of people. Kant, on the other hand (at least this is one standard way of reading him), explicitly denies that moral theory has to do with maximizing happiness. A theory committed to denying that maximizing happiness is the purpose of moral philosophy cannot, of course, logically contain a theory that is committed to maximizing happiness.

However, in the fullest discussion of the philosophical content of his moral stages, Kohlberg is careful to point out ways in which stage 6 diverges from the Kantianism of Kant. Kohlberg, in fact, identifies certain conservative, morally rigid features in Kant's philosophy, features which embody a stage 4 perspective.[62] He writes as if stage 6 is Kantian only in the sense that it has elements which lie at the heart of Kant's position: humans are valued unconditionally, and moral decisions must be universalizable and consistent in the sense that the person making the decision would make the same decision even if he held a different role in the morally problematic situation. For example, whether or not a stage 6 person puts himself in Heinz's place, that of his wife, or that of the avaricious chemist who invented the drug that could help Heinz's wife, the stage 6 person will still think that the chemist should sell the drug at a fair price.

This enables Kohlberg to describe stage 6 in modified Kantian terms and thus overcome its incompatibility with utilitarianism. For example, in speaking of one stage 6 subject, Kohlberg says, "He accepts Stage 5 rule utilitarian and social contract reasoning in its place but asserts two moral principles as defining a higher 'moral law' . . . the *first principle* is that *'people are of unconditional value,'* translatable into the Kantian principle 'act so as to treat each person as an end, not as a means'. The *second related principle* is individual *justice*, 'the right of every person to an *equal* consideration of his *claims* in every situation, not just those codified into law.' "[63]

Described this way, the claim that stage 6 integrates stage 5 is much more plausible. The stage 6 individual is concerned with promoting the greatest amount of happiness altogether but in addition wants to make sure that no one is used as a means, and that the rights of all parties are considered equally. The basic idea is that each stage integrates the principles of the previous stage, but constrains them with new principles.

Does stage 5 then contain stage 4, and does stage 4 contain stage 3, and 3 contain 2, and 2 contain 1? Again it depends on exactly how the stages are described, but a plausible case can be made that they do. The stage 5 concern for the greatest amount of happiness altogether integrates the stage 4 concern for one's social group; the stage 4 concern for one's social group integrates the stage 3 concern for one's family and friends; and the stage 3 concern for one's family and friends integrates the stage 2 and 1 concern for oneself.

Thus it looks as if Kohlberg's stages can pass the integration test. But there is one possible snag, having to do with the relativistic substage 41/2. Especially in his more recent writings, Kohlberg lays heavy emphasis on the importance of this transitional stage. It is the stage in which conventional morality is thrown into question and thus the stage that makes possible the transition to principled postconventional morality. But recall what stage 41/2 is like. Kohlberg calls stage 41/2 "ethical egoism" and says, "It characteristically rejects the meaningfulness of normative moral terms like 'morally right' or 'duty' and is strongly relativistic and emotivistic."[64]

The worry regarding integration is simply this: it is hard to see how stage 41/2 integrates the concern with doing one's duty, the acknowledgment of social responsibilities, and the nonegoistic features of stages 3 and 4, all of which return at stages 5 and 6. It is hard to see how a stage in which "the meaningfulness of normative moral terms" is denied can integrate stages in which the meaningfulness of such terms is assumed. As things now stand I see no way for Kohlberg to meet this objection and claim that his theory genuinely satisfies the integration criteria.

In sum, then, with regard to the first five of Piaget's stage criteria, Kohlberg's theory meets with very limited success. The summary scorecard looks like this: universality—fail; structured wholes—maybe, awaiting more data on response consistency; invariant sequence—maybe, also awaiting more data on response consistency; no regression—fail; integration—fail.

The scorecard, of course, could improve depending on how data gathered by independent researchers turns out. But in the meantime one should ask: why should we care so much about a theory of moral development meeting Piaget's stage criteria? Admittedly, Kohlberg worries a good deal about it, but it is not clear why he cannot just acknowledge the differences between the two theories and still claim that it is useful to talk about moral reasoning in terms of stages, some of which are rarely found, some of which involve regression, and so on. I will leave the answer to that question to Kohlberg. Now I want to discuss the philosophically most interesting claim he makes for his moral stage theory, the claim that the last stage of moral development is also the most adequate from an ethical point of view.

Kohlberg's Adequacy Thesis

One general problem regarding the proper interpretation to give to Kohlberg's claim for the adequacy of the last stage of moral development relates to the question of what exactly is the last stage. Kohlberg has recently revised his theory and admitted that he has not been able "to confirm the existence of, or define, a sixth stage. . . . our sixth stage remains a theoretical hypothesis rather than an empirically confirmed stage. Given this state of the research I would not want to press claims about the greater moral adequacy of a sixth stage distinguishable from a fifth stage of moral reasoning—which latter often express utilitarian principles."[65] This might seem to imply that we should take the claim for the adequacy of the highest stage to be a claim for the adequacy of stage 5. On the other hand, Kohlberg continues to talk of both stages 5 and 6 throughout the paper in which he makes the latter admission. On the basis of his continued mention of stage 6 and on the basis of the remark that he does not "want to press claims for the greater moral adequacy of a sixth stage distinguishable from a fifth stage. . ." I will interpret the adequacy thesis as the claim for the adequacy of a combined stage 5-6. What exactly such a stage would look like, for example, whether stage 6 considerations override stage 5 considerations, I will leave to Kohlberg.

In any case, Kohlberg's argument for the adequacy thesis has four main strands. He does not intend for us to think that these four strands add up to a definitive proof of the adequacy thesis but merely that they provide strong grounds for thinking the adequacy thesis is true.[66]

I will first briefly describe each strand in the argument and then conclude with a discussion of a series of difficulties faced by the overall argument for the adequacy thesis.

The first strand in Kohlberg's argument for the adequacy thesis rests on the Piagetian belief that humans continually search for more adaptive ways of dealing with the environment. That is, in all aspects of our lives, we seek the most adaptive cognitive relation with the external world. We seek equilibrium with the moral world in the same way we seek equilibrium with the spatial world. Kohlberg says that "moral judgments that are not reversible . . . are not in equilibrium . . . . This search for equilibrium is a basis for change to the next stage."[67]

Following philosophers like John Rawls, Kohlberg means "reversible" in the sense that the moral decision one makes is the one that one would (want to) make no matter what role one was in (for example, that of Heinz, Heinz's wife, or the chemist). Kohlberg asserts that humans experience cognitive conflict when they become aware of the lack of reversibility of one of their principles. Thus a moral perspective which involves treating all persons' interests equally and in which the reasoner is proficient at putting himself in the place of all the different parties affected by a dilemma is in maximal equilibrium with the moral world—the nature of the moral world being legislated from both without and within, from one's particular social world and one's natural moral sense.

The second strand in Kohlberg's argument for the adequacy thesis is that each stage of moral development culminating in the highest stage is better integrated and differentiated than its predecessor which it logically absorbs. Each stage logically absorbs the competencies of the previous stage (integration) and incorporates new ones (differentiation). Furthermore, the patterns of integration have the following important feature: "overarching reasons given for moral judgments at earlier stages (e.g., 'because it gives you a good reputation,' or 'because you promised') are later viewed merely as relevant considerations or components of more general rationales ('Promises are especially important obligations which must be kept to be equally fair to all members of one's society,' 'A good reputation should be established by treating people fairly, keeping promises, respecting people's rights,' etc.)."[68]

The third strand in Kohlberg's argument is intimately related to the previous one, namely, people "prefer the highest stage they comprehend."[69] For example, if you ask a stage 3 individual which is better, stage 3, 2, or 1, he will rank 3 ahead of 2 and 2 ahead of 1. Since an individual comprehends the stage he is in, as well as the earlier stages he was in, his preference for the highest stage is evidence that he considers the higher stage to be in greater equilibrium.

The fourth strand in Kohlberg's argument is that the best philosophical wisdom independently depicts Kohlberg's highest stage as *the* highest stage. Kohlberg claims that his highest stage converges with the moral philosophies of Kant, Hare, Baier, Frankena, and Rawls. In an important paper, "The Claim to Moral Adequacy of a Highest Stage of Moral Judgment," Kohlberg says:

> The assumptions of our psychological theory are naturally allied to the formalistic tradition in ethics from Kant to Rawls. This iso-morphism of psychological and normative theory generates the claim that a psychologically more advanced stage of moral de-velopment is more morally adequate, by moral-philosophic cri-teria. . . . [T]his implies that the philosopher's justification of a higher stage of moral reasoning maps into the psychologist's ex-planation of movement to that stage and vice versa.[70]

Does this four-strand argument for the moral adequacy of the highest stage work? I see several possible objections, some minor, some major.

First, it is easy to think up alternative explanations for the fact that people prefer the highest stage they comprehend that do not require the conclusion that people prefer the highest stage because they prefer the most adequate stage. That is, one might argue that because people generally comprehend the stage they are in plus the stages they used to be in, their preference for the highest stage is typically just the preference for the stage they currently are in. This preference, however, might be explained in terms of ego involvement or social reinforcement. People generally prefer traits they now possess to ones they have yet to conceive of or ones they have given up. Or alternatively, people tend to prefer traits for which they are most reinforced by those around them (or in cases where people prefer stages higher than the stage they occupy we might argue that they see that they would be more reinforced by the moral community if they were to reach the higher stage). I am not sure how far the argument locating the preference data in ego identity or reinforcement patterns could get. But to the degree that such an account has credibility, to that degree we will need in-dependent arguments for the ethical adequacy of the preferred stages. Kohlberg, of course, recognizes this. He does not make the mistake of thinking that the preference data is sufficient to prove adequacy, but he does sometimes conflate ethical adequacy with psychological equilibrium.

Second, it is easy to think of more integrated and differentiated stages which are not morally more adequate than their predecessors. In fact, Kohlberg himself once inadvertently produced such a stage, when in a weak mystical moment, he wrote a paper on a seventh stage of moral development. According to Kohlberg and Power, "In the state of mind we have metaphorically termed Stage 7 we identify ourselves with the cosmic or infinite perspective itself; we value life from its standpoint."[71]

I submit that if we were to take the perspective of every living thing when reasoning about actions, we would not dare breathe, let alone move, for fear of destroying some microorganism with an equal right to life. Yet such a perspective does absorb logically the universal concern for humans of Kohlberg's highest stage and goes beyond it. We could reason this way but we could not act on our reasons.

Third, one might wonder about Kohlberg's use of Piaget's equilibrium concept in his argument. Kohlberg sometimes talks as if moral judgments which are not reversible in the Kantian or Rawlsian sense are not in equilibrium. He says that when "people become *aware* of the lack of reversibility of their judgments, they will change these judgments or principles to reach a more reversible solution."[72] Elsewhere he says "Another word for reversibility is 'ideal role taking' or 'moral musical chairs.' Moral musical chairs means going around the circle of perspectives involved in a moral dilemma to test one's claims of right or duty until only the equilibrated or reversible claims survive."[73] By speaking this way, Kohlberg implies that humans are wired so that they naturally desire to become maximally consistent ideal role takers. When a person discovers that he has not considered someone else's point of view he tries to do so. The higher stages then are more adequate than the lower ones relative to this natural desire to take the most reversible perspective.

There are reasons to be suspicious about this story. From Kohlberg's own description of the early egoistic stages it does not sound as if humans naturally desire to take the widest possible perspective. What seems more plausible is that we receive feedback from the social world which indicates that we will have to compromise our (at least somewhat) selfish perspective. We are asked to consider "What if everyone did that?" and we are told "to put ourselves in the other person's shoes." All this makes sense from the social point of view—from the point of view of all the other people who will have to deal with us.

But if such a social learning story is right, then a particular moral perspective is in equilibrium only relative to the sorts of compromises required in some particular social system. The acid test of whether a moral perspective is equilibrated rests then on the degree of harmony between it and the manner in which the larger social environment doles out admiration, respect, and disapproval, not on whether the perspective meshes with some natural desire to be consistent ideal role takers. On the social learning view, that desire, if one has it at all, is an acquired trait.

The way this alternative story about equilibrium undermines the adequacy thesis is this: if a moral perspective is in equilibrium relative to a social context, then the fact that it is in equilibrium says nothing, by itself, about the ethical adequacy of the perspective—it is possible to have a harmonious relation with a morally corrupt society by sharing its bad values.[74] This brings me to the set of more major concerns.

Kohlberg claims that his highest stage converges with the moral perspective put forward by the most respected moral philosophers. The main problem with this strand of the argument is that there is quite a bit more disagreement among moral philosophers, including the ones Kohlberg cites, about the nature of morality than Kohlberg lets on.[75] In fact, if one casts one's net more widely into the circle of respected moral philosophers, one will see deep differences about the best moral theory. Several widely respected contemporary moral philosophers claim to reject both Kantianism and utilitarianism and thus could not possibly be counted as supporters of the adequacy of stage 5-6.[76]

My second major concern follows indirectly from the first. The combined stage 5-6 incorporates features of stage 5 utilitarianism and stage 6 Kantianism; it stresses maximizing utility and protecting universal human rights. But it is widely held that the concepts of "utility" and "rights" are recent conceptual inventions. The meaning of these terms was solidified over the course of the past two and one-half centuries, and their appearance is historically associated with the breakdown of traditional communities and with the rise of capitalism, industrialization, and individualism. This might lead one to argue that Western culture has itself moved through stages of moral development—only recently discovering the highest stage.[77] Alternatively, one might argue, as for example Alasdair MacIntyre does, that utility and rights theories are merely ways of dealing with the moral deficiency of living in social groups without clear-cut social roles and a genuine sense of community purpose. On this view Kohlberg's highest stage is, at best, an adaptive way of dealing with a world which is in certain respects less morally adequate than its predecessors. At worst, the highest stage is adaptive merely because it deploys the vocabulary with which, perhaps driven by inexorable socioeconomic forces, we have unwittingly consented to talk about our world. But if either situation is the case then it would be peculiar to think of the "highest" stage as the morally most adequate stage in some absolute, atemporal or ahistorical sense.

This brings me to two closely related points. A stage of development in Piaget's or Kohlberg's theory is always adequate relative to something else. For example, the Aristotelian-Euclidean-Newtonian understanding of space of the average twelve-year-old is more adequate than the preoperational spatial understanding of a five-year-old because the spatial world all humans have commerce with has (roughly—and only for nonphysicists) an Aristotelian-Euclidean-Newtonian structure, always has and, as far as we know, always will. Thus, the understanding of space all mature humans have is adequate relative to the way the spatial world is.

The question arises: a stage of moral development is adequate relative to what? As we have seen, Kohlberg sometimes speaks as if it is adequate relative to some internal moral sense we have, some drive we have to reach the maximally consistent, reversible moral conception. The view that there is such a drive is somewhat implausible, as we have seen. At other times Kohlberg speaks as if a moral stage is adequate relative to the way the social world is. We want after all to be in maximal equilibrium with social reality. But the trouble with this way of assessing adequacy—not to mention the fact that the social world is sometimes incredibly corrupt—is that there is no one way the social world is. Social worlds change dramatically over time and culture, frequently even across town. The question then arises for Kohlberg, in a way it does not for Piaget: which among the many possible and actual social worlds should we be trying to adapt to? Kohlberg's answer to that question is that we should seek to achieve the moral perspective which incorporates most fully the "moral point of view," the most reversible moral perspective; this he goes on to tell us is best done by utility and rights theories.[78]

But this brings us back to the concern we voiced above. The ideas of maximizing utility and inalienable individual rights arose in response to certain social, economic, and political conditions. Many thinkers have raised serious doubts about the initial moral wisdom of giving up the view that individuals are inseparable parts of a social community for the sort of Robinson Crusoe individualism which permeates the modern world and which logically supports the notions of individual rights and the conception of persons as individual happiness-maximizing units. Kohlberg has very little to say about the relation between social phenomena and morals. The logic of his highest stage, however, presupposes the superiority of the kind of world we have, the kind of world that gives rise to the concepts of rights and utility. But this means that from the perspective of Kohlberg's highest stage, we will not be able to raise critical questions about the relative goodness of a world whose characteristic economic and social relations give rise to the concepts of rights and utility from a world which does not give rise to these concepts, precisely because his highest stage requires the concepts of rights and utility.

I can make this point more concretely: it is widely known by now

that people in undeveloped countries do not reach the higher stages
of moral development as plotted by Kohlberg. As Bill Puka, one of
Kohlberg's staunchest supporters, says, "In simple cultures most people
will not reach high stages, they will not have an amply complex environment to grapple with."[79]

The problem seems to be that the preindustrial, pretechnological
world simply does not make stage 5-6 concepts available to its citizens.
Because these higher-stage concepts are only available in industrialized
societies it would seem to follow that the features of industrialized
societies (complexity, individualism, anonymity) which give rise to these
concepts are, in some sense, morally superior to the features of undeveloped societies which do not give rise to these concepts. But this
is a disturbing consequence, since there are many ways in which the
models of community operative in undeveloped societies seem morally
superior to our own, for example, in family and community loyalty
and concern for future generations.

Just as we come upon what is, I think, a major weakness in Kohlberg's
argument for the adequacy of the highest stage, we hit on an area of
strength. Kohlberg is right that his highest stage is, in some important
sense, the most reasonable approach to adjudicating questions of distributive justice in a world in which socioeconomic transactions take
place more and more frequently between anonymously interacting individuals (often culturally removed) who have no special affection for
each other and no noneconomic affiliation with each other. As John
Rawls has shown in *A Theory of Justice*, the rational thing to do if
asked: "How would you want to construct the moral rulebook if you
could end up in any position at any time?" is, "Very fairly with equal
protection for all and I wouldn't want to ever maximize utility for the
best off if it required hurting the worst off (because the worst off might,
after all, be me!)."

But seeing what is right about Kohlberg's argument for the adequacy
thesis puts in sharper relief what is wrong with it. Kohlberg's argument
is really an argument for a certain conception of how to resolve justice
disputes in a certain kind of world. This comes out in the very type
of moral dilemmas he uses to test his subjects' moral stage—dilemmas
involving decisions about the fair distribution of property and burdens,
the upholding of contracts, and the like. But considerations of justice
are only part of the moral domain. There are issues having to do with
the good life—with things like friendship, family, love, kindness, courtesy, and altruism. A theory of justice, as Rawls would be the first to
admit, does not provide answers to questions in these areas. Two hypothetical examples can give a sense of the inapplicability of justice

considerations in certain morally difficult situations; we might call these the canoe counterexamples.[80]

Suppose there is a mother on the lakeshore who suddenly notices that her young child and a friend the same age, both nonswimmers, are paddling a hijacked canoe in the middle of the lake. Suddenly the canoe tips over and the two children start to drown. The mother is equidistant from both, and she is a good swimmer but only good enough to save one child. The mother quickly flips a coin saying, "heads my child, tails the other." Tails appears and she swims off and saves the other child. After the fact, the mother explains her action by claiming to have been following a Kantian principle to "give every life equal consideration."

My conjecture is that most people would feel morally uncomfortable around such a mother. She applied an abstract principle of justice that would have been applicable were it a question of giving the last morsel of food to two equally hungry strangers but is not applicable in this case. Parents have special responsibilities to their children, and to their families in general.

Suppose, to vary the example, we now put three young children in the canoe, one the mother's child, the other two not. The canoe tips over, and this time the mother is a good enough swimmer to save two children if they happen to end up next to each other. So suppose that the two children unrelated to her go over the left side of the boat and stay together, while her child goes over the right side alone. The mother swims off and saves the two children on grounds that she is following a utilitarian principle to "maximize the greatest amount of happiness for the greatest number of people."

I think this case is the same as the first. The utilitarian principle is being applied in the wrong place at the wrong time. Nor do I think the numbers matter—suppose there were three unrelated children, or four, or five.[81]

The purpose of these examples is to show that Kohlberg's moral stages do not give us a comprehensive picture of the moral sphere. Without such a comprehensive picture the claim to have identified the highest stage of moral development is grossly inflated. At best Kohlberg has identified an adequate stage for reasoning about issues of distributive justice. His stages are stages of justice; they are not sufficiently comprehensive to pass for stages of morality. Furthermore, if situations like the canoe cases turn out to be common, we will end up with so many different kinds of moral reasoning in different situations that we will have to conclude that moral reasoning, like other kinds of reasoning, is highly task-specific and content-sensitive. In that case it will not make sense to talk about moral stages in general, even if the claim for stages of reasoning about issues of distributive justice stands up to scrutiny.

I have one additional worry about the lack of comprehensiveness of the underlying conception of morality. It relates to the concern voiced earlier that Kohlberg's theory has virtually nothing to say about actions. This is a fairly serious shortcoming for a theory that claims to have identified the most adequate stage of moral development. The problem can be brought out in the following way. It is utterly conceivable that a given individual might be able to pass a test of stage 5-6 reasoning on hypothetical justice dilemmas, but lack altogether the traits of being a good and loyal friend, of being reliable, and being respectful of others as persons. But I take it that one of the main commonsensical tests for the moral goodness of a person has to do with his reliability, with whether or not he is respectful of others, capable of stable, loyal relationships, and with whether he goes out of his way to help others.

Kohlberg has virtually nothing to say about stable character traits such as these which show up in action, and that is a serious deficiency. We shall need to know how such traits arise and are maintained if we are going to be able to create a more moral world. Inquiry into that question, however, will require that we look more closely at the social worlds from which people's moral visions ultimately come and in which they do their good and harm. Unfortunately, as we have seen throughout, Kohlberg's rationalism keeps him from engaging in inquiry into the social world, so transfixed is his research program on what people say about issues of justice.

In the end then, Kohlberg cannot secure the adequacy thesis for three basic reasons. First, his conception of morality is limited. Second, he pays insufficient attention to actual behavior, but however moral adequacy is ultimately defined, it will involve a component of acting well. Third, he pays insufficient attention to the social worlds in relation to which our moral perspectives arise, and in relation to which they are criticized and transformed. Having said that much, however, I should say that I see no reason, in principle, why Kohlberg could not enrich his research program to deal with these shortcomings. My firm conviction, however, is that such an expanded research program would make the project of establishing the thesis that there exists a single most adequate stage of moral development seem less, rather than more, plausible.

Conclusion

I can summarize my evaluation of Kohlberg as follows:

(1) Kohlberg models his theory on Piaget's theory of cognitive de-

velopment and thereby makes the plausible assumption that cognitive structures with moral content account for characteristic patterns of moral reasoning.

(2) Kohlberg's experimental paradigm, however, involves a less than comprehensive conception of morality. This shows up in two main ways. First, Kohlberg only tests his subject's verbal behavior on moral dilemmas involving hypothetical third parties. But morality involves not only saying the right things or reasoning in the right ways, but performing the right deeds as well. Second, the standard sorts of dilemmas Kohlberg gives his subjects are dilemmas involving issues of distributive justice. Problems of distributive justice, however, constitute only a portion of the set of common moral problems, and they may well be atypical in their logical structure.

(3) Furthermore, (2) raises methodological concerns about what exactly is being tested when we ask subjects to reason about hypothetical third-party dilemmas. Are the subjects telling us how they think the third party should act or are they predicting how they think they themselves would act? Are they expressing how they think they themselves should act or are they just saying the right things? Also, what is the connection between what they say and what they do? Kohlberg is, by and large, insensitive to concerns such as these.

(4) In addition, Kohlberg's theory has problems of varying degrees in satisfying the criteria Piagetians normally lay down for membership in the class of bona fide stage theories, namely, universality, structured wholes, invariant sequence, no regression, and integration.

(5) Finally, Kohlberg has difficulties in supporting his version of the adequacy thesis, the thesis that the highest stage of moral development is also the ethically most adequate. First, there is Kohlberg's lack of clarity about what exactly the highest stage is. Second, there is the asymmetry between the Piagetian case for epistemological adequacy and Kohlberg's case for moral adequacy. Piaget can claim adequacy on grounds of convergence between, for example, the highest stage of spatial development and the way the spatial world actually is across the entire earth. But there is no correspondingly constant social or moral world for Kohlberg to claim convergence of his highest stage with. Third, there is the problem that Kohlberg's highest stage presupposes a particular kind of social world, namely, the technologically developed one Americans and Western Europeans happen to live in. Fourth, there is the problem that follows from (2), namely, that the highest stage of moral development cannot be the most adequate if it is underwritten by a conception of morality which is not comprehensive.

In the next chapter, I continue the discussion of cognitive psychology in what might be called its post-Piagetian form. It should be obvious by now that both Piaget and Kohlberg analyze cognitive processes at the macroscopic level, at roughly the level accessible to direct observation and occasionally to introspection. Furthermore, although both theories shed light on the cognitive structures that mediate behavior, they have little to say about how exactly the cognitive processing is done.

The burgeoning fields of cognitive psychology and so-called cognitive science—an amalgam of psychology, linguistics, philosophy, neuroscience, and computer science—are designed to answer questions about the precise nature of cognitive processing. A wide array of important philosophical assumptions guides these new enterprises, most notably the assumption that the human mind is a computational system. An equally wide array of important philosophical implications relating to the problems of innateness, self-knowledge, personal identity, and the unity of consciousness follows from working out the details of the guiding computational metaphor in experimental settings.

Suggested Readings by and about Piaget

General Overview

Boden, M. (1979), *Jean Piaget*.
Gardner, H. (1973), *The Quest for Mind: Piaget, Lévi-Strauss, and the Structuralist Tradition*.
Ginsberg, H., and Opper, S. (1969), *Piaget's Theory of Intellectual Development: An Introduction*.
Gruber, H., and Voneche, J., eds. (1977), *The Essential Piaget*.
Inhelder, B. and Piaget, J. (1958), *The Growth of Logical Thinking from Childhood to Adolescence*.
Piaget, J. (1970), *Genetic Epistemology*.

Criticisms of Piaget's Theory

Brainerd, C. J. (1978), "The Stage Question in Cognitive-Developmental Theory."
Carey, S. (1983), "Are Children Fundamentally Different Thinkers and Learners than Adults?"
Haroutunian, S. (1983), *Equilibrium in the Balance: A Study of Psychological Explanation*.
Macnamara, J. (1978), "Another Unaccommodating Look at Piaget."
Piattelli-Palmarini, M., ed. (1980), *Language and Learning: The Debate between Jean Piaget and Noam Chomsky*.

Suggested Reading by and about Kohlberg

Collected Papers

Kohlberg, L. (1981a), *Essays on Moral Development*, volume 1, *The Philosophy of Moral Development*.

Kohlberg, L. (1984), *Essays on Moral Development*, volume 2, *The Psychology of Moral Development*.

Major Philosophical Essays

Kohlberg, L. (1973), "The Claim to Moral Adequacy of the Highest Stage of Moral Judgment."

Kohlberg, L. (1981b), "From 'Is' to 'Ought': How to Commit the Naturalistic Fallacy and Get Away with It in the Study of Moral Development."

Kohlberg, L. (1982), "A Reply to Owen Flanagan and Some Comments on the Puka-Goodpaster Exchange."

Criticisms of Kohlberg's Theory

Flanagan, O. J. (1982d), "Virtue, Sex, and Gender: Some Philosophical Reflections on the Moral Psychology Debate."

Flanagan, O. J., and Adler, J. E. (1983), "Impartiality and Particularity."

Flanagan, O. J. (1982c), "Reply to Lawrence Kohlberg."

Flanagan, O. J. (1991), *Varieties of Moral Personality: Ethics and Psychological Realism.*

Gilligan, C., and Murphy, J. M. (1979), "Development from Adolescence to Adulthood: The Philosopher and the Dilemma of the Fact."

Gilligan, C. (1982), *In a Different Voice.*

Kohlberg, L. (1982), "A Reply to Owen Flanagan and Some Comments on the Puka-Goodpaster Debate."

Shweder, R. (1982), "Liberalism as Destiny."

Chapter 6

Cognitive Science and Artificial Intelligence: Philosophical Assumptions and Implications

---

Last week I saw a former student whom I had neither seen nor consciously thought of since the time of her graduation four years before. Nonetheless, the instant she came into my visual field I experienced a mental cramp and found myself saying, "Hi, Nancy, are you still working in Washington, D.C.?"

Such experiences are commonplace, but nevertheless remarkable. What exactly did I do when I remembered Nancy's name and where she had gone off to work?

One possibility—and one of the more popular ones, judging by the dominant metaphors in the field—is that the mind is organized like an automated office and contains an elaborate filing system. Given the visual cue of Nancy's face, I matched it with a name and then went to a file that contained propositional information about her.

Supposing for a moment that the office metaphor is remotely correct, more questions arise. How is the office organized? Are the files coded by faces or names, or both? Can names get you to faces as easily as faces can get you to names? If not, why not? If the files are coded by names are they simply alphabetical, or alphabetical by date (so that Nancy was in the 1979 batch)? Is there one set of files for students I have taught, another for friends from my college days, and another for my immediate family?

Why don't I remember what Nancy's job is? I seem to remember that she told me what her job would be at the same time she told me

The best introduction to cognitive psychology is John Anderson's *Cognitive Psychology and Its Implications* (1980). For cognitive science, see Neil A. Stillings et al., *Cognitive Science: An Introduction* (1987), and Philip N. Johnson-Laird, *The Computer and the Mind: An Introduction to Cognitive Science* (1988), and for an excellent history of the field, see Howard Gardner, *The Mind's New Science: A History of the Cognitive Revolution* (1985). For traditional Artificial Intelligence, see John Haugeland, *Artificial Intelligence: The Very Idea* (1985), and for the classical statement of the new connectionist AI, see D. Rumelhart, J. McClelland, and the PDP Research Group, *Parallel Distributed Processing: Explorations in the Microstructure of Cognition*, two volumes (1986).

where it would be. Are the files, therefore, not comprehensive or are they sloppily organized, and if so, whose fault is that?

Further questions arise about how the searches and information retrieval get done. Who or what performs the match of face to name and who or what goes to the file which contains the further propositional information? I certainly did not experience my conscious self doing any of this.

Perhaps this is evidence for a secretarial homunculus, a sort of mental office manager, who races around performing the boring matches and searches and only passes on information to me when I, as the executive director of the operation, really need it. But if there really is such an office manager in my mind, he or she or it is really quite a bit smarter than I am, and possesses skills that I certainly don't have. It is inconceivable to me that I could figure out a filing and retrieval system, as well as perform the filing and retrieval, for the 100 trillion bits of information which, according to some estimates, are encoded in my brain.

Perhaps there isn't just one superintelligent secretarial homunculus in my mind, but instead a multifarious force of low-level specialists—what Dennett calls an "army of idiots"—who run around at high speed, passing around the information that I, the commander-in-chief, need.

Thinking of this army of idiots as comprised of the various components of the brain helps refine the well-run office analogy. After all we know that there are no ordinary files, and nothing written in English in our brains, nor are there little people running about performing information-processing tasks.

This more neuroscientific and less anthropomorphic view, however, gives rise to puzzles of its own. Suppose we assume, as many do, that the neural network stores things in a code—call it neuronese—that it understands. Notice first that if the brain understands a code, it is not so idiotic after all. Furthermore, if all brain messages are written in neuronese rather than in English, it's hard to understand how it is that what I remember, I remember in English. The conclusion that suggests itself is that there has to be a mechanism which translates messages back and forth from neuronese to English. Who or what does the translating? *Ex hypothesi* it cannot be the neurons because they only understand neuronese, and I cannot be doing it because I only understand English. It looks as if we need a bilingual homunculus who can translate messages between neuronese and English.

This exercise is not intended to establish any particular substantive view about how people remember, nor to make you worry that your mind is more like a committee than a unified whole (although I think this is true). It is simply intended to indicate how extraordinarily difficult it can be to account for some very basic things we do, and for some fundamental capacities we have. Wondering and worrying about such matters and taking pleasure in the philosophical knots to which they lead is at the heart of contemporary work in cognitive science. Cognitive science is not a discipline so much as it is an increasingly well-organized committee of disciplines and subdisciplines, all of which claim to have something to contribute to our understanding of mentality. More specifically, cognitive science is a confederation of philosophy (especially philosophy of mind, philosophy of language, epistemology, and logic), cognitive psychology, neuroscience, linguistics, and computer science.

Cognitive Science: The Basic Program

Surprisingly, cognitive scientists start by sharing an assumption with behaviorists to the effect that there are lawlike regularities between stimuli and responses. They part company with behaviorists, however, by claiming that any theory of mind that fails to talk about the intervening mental processes that link these stimuli and responses will be unacceptably incomplete.

It is a remarkable fact, for example, that in conversation people generally respond in appropriate ways to the verbal stimuli produced by those with whom they are conversing. This generalization, however, tells us nothing about how people understand the words they hear, how they process and generate speech so rapidly, or why people but not dogs are so good at this sort of thing.

In one of the founding documents of contemporary cognitive science, *Plans and the Structure of Behavior,* Miller, Galanter, and Pribram quote approvingly from a seminal paper by E. C. Tolman in which this point is made forcefully:[1]

> [The brain] is far more like a map control room than it is like an old-fashioned telephone exchange. The stimuli, which are allowed in, are not connected by just simple one-to-one switches to the outgoing responses. Rather, the incoming impulses are usually worked over and elaborated in the central control room into a tentative cognitivelike map of the environment. And it is this tentative map, indicating routes and paths and environmental relationships, which finally determines what responses, if any, the animal will finally release.[2]

Although Tolman's specific metaphor of the map room is by no means universally accepted, his emphasis on the complexity of men-

tal processes, on the remarkable degree to which stimuli are transformed, elaborated, and related to each other before intelligent action
occurs, is the guiding assumption of contemporary cognitive science.
John Haugeland puts it this way: "Cognitivism in psychology and
philosophy is roughly the position that intelligent behavior can (only)
be explained by appeal to internal 'cognitive processes.'"[3]

Another important assumption of cognitive science is also contained in the quotation from Tolman, namely, that the mind is a representational system. The basic idea is simple, although as we will
see, as philosophically slippery as they come. Think of a banana.
Now think about the beliefs you have about bananas, for example,
about what they look like, what kinds of creatures like to eat them,
where they grow, and so on. Notice that you not only have a complex
set of beliefs about bananas, but that your very ability to entertain my
suggestion that you think about a banana means you have a specific
idea as to what the printed word "banana" means. This external representation—"banana"—is a meaningful symbol to you.

Beliefs and ideas are mental attitudes which invariably lie in
"aboutness" relations to specific meaningful contents. For example,
suppose you believe—that is, you are in a believing attitude as opposed to a hoping or expecting attitude—that monkeys love bananas.
That monkeys love bananas is the content of your belief; it is what
your belief is about. Your belief represents the world in the sense that
you would do well to act on the basis of this belief if, say, you were
to have a monkey as a pet.

Notice that we confront here our old friend *intentionality*, the property of mental states being essentially related to meaningful content.
The idea that the mind is a representational system, then, is the idea
that the mind is an intentional system.

It should come as no surprise, given the very general and (except
to behaviorists) uncontroversial assumptions about regularities and
intentionality, that cognitive scientists cast their explanatory nets very
widely. For example, in the first significant text in cognitive psychology proper, published in 1966, Ulric Neisser says,

> As used here, the term "cognition" refers to all processes by
> which the sensory input is transformed, reduced, elaborated,
> stored, recovered, and used. It is concerned with these processes
> even when they operate in the absence of relevant stimulation,
> as in images and hallucinations. . . . [G]iven such a sweeping
> definition, it is apparent that cognition is involved in everything
> a human being might possibly do; that every psychological phe-
> nomenon is a cognitive phenomenon.[4]

In a more recent text, John Anderson simply says that "cognitive psychology attempts to understand the nature of human intelligence and how people think."[5]

Insofar as the cognitivist research program is unified primarily by the core assumptions about the complexity and the representational nature of mind, and very little by shared substantive doctrine, it is not surprising that almost nothing is excluded from the possible domain of cognitive science by its major proponents. To whatever extent cognition, broadly construed, turns out to be relevant to the explanation of emotion, social behavior, psychopathology, or physical skills, the cognitive scientist will be interested.

With respect to style of explanation, cognitive scientists mix what Dennett calls the *design* and the *intentional* stances. Design-stance analyses, according to Dennett, are "all alike in relying on the notion of *function*, which is purpose relative or teleological. That is, a design of a system breaks it up into larger or smaller functional parts, and design-stance predictions are generated by assuming that each functional part will function properly."[6]

Design-stance analyses are especially appropriate for talking about cognitive mechanisms operating at subpersonal levels (subpersonal in the sense that the processes in question are inaccessible to the person herself). If, for example, I explain your comprehension of this sentence in terms of a mechanism that encodes information about visual arrays, organizes a search of the mental lexicon, comes up with semantic and syntactic analyses of the visual arrays, and comprehends, I have given a design-stance account by dividing comprehension into smaller functional components and submechanisms.[7]

The intentional stance, unlike the design stance, involves open use of ordinary mental concepts: belief, desire, hope, expectation, imagining, and the like. Take the phenomenon whereby people tend to generalize from familiar and easily accessible cases—Tversky and Kahneman call this the "availability" bias—so that, for example, if I ask someone to estimate whether it is more common for English words to being with *k* or have *k* in the third slot, most people will answer that *k* is more common in the first slot. This is, as it turns out, false.

The explanation for the phenomenon is that people answer by imagining words like "kid" and "pike," find that they can think up more words that start with *k* than have *k* in the third slot, believe that what they can think up is relevant to the task and guess in favor of the first slot. This explanation is, as philosophers like to say, shot through with the intentional idiom.

Cognitive scientists often weave the two explanatory styles together. For example, the design-stance explanation of sentence comprehension might well advert to a full-blown intentional state, such as your desire to understand, in order to account for why the subpersonal sentence comprehension mechanism is activated in the first place. Alternatively, the intentional explanation of the availability bias with the letter k presumably calls for a design-stance account of why it is easier to remember words on the basis of first letters than on the basis of third ones.

There is one additional point worth emphasizing regarding explanation. Most cognitive scientists are not primarily interested in offering analyses of the mind at the neural level, even though most think that mental processes are ultimately neural processes. They are not interested in providing an analysis from the perspective of what Dennett calls the "physical stance." Perhaps surprisingly, neither design-stance nor intentional-stance explanations require mentioning the actual physical and chemical properties of the nervous system.

The standard defense of this preferred, so-called functional, style of explanation comes by way of analogy with computer science. In computer science there are two well understood levels of explanation: the level of software and the level of hardware. If I ask you how a particular computer performs some arithmetic calculation, why, for example, given the input 9 it gives the output 81, you can either tell me a very long story about the electrical and mechanical properties of the physical device, or you can tell me about its program, for example, that, given any number n, it performs the operation $n \times n$.

The first answer is the one most relevant from the point of view of the electrical engineer, the second from the point of view of the programmer. One might think of the cognitive scientist as being interested in offering an abstract functional description of the mind. He is interested in offering an analysis of cognitive processes in functional terms, at the level of the mind's program(s), not at the level of hardware.

The widespread confidence in this explanatory approach, in the idea that the level of functional explanation can operate in total independence of explanation at the physical level, has become harder to maintain recently. First, new connectionist models in computer science have called the distinction between software and hardware into question. Second, challenges from both connectionists and neuroscientists have shown that the best protection against bad theorizing at the level of cognition is to try to maintain maximal consistency among all levels of explanation. There are always indefinitely many functional stories compatible with the input-output relations. Constraints on such stories and choices among incompatible contenders require attention to our best theories at the physical level. Therefore, we must demand that explanations of mental function cohere as best they can with the best current models of brain function, and this can only be done if we firmly commit ourselves *qua* cognitive scientists to making use of all levels of explanation at once.[8]

Kant, Cognitive Science, and the Anticipation of Experience

When cognitive scientists discuss their philosophical forebears one hears the name of Immanuel Kant more than any other. (Descartes is the only competition, and he wins only at MIT.) This, as I see it, is just right. Kant laid both the substantive and methodological foundations for modern cognitive science. On the substantive side, Kant was responsible for what he himself called the "Copernican revolution" in epistemology, the revolution of construing the mind as active in the construction of knowledge. On the methodological side, Kant spelled out the logical structure of the still-canonical method for inferring hidden mental processes. Kant called his method of inference from words, behavior, and pieces of knowledge to hidden mental processes, *transcendental deduction*. We will look at both his substantive and methodological contributions in turn.

On the substantive side, Kant saw his philosophy of mind as an alternative to Hume's empiricist model of mind. Kant took his empiricist rivals to be promoting two main theses, one psychological, the other epistemological.

The psychological thesis was that all knowledge originates with sense impressions. Higher-level ideas and concepts are simply complex associations of sense impressions. The epistemological thesis was that complex ideas correctly represent the world to the extent that they can be traced back to sense impressions in the right sort of way. The idea of a unicorn, for example, involves the association of the impression of a horse with an impression of a horn. That is its psychology. "Unicorn" fails to refer, however, because at the level of our sense impressions, horses and horns fail to occur together. This is why we say that unicorns don't exist.

Kant saw Hume's philosophical skepticism as the result of these two theses. Take the concept of causality. Hume notices that when we take a complex judgment such as "The sun causes the sand on the beach to get hot" and trace it back to its sensory components, all we end up with are sense impressions of the sun shining and hot sand occurring together; all we experience is the "constant conjunction" of the sun and hot sand (actually not even that, because the sun does not make the sand hot in winter). Nowhere, however, in sense experience do we see the causality between the sun and the hot sand. Causality then is not so much a phenomenon in the real world as it is a concept we as subjects add to sense experience. Hume concluded that because metaphysics (literally the study of what is beyond physics) is the science which is supposed to give certain knowledge of the way the world is from the God's-eye view, and because concepts like causality are subjective, that is, mental, there simply is nothing metaphysically interesting, that is, ultimate and objective, to say about them.

Kant's strategy is to take Hume's hint that certain concepts are superadded to sense experience, and to frame this idea in an entirely different, revolutionary way. Kant accepts Hume's argument that we never experience causality as such, or space and time as such or material substance as such, or the principles of logic as such. But he insists that the fact that all humans talk about the world in logical terms—as if it were comprised of distinct material objects, occupying space and time, and interacting in accordance with causal principles—is reason to think that we supply these forms, concepts, and categories a priori.

The concepts of logic, causality, substance, space, and time are, of course, subjective. Other creatures, paramecia, for example, probably do not construct their world in terms of these concepts and categories. But these mental structures are subjective in an utterly healthy sense. They are universal species-specific ways in which we organize reality. Without these structures operating as a system of expectations about the world, in anticipation of experience, we would never be able to build up the fantastically complex, adaptive, rule-governed picture of the world we achieve at a very young age.

In speaking of Hume and his fellow empiricists in the preface to the second edition of the *Critique of Pure Reason,* Kant says,

> Hitherto it has been assumed [by the empiricists] that all our knowledge must conform to objects. . . . We must . . . make trial whether we may not have more success in the tasks of metaphysics, if we suppose that objects must conform to our knowledge. . . . We should then be proceeding precisely on the lines of Copernicus' primarily hypothesis. Failing of satisfactory progress in explaining the movements of the heavenly bodies on the supposition that they all revolved around the spectator, he tried whether he might not have better success if he made the spectator to revolve and the stars to remain at rest.[9]

Kant's Copernican revolution then comes to this: we supply form and structure to experience by way of a rich system of a priori mental structures. Were it not for the rich initial state of the cognitive system, experience would simply go in one ear and out the other.[10]

One caveat is in order: there is no need to read Kant as an extreme nativist. (Piaget has seen this most clearly.) No doubt we need a rich innate rule system to get started, but then the system can enrich itself. One might distinguish, therefore, between two senses of "a priori": as referring to the structures and concepts in the initial rule system, such as the propensity to think inductively; or as referring to structures and rules which subsequently join the system, such as my expectation that it will be cold in Boston in February. The second type of structure is a priori in the sense that once it joins the system it functions anticipatorily. Reading Kant as a moderate on the nature-nurture, learning versus preformation issue is just right. Those cognitive scientists looking for nativistic philosophical inspiration invariably choose Descartes over Kant.

In any case, once we take the Copernican turn in the philosophy of mind, the question naturally arises: what method should we use to draw up an accurate map of mental terrain? Given that the underlying features of mind are not directly visible, how should we infer the nature of mind?

This is where transcendental deduction comes in. A transcendental deduction, in the Kantian scheme of things, is an inference strategy that allows us to start with observables and go behind the scenes. Strictly speaking, a transcendental deduction is a misnomer, since all transcendental deductions are instances of inductive reasoning, specifically, eliminative induction. Conclusions of transcendental deductions are always probabilistic, never certain. The basic form of a transcendental deduction is as follows:

1. Start with a fact or set of facts.
2. Ask how the fact or set of facts could be as they are. That is, ask how the state of affairs in question is possible, how it could have come to be the way it is.
3. Calculate the contribution observable events and processes make to the solution of the "how is this state of affairs possible" question. If the observable events and processes provide a satisfactory solution, Stop. Otherwise, proceed to (4), the transcendental deduction proper.
4. Cautiously infer the necessary unobserved or unobservable events and processes to fill out the answer to the "how is this state of affairs possible" question.

Reasoning transcendentally is a general feature of reasoning in situations where there are no eyewitnesses. Thus transcendental reasoning is common in criminology and history as well as in psychology and physics.

Sherlock Holmes was forever performing transcendental deductions. When Dr. Watson says "Brilliant deduction, Holmes," he is almost always referring to this kind of inductive reasoning.

Holmes usually starts with some mysterious state of affairs, say, a murder in which there are no fingerprints or footprints. There is, however, a cigar ash next to the dead person's body. The dead man smoked, but he did not smoke Cuban cigars, and this is a Cuban cigar ash. Holmes wonders, How is it possible that there is a Cuban cigar ash next to the dead man's body? He infers that the murderer must smoke Cuban cigars. Since the jealous stepson is the only person in all of Britain who smokes Cuban cigars, he must have committed the murder (or been set up by his sister who had access to his cigar box, or whatever).

There is, however, an epistemologically significant difference worth emphasizing between the use of transcendental reasoning in criminology and in the science of the mind. Notice that transcendental reasoning is required in criminology when there are no eyewitnesses or when the eyewitnesses are not talking. In criminology the transcendental step is normally required because of practical difficulties; no one saw or reported what transpired. There is reason to think that the necessity of transcendental reasoning in the science of the mind, as in subatomic physics, is necessitated by an "in principle" difficulty. The difficulty is simply this: of all possible observers, each person is the only candidate in a position to provide direct testimony about the structure, content, and processes of his or her own mind— to give the sort of eyewitness accounts which would obviate the need for transcendental reasoning. But all the available evidence indicates that we are notoriously bad at providing accurate self-assessments, especially, but not exclusively, at the level of cognitive processing. But if no one, including its owner, is in a position to given an eyewitness account of mind, it makes sense that transcendental reasoning would, of necessity, be the canonical procedure in cognitive science.

Kant invariably proceeds transcendentally when treating matters mental. One of Kant's most important transcendental deductions is the one locating the concept of causality in the a priori conceptual system. The explicit version of his argument runs as follows: First, Kant points out that causal talk is pervasive in ordinary discourse as well as in physics (where principles like "every effect has a cause" are considered self-evident). Next, Kant acknowledges the force of Hume's argument that we never see causality as such, we only see constant conjunctions between events; and that no beliefs based wholly on sense data are self-evident. Finally, and this is novel, Kant asks how our concept of causality is possible if neither its substance nor its epistemic character originate in sense data. His answer is that it must be supplied a priori by us.

Throughout the *Critique* and the *Prolegomena* Kant offers similar sorts of arguments for his view that the notions of time, space, substance, number, logic, self, and many others, cannot be accounted for in purely sensory, a posteriori terms and that, therefore, they must have a priori components.[11]

The point I want to make here is the following: Kant made the crucial substantive and methodological moves which make cognitive science as we know it today both possible and respectable. He took the stance that the mind actively and surreptitiously contributes to the organization of knowledge and behavior, and he promoted the "transcendental" method as a respectable but fallible tool for revealing this contribution.

Transcendental Reasoning: Two Experiments

Here I want to discuss two sets of experimental data and look at the transcendental deductions cognitive scientists perform on these data. This will help us get clearer on some of the difficulties, especially the so-called underdetermination associated with the transcendental method, and it will give a preliminary sense of just how radical a reconceptualization of mind cognitive psychology might require.

Sternberg on Symbolic Memory
In an important paper, "High-Speed Scanning in Human Memory," Saul Sternberg asks: How is information of recently encoded memories retrieved?[12] Notice (by way of getting clear on the changing nature of scientific intuitions) how much this perfectly sensible question itself assumes: first, that memory exists; second, that memories are representationally encoded; third that there are mechanisms which retrieve information from memory; and fourth, that these mechanisms operate in a rule-governed way. Both Cartesian and behavioristic theories would have had trouble with at least one of these assumptions, as would certain connectionists (see below).

Sternberg's experimental procedure involved having subjects memorize lists containing some subset of the numbers 1 to 10. The lists varied in size from one to six digits. On each trial the subject saw a randomly generated list, for example, 2, 7, 3, 9. The list was visually displayed for just over one second. After a two-second delay a test digit appeared, say, 3. The subject was to pull lever A if the test digit was on the memorized list, lever B if it was not. Sternberg's data consisted of measurements of the time it took from presentation of the test digit to the pulling of the appropriate lever.

Now you might wonder how something as pedestrian as reaction-time data could help us figure out how people perform this (short-term) memory task. Why doesn't Sternberg simply ask people how they perform the task? The answer is that many people have only the vaguest of intuitions as to how they do such things, and even those who have powerful intuitions are often wrong. This will become clear if we look more closely at the experiment. Without knowing anything at all about how memory works, we can think of three possible ways we might perform this task.

(1) Mind's Eye Sees All. On this model the mind simply fetches the entire list and "looks" at it to "see" if the test digit is on it. This model has some intuitive credibility from situations such as this: a house-mate calls from upstairs and asks you if his glasses are on the kitchen table. You walk into the kitchen, look at the table, and say yes or no.

(2) Self-Terminating Serial Search. On this model the mind goes down the list serially from left to right and answers as soon as it makes a match in the case of a positive answer, or as soon as it gets to the end of the list without a match in the case of a negative answer. This model has credibility from situations such as this: You've lost your glasses. You say to yourself "I must have left them on a tabletop, in a coat pocket, or at the office." You start by looking on all the tabletops. Next you start to rummage through the pockets of the coat you wore earlier in the day and find your glasses in the first pocket you reach into. Search terminates. (You do not continue on to the office.)

(3) Exhaustive Serial Search. On this model the mind goes down the list serially from left to right and answers yes or no only when it gets to the end of the list. If the match occurs before the end of the list, it is registered. But the mind still proceeds to the end of the list before answering. It is hard to think of examples of situations where we consciously operate this way. But consider: You are an eyewitness to a crime and are called in to identify a suspect in a police lineup consisting of six people. You start by looking at the first person on your left and proceed to the right. The third person looks just like the criminal; you register this, but continue to the end of the lineup before you point your finger. The exhaustive search takes place, so to speak, just to make sure that you are not mistaken in your match of memory to face.

Fortunately, since allegedly this is science we are discussing, these three hypotheses predict different reaction times. The *Mind's Eye Sees All* model predicts that the reaction time will be the same no matter what the location of the test digit is on the list. For example, if the memorized list is 1, 8, 9, 2, 4, reaction time should be equal for the test digit 1 or 4. The reason is simple: on the *Mind's Eye Sees All* model the entire list is conjured up and "seen all at once," rather than processed from left to right. There either is or is not a match.

The *Self-Terminating Search* model predicts that reaction times will vary depending on the location of the test digit on the list. Responses should take longer the later (in terms of left to right) the test digit occurs on the list, and negative responses should always take longer than positive ones.

Like the *Mind's Eye Sees All* model, the *Exhaustive Serial Search* model predicts that reaction times will not vary with location on a particular list. However, unlike the *Mind's Eye Sees All* model, the *Exhaustive Serial Search* model predicts that reaction times will vary with the length of the list. The reason is obvious: if a search is exhaustive in the sense that we go to the end of a list even after a match has been made, reaction time should take longer, the longer the list.

Results: Sternberg found that the mean reaction time varied linearly with the length of the memorized list and that reaction times were the same for positive and negative responses. We now need to ask a Kantian sort of question about these data. How are they possible? They are possible only if our minds perform exhaustive serial left-to-right searches on tasks such as these. This is exactly Sternberg's conclusion. He claims that we "scan" serially and exhaustively at the rate of about 25 to 30 digits per second. Sternberg uses the "scanning" metaphor in part because the speed here is too fast for the mechanism to involve the left-to-right inaudible vocalization some of his subjects report.

Transcendental reasoning is a variety of inductive inference. This means that Sternberg's conclusions are, as philosophers like to say, radically underdetermined by the available evidence. A skeptic, for example, might argue that the *Mind's Eye Sees All* model is also compatible with Sternberg's data. He could argue that whereas the *Mind's Eye Sees All* model predicts no variation in reaction time, depending on the location of the test digit on a particular memorized list, it does not necessarily predict against reaction-time differences for lists of different lengths. Thus, it might take longer—for reasons having to do with the access mechanisms—to conjure up longer lists for scanning, but once conjured up the response could be all or none.

Most physical theories are similarly underdetermined by the evidence. Nevertheless, skeptical doubts about logically possible alternatives do nothing to undermine credible inferences from carefully controlled experiments.

Now, I take it that most people's intuitions, insofar as they have them, would have predicted against the *Exhaustive Serial Search* model. First, there are relatively few good examples of this sort of model operating in intuitively familiar domains. Second, and this is related to the first, the *Exhaustive Serial Search* model is not optimally efficient, or rather it is only optimally efficient if there are preexisting nonoptimal features of the system. For example, an exhaustive search of a police lineup is only optimal for a system which is prone to making matching errors. If one were an omnipotent and omniscient designer one would surely make us infallible at memory matches and then wire us in accordance with the *Mind's Eye Sees All* model or the *Self-Terminating Search* model. They just have to be faster.

Two philosophically important points begin to emerge. First, our intuitions are not to be trusted very far in generating knowledge of mental mechanisms. Second, our minds have design constraints; we may well not be designed by an omnipotent and omniscient designer.[13] The mind may turn out to be something of a Rube Goldberg device, what Marvin Minsky calls a "kludge."

Shepard and Metzler on Imagistic Representation
Although it seems utterly plausible to assume that the mind is a representational system, it is much harder to say how it goes about representing what it represents when engaged in higher-level mental processes such as thinking and remembering.

Let me try to make the difficulty clear. In the world of everyday objects the two most common modes of representation are pictures and words. The picture on your driver's license represents you, as does the name on your driver's license. The predominance of visual and linguistic representation in our everyday world reflects a common and quite possibly justified epistemological prejudice, namely, that vision is the primary sensory modality, and language the cognitive capacity par excellence.

On the other hand, most people will also acknowledge the existence of mental representations which strongly resemble perception in the other four sensory modalities: taste, touch, hearing and smell. My current memories of the taste of orange juice, the smell of a skunk, the opening bars of Beethoven's Fifth, and the feel of a baseball seem to strongly resemble the original sense experiences.

Taken as a whole, the introspective data support what I will call the *six-code* theory of higher-level mental representation. The underlying idea is that our minds represent things in a total of six different ways. Five of these ways are tied to the sensory modalities; the other is abstract, propositional, and quasi-linguistic.

Because the internal representations that occur in the five sensory codes occur in a form closely tied to the sensory modality from which they originated, they can be described as imagistic. Because those that occur in the propositional code occur in a form closely tied to representation in natural language, they can be described as non-imagistic. (The six-code theory, of course, still allows the visual code and the propositional code to be dominant.)

For all its intuitive plausibility there are problems with this theory, especially if it is taken literally. There simply are no actual pictures, sounds, odors, or words inside people's brains. If we ask a person to visualize her mother's face, imagine her favorite piece of music, or think of the smell of milk chocolate, we will not be able to discover any sights, sounds, or smells in her brain. Furthermore, we will not find that her eyes, ears, and nose are in anything like the states they are in when she is experiencing the real things.[14]

Many philosophers and cognitive scientists think that all versions of the six-code theory fall right into an "introspective trap."[15] I will refer to the opposing theory as the *unified-code* theory of higher-level mental representation. The basic idea is this: all mental representation occurs in a single code which is abstract and quasi-linguistic.[16]

In its most extreme form the view has consequences such as the following: when you picture Main Street of the town in which you grew up, you are conjuring up a bunch of sentence-like entities that contains information such as: the five-and-dime store is next to the supermarket which is across the street from the florist. Your introspective intuitions notwithstanding, you are not entertaining any kind of picture at all. Alternatively, when you go to an Italian restaurant, examine the menu, mull over the possibilities, and say "I'd love the lasagna," you should not be misled into thinking that you conjured up all the alternative tastes and smells and picked the one which tasted best. That view is preposterous. What happened was that you remembered (propositionally) that you like lasagna more than you do the other choices. The same sort of analysis goes for sound and touch.[17]

The issue dividing the six-code theory and the unified-code theory cannot be resolved, at present anyway, by peering into our brains, nor can it be resolved a priori. We need to look at the experimental evidence and ask: are there or are there not modes of mental representation which are analogous to sensation, and thus in some sense imagistic? Or is all mental representing done in the same way, and is that way quasi linguistic and therefore nonimagistic?

The Shepard and Metzler experiment is crucial in trying to answer this question.[18] Subjects were presented with three pairs of two-dimensional pictures of three-dimensional objects. (See figure 6.1.)

The task was to decide whether or not the paired objects were the same. In situations A and B there is a match. In A the rotation is on the plane of the page, and therefore in two dimensions, while in B the rotation is into the third dimension. In C there is no match.

The subjects were tested with additional pairs in which the degree of rotation between the two figures varied. As in Saul Sternberg's experiment, reaction time was measured.

The introspective reports here are interesting. Almost all subjects claimed that they performed the matches or discovered the mismatch by mentally rotating one of the figures until it was congruent with the other. Was there an introspective trap lurking here?

This is where the reaction-time data come in handy. Shepard and Metzler found that the reaction times were a linear function of the degree of rotation. That is, a positive answer in a situation where the figures were at a 160-degree rotation distance took twice as long as one in which the figures were at an 80-degree rotation distance. Shepard and Metzler also found that tasks A and B took the same amount of time. That is, processing a two-dimensional problem takes no longer than processing a three-dimensional one.

Now we can ask our Kantian question: How are these data possible? Shepard and Metzler's transcendental inference is that they are possible only if people in fact mentally represent and then rotate the figures in some medium which is representationally analogous to three-dimensional space.

There is no need to think that subjects rotate actual pictures, but merely that they are doing something more spatial than linguistic. Why else would the reaction times vary linearly with the degree of rotation?

It is worth emphasizing that the data warrant a spatial interpretation rather than a pictorial one. People blind from birth can solve the identical rotation problems by analyzing blocks tactilely. They too introspect an abstract process of spatial rotation, but clearly in their case the mode of representation cannot be visual or pictorial.

How comfortable one feels about Shepard and Metzler's transcendental deduction will depend in part on one's attitude about the degree to which introspective reports should or should not be allowed to add to or detract from the credibility of experimental data. Notice that Shepard and Metzler's interpretation that some kind of spatial transformation takes place is more plausible the more credibility we assign to the subjects' reports that they are in fact mentally rotating

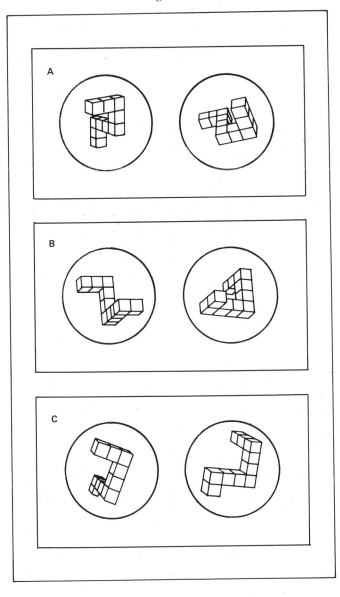

Figure 6.1
Three pairs of two-dimensional pictures of three-dimensional objects. (Reprinted with permission from Shepard and Metzler 1971.)

images. If we bracket or dismiss these reports as irrelevant, it is less clear how to interpret the data.

For example, a unified-code theorist who was also an anti-introspectionist might argue along the following lines: we know that all geometrical spaces can be represented in the language of analytic geometry, a language that makes no essential use of spatial displays. For example, in the language of analytic geometry, the equation $x = y$ designates a straight line which bisects the x and y axes in Cartesian coordinate space. This is the possibility proof that the mind could conceivably function by analyzing the Shepard and Metzler figures and representing their spatial properties in some linguistic mode comparable to analytic geometry; the mind could then compute congruence in roughly the way one would in the language of analytic geometry, that is, by manipulating sentences.[19]

I have no intention of trying to resolve the question of the number and types of representational modes here, although I do think the unified-code theorist has the harder, although by no means an impossible, case to make. I do want to emphasize an epistemological point, however. Transcendental reasoning is always radically underdetermined by the available evidence. There is always an enormous number, in some cases an infinite number, of possible hypotheses compatible with some set of reaction-time data. Now, if there is an infinite number of hypotheses compatible with any data set, it would seem that we cannot even be sure that we are getting closer to the truth by eliminating extremely implausible hypotheses because there will always be an infinite number of viable candidates remaining.

It is easy to give in to worries such as these and conclude that cognitive science is, strictly speaking, impossible. But here one has to be careful. First, it is true of all observation and inference that we cannot ever be absolutely certain we are right. Second, the extremely inferential nature of transcendental reasoning is worth noting, but it cannot be a reason for abandoning all hopes for a science of mind. After all, one of our most respected sciences, subatomic physics, is as radically transcendental as cognitive science. Third, some of the worries about infinite numbers of hypotheses are worries about substantively identical, but notationally different hypotheses. Fourth, all the usual normative constraints on scientific reasoning can be applied to transcendental reasoning in psychology and cognitive science. The project is to postulate the simplest, most comprehensive, and predictive hypotheses about cognitive mechanisms compatible with the data and with the rest of science. These hypotheses will be rejected or refined as the data or the state of the sciences as a whole change. Transcendental inferences in cognitive science, therefore, suffer from no unique epistemological afflictions. They are as subject both to error and to the mechanisms of critical self-correction—which, happily, are partly constitutive of the enterprise—as the rest of science.

Cognitive Science and Self-Knowledge

In discussing both Sternberg's and Shepard and Metzler's experiments I mentioned the issue of the status of introspective reports. In Sternberg's study most subjects report engaging in "subvocal" self-terminating searches; no one reported doing an exhaustive serial search. Nevertheless, all the data point to the latter hypothesis. Sternberg's experimental conclusion, therefore, requires treating his subjects' introspective reports as irrelevant, indeed as simply wrong.

The Shepard and Metzler paradigm, on the other hand, uses subjective introspective data and objective reaction-time data to support each other. Without the introspective support for the mental rotation hypothesis, it is, as we saw above, not clear how we should interpret the reaction-time data.

Here I want to ask, What implications does work in cognitive science have for the problems associated with self-knowledge? Are there areas in which we have reliable conscious access to our minds, and areas in which we do not? Can introspection obviate the need for transcendental reasoning by providing direct information about the mind?

Dennett suggests a useful taxonomy for talking about these matters. He distinguishes between *autophenomenology* and *heterophenomenology*.[20] Autophenomenology is commentary on a psychological system from the inside, by an insider, namely, the owner. Autophenomenology is necessarily performed from what Thomas Nagel calls the "subjective point of view."[21] Heterophenomenology, on the other hand, is commentary on a psychological system from an outsider's point of view (even the owner can take this point of view). Heterophenomenology, therefore, is performed from what Nagel calls an "objective point of view."

The "phenomenology" is by way of emphasizing that whether we take the "auto" or "hetero" point of view, we are dealing with appearances—from which we will then try to infer transcendentally the hidden realities.

The advantage of this "auto-hetero" taxonomy is that it carries no connotations and begs no questions regarding the relative accuracy or relative degree of eyewitnessing involved in the two forms of studying mind. Borrowing from literary theory, Dennett suggests that we think of both the autophenomenology and heterophenomenology as producing a text or a story. The epistemological project is to discern any patterns in the relative veridicality of the two sorts of stories, and to be open to the possibility that in certain cases the outsider, that is, the critic, may understand the story better than the author does.

The question, therefore, can now be put this way: what do we know about the relative reliability of autophenomenological and heterophenomenological reports? What should we do when the reports conflict?

The traditional philosophical and commensensical answer to this question has an explicitly Cartesian cast: each person is in a special epistemic position to observe the goings-on of his or her own mind. Autophenomenology is, if not completely infallible, the only reliable method by which to understand mentality; it certainly cannot be overridden by heterophenomenology. For the sake of clarity I will distinguish among five logically distinct forms of Cartesianism regarding self-knowledge.

(1) Simple Cartesianism (this is the only one I am certain Descartes espoused). One knows for sure that one has a mind, that one is a thinking thing.

(2) State Cartesianism. In addition to knowing that one has a mind, each person has infallible and privileged access to the intentional and phenomenal states she is in. Every normal person is in unique and perfectly reliable touch with whether she is in a state of belief, desire, hope, happiness, or fear. We know our own moods, itches, pains, and afterimages for what they are and as they are.

(3) Content Cartesianism. In addition to knowing that one has a mind and what state it is in, each individual has privileged and perfect access to the contents of the intentional states she knows herself to be in. So in addition to knowing that I am in a state of desire rather than a state of belief or horror, I also know what I am desirous of, I know that the content of my desire is a cold drink, that I desire [a cold drink]. It is not a desire that you have a cold drink or that Gorbachev sleep well tonight; it is a desire whose content is that I have a cold drink.

(4) Causal Cartesianism. One has special epistemic access not only to the mental states one is in, and in the case of intentional or propositional-attitude states to the contents of these state; one also has special access to the causes of the states and their contents. For example, I know that I desire a cold drink because I have just exercised and exercising causes water loss, which causes thirst.

(5) Process Cartesianism. One has privileged access (at the functional level, not at the neural level) to the internal mental processes.

For example, if I ask you how many windows there were in the house you grew up in, and then after you answer, ask you how you figured out the answer, you will tell me that you pictured the house in your mind's eye, and then went from room to room counting windows. If Process Cartesianism is true, you know what you are talking about.

The very existence of an experimental cognitive psychology whose main experimental procedure consists of transcendental deduction is a challenge to the latter constellation of beliefs. No one, however, as far as I can tell, seriously challenges Simple Cartesianism. The universal certainty that we are each the location of a mental life is in some important sense the fact that makes sense of the enterprise of the science of the mind. Therefore, let us examine the other four Cartesian views on self-knowledge.

Virtually no cognitive scientists espouse Process Cartesianism. The reason is that the evidence for it is so bad. Take Sternberg's study, a case where the task is simple, people are excellent at performing the matches between the test digits and the short memorized list, and there is nothing emotionally loaded about the task. Most subjects, however, are seriously mistaken in their descriptions of the mechanisms underlying performance on the task: no one ever claims to be performing an exhaustive serial search.

At a more intuitive level, what mental processes account for your understanding of the words in this sentence? How is the alphabet stored in your long-term memory? Complete this word: **ppy. How did you do that? What number comes before 2,437? How did you do that so fast? Picture your own face upside down. How did you do that? How do you recognize msspilled wurds? Ha! You had a little trouble with that one, didn't you? How come? The point is that most people haven't a clue as to how they do any of these things.

In the end there are three sorts of evidence regarding Process Cartesianism, one pro, two con. First, there are cases where there is reason to think that the autophenomenology is close to the mark. For example, in the Shepard and Metzler study, "mental rotation" looks to be the right functional description of the underlying process. Second, there are the Sternberg-type cases where, the subjects' confidence notwithstanding, they are seriously mistaken about the underlying processes. Third, there are cases such as the intuitive ones I just mentioned, in which there is no privileged access about underlying processes—there is simply no access at all. Process Cartesianism, therefore, is false.[22]

State Cartesianism, the view that I know what state I am in and Content Cartesianism, the view that I have special access to the contents of my mind, seem more plausible than Process Cartesianism.

But we can cause immediate difficulties for State Cartesianism. First, because consciousness is serial, we tend to be aware of only one state at a time. But the mind is usually in more than one state at a time. I may know that I am now typing English sentences, but my mind is in many more states than that single belief state. It is also in states relevant to the production of English sentences by way of my fingers rather than by way of my speech mechanisms. From a scientific perspective I have reason to think that I am in these other states as well as the ones I am occurrently or serially aware of. But I am hardly in natural, immediate, or infallible touch with these states or with what they are like. Second, people sometimes express confusion about what state they are in fact in. There are uncertainties about whether some sensation is a pain, a tickle, or an itch, and it is often notoriously hard to distinguish among certain moods or to describe them. Finally, third parties sometimes reject sincere first-personal state reports, and first persons sometimes become convinced that these third parties are correct in so doing.

If you honestly insist that you are very happy but systematically fail to act as if you are, the heterophenomenological data will justly override your state claim, your sincerity notwithstanding. I can accept that happiness is the state that springs to mind and that its springing to mind provides you with a powerful intuitive motive for saying, "I am happy." I can nevertheless deny that this is the state you are in. So State Cartesianism is false.

If I cannot be sure what state I am in, then Content Cartesianism is also in trouble. On one interpretation the truth of Content Cartesianism depends on the truth of State Cartesianism. This is the relational interpretation, according to which one only knows the content of an intentional state if one knows it as the content of the propositional-attitude state it is in fact associated with. So if Mary does not know whether she desires, fears, loathes, admires, or loves John, then Mary does not knows what intentional state she is in. On a nonrelational interpretation Mary might be said to know the content in each of these cases. She is in complete confusion about which state [John] is the content of. But at least she knows that [John] is the content of whatever state it is that she is in.

It is not clear whether the nonrelational interpretation holds any interest. Even if it does, Content Cartesianism has other problems. First, there are confusions that are unlike Mary's in the following respect. One seems to know that one desires something but does not know what it is that one desires. In such cases we lack the alleged intimate epistemic access to the contents of our minds. Different contents are compatible with the state we are in, and we cannot choose among the contenders. Second, even if we set aside all the latter scenarios of state or content ambiguity and consider only a person's system of declarative, non-emotionally-loaded beliefs, Content Cartesianism still has trouble getting off the ground. This is easy to see. If Content Cartesianism is true, then you should be able to name all your declarative (non-emotionally-loaded) beliefs.

Of course, this cannot be done. The problem is not merely the problem of finding the time to recite all your beliefs; it is simply that you would never be able to remember all your beliefs (nor to infer all the beliefs you are logically committed to hold by virtue of the fact that they are consequences of your other beliefs). But surely the beliefs you fail to remember now are contents of your mind, and you may well remember them at some other time. Thus Content Cartesianism is false; people have no privileged access to the contents of their minds.

One might object that this sweeping naming-test is simply too strong, and suggest an assenting-test in its stead. Thus it might be argued that sufficient evidence for the truth of Content Cartesianism should not depend on a person's ability to conjure up and name all his beliefs, but rather on his ability to assent and dissent to prospective belief candidates. The assenting-test works as follows: I ask you questions, such as "Do you think elephants wear dresses?" and your job is simply to answer yes or no. Your ability to give accurate answers will provide sufficient evidence that you know what is in your mind.

The assenting-test, however, cannot save Content Cartesianism. First, the assenting-test dramatically waters down the degree of privileged access being claimed. After all, the test assumes that one needs another person's (the questioner's) assistance to get to the contents of one's own mind.[23] Second, there are cases where people clearly fail the assenting-test. Consider the Lackner and Garrett experiment discussed earlier.[24] Subjects were divided into two groups: they were all instructed to listen to the left channel on a set of headphones and to ignore the right channel. Both groups heard target sentences such as "The lieutenant put out the lantern" in the attended channel. Meanwhile, in the unattended channel, one group heard sentences which would help fix the meaning of the ambiguous words "put out" in the target sentence, for example, "The lieutenant extinguished the lantern." The other group heard semantically unrelated sentences, such as "The space shuttle blasted off this morning."

Afterwards, all subjects were asked what they had heard in the unattended channel. Answer: "Nothing, I was told not to pay attention to that channel!" (This well-known phenomenon is called the

"Broadbent filtering effect.") Subjects were then given tests which required them to interpret the meaning of the target sentence. Members of the group that heard the semantically unrelated sentences in the two channels divided over the interpretation that the lieutenant snuffed out the lantern, and the interpretation that the lieutenant placed a lighted lantern outdoors. Members of the group which heard the semantically related sentences overwhelmingly preferred the former interpretation.

The irresistible conclusion is that the sentence that occurred in the unattended channel, and that the subjects claimed not to know about, was not only acoustically processed, but was semantically processed as well. The noise in the unattended channel was processed as a contentful intentional object in the cognitive system, and it was causally, albeit unconsciously, relevant qua intentional object to the interpretations the subjects consciously provided on the posttest.

In the face of such data the obvious move for an advocate of Content Cartesianism is to weaken his thesis to the view that each person has epistemically privileged access to the contents of states of which he or she is consciously aware, to the current contents of his or her consciousness. The trouble with this revised version of Content Cartesianism is that it is a very weak thesis. Furthermore, it is not obviously true. First, there are cases of conscious ambiguity, mentioned above, where, for example, Mary desires, fears, loathes, admires, or loves John but is not sure which it is. Second and relatedly, there is the ever present possibility of self-deception. Even if one does not accept Freudian views on the unconscious, most individuals are familiar with cases in which some confident autophenomenological description of their state of mind seemed upon reflection and from the point of view of hindsight to be wrong. Third, and this is related to the second point, the problem of self-knowledge has to do with the accuracy of autophenomenological reports, not with people's willingness to generate such reports. The mere fact that people are forever confidently reporting the alleged contents of consciousness proves nothing about the accuracy of their reports. Content Cartesianism, therefore, is woefully implausible in its strong and interesting form as well as in its weaker, more commonsensical form.

We come to Causal Cartesianism; since this thesis is even stronger than State or Content Cartesianism (it assumes access to states, contents, and their causes) we already have strong grounds for skepticism. Most of the interesting work on Causal Cartesianism comes from cognitive social psychology. The classic paper on the topic, by Richard Nisbett and Timothy Wilson, comes with the inauspicious title, "Telling More than We Can Know: Verbal Reports on Mental Processes."[25]

Nisbett and Wilson and Nisbett and Ross present many examples of experiments which undermine Causal Cartesianism.[26] Two will suffice to make the point.

(1) A large number of experiments have shown that people are increasingly less likely to assist others in distress as the number of bystanders increases. The heterophenomenological data point overwhelmingly, therefore, to the causal influence on helping behavior of the number of others who are present. Subjects, however, systematically and emphatically deny—even when directly asked—that this variable (number of bystanders) had any effect on their helping behavior.

(2) In one of Nisbett and Wilson's experiments, subjects were divided into two groups: subjects in both groups saw filmed interviews with the same college professor who had a medium-thick Belgian accent. One group of subjects saw the professor speaking in a warm, pleasant, and respectful manner; the other group saw him acting aloof, rigid, and intolerant. Subjects were asked to indicate how likable they found the professor, and to rate three attributes which were (allegedly) invariant in the two films: his physical appearance, his mannerisms, and his accent. Subjects in the first group found the professor likable and his physical attributes appealing, while those in the second group found him unlikable and his physical attributes irritating. Because the three attributes were invariant across films, the most plausible conclusion is that the degree of overall likability affected the ratings of the specific attributes. This widely known phenomenon is called the "halo effect."

When subjects in both groups were queried, however, they emphatically denied that their overall attraction to the professor had any effect on their evaluation of the three attributes. The only causal principle widely reported was by subjects who saw the film depicting the professor as intolerant. But they got everything backward, and claimed that their negative evaluation of the three attributes decreased the degree to which they found the professor likable.

The three experimenters point out (I think correctly) that even when people make correct causal self-attributions it is not usually because of some special introspective access they have to the contents and causes of their mental states; it is because they have discovered the (objectively) correct causal generalizations. Thus when I tell you that I am going to answer the phone because it is ringing, or that I try to exercise in order to stay in shape, I am almost certainly correctly identifying the cause of my behavior; but it is not remotely plausible to think that I am introspecting.

In speaking of the ordinary person, Nisbett and Ross say,

> knowledge of the self is produced by the same strategies as knowledge of other social objects. . . . [A]ccurate perception of self and accurate perceptions of others ultimately depend on the successful performance of the same "scientific" tasks—that is, collecting, coding, and recalling data, assessing covariations, inferring causal relations, and testing hypotheses.[27]

A series of important conclusions seem to follow. First, the criticisms of Content Cartesianism show that we often know more than we can tell. Second, the criticisms of Process, Content, State, and Causal Cartesianism show that we often tell more than we know. Third, it may well be the case that when we make correct process, content, state, and causal judgments about ourselves, it is not so much because we are introspecting correctly as that we believe in the correct psychological generalizations.

The surprise is that, contrary to the received philosophical tradition, getting the autophenomenological story right often, perhaps usually, requires getting the heterophenomenological story right. The important methodological consequence for cognitive science is that when an autophenomenology and a heterophenomenology conflict, the heterophenomenology will normally win epistemically.

Lest you despair of the entire project of trying to attain self-knowledge, remember three things. First, nothing follows from what I have just said about the degree to which any particular individual has or lacks self-knowledge. Second, the argument in no way denies that you and I know all sorts of things about ourselves; it simply denies that we know most of these things by introspecting. (Spinoza pointed out that we know our birthdates and who our parents are by hearsay.) Third, the argument is perfectly compatible with two widely shared assumptions of clinical psychology: that one's self-conception is causally significant with respect to one's behavior and general state of mind, its accuracy or lack thereof notwithstanding; and that an accurate self-conception is desirable.

Cognitive Science and the Unity of Mind

A cluster of traditional philosophical views, taken together, constitutes what I will call the *thesis of the unity of mind*. The thesis of the unity of mind is very general, comes in various forms, and is closely associated with the view that one's existence as a mental entity is absolutely certain. To many it has seemed equally certain that the particular kind of mental entity one is, is a simple and undivided whole.

The thesis of the unity of mind is connected (historically and conceptually) to a cluster of traditional views on the mind-body problem, the problem of personal identity, and the problem of self-knowledge. Descartes, for example, explained the mind's indivisibility in terms of its incorporeality: physical things are divisible, incorporeal things might be, but need not be. Furthermore, the incorporeality of mind explains how my mind is unified over time, that is, how I remain exactly the same person from birth to death and beyond; my identity does not depend on this changing, divisible, and destructible system known as my body. Finally, my mind is subjectively unified by the omniscient relation my consciousness has to its contents.

Many traditional proponents of the thesis of the unity of mind were also faculty psychologists. Descartes, for example, believed that the unified and indivisible mind was comprised of several functionally distinct faculties—imagination, will, understanding, and so on. Prima facie, faculty psychology would seem to be inconsistent with the thesis of the unity of mind since it seems to divide that which is claimed to be indivisible.

Unity was maintained, however, in two ways. First, the faculties are, to use Jerry Fodor's terminology, horizontal; that is, they all communicate openly with each other and share the same material. The same mental object that is in my imagination one moment is in my understanding the next, and at some third moment activates my will. Second, all the faculties are unified by consciousness which courses through them all in equal and basically unlimited amounts. In this way, all the faculties "know" what their fellow faculties are doing.

It will be useful to refine the discussion somewhat by distinguishing between two versions of the thesis of the unity of mind: the simple thesis of the unity of mind, and the modified thesis of the unity of mind.

The simple thesis is associated with the view that the mind is the soul and, therefore, one simple, indivisible, incorporeal, and completely self-aware unity. The modified thesis allows some subdividing of mental operations, as in classical faculty psychology, but sees consciousness as a pontifical, unifying force. Indeed, on the modified view, consciousness has both access to all mental happenings and power over them. The access might be construed as omniscient access or, more credibly, if one accepts some version of the argument offered previously, as a type of omnipresence; consciousness is always in the vicinity of other mental happenings, and has a more or less accurate sense of what the rest of the system is doing.

Similarly, the power of consciousness can be thought of as virtual omnipotence as, for example, in Descartes' conception of the power of conscious will, or alternatively as subject to various constraints because we possess finite corporeal bodies. In either case, on the modified view, consciousness keeps track of and orchestrates the behavior of the entire system. One advantage of the modified view is its metaphysical neutrality. Unlike the simple thesis, it is compatible with both dualism and materialism.

There is an important psychological thesis which, although logically independent, nevertheless often accompanies the modified philosophical thesis of unity of mind. The psychological thesis maintains (roughly) that the principles in accordance with which the mind functions share a unified underlying logic. One sees this thesis in the work of psychologists as otherwise different as Skinner and Piaget.[28]

Skinner, for example, sees the mind as a unified general-purpose mechanism which functions in accordance with the same two conditioning principles in all domains. Piaget sees the mind as operating in accordance with the principle of assimilation and accommodation in all domains, and as moving as a unified whole from one cognitive stage to the next.

One of the most interesting questions in the philosophy of psychology has to do with the truth of the various philosophical and psychological views which comprise the modified thesis of unity of mind. Is the mind organized in a unitary way, or is it better viewed as having a committee structure wherein each committee has a special, nontransferable, domain-specific role? If there are various domain-specific mental faculties, to what extent does consciousness course through them all keeping track of the entire cognitive processing system?

I will confine my remarks to two otherwise unrelated research programs, *Massachusetts Modularism* and *Split-Brain Research*, to indicate why there is a growing consensus that the modified thesis of the unity of mind is, at the very least, overstated.

Massachusetts Modularism
Since the late 1950s Noam Chomsky of the Massachusetts Institute of Technology has been performing transcendental deductions on linguistic data in order to generate a theory of the principles subserving language acquisition, understanding, and production. Chomsky insists that the evidence points in the direction of a genetically determined and unique mental faculty whose one and only function is language acquisition, processing, and production. A unique, domain-

specific language processor is, Chomsky insists, the only plausible way to account for the (alleged) facts that all biologically normal children reach a "steady state" of linguistic competence by the time they reach puberty; and that reaching this "steady state" has surprisingly little relation to "general intelligence" or the possession of other talents and skills. Chomsky conjectures that the language-acquisition device is only one of many such special-purpose mental processors.

> We may usefully think of the language faculty, the number faculty, and other "mental organs," as analogous to the heart or the visual system or the system of motor coordination and planning. . . . In short, there seems little reason to insist that the brain is unique in the biological world, in that it is unstructured and undifferentiated, developing on the basis of uniform principles of growth or learning—say those of some learning theory, or of some yet-to-be-conceived general-purpose learning strategy—that are common to all domains.[29]

Let's call the thesis that the mind is modular, in approximately Chomsky's sense, *the modularity thesis*. The foremost advocate of the modularity thesis is Chomsky's former colleague at MIT, Jerry Fodor. In his book *The Modularity of Mind*, which evolved from a graduate course he taught with Chomsky, Fodor makes his case.[30]

Fodor starts by distinguishing between horizontal and vertical faculties. Horizontal faculties (if they exist) are functionally distinct, pass information back and forth to their fellow faculties, and are domain-nonspecific. If the mind is organized horizontally, then one and the same memory faculty is deployed in memorizing phone numbers, French vocabulary, and tastes of wine. On the horizontal view, when I need to call my wife at her office I go to my unified memory faculty—ignoring all the information about philosophy, sports, wine, and French—fetch her work number, pass it on to my (unified) will, which tells the (unified) motor faculty to set the fingers dialing.

Vertical faculties (if they exist) are also functionally distinct, but they do not cross content domains, and they are "computationally autonomous," that is, they "do not share—and hence do not compete for—such horizontal resources as memory, attention, intelligence, judgment, or whatever."[31]

To get the relevant idea, imagine that the mind has separate modules for dealing with, say, phone numbers and chess. The phone number module is responsible only for phone numbers, for detecting them, for memorizing them, perhaps even for getting the fingers to start dialing. The chess module, on the other hand, is responsible only for chess, for detecting possible moves, for memorizing chess strategies, and perhaps even for getting the fingers to move the pieces. The two systems do not communicate with each other, and they do not share one general-purpose memory or motor faculty because they have, *ex hypothesi,* their own individualized content-specific memory and motor systems.

Fodor claims that, contrary to popular wisdom, there is considerable evidence for vertical faculties. His favorite candidates are what he calls "input systems." "Input systems function to get information into the central processors."[32] Fodor asks how many special-purpose input systems there are. He answers,

> The discussion thus far might be construed to suggest an answer somewhere in the vicinity of six—viz., one for each of the traditional sensory/perceptual 'modes' (hearing, sight, touch, tastes, smell) and one more for language. This is *not,* however, the intended doctrine. . . . I imagine that within . . . the traditional modes there are highly specialized computational mechanisms in the business of generating hypothesis about the distal sources of proximal stimulations. . . . [C]andidates might include, in the case of vision, mechanisms for color perception, for the analysis of shape, and for the analysis of three-dimensional spatial relations. They might also include quite narrowly task-specific *'higher level'* systems concerned with the visual guidance of bodily motions or with the recognition of faces of conspecifics.[33]

Because Fodor's argument is more programmatic than experimental, nothing essential rests on his being exactly right about particular cases. His purpose is to provide a general theory of the sorts of evidence which are relevant to establishing the existence of special-purpose cognitive modules. Several species of evidence stand out.

First, "the more eccentric a stimulus domain, the more plausible the speculation that it is computed by a special-purpose mechanism."[34] It is hard to see how the processes underlying success in, say, Shepard and Metzler's rotation experiment could be recruited for sentence comprehension. That is, three-dimensional objects and sentences seem, prima facie at least, like very different kinds of stimuli.

Second, if special-purpose modules exist, their operation is likely to be mandatory. Take the Lackner and Garrett experiment: how do we explain the fact that the noise in the unattended channel was semantically processed—despite the subjects' success in keeping its semantic interpretation out of consciousness—except by postulating a mandatory processor which takes acoustic features of human speech as input and gives semantic interpretations as output?

Third, special-purpose modular systems are fast. Fodor gives this excellent example:

Appreciable numbers of subjects can "shadow" continuous speech with a quarter-second latency (shadowing is repeating what you hear as you hear it) and . . . there is good evidence that such "fast shadowers" understand what they repeat. . . . [T]his finding is mind-boggling. And, mind-boggling or otherwise, it is clear [because shadowing requires *repeating* what one is hearing] that shadowing latency is an extremely conservative measure of the speed of comprehension.[35]

The speed and mandatory nature of special-purpose modules contrasts sharply with paradigm cases of general-purpose, central processing. Suppose I ask you for advice on the best way to invest $50,000 so as achieve maximum profits in twenty years. Your advice—your solution to my problem—will, of course, be both slow and nonmandatory. That is, unfortunately for me, there are numerous credible ways for you to give me "sound" financial counsel.

The fourth feature one would expect from special-purpose cognitive modules (if there are such things) is "informational encapsulation"—what Zenon Pylyshyn calls "cognitive impenetrability."[36] The basic idea is this: although special-purpose modules can send information upward for central processing, they are likely to be relatively immune to top-down effects. This is because *ex hypothesi* the modules are designed to take very limited and idiosyncratic classes of stimuli as input. For example, the next time you are in a room where others are talking, try to hear what they are saying as "noise." It is easy to tune out speech from conscious awareness, but when you actually try to hear a conversation as noise you will find that it simply can't be done. The alleged reason is that the mandatory processor that provides semantic interpretations to the particular class of acoustic stimuli known as human speech is in operation. It apparently is not designed to accept, recognize, or in any other way process your conscious wish that it turn itself off!

Fodor convincingly recommends several other sorts of evidence as support for modularity claims, such as the association of some competence with fixed neural architecture, and characteristic (that is, modular), individualized breakdown patterns.

I call the research program that advocates modularity Massachusetts Modularism rather than MIT Modularism, because Howard Gardner of Harvard University and the Boston Veterans Hospital develops a related modularity thesis in his *Frames of Mind: The Idea of Multiple Intelligences*.[37] Gardner's argument is complementary to Fodor's in that it makes a case for modularity at even higher levels.

Gardner is an admirer of Piaget; nevertheless he takes aim at Piaget's view that intelligence is all of one piece. Gardner sees a prejudice—reflected in Piaget's work and in the IQ-testing tradition—that involves viewing intelligence as a single, generalizable set of logical-mathematical abilities operating across all domains.

Gardner looked at three different kinds of data: (1) data linking breakdowns of certain mental competences, for example, linguistic competence, with certain kinds of physiological breakdown, for example, damage to Broca's or Wernicke's area; (2) data on the abilities of special populations, for example, mathematical and musical geniuses, and *idiot savants;* and (3) cross-cultural data on the types of intelligence that are identified as "independent" in different cultures. His project is designed to see if there is evidence for separate, domain-specific, higher-level intelligences.

On the basis of the evidence, Gardner hypothesizes the existence of seven different kinds of intelligence: two "object-free," linguistic and musical; three "object-related," logical-mathematical, spatial, and bodily-kinaesthetic; two "person-related," interpersonal and intrapersonal.

One can easily imagine forms of these intelligences embodied respectively in the poet, the musician, the mathematician, the geometrician or architect, the athlete, the peacemaker, and the person with great self-knowledge.

Gardner cautiously conjectures that these seven intelligences have strong innate components; that not everyone has all of them to the same degree; that different intelligences support different talents and abilities; and that each kind of intelligence is semiautonomous in the sense that it may not be subserved by one general-purpose horizontal memory or comprehension faculty.

According to Gardner's model, if you have a great memory for music and a poor one for geometry it may not be because you are more interested in the former than the latter; more likely you have a (domain-specific) musical memory that is more subtly honed to begin with than your (equally domain-specific) spatial memory.

Taken together, Fodor's and Gardner's distinct but compatible versions of the modularity thesis undermine the view that the mind is a general-purpose device that performs all tasks the same way, and that is equally competent across domains. Fodor and Gardner, however, would be the first to admit that their respective modularity theses have many loose ends, and that many details need to be worked out before we are clear as to exactly what extent, and in what areas, the mind ought to be viewed as modular.

Split-Brain Research
Individuals with so-called split brains have had their cerebral commissures severed. The operation, known as a commissurotomy, cuts

the nerve network that normally connects the right and left cerebral hemispheres, and has been performed on over a dozen patients with a severe form of epilepsy. The operation not only stops the epilepsy, but, surprisingly, seems to have no deleterious effects on the patients' mental or behavioral functioning in everyday life.

In experimental situations, however, there are startling findings. (1) If a word, say, *ring*, is displayed for a very short time in the right half of the visual field, or if an actual ring is felt by the right hand but concealed from view, split-brain patients can report what they have seen or felt. However, if the word is displayed in the left half of the visual field or if an actual (but visually concealed) ring is felt by the left hand, patients cannot report what they have seen or felt. (2) If the word *key*, is flashed on the left side of the visual field the left hand will (upon request) retrieve a key from a number of objects; at the same time the person will insist that he saw nothing. (3) If *key* and *ring* are flashed on the left and right sides of the visual field respectively, and the person is told to retrieve what she saw from a group of objects behind a screen, her two hands will work independently. The right hand will reject the key and settle on the ring; the left hand will do the opposite.

Research on split-brain patients has helped clarify certain features of the functional organization of the brain. The well-understood facts are these: The left and right cerebral hemispheres are associated (to a significant degree) with opposite sides of the body. Thus tactile stimuli from each side of the body are processed by the opposite side of the brain (except stimulation of the head and neck, which is processed by both sides). The left half of each retina (which scans the right half of the visual field) sends impulses to the left hemisphere; the right half of each retina does the opposite.

Language (speech and writing more than comprehension) is usually controlled by the left hemisphere (and this is imperfectly related to handedness). Olfaction is ipsilateral: the left nostril is connected to the left hemisphere, the right nostril to the right hemisphere. Audition is the most hemispherically nondiscriminatory modality, sending its messages to both sides of the brain. Nevertheless, even audition involves some favoring of the opposite hemisphere.

Philosophically, much ado has been made of the split-brain phenomena. One philosopher, Puccetti, has argued that split-brain patients have two independent streams of consciousness, and therefore have two minds and are two persons.[38] Thomas Nagel has argued that the conception of mind suggested by the split-brain results is incompatible with the traditional view that the mind is unified by a single (omniscient) consciousness.[39] Even Roger Sperry, the cautious Nobel Laureate who generated much of the split-brain data, thinks that split-brain patients have a disunified consciousness and are unaware of this disunity.

It is important to realize that normal individuals are like split-brain patients in all relevant respects except that their commissures are intact. The commissures allow the two hemispheres to communicate and thereby to spread awareness of what the other is doing and "knows." This means that if the words *key* and *ring* were flashed before your eyes so rapidly that eye movement was impossible, there would be a very short span of time during which it would be fair to say that one side of your brain was aware that it saw the word *ring*, the other side that it saw *key*. This would seem to imply that even in normal people consciousness is not always unified.

Assuming that all this is right, several important conclusions emerge. First, there is a considerable amount of functional localization in the brain; different systems do different sorts of processing. Second, conscious introspection gives us virtually no access to these processes and processors. Third, consciousness does not so much course through, and thereby unify, all the different parts of the mind, as it occurs, when it occurs at all, as an end product of massive amounts of cognitive processing. The feeling of a unified consciousness that omnisciently orchestrates all lower-level goings-on is just that—a feeling. Consciousness is, so to speak, often the last to "know" what other parts of the system have "known" all along. This is not to deny that consciousness often initiates mental activity; it is simply to deny that it does so as often or as omnipotently as we are consciously inclined to think.

In sum, then, Massachusetts Modularism and Split-Brain Research undermine the modified thesis of unity of mind and its partner, the psychological thesis of unified processing, in several related and complementary ways. They present a serious challenge to the views (1) that the mind is a unified general-purpose device that performs all tasks the same way and is equally competent across domains, (2) that consciousness has access to all mental goings-on, (3) that consciousness has power over the rest of the system, and (4) that awareness is one unitary thing.

Cognitive Science and Rationality

During the Enlightenment—and only among intellectuals and scientists—rationality replaced faith as the primary epistemic virtue. The human project was reconceived as the project of coming to possess justified true beliefs, as opposed to beliefs that were edifying and comforting, but nevertheless unsupportable and superstitious. Rationality was to be the road to these justified true beliefs and thereby to the good life for *Homo sapiens*.[40] The first problem, of course, was to specify what rationality is.

Often rationality is taken as equivalent to logicality. That is, you are rational just in case you systematically instantiate the rules and principles of inductive logic, statistics, and probability theory on the one hand, and deductive logic and all the mathematical sciences, on the other.

The trouble with identifying rationality with the formal canons of logic *simpliciter* is that rationality is a broader and more complex notion than logicality. Rationality is tied up with issues related to the meaning and quality of our individual lives in a way logicality is not.

Almost everyone agrees (1) that it is rational to be concerned about one's own welfare and happiness and (2) that it is rational (not to mention good) to be concerned about the welfare and happiness of others. No one, however, knows exactly how to weigh (1) and (2). We do in fact assign differential weights to (1) and (2) all the time; the point is that no one is terribly confident about the particular weightings.

Furthermore, because logic is formal it is of no help whatsoever in assigning the differential weights to (1) and (2). Where logic can be of help is in coming to complex conclusions about beliefs or actions once we have assigned the weights to (1) and (2).[41] Beware, therefore, of discussions of rationality which identify it with logicality *simpliciter*.

Actually there are those, I'll call them *logicists*, who claim that the ideals internal to formal logic, in particular, impartiality, consistency, and objectivity, are the standards for all rationality. According to the logicist, my mistake a moment ago was to assume that there is a problem about weighing my own interests versus the interests of others. There is not. The rational, that is, the logical, thing to do is to weigh the interests of all people (including one's own interests and those of one's loved ones) equally. On the logicist's view, people could be fully rational, that is, logical, if only they would get over certain subjective, emotional biases, such as self-interest.

I am not going to argue against the logicist's view here. I am just going to assume that he is wrong, and that the view of rationality he presupposes is too restrictive.

What I intend to defend is what I will call the *Enlightenment Competence Theory* (ECT), namely, that all normal people ('normal' excludes only idiots, the insane, and the like) are capable of reasoning in a highly rational manner, that is, in a manner which integrates the demands of logic, statistics, and probability theory with legitimate claims to pursue life plans of one's choosing and to maximize one's defensible talents, interests, and values.

The basic idea behind ECT is that although most people do not, as a matter of fact, always reason well, they have the underlying ability or competence to do so. The theory is optimistic in the sense that it bets there are no insurmountable psychological obstacles to a world in which right reasoning, in the sense specified above, is not merely ideally but is actually the norm.

The question is, Is ECT true? Can human reasoning performance converge with the alleged underlying competence? That is, can we systematically instantiate the principles of right reasoning?

The data from cognitive science provide some grounds for concern. It is important to point out that although cognitive scientists, as well as the philosophers who discuss their work, talk of its implications for human rationality, the experimental research is really cast fairly narrowly. Probably wisely, cognitive scientists have focused almost exclusively on logicality, on rationality in the narrow sense. Their experiments intentionally involve tasks that normally can be solved by agreed-upon logical canons and are non-ego-involving, that is, they allegedly have no connection to the subjects' moral values, life plans, loves, hates, phobias, and the like.

Although logicality is not equivalent to rationality, it is important to the issue of rationality in the wider sense. One reason is this: given some defensible assessment of our personal projects and plans, it would be best if we logically assessed the probability of our success in carrying them out. The fruition of our plans, after all, usually depends on factors outside our control. If we fail, therefore, at accurately assessing objective states of affairs because of some fundamental logical incompetence, we will have trouble attaining the sort of rationality that integrates our life plans with the demands of logic. A further reason for taking a close look at research on logicality is that intuitively one would think it should be easier for people to be rational in the narrow sense, that is, to logically assess impersonal states of affairs, than it would be for them to be rational in the broader sense that ties rationality to the intricacies of their personal lives. If humans have trouble on narrow logical tasks we have prima facie grounds for worrying about their wider rationality (on the other hand, one might argue that performance on purely logical tasks is unrealistic and, therefore, irrelevant to the assessment of real-life reasoning).

Research on deductive reasoning indicates that even trained logicians sometimes have trouble applying such standard rules of inference as *modus ponens* (if A implies B and if A is true, then B is true) and *modus tollens* (if A implies B and B is false, then A is false). They get confused by quantifiers ("all," "some," "each") and they have trouble processing negative sentences.[42] These data undermine any naive platonic confidence that all people need is a gentle academic reminder of the deductive logical principles that they already, in some sense, "know."

Furthermore, psychologists like Daniel Kahneman and Amos Tversky have found that inductive reasoning is similarly prone to certain characteristic errors. Because much of Kahneman and Tversky's research has been done on very talented students at Stanford and elsewhere, as well as replicated on professional scientists, their research provides additional prima facie grounds for worrying that ECT may indeed be too strong.

Kahneman and Tversky claim that the rules of thumb most people rely on in reasoning are economical and probably lead to correct judgments much of the time; but these strategies are also biased, insensitive, and myopic when it comes to certain tasks. I will focus on two commonly utilized reasoning strategies: representativeness and availability.

Representativeness is used in categorization problems. It is a catch-all technique for deciding whether a novel instance is or is not a member of some class on grounds of its degree of resemblance to known members of the class. Availability is a heuristic in which the frequency or probability of some event or object, or set of events or objects, is judged in terms of the relative availability of the objects or events to memory, perception, or imagination.

Representativeness   Consider the following biographical sketch: Mary graduated from Berkeley in the late 1960s. She was active in both the civil rights movement and in the antiwar movement. Mary now lives in Cambridge, Massachusetts. Question: Which is more probable, that Mary is a bank teller or that Mary is a bank teller and a feminist?

The correct answer is that it is more probable that Mary is a bank teller. The reason is simple: in either eventuality—that is, whether or not Mary is a feminist—she must be a bank teller. Remember the question: which is more probable, that she is a bank teller or a bank teller *and* a feminist? It is a trivial principle of the probability calculus that A & B cannot be more probable than A.

You were misled no doubt, if indeed you were misled, by the fact that the description says nothing representative about bank tellers, but it does say something representative about the category of feminist. That is, the sort of background Mary has is more representative of feminists than of bank tellers.

Representativeness is a particularly stubborn reasoning strategy. In one study, Kahneman and Tversky gave subjects personality sketches allegedly taken at random from a group of a hundred engineers and lawyers. The subjects were asked to assign the people to the appropriate professional category on the basis of the personality sketches. One group was told (and reminded throughout) that the ratio of engineers to lawyers was 7 to 3; another group was told, and similarly reminded, that the ratio was the opposite: 3 to 7.

Correct reasoning here would involve some kind of integration and weighting of the prior probabilities with the evidence provided in the particular sketches. "Bayes' theorem" is widely believed to be a formal rule for such integration and weighting. If subjects used Bayes' theorem, or some informal analog, the answers of the two groups should show the effects of having weighted the prior probabilities, the so-called base rates.

Tversky and Kahneman comment,

> The odds that any particular description belongs to an engineer rather than a lawyer should be higher in the first condition . . . than in the second condition. . . . In sharp violation of Bayes' rule, the subjects in the two conditions produced essentially the same probability judgments . . . with little or no regard for the prior probabilities of the categories.[43]

Tversky and Kahneman found that their subjects did apply Bayes' theorem correctly in certain situations. For example, when asked before reading a particular sketch what the a priori probability was that it was a sketch of a lawyer, subjects correctly answered .3 or .7 depending on which group they were in. Tversky and Kahneman, found, however, that even completely uninformative verbal information seemed to turn attention away from the statistical base rate information. For example, subjects were given one description that said: "Dick is a 30-year-old man. He is married with no children. A man of high ability and high motivation, he promises to be quite successful in his field. He is well liked by his colleagues."

The subjects in both groups assigned this uninformative sketch a .5 probability of describing an engineer. To me this suggests that the description activated some sort of representativeness search, which failed to find decisive evidence for either (unweighted) possibility. Having failed to find evidence representative of either profession in the sketch, however, the reasoning mechanism did not revert to the base rates. Instead it simply called the sketch a toss-up.

Availability   To get the intuitive idea behind the availability heuristic, consider the following experiment:

> Subjects heard a list of well-known personalities of both sexes and were subsequently asked to judge whether the list contained

more names of men than of women. Different lists were presented to different groups of subjects. In some of the lists the men were relatively more famous than the women, and in others the women were relatively more famous than the men. In each of the lists, the subjects erroneously judged that the class (sex) that had the more famous personalities was the more numerous.[44]

What happened here? Kahneman and Tversky claim that the variables of fame and recognition are apparently (in this case at least) processed as more salient, interesting, and worth remembering than the unnoticed variable, number. The greater availability of the former variables over the latter lead the frequency judgment astray.

Or consider this experiment: Subjects were asked to suppose that a word (three letters or more) was picked at random from some English text, say page 147 of this book. Is it more probable that the word starts with r or that r is its third letter? Tversky and Kahneman comment that

> People approach this problem by recalling words that begin with r (road) and words that have r in the third position (car) and assess the relative frequency by the ease with which the two words come to mind. Because it is much easier to search for words by their first letter, most people judge words that begin with a given consonant to be more numerous than words in which the same consonant appears in the third position. They do so even for consonants, such as r or k, that are more frequent in the third position than in the first.[45]

These and other evidence of faulty logical reasoning could be, and are, multiplied endlessly in the literature. The question is, what interpretation should we give to these data? How are these data possible? How do they affect the credibility of ECT? Are the errors due to certain built-in and therefore necessary features of the cognitive processing equipment, or are they acquired disabilities?

Let us look more closely at several features of the actual experimental evidence to see why ECT, realistically conceived, is still plausible, and how research exposing characteristic weaknesses in reasoning can actually assist in helping performance get closer to what from a normative point of view we might think of as ideal.

I will focus on evidence of problems in the innate cognitive equipment, as opposed to evidence of acquired bad reasoning habits. Evidence of innate liabilities, if such exists, is the strongest sort of evidence that can be brought against ECT.

Some of the errors discussed by Tversky and Kahneman look as if they may have to do with the wiring. For example, in the experiment where subjects are required to estimate whether more English words begin with r or have r in the third position, the inability to guess correctly has to do with certain idiosyncratic features of the memory and the search mechanisms, for example, first letters are easier to conjure up than third ones, letter counts are normally not made during semantic encoding, and so on.

The temptation here is to say that this is a case where we lack an underlying competence. I think this is right. It is not obvious, however, that the competence we lack is a rational competence. What I mean is this: if the mind happened to be wired to count letters, encode the counts in memory, and retrieve these counts, we might well deploy the correct statistical canons over the accurately memorized and retrieved evidence about r's and k's, and get the questions about them right. The limitation here, to be sure, is a cognitive one, but it is not obviously a limitation of logical reason; it is only a limitation of memory.

One might respond that surely an underlying logical competence cannot be claimed if we have the right formal principles but altogether lack the procedures to gather the evidence over which the principles are to perform their inferences. This strikes me as basically right, but it cannot be brought to bear in the case under discussion. The reason is that in fact there are procedures for correcting and avoiding the error alleged in the latter experiment. The experiment artificially restricts (this of course is the psychologist's standard tactic) the possible means of estimating whether there are more r's in the first position than in the third. The way around the error, of course, is to count words on pages rather than in the head, just as the experimenters who know the answer did.

This argument is somewhat harder to bring against several other alleged competence problems. For example, Tversky and Kahneman attribute the common failure to apply statistical principles, such as regression toward the mean and weighing the relevance of sample size, to the fact that the cognitive system simply is not wired to be sensitive to these features; that is, it fails to encode the plentiful objective data pointing to the genuine reality of the regression phenomena and the effects of sample size. Both these disabilities seem more relevant to the assessment of underlying logical competence than mere memory limitations because they relate directly to our inductive abilities.

However, it cannot be right that we are constitutionally incapable of drawing the right inferences, since statisticians and logicians have, in fact, extracted the allegedly correct principles from patterns of data. Furthermore, thanks to the work of these very same statisticians and logicians, the problems can be corrected for. How? Drill into people's heads that they should be aware they are prone to forget about these principles, and tell them to be sure to look and see if the principles are applicable before making judgments.

The data showing that psychologists with backgrounds in statistics attach inordinate credibility to inferences from small samples does not prove that the latter sort of exhortation will not work. It might be that the psychologists have been improperly educated, have forgotten statistics, or were insufficiently exhorted.[46]

What about the data on seemingly acquired biases having to do, for example, with the representativeness heuristic? Tversky and Kahneman are by no means the first to notice this bias. David Hume sent chills down the spines of the earliest proponents of ECT by pointing out, first, that the canons of logic are themselves not rationally justifiable (you need to use logic to justify logic), and second, that in many areas of life, local customs and habits serve us better, on the whole, than would impeccable, but time-consuming, use of the canons of logical reason.

The concepts of "on the whole" and "time-consuming" are important. In all likelihood certain reasoning heuristics are compromises privately struck (perhaps evolutionarily struck) among the demands of logic, the demands of cognitive economy (that is, the demands to keep track of as many important things as possible given the constraints of memory), and the demands of practical life.[47]

For example, one canon of informal logic is that one should maximize information before action. The trouble with the rule is that it would utterly immobilize us, not just occasionally, but all the time. On the other hand, by expanding our information-processing capacities, say by sensible use of small mobile personal computers—prosthetic electronic reasoning assistants, one could call them—we might start to compensate for some of our design constraints and their related biases. In the meantime, we can exhort: Remember the base rates! Watch out for the availability bias! and so on.

All my talk about compensating procedures, exhortations, and improving our reasoning by attaching ourselves to artificial intelligences does, I think, involve an admission that when one looks at cognition as a whole, one sees a system with limitations of memory and imagination that is prone to a variety of (understandable) biases. This admission, in turn, seriously undermines the view of persons as naturally competent, intuitive logicians.

But it does not defeat ECT. ECT, as I have described it, is neutral on how rational competence comes about. It is compatible with ECT that full rationality might require the internalization of the knowledge and skills articulated by logicians, statisticians, and probability theorists over the ages, with or without hand-held or implanted artificial memories and computational devices, equipped (of course) with Bayes' theorem!

This, however, would still do only part of the job. Remember rationality is closely connected to logicality, but it is not identical to it. Even if we could learn to be perfectly logical, there is still the matter of acquiring strategies for choosing sensible moral values, life plans, friends, spouses, and political systems. All these things require rationality, but the sorts of considerations which are relevant to choosing rationally in these areas are not amenable to purely formal or quantitative analyses. I maintain, however, that what goes for logicality also goes for rationality in the broad sense. Our successes will come from paying attention to our externalized species memory, to the knowledge of past successes and failures in human endeavors as depicted in historical, literary, political, economic, and philosophical accounts. Intuitions and gut reactions are not enough; they are not even trustworthy.

I have argued that accurate self-understanding cannot be based solely or even mostly on self-observation, on the deployment of some allegedly omniscient mind's eye. Accurate self-understanding requires understanding and internalization of the best available scientific theories about the kind of creatures we are, as well as collective cultural wisdom about human nature and human history.

A parallel conclusion suggests itself here. Rationality—to whatever extent we can instantiate its canons in view of our fallibility, the bounds of rationality, and real-world constraints—will not always or even often come naturally. It will come, if it comes at all, as a result of our very best efforts to internalize the canons articulated by experts. Happily for the Enlightenment Competence Theory, we have no reason to think that this cannot be done.

Cognitive Science and the Mind-Brain Problem

The discussion thus far has been decidedly nonmetaphysical; it has been concerned with some of the central philosophical assumptions and implications of cognitive science with little mention of the question of the nature of the mind.

This is not merely an artifact of my mode of presentation. Cognitive scientists, by and large, simply seem not to worry about the mind-brain problem. It is not entirely clear why this is, but I suspect there are two main causes. First, in some quarters there is the view that the mind-brain problem can simply be ignored. New lawlike generalizations about cognition are being discovered every day by scientists who worry not one iota about the metaphysical nature of the underlying processes. Second, there are those who consider some form of materialism to be established, and who, in addition, take the software-hardware distinction in computer science to have provided, once and for all, convincing proof for the permissibility and usefulness of scientific talk about a material system in a language which does not ever directly refer to the materials themselves.

Philosophers interested in reconstructing the metaphysical commitments of cognitive scientists often claim that some form of functionalism is the canonical position in the field. One has to be careful here. Among cognitive scientists, functionalism often refers to an epistemological position, to a view on how mental states are picked out and on how psychological explanations are most appropriately framed. According to epistemological functionalism, mental states are identified in terms of the characteristic causal relations which hold among environmental events, other mental states, and action. Anger, for example, characteristically results from some unjust act; it is usually accompanied by annoyance and the desire to retaliate, and it often results in harsh words or actual physical violence.

The main difference between the functionalist's and the behaviorist's way of picking out mental states is twofold. First, the functionalist, unlike the behaviorist, does not try to characterize mental states solely in terms of nonmental ones, such as, S is angry means S is acting angry; rather the functionalist is interested in characterizing mental events in terms of stimuli, responses, and other mental states. Second, the functionalist believes that in intelligent organisms such as ourselves, the causal relations between mental states are causally significant processes and not mere side effects or end products of more interesting processes taking place in the environment.

It is easy to wonder and sensible to ask how epistemological functionalism has any bearing on the mind-brain problem. After all, the brain was never mentioned in what I just said; and, as I pointed out above, many psychologists and cognitive scientists happily ignore metaphysical questions of the form: What is the essence of mentality? Philosophers, of course, are notorious for taking the plunge. Nevertheless, even philosophers committed to a more obviously metaphysical brand of functionalism are cagey on the mind-brain problem. Explaining their caginess requires repeating a little philosophical history.

First—among opponents of dualism—there was *identity theory.* Identity theory is the claim that each *type* of mental state is identical to some *type* of brain state. The fundamental idea is that the kinds of things picked out by our ordinary mental concepts (belief, desire, hope, love, and so on), are actually identical type-for-type with kinds that neuroscientists will someday discover. The identity theorist is, therefore, a *type-physicalist*. Happily for the identity theorist, the history of science is replete with examples of discoveries of type-type identities: Clouds are collections of water droplets, water is H_2O, temperature is mean molecular kinetic energy.

Identity theory assumes one important philosophical thesis and implies another. The assumption is that the taxonomy of our commonsense psychological framework, our so-called folk psychology, is on the mark. That is, folk psychology accurately picks out types of entities that will be definable completely in terms of the yet-to-be-discovered types of a mature neuroscience. The bet is that someday people will formulate type-type identity statements such as "Beliefs are just xzqry firings at velocity v and rate r in sector 2304."

The implication that follows from the latter assumption is this: if type-type identity theory is true then reduction of psychology to neuroscience will eventually be possible. It is easy to see why reduction requires that all the concepts of the science to be reduced be translatable into the concepts of the reducing science. These translations are called "bridge laws" and once they are in place reduction merely involves replacing, synonym for synonym. Type-type identity statements, of course, are precisely the necessary bridge laws.

In the heyday of identity theory one would hear questions as to why reduction was urged in the direction of neuroscience if indeed both psychology and neuroscience were about exactly the same thing. There were two sorts of replies. First, it was often said that the concepts of psychology were a bit loose and vague, while those of neuroscience were more precise. The trouble with this reply is that it seems to deny what identity theory assumes, namely, that there is a perfect mapping between ordinary psychological types and neuroscientific ones. How can sloppy concepts map onto neat ones?

A second, and better reason for urging reduction in the direction of neuroscience is this: although all psychological terms eventually will be definable in terms of neuroscientific terms, there are sure to be additional neuroscientific terms for which there are no corresponding psychological ones, for example, terms describing states and processes to which we have no conscious access. In this way, neuroscience will be richer than psychology: it will absorb psychology and go beyond it. It will say everything psychology can, and more.

Now the metaphysical functionalist comes in; his strategy is to try to accept the identity theorist's physicalism without accepting his reductionism. The functionalist starts by pointing out that there are many interesting kinds of things for which there are no coherent underlying physical types. Take the type, mystery story. Go through the library gathering all the books and short stories that are instances of the genre "mystery story." Pile them in a room. Now tell me what physical properties underlie the type "mystery story" and distinguish it from other literary genres that also appear in book form.

Or take the kind "clock." Big Ben is a clock, a sundial is a clock, my wristwatch is a clock, you would be a clock if you stood in the middle of a desert. What physical properties do all clocks have in common by virtue of which they are clocks?

Or take the kind "calculator." There are hundreds of different brands. They come in assorted shapes and sizes. Some are made of metal, some of plastic, and some are mixed. They vary widely in their wiring diagrams. But they all do arithmetic.

Notice two things about the examples. First, all the tokens (the individual members) of the types are physical. That is, each and every individual mystery story, clock, and calculator is a physical thing. But even within types, they are not even remotely the same kind of physical thing.

The examples, therefore, provide the functionalist with motivation for espousing token physicalism, the view that each thing that exists is physical, without accepting reductionism (which requires type-type bridge laws).

The second thing to notice about the examples is that all the types cited as being irreducible to homogeneous physical types are functional types; they are normally characterized in terms of what they can do, how they work, what function they have, what effects they have, and so on.

With the confidence generated by such examples the functionalist claims, in the words of Jerry Fodor, that

> The reason it is unlikely that every kind corresponds to a physical kind is just that (a) interesting generalizations . . . can often be made about events whose physical descriptions have nothing in common; (b) it is often the case that *whether* the physical description of the events subsumed by such generalizations have anything in common is . . . entirely irrelevant to the truth of the generalizations, or to their interestingness, or to their degree of confirmation, or indeed, to any of their epistemologically interesting properties.[48]

The functionalist claims that because we have every reason to believe mental states are individuated functionally, and because we have no reason to believe that most functional types map neatly onto homogeneous physical types, we have no reason to think that psychological kinds will map onto neuroscientific kinds. We can be (token) physicalists without being reductionists. We have, in effect, a principled, as opposed to a state of the art, defense of the autonomy of psychological explanation which also happily coheres with a commitment to metaphysical materialism.

Furthermore, metaphysical functionalism helps legitimize the cognitive scientist's preferred style of explanation (this is why many philosophers recommend metaphysical functionalism in addition to epistemological functionalism). The metaphysical functionalist offers a principled reason as to why the cognitive scientist should offer functional explanations from the design or intentional stances, without bothering with physical-stance accounts. Consider the generalization that, on the average, people who believe in God attend religious services more often than those who do not. The metaphysical functionalist accepts that all beliefs for or against God are physical events and processes, but he doubts that they are any one particular kind of physical event or process in all people. Person A and person B might share a belief in one and the same God, say Zeus, and thus be in the same intentional state, while their brains are in very different states. According to the token-physicalist, one and the same functional state can be realized in many different ways.

This last point has given rise to a heated debate that is central to the question of artificial intelligence. The metaphysical functionalist is committed to the view that you and I can have the same belief about, say, the date of Columbus's discovery of America, without being in exactly the same brain state (although we need to be in some brain state or other). Now suppose some Martians land on earth, looking like Martians in comic books. Suppose that several of these friendly visitors learn our language, enter our schools, and learn history the way we do. The Martians come to say things like "Columbus discovered America in 1492," and we come to think of them as knowledgeable in the same ways we are. Cognitive scientists do research on them and find that Sternberg's, Shepard and Metzler's, and Tversky and Kahneman's results all generalize to Martians.

Now suppose that one of the Martians dies and we do an autopsy and discover that the Martian's nervous system is not spine- and brain-based like ours, but appears to involve neuronlike cells spread throughout the circulatory system.[49] Do we still attribute consciousness and beliefs to the living Martians? The functionalist, of course, says yes. The Martians' beliefs and mental processes are realized differently from ours; but from a functional point of view they are the same.

Suppose instead that the scenario differs in the following way. The autopsy reveals that internally the Martian functions hydraulically; there are minute pieces of some sort of organic metal, unknown in Earthly chemistry, mixed with what looks like water, but is really XYZ (also heretofore unknown on earth), coursing through the pliable tubes which make up his internal anatomy. Do we still attribute consciousness and beliefs to the living Martians? Again the functionalist says yes. The way the Martians' beliefs and mental processes are realized is admittedly unexpected, but their beliefs and mental processes play the same functional role as ours, and thus they are the same.

Third scenario: the autopsy reveals that the Martian has only an organic exterior, which, it turns out, has a designer label on the inside that says in Martian (which we now understand) "Made by Organic Exteriors, Inc. Wear only in sunny oxygen-rich environments." Further inside, however, the Martian is entirely inorganic, filled with plastic, silicon chips, copper, and a dead nuclear battery. Do we still attribute consciousness and beliefs to the living Martians, all of whom, we have now discovered by X-ray, have the same kind of body?

Here things get harder. Some functionalists agree that they are committed to attributing mentality once again, and view this as the possibility proof for the existence of genuine artificial intelligence. Others reject the fantasy on grounds that it is simply too implausible. To be sure, mental states can be realized in a variety of ways in a nervous system, but the nervous system has to be made of the right stuff, minimally organic stuff.

To some, all this science fiction is an indication of the cost of metaphysical functionalism. The functionalist claims to be a card-carrying materialist, but has gone so far overboard with his insight about the possibility of multiple realizations that he acts as if the particular kind of body we have is irrelevant to our mental life.

At this point we meet the eliminative materialist; the eliminativist is a critic of functionalism and worries about the assurances metaphysical functionalism gives the cognitive scientist about the legitimacy of his preferred style of explanation.

Like the functionalist and unlike the identity theorist, the eliminativist doubts that there will ever be a neat reduction of psychology or cognitive science to neuroscience. His reason is that he doubts there will ever be a remotely true or coherent psychology to reduce!

The eliminativist is skeptical of an assumption which he claims the identity theorist and the functionalist share, namely, that the concepts, categories, and laws of folk psychology are fundamentally correct. The eliminativist thinks our ordinary commonsense psychology is seriously misguided and worth outright elimination. The twist is that he thinks so-called scientific psychology has appropriated the concepts and principles of folk psychology hook, line, and sinker, and thus is worth deep-sixing as well.

Paul and Patricia Churchland are the most able and articulate contemporary defenders of eliminativism. Paul Churchland says,

> FP [Folk Psychology] suffers explanatory failures on an epic scale. . . . [I]t has been stagnant for at least twenty-five centuries. . . . [I]ts categories appear (so far) to be incommensurable with or orthogonal to the categories of the background physical science whose long-term claim to explain human behavior seems undeniable. Any theory which meets this description must be allowed a serious candidate for outright elimination.[50]

According to the eliminativist, the main problem with functionalism, as with identity theory, is its uncritical confidence in the types of ordinary folk psychology: belief, desire, love, hope, pain, and so on. The eliminativist believes that this typology and its accompanying theory have led only to vacuous and contradictory generalizations (such as "out of sight out of mind" and "absence makes the heart grow fonder"), and to absolutely no scientific progress whatsoever. Folk psychology, and its first cousin, scientific psychology, will eventually go the way of phlogiston, witches, and the geocentric theory of planetary motion. All these theories were once widely accepted, but were eventually simply eliminated; they were shown not to be even approximately true. It is time to do neuroscience and stop playing games.

Churchland argues that once neuroscience is complete we can

> set about reconceiving our internal states and activities, within a truly adequate conceptual framework at last. Our explanations of one another's behavior will appeal to such things as our neuropharmacological states, the neural activity in specialized anatomical areas, and whatever other states are deemed relevant by the new theory.[51]

The eliminativist raises a very important point: Folk psychology is a theory, and it is conceivable that it could turn out to be false, not only at the level of its laws, but even at the level of its typologies. Maybe there just are no beliefs, desires, hopes, and so on, as we conceive of them.[52] Marvin Minsky, another skeptic about folk psychology, puts it this way: "Though prescientific idea germs like 'believe,' 'know,' and 'mean' are used in daily life, they seem technically too coarse to support powerful theories; we need to supplant, rather than support and explicate them."[53]

If we take seriously the possibility of the demise of folk psychology, it is worth reflecting on what the consequences might be for the preferred style of explanation in cognitive science. Fortunately for the cognitive scientist, things are not nearly as bleak as the eliminativist paints them.

Eliminativists sometimes talk as if cognitive scientists simply appropriate the concepts, categories, and laws of folk psychology straight out, but this is not quite right. Cognitive scientists tend to offer explanations from both the design stance *and* the intentional stance.

Intentional-stance explanations openly appropriate traditional belief-desire concepts from folk psychology, and thus can be expected to suffer from whatever liabilities these concepts bring. On the other hand, folk-psychological concepts function differently in the hands of cognitive scientists than in the hands of the person on the street. In large part this is because folk-psychological concepts are being deployed in experimental settings in which enrichment as well as revision of our commonsense understanding is the goal. Furthermore, it is simply not true that in accepting the basic conceptual scheme of folk psychology, the scientist who takes the intentional stance, the cognitive scientist, also accepts the generalizations of folk psychology. Many of the experiments I have discussed here completely undermine traditional folk-psychological wisdom, for example, the view that people have privileged access to their own minds, or that the mind is one simple unity, or that we are by nature completely rational animals.

When cognitive scientists study the mind at the subpersonal level, explanations tend to move in the design-stance direction. The process being studied, say, sentence comprehension, is divided into a series of smaller functions—visual or auditory processing, semantic and syntactic analysis, and so on. Such explanations appropriate folk-psychological concepts far less than full-blown intentional-stance explanations. Furthermore, design-stance explanations rarely appropriate folk-psychological generalizations, in part because normally there are no extant folk-psychological generalizations about the processes under study. The eliminativist acts as if the cognitive scientist has made a completely uncritical pact with folk psychology. This is simply not true.

The eliminativist does raise an important point, however. To whatever extent theorizing in cognitive science is constrained by alleged truths of folk psychology from above, it is also constrained by known truths about the nervous system, from below. It would be dangerous for cognitive scientists to entertain even for a moment the belief that research in brain science is irrelevant to their functional pronouncements, or to take metaphysical functionalism as proof that there are no interesting mappings of psychological processes onto brain processes. The amount of important work indicating all sorts of localization of function makes this view untenable. Furthermore, it would be a parallel error to think that neuroscience will never lead us to reconceptualize phenomena at the functional level. It seems to me that work on the biochemical bases of certain types of mental illness, such as manic-depressive psychosis and schizophrenia, has already produced not only better understanding of the cases of these illnesses, but has also led to a reconceptualization of their nature.

It is worth emphasizing that for all their bravado, identity theory, functionalism, and eliminativism all involve more or less a priori stances about the way the relations among the different sciences will work out. The three views share a commitment to metaphysical materialism. They differ, however, in that the identity theorist bets that psychology will someday be smoothly reduced to neuroscience; the functionalist that psychology will remain an autonomous special science; and the eliminativist that psychology will simply go the way of alchemy and be replaced by neuroscience. The important point is that the issues here cannot be settled a priori. They will depend for their resolution on how the various research programs guided by the three points of view turn out. In the meantime, the cognitive scientist is on epistemologically sound ground in proceeding to analyze mental processes at levels above the neural.

Cognitive Science and the Charms of Good Old-Fashioned Artificial Intelligence

Sherry Turkle has written, "Under pressure from the computer, the question of mind in relation to machine is becoming a central cultural preoccupation. It is becoming for us what sex was to Victorians— threat, obsession, taboo, and fascination."[54] In this section I focus on work in computer science—specifically work in Artificial Intelligence—not only because of its intrinsic philosophical importance but because AI has been warmly embraced by many cognitive scientists as a partner in the struggle to understand the nature of human intelligence. I first discuss the attractions of traditional AI, what John Haugeland calls "Good Old-Fashioned Artificial Intelligence" or

GOFAI. Then in the next section I discuss a compelling, powerful, and novel approach to AI known as "connectionism" or Parallel Distributed Processing (PDP), PDPAI for short.

GOFAI inspires and is inspired by the representational theory of mind (RTM). According to RTM, the human mind is a device that performs computations over mental representations. Thinking takes place at the lowest level in a common code shared by all members of our species. This common code is what Jerry Fodor, the major proponent of the representational theory of the mind (RTM), calls "the language of thought." Fodor thinks that it is necessary to postulate a language of thought if one is to explain how concept acquisition of any sort (in one's native language) is possible. Concepts, words, public symbols can be learned only if there is something symbol-like in the mind onto which they can be mapped. Fundamentally, computation over representations in the common code is what thinking is.

GOFAI operates with a kindred insight. Thus Haugeland writes that "the thesis of GOFAI . . . is not that the processes underlying intelligence can be described symbolically . . . but that they *are* symbolic."[55] Although the computer manipulates uninterpreted symbols, these symbols are manipulated in accordance with the syntax of the computer's machine language. The machine language of a computer consists of the procedures, operating at the very lowest level, for manipulating symbols of the right kind in a way that can (eventually) be understood at the top level. Fodor explicitly recommends the analogy between a language of thought that subserves human cognition and the machine language of a digital computer.[56]

The symbols a computer manipulates are meaningless to it, but they receive an interpretation from us. Depending upon the interpretation, an arbitrary string of symbolic output can represent numbers, chess moves, words, or weather patterns. The machine itself operates according to strict syntactic rules. Happily, these rules will result in the preservation of the right semantic interpretation throughout, since the syntactic rules allow only certain clearly specified transformations of one set of symbolic structures to another. If the system starts with sense and the rules are clear, the system will produce sensible output. A computer that doesn't know Socrates from Plato, *Homo sapiens* from Martians, or mortality from immortality and hasn't a clue as to what its internal symbols mean will nonetheless produce the proper syllogistic conclusion "Socrates is mortal" from the premises "Socrates is a man" and "All men are mortal" so long as it is provided with the right inference schema and translation rules that allow these English words to become values for the variables in that schema. The power of syntactic devices manipulating symbols or symbol-like tokens leads John Haugeland to this simple and elegant definition of a modern GOFAI computer: "A *computer* is an interpreted automatic formal system—that is to say, a *symbol-manipulating machine*."[57]

It will become clear as the discussion proceeds that the connectionist models dominant in PDPAI reject the shared assumption of RTM and GOFAI that it is necessary to postulate linguistic or quasi-linguistic processes at every level of processing in "intelligent" systems. Indeed, existing connectionist systems are not illuminatingly viewed as symbolic or representational all the way down, at least not in any obvious way.

In any case, GOFAI models human intelligence in von Neumann systems that have the following main features: first, computation operates over *abstract symbolic representations;* second, computation is governed by a *stored program* that contains an explicit set of instructions or rules in accordance with which the symbolic representations are to be transformed into new symbolic structures; third, computation is carried out by a *serial central processing unit* that has access to information stored in the computer's *permanent memory.*

The attraction of GOFAI derives from five main sources. First, there is the impressive state of the art. AI has effortlessly captured the attention of mind scientists because of the amazing things computers can now do. Modern automata can perform humanlike motor, perceptual, and conceptual tasks. They can orchestrate a spaceship landing and then carry out biochemical analyses of the soil and atmosphere of a distant planet. They can discriminate between exceedingly subtle differences in visual patterns. They can play chess well, backgammon very well, and checkers faultlessly. They can prove the theorems in Whitehead and Russell's *Principia Mathematica.* They can read and give fair plot summaries of stories and newspaper articles and they can interact with humans who communicate with them in programming languages which approximate ordinary language. And, of course, they can do arithmetic in a way that staggers the imagination.

The second reason GOFAI is attractive to cognitive scientists is that the concept of computation, the fundamental concept of the field and instantiated in every computer program, rigorously captures the ideas of information processing and rule following which figure centrally, though often metaphorically, in cognitive science.

The third attraction of GOFAI comes from the fact that modern automata are symbol-using entities. Unlike machines such as automobiles, sewing machines, and ordinary clocks which function by the turning of gears and motors, computers function by manipulating what, to us anyway, can only be described as symbols. A modern digital computer is essentially a machine that interacts with symbols at several different levels; it is a semantic engine.

Fourth, commitment to certain forms of AI coheres nicely with the metaphysical functionalist's commitment to token-physicalism, the view that although every mental event is some physical event, mental events can be realized in many different ways, in many different kinds of physical devices. According to standard functionalism, the particular physical embodiment of a cognitive process is not necessarily what makes it a cognitive process of a certain kind (although it must be embodied in some sort of physical process). What determines, for example, that a particular cognitive process is a wish for an ice-cold drink as opposed to a belief that the Yankees will win the pennant is not its physical embodiment or location (which in the case of the wish and the belief might overlap or coincide), but its role in a system of functional states. If one accepts functionalism, one is committed to the theoretical possibility that some, perhaps all, cognitive states, which in normal humans require real flesh and blood, can be carried out by an inorganic electrical device made of metal and plastic.

Finally, GOFAI is attractive because it lends credibility to the cognitive psychologists' choice of a level of analysis above the level of hardware. Within GOFAI itself the distinction between hardware (the system constituted by the Central Processing Unit (CPU), the memory grid, and the terminals and printers) and software (the set of instructions loaded into a computer's active memory that tells the hardware what special-purpose computations it is to perform), is well established. Explanations at both levels are considered valuable and illuminating.

How was GOFAI able, in such a short time, to make information-processing mechanism a respectable model of mentality? Paradoxically, it was an abstract and supposedly nonpsychological discipline, logic, that made this possible by clarifying the notion of a formal system.

A formal system consists of a set of basic elements or pieces and a set of rules for forming and transforming the elements or pieces. For example, in propositional logic, p, q, r, $\&$, $\vee$, $\rightarrow$, $\sim$, and so on, are elements, and $p \& q$ is a legitimate expression, what logicians call a well-formed formula (wff). The transformation rules allow the inference p to be drawn from $p \& q$. All the mathematical sciences are formal in exactly the specified sense.

It is a truism that a formal system is meaningless until meaning is assigned to its elements. Until then a formal system is all syntax and no semantics. The sense of a formal system is provided by what is known as its "interpretation." The basic idea is this: manipulations of formal systems—for example, $1 + 1 = 2$ or $p \rightarrow q$, not q, therefore not p—are meaningless until we are told that numerals stand for numbers and that 'p' and 'q' can stand for any proposition in any natural language. The interpretation of a formal system is crucial if the system is to be about anything.

It turns out that many (some say all) systems can be treated profitably as formal. For example, games are formal in the sense that one normally starts with a set of basic pieces, such as checkers, or chessman, or the X's and O's of tic-tac-toe. The pieces are arranged in a certain canonical manner at the opening of the game, and all permissible moves are specified by the rules.

A computer programmed to play tic-tac-toe, checkers, or chess is an automatic formal system. Modern GOFAI computers are just automated, self-regulating imitators of some formal system or other. Owing to the important work of Alan Turing, philosophers often refer to any device that automatically instantiates some formal system as a Turing machine. Turing machines are primitive theoretical ancestors of von Neumann machines—the apple of GOFAI's eye.

Compared to modern computers, a Turing machine is a primitive, somewhat awkward device. It comes equipped with a limitless supply of paper with has 0's and 1's written on it. The executive unit scans the paper, and (depending on its program) either ignores, or erases and replaces the 0's and 1's with other 0's and 1's.

The primitiveness of Turing machines notwithstanding, it turns out, according to a theorem proved by Turing, that there exist Universal Turing Machines which can be programmed to imitate all special-purpose Turing machines. Thus if there exists one Turing machine which plays chess, another which plays checkers, and a third which plays tic-tac-toe, there exists a universal machine which can do all three, as well as any other automated formal task.[58]

It is the most widely shared article of computer scientific faith that every formal system can be automated. This article of faith is called "Church's thesis" after the great logician Alonzo Church, and it has been proven true for every well-understood formal system.

It should be clear by now that the hopes for GOFAI as a psychological research program rest on the credibility of viewing mentality as a causally realized set of formal systems. Taken together, Turing's theorem and Church's thesis imply that if our minds are formal systems or collections of formal systems, there exists an infinite number of automatic universal machines which are formally equivalent to them. John Haugeland puts the point this way: "The basic idea of cognitive science is that intelligent beings are *semantic engines*—in other words, automatic formal systems with interpretations under which they consistently make sense. . . . [P]eople and intelligent computers turn out to be merely different manifestations of the same underlying phenomenon."[59]

Fancy formal work notwithstanding, most people remain puzzled as to how it could be possible for a dumb electrical device to imitate every conceivable formal system, and how it is remotely credible to think of a person as a set of interpreted formal systems. A brief explanation of how a computer works might help to give us some leverage toward removing such suspicions. Even among the so-called "computer literate," the workings of computers are often a deep dark secret.

A standard digital computer has the following sort of (von Neumann) architecture. The central processing unit, CPU, consists of a series of hard-wired pathways called logic gates that distinguish electrical pulses from nonpulses. The pulses can be viewed as representing 1's and the nonpulses 0's. The CPU is hard-wired to take strings of 1's and 0's at the entry ports of its logic gates and transform them into any variety of new strings of 1's and 0's before they exit. In an ordinary computer the CPU can perform as many as a million transformations per second. The CPU also has access to and interacts with its memory. The memory consists of an electronic grid. Typically the grid is comprised of over 250,000 "words." Each word is composed of approximately 32 "bits." Each word on the grid is uniquely addressable by the CPU; each bit in memory contains a unique piece of electrical information—in particular, each bit of memory is in a charged (1) or uncharged (0) state.

The CPU is limited to registering and operating on information from the memory. Typically the first few bits in a word tell the CPU what operation it is to perform; the rest tell it what other words it should seek out to perform these operations on. This is where the software, or program, comes in. The CPU is responsive to software loaded into its memory. The program—usually encoded as a sequence of control words—gives the CPU specific instructions on how to transform electrical patterns—sequences of 0's and 1's—into new electronic patterns. A program in effect turns the CPU of a universal Turing machine into a special-purpose device.

At bottom, then, it is fair to say that a computer only understands electricity. The electronic code—the strings of pulses and nonpulses—that the CPU is built to understand and manipulate is called the machine language. If you harbor any doubts about the representational capacity of variously sequenced strings of pulses and nonpulses in a 250,000-word vocabulary each made up of 32 bits, consider the representational capacity of the 26 letters of the alphabet!

In any case, because the CPU is monolingual, that is, it only operates in machine language, all programs ultimately must be encoded in machine language. But programmers write programs in languages such as BASIC, Fortran, Pascal, LISP, and so on, that are closer to natural language than to machine language.

The reason they can do this runs as follows: The keyboard of a cathode-ray tube (CRT) is wired so that when a character is typed it is sent to the CPU as a unique electrical string, typically an eight-unit string of 0's and 1's. Sequences of these strings are then worked over by a program permanently stored in the computer's memory and meticulously translated into machine language. This program is called an "interpreter" (or "compiler" or "assembler") and it takes eight-unit strings of 1's and 0's and transforms them into other strings of 1's and 0's so that the actual computing can take place.

Suppose, for example, that at monitor level—that is, at a keyboard in front of a CRT—we ask a suitably programmed computer to add 1 + 2 by typing, say, "(add 1, 2)". In a system that uses 8 bit ASCII (that is, each character we type is internally represented as an eight-unit string of 0's and 1's), the CPU first gets this problem in the form (00110001, 00110010). Next the CPU consults the interpreter as to the rules for transforming these still unfamiliar eight-unit strings into its vernacular (picture yourself in a foreign country with a dictionary). Often this will involve transforming (00110001, 00110010) into a binary representation of 1 and 2, say, (1,10). Now the CPU is ready to perform the computation proper. Once it gives its answer, which in its binary language is 11, the CPU consults the interpreter for further instructions on how to turn 11 (which represents 3 to us) into the appropriate eight-bit ASCII sequence so that the answer will show up in a "user-friendly way" on the screen or printer, that is, as 3.

An additional reason why modern computers offer a tempting model of the human mind begins to emerge. Brains appear to function in a way somewhat analogous to machine language. Brains are essentially electrochemical processors containing about 100 billion neurons, many of which are specialists and all of which can spike at rates exceeding 100 times per second. If we assume, as many members of the GOFAI establishment think we should, that the brain encodes and processes information in some electrochemical code, the question arises as to how and why I understand English but haven't a clue as to the semantic and syntactic features of this code. After all, it is likely that all my conscious thoughts in English are effected by some brain process carried out in neuronese. Without answering this question directly one can see how computers give a purchase on the possibility of a solution to this conundrum.

Both humans and sophisticated computers can receive inputs and represent outputs in a language utterly different from the languages in which they process these inputs and outputs. This suggests that human systems, like computational systems, require interpreters and involve several different levels of processing.

The situation of the programmer who instructs a computer to do all sorts of things without the faintest knowledge of machine language is interestingly analogous to our everyday situation of getting ourselves and each other to do all sorts of things without the faintest knowledge of the properties of our own or each other's brains. Furthermore, the mysterious fact that I understand English while my brain operates in a code of its own is explained by the fact that an entire system (in this case me) and a subsystem (my brain) can have different properties. My cells, after all, are small but I am not. This table is hard but its constituent molecules are not.

To reiterate, GOFAI systems operating with standard von Neumann architecture contain a single powerful CPU that responds to input by performing serial high-speed transformations of symbols into new sets of symbols in accordance with the rules specified in a stored program that has access to its memory bank.

Parallel Distributed Processing, Connectionism, and Biological Realism

So far in discussing GOFAI, I have been describing the standard Turing and von Neumann computer architecture. An exciting new computer architecture has emerged in the last decade to compete with the standard model. *Parallel Distributed Processing* (PDP) or *connectionism* is the name of this competitor.[60]

As we have seen, the standard GOFAI model involves a single, relatively powerful CPU that performs operations *serially* on abstract representations in accordance with the rules specified in a program. The program itself is retrieved from permanent memory. It is loaded into working memory and has on-line access, as needed, to other knowledge stored in permanent memory. Allen Newell and Herbert Simon are major proponents of a picture of human knowledge that was made, one might say, to be implemented on standard von Neumann architecture. Knowledge, according to them, is represented by an enormous set of conditional rules called "productions." Productions have the form "condition → action." If such and such condition obtains, for example ⟨square root, 81⟩, then do such and such, i.e., compute the square root and produce ⟨+/−9⟩. It is easy to imagine production systems doing mathematical problems and playing chess. Indeed, they are terrific at doing both. The production rules are stored in long-term memory. The program being run retrieves the relevant production rules into working memory and follows them *seriatim.*

But standard von Neumann architectures have several shortcomings. First, they are ultimately, despite certain tempting analogies cited above, biologically unrealistic, and this for a host of reasons. For present purposes, the most important source of this lack of biological realism is that there is no anatomical area of the brain that plays the role of permanent memory. To be sure, there are domain-specific memory losses (losses of memory for faces or linguistic memory) that are tied to destruction of particular brain areas. But even in these cases, localization of memory function is by domain, by memories of a particular kind. There is no one place where memories of every kind are stored. There is no single brain area that plays the role that the ubiquitous box labeled "long-term memory" plays in standard flow-charts of the mind.

Not only is the capacity to remember different kinds of things distributed throughout the brain rather than dependent on one large localized memory store, but some evidence suggests that even within each domain there is no specific anatomical location that plays the role of storing, on a permanent basis, things that are memorable in that domain. Not only is there no all-purpose memory warehouse in the brain; there are no smallish, domain-specific long-term memory stores either. There are no stores stocked with memories, period.

Consider face recognition. The metaphor of the well-run office with permanent files might lead us to imagine that what happens when one recognizes a familiar face is that my superspeedy and superefficient secretarial homunculus fetches my face files and searches for a match with the one before it. Since damage to the right parietal lobe can produce prosopagnosia—the inability to recognize or remember faces, possibly even to see faces as such—one might hypothesize that such damage destroys the files or the fetcher. Unfortunately, no facts about the brain support this way of thinking about the process. Even for those of us with intact parietal lobes, there is nothing in the relevant parts of the brain that is anything like a file full of pictures of faces I have known, nor is there any processor to play the role of the secretarial homunculus. A familiar face activates a complex but characteristic pattern of neural activity. The brain is *disposed* to activation of a certain sort when a familiar face appears.

Where is my memory of your face when you are not in front of me or I am not imagining your face? The answer, it appears, is nowhere.

Memories exist as dispositions, not as permanent states or files. Memories, inactive or active, are *distributed* in two respects. First, when inactive, they exist only as dispositions to activation spread throughout different areas of the brain. The nature of particular dispositions depends on the nature and strengths of various connections among systems of neurons. Second, remembering just is the activation of the relevant populations of neurons distributed through many layers of the brain. It does not involve some secretarial homunculus's retrieving the information in a preexisting file and comparing it to the current stimulus array.

The second problem with thinking of the mind as a standard serial von Neumann device is related. It has to do with the fact that although conscious problem solving may be serial and governed by something akin to a central processor, most problem solving, perceptual processing, and motor activity are probably neither serial nor governed by a single CPU. This point was originally brought home to AI workers when it was noticed that whereas chess playing was easy for production systems operating on von Neumann machines, simple visual recognition tasks were extraordinarily difficult and could take a ridiculously long time. How could it be that computers could play chess and do arithmetic faster and more accurately than a human but were absurdly slow at simple recognition tasks? One plausible answer is that systems like us that can do such things fast and accurately perform computations in parallel.

A standard CPU performing 10^6 computations per second can do arithmetic at blazing speed. But many visual-recognition tasks take on the order of a billion (10^9) steps. For such a CPU, the task of distinguishing two visual patterns, say a cat from a ball of yarn, might take as long as 1,000 seconds, that is, about 15 minutes. As Paul Churchland says, a "mouse who cannot recognize cats faster than that is doomed to be lunch."[61] The way around the CPU bottleneck problem is to introduce parallelism.[62] A neural system with 10^9 neural processors working in parallel can recognize a face, a cat, or a degraded word in a fraction of a second. This is the result we want, since that is how fast we do in fact recognize such things.

But wait, one might complain, it cannot be that 10^9 neural processors are involved in such tasks. There are, after all, only 10^{11} neurons, and using 10^9 is using most of the system. The first point is that using this many processors does not involve using most of the system. If 10^9 processors are in play in a system with 10^{11} processors, this is only 1 percent of the system. Second, we should not think of neural processors as equivalent to individual neurons. It is better to think of them as involving populations of neurons. A typical neuron has synaptic connections emanating from on the order of 3,000 other neurons (some neurons are on the receiving end of 10 thousand synaptic inputs, most have fewer, but some have as many as 100 thousand synaptic inputs). This makes for an order of 10^{14} synaptic connections in the brain. If we assume that each connection is capable of one of only ten possible weights at any given time (this is a conservative estimate), the total number of distinct possible neural configurations is $10^{100,000,000,000,000}$. Paul Churchland puts these numbers in perspective. "To get some idea of the size of this number, recall that the total number of elementary particles in the universe is generally estimated to be about 10^{87}."[63] Suppose that 99 percent of these possible brain states are totally useless from a cognitive point of view. Remember the old adage that people only use 10 percent of their mind? Well, make believe it is only 1 percent (10^{-2}). Even if 99 percent of brain activity can give rise to nothing functional or thoughtlike (these being different), this would still mean that on the order of $10^{99,999,999,999,999,998}$ brain states are potentially fungible in cognitive coin. Even if 99.9 percent of the possible states are useless and only .1 percent (10^{-3}) potentially useful, that still leaves us with $10^{99,999,999,999,999,997}$ functional mental states. The brain obviously has enough room for our mental life!

The lesson is this. Since there are absolute constraints on the speed of serial computation set by the speed of light (186,281 miles per second in a vacuum), the best strategy for breaking up the computational bottleneck of a serial device would be to introduce massive parallelism and connectivity. One way to do this is to dedicate lots of different CPUs to handling different aspects of some input and to then have them pass on the products of their labor to some more central location that prepared the overall global computation for dissemination. Each CPU can be significantly dumber than the CPU of a standard high-powered serial device since its job involves doing only one small piece of a monstrously complex job. Massively parallel von Neumann devices do exist.[64] These devices solve the bottleneck problem, and they gain thereby in biological realism. Such devices, however, still make use of permanent memory stores. Memory is sometimes allotted in domain-specific ways, so that each special-purpose CPU has access only to its own special-purpose memory store, or only to the part of global memory relevant to its job description. But the memory systems are not fully or truly distributed, since they are firmly localized and they involve permanent dedicated states rather than activation dispositions. To get an idea of the difference between a dedicated informational state and an information-bearing dispositional state, consider this analogy. A book on your shelf is localized, and the print on its pages involves informational dedication.

The whole book can be moved, but the information it contains goes with it. But other real things are not like this. Solubility, flammability, courage, honesty, seeing, and remembering, to name just a few, are dispositions. Logically, a disposition can be analyzed in counterfactual terms. To say that P is courageous means among other things that *if* P were in a situation of great danger that required action rather than inaction or passivity, P *would* be disposed to act. To say that P remembers that Columbus landed in the Americas in 1492 is to say that *if* faced with the relevant question or placed in a situation in which that knowledge is relevant, P *would* be disposed to think or say that Columbus landed in the Americas in 1492. But there is no book on P's mental shelf that P fetches and looks up this information in. P is simply disposed to go into a certain information-bearing state in certain appropriate situations, akin to the way water is disposed to freeze at 32°F. The freezing isn't kept in some place while the water isn't frozen. Freezing is just one of the states water goes into in certain circumstances. The same goes for remembering some fact.

We tie ascriptions of dispositions to predictions in the relevant counterfactual situations and in this way make sense of ascriptions of courage, sight, and memory to persons, solubility to sugar, and flammability to gasoline. But we are asking the wrong question if we ask—expecting a literal answer—for the *location* of the courage, or if we ask where the courage (or sight or memory) is kept when P is not being courageous (or not seeing or not remembering). Dispositions are characteristic patterns of activation. Bona fide dispositions display precisely the counterfactually predicted features once activated. Furthermore, active dispositions are physical. But they are not physical *things* in the standard sense, and thus they do not reside in some tangible location when they are not active.

The bet of PDP researchers is that most of cognition—sensory experience, perceptual recognition, possibly scientific theorizing itself—is to be analyzed in terms of dispositions to experience, recognize, and classify incoming signals in terms of certain characteristic neural-activation patterns.[65] Here are two examples of connectionist networks.

The Mine-Rock Detector
This first example is based on work by Gorman and Sejnowski,[66] and it is illuminatingly described by Paul Churchland.[67] The network's job is to distinguish mines from rocks by sonar in the way in which a submarine might want to do. What is nice about the problem is that it was not known a priori whether there is any acoustical pattern in nature that distinguishes rocks from mines. The first task was to

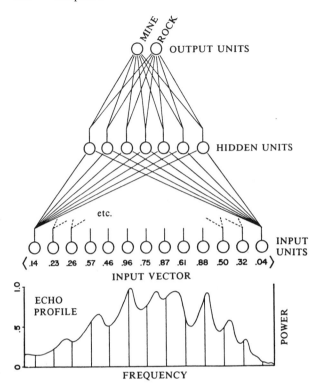

Figure 6.2
Perceptual recognition in a large network, here a rock-mine detector. (Reprinted with permission from P. M. Churchland 1989, p. 203.)

gather huge numbers of sonar recordings of rock echoes and mine echoes. The second step was to set up a connectionist network with thirteen units at the input level. Figure 6.2 shows what the system looks like. The units at the input level compute in parallel the energy levels of the recording at thirteen different frequencies. The results of this set of computations (expressed as a fraction between 0 and 1) are projected or propagated upward to the second level, the level of the so-called "hidden units," which in this case is comprised of seven units. The level of activation of each unit at the hidden layer is determined by the sum of all the values reaching it. The activity of the entire hidden layer can be captured as a vector that expresses the total level of activation at that layer, this being determined by the connections from the input layer to each hidden unit and the weights or strengths of the inputs received by each hidden unit. The activation pattern achieved at this level is then propagated upward to the out-

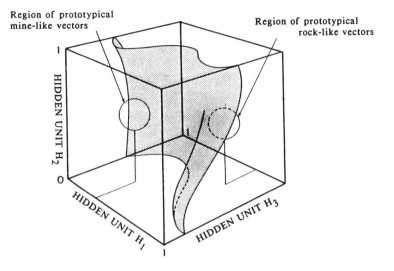

Figure 6.3
Learned partition on a hidden-unit activation-vector space. Axes are shown for
only three of seven hidden-unit activation levels. (Reprinted with permission from
P. M. Churchland 1989, p. 203.)

put level, which computes its activity level. In this case, only two
output units are required, one for mines, another for rocks. The aim
is to get the system to produce a vector at the output level near
⟨1, 0⟩ when a mine echo is heard and near ⟨0, 1⟩ when a rock echo is
heard—if, that is, there is some principled natural distinction between sonar recordings of mines and rocks.

Initially the system randomly gives correct and incorrect responses.
But here a second computer enters to "train up the network." This
teacher knows whether the network was fed a mine or a rock recording. It reads the network's guess, and it gives the network feedback
about how it is doing. In particular, it gives the network detailed information about how far off it is from the desired result by subtracting
the output vector produced from the vector desired. A simple differential equation, called the "generalized delta rule" sends this information back into the system (this is so-called "back propagation")
with the sole aim of getting the system to nudge the weights at the
various connections at the hidden level in the right direction. If the
proper discrimination is possible at all, we want the system to reach
a point where the hidden-level vector partitions mines with mines
and rocks with rocks (as in figure 6.3).

Amazingly, after sampling a mere 100 recordings and getting detailed feedback about its mistakes in the form of the back propagation

of the magnitude of the erroneous guesses, this network will correctly discriminate both the original sample set plus new samples!

There are five main features of the network that distinguish it from a standard von Neumann device and deserve notice. First, there is no CPU. Second, inputs are processed in parallel. Third, "representations" have no unique location but are distributed throughout the system. Fourth, "representations" are not stored anywhere. They exist as dispositions of the system to take on certain activation patterns. Fifth, the system does not operate in accordance with a fixed program. There are "selection" pressures that operate on the system and nudge it toward an equilibrial state. But these pressures are not well described as driven by software, and thus the software-hardware distinction finds less of a foothold in such systems.

NETtalk

NETtalk, created by Terry Sejnowski and Charles Rosenberg, is another network that works by back propagation.[68] NETtalk more or less learns the correct pronunciation of American English after exposure to a set of 1,000 words, repeated about 50 times over a ten-hour period. Before describing how NETtalk learns how to speak, it will be useful to compare NETtalk to a system developed by engineers at Digital Equipment Corporation to do the same job.[69] DECtalk is a GOFAI system that contains a large dictionary of word-pronunciation pairs in memory. For any input string, DECtalk first searches its dictionary for a word match and follows the associated pronunciation instruction. If the word is not in the dictionary, abstract pronunciation rules are applied. DECtalk is a competent pronouncer. But its abilities reside totally in the dictionary pairings stored in memory and in its abilities to carry out the instructions for generating correct speech for words not in the dictionary.

NETtalk, unlike DECtalk, "learns" correct pronunciation. NETtalk is a three-level system like the mine-rock detector. But it possesses many more input units (203), hidden units (80), and output units (26). Since each unit is connected with every unit above it, the system contains over 18,000 connections. Differential weights on the units propagate different patterns upward and produce different sounds on the speech synthesizer that reads the output layer. The system is designed to "read" seven-unit strings of letters, or letters and spaces (represented here by dashes, e.g., "pho*n*eme" or "– – –*b*oy–" or "–a–*c*up–") and to try to pronounce the middle letter (these are italicized) in the string. To simplify the task, the 203 units comprising the bottom layer are organized into 7 groups of 29 units each. The first unit in each string is activated if "a" is input, the fifth unit if "e" is input, the twenty-fifth if "y" is input, and so on. The three extra units in each group are for spaces (dashes), commas, and periods. Suppose that "pho*n*eme" is entered. Each letter activates a different input unit in each group: "p" the sixteenth unit, "h" the eighth unit, and so on. When the target letter "n" in "pho*n*eme" is entered, the fourteenth unit is active in each group. The surrounding letters provide the context for phonetic detection, so that, for example, the "c" in "car" will be eventually pronounced as /k/, while the "c" in "race" will be pronounced as /s/. The weight of each unit is initially randomly set at some moderate value, and the system produces dopey sounds.

Now American English is not easy to learn to speak, for although the alphabet contains only 26 letters, this alphabet requires 79 distinct letter-to-phoneme associations (there is hard *c* and soft *c*, as in "car" and "race," long *a* and short *a*, as in "brave" and "hat," and so on). Thus, unlike the binary partition required in the rock-mine case, the hidden layer for American speech needs to partition sounds in precisely the 79 different ways required. Amazingly, NETtalk learns to do this by being given feedback. The feedback consists of a comparison of the desired sound with the sound produced. On the basis of this comparison a vector is computed representing how far off the actual sound is from the target. This information is propagated backward through the system to incrementally nudge the weights of the units in the desired direction. After 50 exposures to the 1,000 words, NETtalk is as competent as DECtalk, that is, about as competent at pronunciation as a young child. No Henry Higgins to be sure, but no Tower of Babble either.

One especially nice result is that the 79 vectors partitioning the phoneme space at the hidden level, partition things in such a way that the values of the vectors producing distinct sounds are numerically proximate to the degree that the sounds are acoustically similar, so that, for example, vowels and consonants are very far apart from each other, but the vowels themselves lie close together in vectorial space.

Two other features of the system are worth noticing. First, the feedback the system receives results in its learning how to pronounce sounds as they are pronounced in context. If the system pronounces the "c" in "race" as the "c" in "car," the information it receives about the nature of its error is information about how "c" is pronounced in a particular phonetic context (remember that the target letter was part of a seven-unit string "read" by the system), not simply how "c" is pronounced. Since there is no one way in which "c" is pronounced, there is, so to speak, no such information to give. Second, when one looks into the hidden layer, one finds, as with brains (and there one also finds it at the input and output levels), that no single unit is responsible for a single phonetic production. One and the same unit will serve on many different pronunciation committees. This explains why in both connectionist systems and real brains, the degradation or misbehavior of a single unit needn't lead to noticeable changes at the level of performance (see chapter 8 for more on real brains in this regard).

Connectionist AI is exciting not only because of the actual results it has produced in cases such as the rock-mine detector and in NET-talk but also because it provides an alternative picture of the way in which the human mind operates, a picture more in tune with what is known about the brain. The standard von Neumann picture is modeled too closely on conscious rule following or problem solving, which does seem to be serial.[70] But how things *seem* at the level of conscious processing may be a very unreliable indicator of how the system as a whole is operating. It would be a mistake, for example, to think that because visual consciousness is serial, visual processing is serial. All the evidence points in the direction of massive parallelism for visual cognition.

GOFAI also projects too relentlessly the familiar intuitive ideas of symbol manipulation, rule following, and memory storage onto our vision of underlying processing. To be sure, powerful, intelligent computation can be performed by serial systems that function like corporations with powerful CEOs who command armies of linguistically competent underlings (their workers) who have access to masses of filed information. But if we are interested in AI because it might disclose the secrets of human and other biological minds, it is important to remember that the brain does not obviously operate on anything that fits the description of symbolic representations and that the brain does not store rules or memories in the way old-fashioned offices or standard von Neumann architectures tempt us to envision. Furthermore, it is hard to find a candidate for the CEO in the brain, let alone to watch her orchestrate corporate operations.

PDPAI shows the power of models that dispense with the idea that thinking is symbol manipulation all the way down. And it shows the possibility and power of systems that, through massive parallelism, forward and backward propagation, bring themselves into an equilibrial state. If the mind-brain runs in accordance with a program, it is one that changes over time and in whose construction it, or it in interaction with the world, plays a major role. The existence of running connectionist systems have broken the hegemony of mental models that posit, as a necessary condition of intelligent processing, computation over mental representations encoded at the bottom level in a language of thought.

It is too early to claim that either GOFAI or PDPAI adequately models the mind. Indeed, the ideas that the mind can be analyzed at several different levels and that cognition may involve different kinds of processors and processing in different domains suggest that both approaches may be useful. Many philosophers and cognitive scientists who are convinced that the mind is at bottom a connectionist device still think that it is necessary to posit a von Neumann device at the top level. Certain phenomenological and control features of consciousness, it is thought, beg for a serial von Neumann overlay (see chapter 8 for a discussion of this idea). The exciting news for now is that we have in GOFAI and PDPAI two radically different models for thinking about the architecture of cognition. The science of the mind stands to be the beneficiary of the heated debate between proponents of the two models.

Four Kinds of Artificial Intelligence

Because I am primarily interested in the nature of human and other biological minds, I have just expressed sympathy with a vision of AI as an arm of cognitive science and neuroscience. But it is crucial to point out that among workers in AI there is some difference of opinion as to the nature of the enterprise and its relation to the science of the mind. We might distinguish among four kinds of AI.

Nonpsychological AI

Research of this kind involves building and programming computers to perform tasks which, to paraphrase Marvin Minsky, would require intelligence if they were done by us. Researchers in nonpsychological AI make no claims whatsoever about the psychological realism of their programs or the devices they build, that is, about whether or not computers perform tasks as humans do.

Weak Psychological AI

Research here is guided by the view that the computer is a useful tool in the study of mind. In particular, we can write computer programs or build devices that simulate alleged psychological processes in humans and then test our predictions about how the alleged processes work. We can weave these programs and devices together with other programs and devices that simulate different alleged mental processes and thereby test the degree to which the AI system as a whole simulates human mentality. According to weak psychological AI, working with computer models is a way of refining and testing hypotheses about processes that are allegedly realized in human minds.

Strong Psychological AI
Research in this area is guided by the view that "the computer is not merely a tool in the study of mind, rather the appropriately programmed computer really is a mind, in the sense that computers given the right program can be literally said to *understand* and have other cognitive states."[71] According to this view, our minds are computers and therefore can be duplicated by other computers. Sherry Turkle writes that the "real ambition is of mythic proportions, making a general purpose intelligence, a mind."[72] The authors of a major text announce that "the ultimate goal of AI research is to build a person or, more humbly, an animal."[73] Most of the recent philosophical literature has focused on strong psychological AI, in part because it is so controversial, carrying with it visions of computers with consciousness, computers with civil rights, computers with families, romances between humans and computers, and computers as heads of state.

Suprapsychological AI
Research in this field, like strong psychological AI, takes seriously the functionalist view that mentality can be realized in many different types of physical devices. Suprapsychological AI, however, accuses strong psychological AI of being chauvinistic—of being only interested in human intelligence! Suprapsychological AI claims to be interested in all the conceivable ways intelligence can be realized. AI programs are descriptions of these conceivable forms of intelligence. Once a program is conceived, written, and run on a computer it achieves psychologically real status in the broadest possible sense. The same holds for any realization of intelligence by a connectionist system.

From here on I will be concerned primarily with weak psychological AI and strong psychological AI. I take it that nonpsychological AI is already an unqualified and unquestionable success. I also think that suprapsychological AI is, in some important sense, uncontroversial, for the following reason. The term "intelligence" is already used to describe all sorts of human and animal activities. The proponent of suprapsychological AI exploits the generality of the term "intelligence" and suggests that there are principled reasons for extending it to new domains. In particular, he argues that every computer program and every computational device realizes a kind of intelligence. I see no reason to argue with this. Suprapsychological AI has put all its cards on the table; it simply proposes to extend the meaning of the term "intelligence" in a way which allows computer scientists to be its creators. What remains philosophically controversial about suprapsychological AI, namely, that some appropriately programmed computers or computational devices actually instantiate human intelligence, can be dealt with by talking about strong psychological AI. Let me set out a bit more fully the arguments in favor of weak psychological and strong psychological AI before examining specific objections to both programs.

The proponent of weak psychological AI views his research as a powerful methodological addition to the cognitive scientist's bag of tools. He sees AI as capable of providing three kinds of badly needed assistance.

First, cognitive science at present is a piecemeal, largely example-driven enterprise. Interesting little experiments are performed on the basis of which cognitive scientists draw transcendental inferences to the effect that people perform exhaustive serial searches on lists of digits, remember words better on the basis of first letters than third letters, cannot hear speech as meaningless, and so on. Cognitive scientists, however, show little sense of how to draw their multifarious experimental results together into a coherent model of mind. AI, on the other hand, takes seriously Allen Newell's advice that "you can't play twenty questions with nature and win."[74] AI promotes the building of more comprehensive models that, on the one hand, are required to come to grips with the solid but piecemeal experimental data, and that, on the other hand, will foster new explanations, predictions, and questions about how the mind works. These predictions can then be tested in artificial or natural settings, that is, on computers or people.[75]

Second, AI requires that the cognitive scientist design formal or mechanical models of alleged cognitive processes and run them on computers. This makes the cognitive scientist's analyses more rigorous and complex than they might otherwise be. Try writing out a complete set of instructions for playing world-class tic-tac-toe to get the relevant idea of what a complex competence underlies success on this simple game. Actually running such programs on computers has the further advantage of making sure that the alleged processes are, in fact, computationally realizable.

Third, writing AI programs (or building computational systems) can also assist in formulating and eliminating certain psychological hypotheses. Suppose we wonder how people produce phonetically correct speech in their natural language. DECtalk models one intuitively plausible hypothesis for how we might do so. The trouble is that although DECtalk can model the production of correct pronunciation, it is a totally inadequate model of how correct pronunciation is learned. This is because every correct pronunciation rule DECtalk knows is stored in its memory from the start. NETtalk is a better model for pronunciation acquisition, since unlike DECtalk it does learn. NETtalk also models correct production. So it models two things we want modeled, not just one. This doesn't mean NETtalk is a good model. Acquisition and subsequent production might operate according to different rules and in ways captured by neither DECtalk or NETtalk. According to weak psychological AI, the usefulness of systems like DECtalk and NETtalk comes from the fact that they provide vivid displays of possible models of aspects of human cognition and thereby enable us to see what various psychological hypotheses commit us to and how various hypotheses fit with other hypotheses, for example, hypotheses about the connection of the phonetic system to the semantic system. In this way they help with hypothesis generation and clarification. Testing for truth, however, is another matter.

Alternatively, suppose we wonder how a grand master plays chess. One possibility is that he exhaustively analyzes all possible moves. The trouble with this hypothesis is that in the average 80-move chess game (40 by each player) there are on the order of 10^{120} possible moves. (By comparison, there have been on the order of 10^{18} seconds since the Big Bang!) Even assuming that the appropriate chess program somehow came to exist, it would take every working computer on earth a minimum of several hundred centuries to perform an exhaustive look ahead for one game of chess! Clearly, then, grand masters do not exhaustively analyze all possible moves. They must use shortcuts—what are called "heuristics." Perhaps these heuristics exist as short-hand rules represented and followed as "production rules," as von Neumann architects imagine, or perhaps they exist as dispositions for pattern recognition, as connectionists propose.

The proponent of strong psychological AI goes further (it should be said that strong AI is a much more central component of GOFAI faith than of PDPAI faith). He believes that an appropriately programmed computer really has a mind. Motivated by fantasies about other possible intelligences such as the Martians with neurons in their circulatory system, the proponent of strong psychological AI claims that there is nothing logically incoherent in the idea of an artificial intelligence that duplicates human intelligence. If you remain unconvinced by *Gedanken* experiments about Martians, consider this possibility. Imagine that someone has a degenerative brain disease and that some great scientist has created synthetic neurons (some of which are specialists, some of which are generalists) which can be inserted in brains and which are immune to the disease. It is easy to imagine this person's brain continuing to work normally after an initial experimental transplant of say, 100 neurons. Next, suppose we start replacing millions of neurons with these synthetic neurons each week. Again, it is not inconceivable that the brain will continue to work normally even at the point of full replacement. Wouldn't you try the operation if you had the degenerative disease? There are already prosthetic hearts and lungs; there seems to be no reason, in principle, why there could not be prosthetic brains.

The overwhelming philosophical question arises: what is it about you and me, the Martians with neurons in their blood, and the person with the synthetic brain, that accounts for the fact that we possess similar kinds of mental life? The proponent of strong psychological AI answers: it is that our minds have the same kind of functional organization; we all instantiate the same set of psychological laws in different kinds of bodies.

Ten Objections to Artificial Intelligence

There are numerous objections to all forms of AI. I have chosen ten for analysis, all of which I think are worth taking seriously.

The Informality Objection

Weak psychological AI is a credible methodological arm of cognitive science to the extent that a human system is a set of formal systems. According to Church's thesis all formal systems can be simulated by an automated formal system. Strong psychological AI makes the additional claim that some of these simulations, perhaps the entire set taken together, will be actual duplications.

The Informality Objection is simply this: a person is not a formal system or a set of formal systems. Because we are not formal systems we can neither be simulated nor duplicated by other formal systems.

This objection can be mustered from a variety of perspectives. First, it is the kind of objection one might expect from a metaphysical dualist who believed that our minds are incorporeal will-o'-the-wisps (actually a dualist could conceivably hold that our minds obey formal mental laws, but this type of dualist would still oppose AI because he would deny that these laws could be realized in a physical device). I trust that the implausibility of dualism is by now established, so we can dismiss that defense of the Informality Objection.

A naturalist—one who believes that the mind is part of nature and that nature consists of lawful relations among physical phenomena—also could express the Informality Objection along the following intuitive lines: it is inconceivable that the way I play chess (I'm a disaster) could result from following a set of formal rules, and it is preposterous to think that falling in love, or making career plans or ethical choices, or developing political preferences are formal processes.

The naturalist, however, will have trouble making the Informality Objection stick in this form. First, he is depending a good deal on intuitions and gut reactions which we know by now are no way to do science. Second, naturalism itself carries with it a commitment to the lawfulness, that is, the rule-governedness, of physical phenomena. The rules the phenomena obey, of course, can be inefficient—as apparently they are in his chess game—and they may be a mystery to conscious reason—as in the case of falling in love. But insofar as the phenomena in question are natural, they will have to be rule-abiding; and insofar as they are rule-abiding it is to be expected that they will be formally specifiable; and insofar as they are formally specifiable the processes in question can be simulated by an automatic formal system.[76] Most of the mental phenomena people point to as prime candidates for informal processes involve the emotions. The trouble with using the emotions as examples of informal processes is that the current bet in psychobiology is that our emotional states and processes are governed by a wide array of hormones and neurotransmitters and thus obey formally specifiable biochemical laws.

Because scientific laws can be formally specified, weak psychological AI can thus easily withstand the Informality Objection. The last point about the powerful link of our emotional life to our physiology might give us pause, however, regarding full-blown computational duplication of persons by machines made of silicon and metal—made, that is, of the wrong stuff. The fact that some system obeys formally specifiable laws does not imply that knowing those laws and running them on some computer will capture every property of the system that operates in accordance with those rules. One is guaranteed a simulation, not a duplication. A system running a program that has embedded in it the rules governing human emotion will behave *as if* it has an emotional life, but it might not feel a thing. Running the right formal program is not sufficient for actually duplicating the properties of the system being mimicked (see "The No Emotions Objection" below).

The No Originality Objection
A computer does exactly what it is told to do; it never does anything creative or new or unpredictable. Its outputs are the result of its physical structure, its program, and the inputs it is fed. Persons, on the other hand, initiate novel, creative, and unpredictable actions.

As with the previous objection this is an obvious one for a proponent of dualism who believes that we have metaphysical freedom of will and can therefore initiate actions ex nihilo, that is, outside of normal causal channels. The dualist's view on freedom of the will was, I like to think, put to rest earlier. On the other hand, the naturalist who puts forward the No Originality Objection will have the same sorts of problems he had with consistently arguing for the previous objection. In particular, the naturalist is committed to the view that human behavior is the lawlike outcome of a person's biology, his cognitive equipment, and his life experiences. To be sure there is novelty and creativity—poetry, music, high art, great literature, and scientific breakthroughs. But there are no metaphysical creations, no leaps across bridges not fully prepared by natural and social necessity.

In speaking of the remarkable flexibility of computers, Douglas Hofstadter puts the point this way:

> The trouble is that somewhere, all this flexibility has to "bottom out". . . . There must be a hardware level which underlies it all, and which is inflexible. It may lie deeply hidden, and there may be so much flexibility on levels above it that few users feel the hardware limitations—but it is inevitably there.[77]

If AI is correct about the analogy between humans and computing machines, then human freedom, creativity, and flexibility have to bottom out somewhere too. Sometimes the No Originality Objection focuses less on failures of creativity than on the inability of computers to learn. But this worry no longer applies. It is easy to build computers that learn. NETtalk is a good connectionist example, but there are many GOFAI systems that learn as well.

Many people take unpredictability as evidence for originality, and fear that if it is true that mentality bottoms out in straightforwardly mechanical processes, we eventually will be able to predict everything about people. At that point human life will lose its joy and mystery.

Although it may be a small consolation, it does not follow from the truth of determinism—either for computers or for us—that everything is predictable. Prediction is subject to epistemic and practical constraints, such as the size and complexity of the system, randomness at the subatomic level, and so on. Many programs already exist—for example, most decent chess-playing ones—in which, because of their complexity, the programmer cannot predict his program's specific moves. In the human case, precise prediction would require not only complete understanding of (individual) biology and cognition but also complete up-to-date information about all the social, political, economic, environmental, and nutritional stimuli that have ever affected the person.

The Reductionism Objection

My formulation of this objection is guided by some remarks by Hilary Putnam. Putnam states that "Reductionism asserts that psychology is deducible from the functional organization of the brain." He argues, though, that reductionism has got to be wrong because "psychology is strongly determined by sociology."[78] Here is a simple example of what Putnam has in mind. Even if people are wired with some sort of innate "Universal Grammar," as Chomsky hypothesizes, nothing at all follows about what natural language any particular individual speaks, or what he uses it to say, until we learn where he was born and lives, how he has been socialized, and so on.

This relates to AI in the following way. One reasonable way of looking at psychologically oriented AI is as a project interested in providing a higher-level account of what Putnam calls "the functional organization of the brain." The Reductionism Objection is simply that this will never be enough. Psychology with or without AI does not have the conceptual resources to fully appreciate the human condition. A complete account of mental life will need to utilize concepts which refer to extrapsychological phenomena.

To adapt an example of Putnam's: no functional analyses (neuroscientific, AI, design-stance, intentional-stance—it makes no difference) of the basic functional organization of Chinese minds and American minds, say in 1945, could ever have yielded information sufficient to explain or predict our radically different life forms. We would have discovered, no doubt, that Chinese and American minds come equipped with similar basic desires, are designed to follow paths that they believe will maximize these desires, have similar memory capacities, make similar reasoning mistakes, mentally rotate geometrical objects, have identical linguistic abilities, fear bodily harm, and so on. But this knowledge could never be enough. The reason is obvious: all the fascinating similarities summed together shed absolutely no light on the remarkable differences.

There is one easy answer to this objection, with which I am sympathetic. Who ever said knowledge about the functional organization of the mind was enough? Who would be so foolish as to claim that the sort of research going on in cognitive science or in AI is sufficient for understanding everything about persons and their social, economic, and political worlds? There is, after all, the small matter of the rest of the cosmos which continually bombards the cognitive equipment!

This strategy of denying that AI is reductionist claim and acknowledging the existence of an intellectual division of labor is, I think, exactly the right response for the cognitive scientist or the proponent of AI to make. The acknowledgment puts programs like cognitive science and AI in clearer perspective relative to the other human sciences. Given that the functional organization of Chinese minds and American minds is very similar, we will need all the resources of geography, agronomy, history, literature, political theory, economics, and sociology to explain why, given similar equipment between the ears, our two life-forms are so different yet simultaneously so clearly human.

Although I have said that this response seems like the right one for the proponent of AI, it is not clear that it is a response that all members of the Artificial Intelligentsia can avail themselves of. Certain proponents of strong psychological AI speak as if psychological duplication is a straightforward matter of discovering and then running the right psychological laws in a complex program. But realism suggests that even a low-level simulation of human psychology will require that the system have commerce with a social world and thus that it be embodied, be able to move, and so on.

The Realism Objection

It is common to read in defenses of AI that the computer is an ideal model of mentality because it is an ideal model of the brain. The Realism Objection is that the analogy between brains and computers is grossly inflated and hence misleading.[79] Von Neumann devices have little in common with brains. Even the claim that connectionist machines are biologically realistic requires a good deal of charity. They are more like brains than von Neumann devices, but they are a lot less like brains than other brains are.

Against strong psychological AI the Realism Objection is simply that it is unlikely that computers will ever come to possess genuine mentality because they have the wrong kind of bodies.

The Realism Objection can also be used to try to undermine weak psychological AI. Proponents of weak psychological AI claim that we can write programs that test the relative plausibility of different psychological hypotheses. For example, we can write programs that purport to describe the cognitive mechanisms underlying language production. The correct program will be the one which passes the test of descriptive adequacy, that is, the one that yields all and only the class of syntactically and semantically well-formed sentences, and which, when it makes mistakes, makes the same ones we do.

The problem with this methodological tactic is that in addition to the question of descriptive adequacy there is also the matter of psychological realism. It turns out that there are an infinite number of descriptively adequate grammars—that is, formal descriptions of the language-production device—compatible with the linguistic facts. The realist claims that weak psychological AI can be of no help whatsoever in picking out psychologically real mechanisms from the class of descriptively adequate ones. Reaction-time data on computers might help if computers functioned like brains, but, according to the realist, they don't, so data on computation time is useless.

The realist has gone too far. The proponent of weak psychological AI does not claim that computer models can resolve all questions about the mind, but only that they can assist in the task of understanding mentality. To be sure, a computer simulation of the psychological rules people allegedly deploy in playing tic-tac-toe might not have all the properties of a real game. For example, the simulation might not be fun or involve manipulating X's and O's. But it might lead to enhanced understanding about our psychology if the computer's behavior was functionally isomorphic with ours, that is, if it made the same sorts of right and wrong moves, learned from past games, and eventually reached a point where it always won or drew.

Second, the proponent of weak psychological AI can point out that because the cognitive scientist working with humans is always reasoning transcendentally, that is, from observables to unobservables, his inferences to psychologically real mechanisms are also radically underdetermined by available evidence. Finally, although the proponent of AI would be foolish to claim that computers that accurately simulate human behavior and do so at the speed people do are proof of psychological realism, he can claim that computers can be given information about the brain, including information about its computational speed. This information can then be used to adjudicate among different psychological hypotheses. Despite the differences between computers and brains, there is no reason to think that computers cannot represent any relevant information we desire about neural processes. The point is that a computational system can simulate a brain system without itself being just like the brain. Furthermore, connectionist systems are—despite their differences from "the real thing"—more like functioning brains than any other systems ever built.

The Frame Problem
This problem is an epistemological one discovered by researchers in AI. Although it is easy to program a computer to do arithmetic better than any person, it is notoriously hard to give a computer the nec-

essary common sense or "world knowledge" to get by. To get the relevant idea consider this scenario, which comes from Roger Schank. Mary goes into a restaurant and orders a hamburger. It is delivered burnt to a crisp. Mary storms out of the restaurant without paying the bill. Question: Did Mary eat the hamburger? Alternatively, consider the question, Do giraffes wear hats and underwear?

The correct commonsense answers, of course, are that Mary did not eat the hamburger and that giraffes do not wear hats and underwear. But notice that the point about Mary not eating the hamburger was never stated explicitly, and I'll bet you never thought about the wardrobe of giraffes before.

A Kantian sort of question arises: how is it that we are so good at making these commonsense inferences? One possibility is that we continually update our system of beliefs so that the store of beliefs gets larger and larger throughout life. Then when we confront a novel situation or question we go to memory—a sort of belief warehouse—and search for an answer. If we don't find the answer in the beliefs explicitly stored in memory we start drawing inferences over the beliefs in the explicit store to see if some logical consequence of them (for example, giraffes go naked, and things that go naked don't wear undergarments) answers the question.

The trouble is that *ex hypothesi* we have enormous numbers of beliefs represented in our mind, so we obviously use some sort of relevance criteria to pick out the right set to consult. It turns out to be extraordinarily hard to establish, and thereby program, the right relevance criteria for computers. This is important because if we or computers tried to speed through the entire data base, drawing all possible inferences every time a novel problem came up, we would face such a combinatorial explosion of information that we would never get to the right answer because we would never finish drawing inferences!

Some philosophers have argued that systematically drawing correct commonsense inferences requires a certain kind of context sensitivity which is only likely to arise from sharing our particular kind of human life—our bodies, our institutions, our tastes in food, our sexual attractions, our appreciation of nature, our natural history, and so on.[80] To whatever extent this is true (and it strikes me as plausible), strong psychological AI, with its fantasies of duplication, decreases in credibility. (Notice how this is connected to the Reductionism Objection.)

Nevertheless, even if the point about shared life-forms is right, we still need an account of how people solve the very difficult class of problems we call "commonsensical." What are the cognitive mechanisms people deploy in solving such problems? The Frame Problem shows that it is inconceivable that our minds run through all our beliefs or draw all possible inferences over them every time a new problem arises. Presumably, however, we are performing some kinds of computation over mental representations. If we are natural phenomena, then there must be some extraordinarily efficient lawlike way we perform commonsense inferences. So, what is it?

Here weak psychological AI has already had much to say that is illuminating about the ways knowledge is represented, relevance criteria are established, and memory searches and inferences are performed.[81] PDPAI has hopes that the Frame Problem will yield to models in which all problem solving involves some sort of pattern recognition. According to PDPAI, we do not solve the frame problem by performing quick searches of propositional memory for situations or facts of the relevant kind. Instead, certain subtle features of the situation that confronts us cause the activation of a population of well-honed neural connections (this neural net could be as complex as a Schankian script, but it will not be stored as an explicit narrative) that respond to the situation with what Aristotle called "phronesis," that is, with precisely the sort of practical wisdom required by *that* situation. Aristotle thought that phronesis was something one developed over time. He did not think that it could be inculcated by simply learning a set of rules. The situations we confront in real life require the acquisition of subtle skills of perception, thought, and action. The person who possesses phronesis possesses the relevant skills, but she has not acquired these by sitting at the feet of elders who teach the rules for the practically wise. In fact, the elders do not even know the rules in a form that can be completely articulated! Gaining phronesis must occur to a certain extent on one's own and in real time. There is no set of rules that one can download and that can thereby shortcut the acquisition process. Perhaps Aristotle was the first connectionist!

The No Emotions Objection
Although a computer might simulate rational decision making, grammatical transformations, mathematical and logical reasoning, and chess play, it is inconceivable that a computer could simulate or duplicate human emotional life. First, it is not plausible to think of emotions and moods as involving computations over mental representations. What mental representations do my good moods or my pains take as their object? Second, emotions have an ineliminable qualitative component, a "raw feel," which (in addition to their functional role) is essential to making each emotional state the kind of emotional state it is.[82] Emotions, therefore, are "program-resistant."[83]

The first thing to notice is that this objection does not necessarily hurt weak psychological AI. Almost everyone thinks that human emotional life is lawlike, albeit often mysterious.

If our emotional lives obey natural laws that can be described formally, then there are computer programs that can simulate the operation of these laws. For example, here are two widely held generalizations about emotions: fear and the powerful inclination to flee are linked; and anger is linked to a desire to retaliate. With such knowledge we could write programs that simulate how the emotional system (intricately spelled out) might react if, for example, a person was angry and therefore wished to retaliate against another person, whom, however, she had reason to fear, and therefore from whom she wished to flee. From the point of view of cognitive science it will be important eventually to embed programs simulating emotions in programs simulating cognition in order to test hypotheses about the way emotions and cognition interact.

In addition to functional generalizations about emotions and their relations to each other and to cognition, there are presumably salient generalizations about emotions at the biochemical level. It is widely held, after all, that emotional states are underwritten by biochemical laws involving hormones and neurotransmitters. The operation of these biochemical laws, of course, could also be mimicked computationally.

The No Emotions Objection, therefore, does not refute a mechanistic view of emotional life, nor does it refute the possibility of computer simulation of certain aspects of emotional life.

However, the No Emotions Objection does seem to undermine strong psychological AI. After all, the evidence is overwhelming that emotional life is tied closely (perhaps type-for-type just as the identity theorist always said) to our extraordinarily complex biochemistry. To be sure, it is conceivable that earthworms and silicon chips and blades of grass might have our emotional life. It just seems unlikely. It is hard to see how the right qualitative character could emerge from the wrong kind of organic stuff, let alone from a plastic and metal electrical device. Would something with the macro properties of water but made of XYZ be a duplication of water? The answer, it seems, would be no. It would fail to possess certain essential qualitative properties of water, namely, having a molecular structure of H_2O!

Our mental life is essentially linked to our distinctive biochemistry. It is conceivable that a mental life qualitatively indistinguishable can be realized in an indefinite number of radically different kinds of material substrates. But it is also conceivable that it can't be. Or that it can be but that we will never in our species' history hit upon the right way of putting the materials that would do the job together.

I fully acknowledge the force of the well-taken objection that two hundred years ago it would have been inconceivable to think that human brains could give rise to a mental life ("Two and a half pounds of gray matter for all *this*? Come *on!*"). But it is important to realize that the discovery of this remarkable fact about our brains has come from a better understanding of our bodies in general, our nervous systems in particular, and evolution. It did not come from some a priori philosophical song-and-dance.

Thus I agree with Georges Rey (who no longer agrees with his earlier self) that

> pure (computational) functional seems to be inadequate as a complete account of our psychology; we seem to need, here and there, to return to some more straightforward materialism. And this then would be the grain of truth in the common reaction that machines can't be persons; they don't have our feelings because they don't possess our relevant physiology.[84]

The point is not that there cannot be some physiological differences among organisms that share our kind of emotional life, nor to deny that emotional states are functional states. It is only to propose that organisms that share our kind of emotional life need to possess a relevantly similar physiology, and to insist that the kind of functional states emotional states are, are embodied in a certain way.

The next four objections are directed primarily at strong psychological AI. Like the previous argument, all four are based on what John Haugeland calls the "hollow-shell strategy."[85] The basic move in the hollow-shell strategy is to claim that although it looks as if computers might someday understand, think, and so on, they won't ever do so because computers necessarily lack some property *x* that is essential to genuine mentality. The most popular candidates for the missing ingredient besides emotions are intentionality, consciousness, point of view, and free will. Let me state the four objections together, and then discuss them as a group.

The No Intrinsic Intentionality Objection
Computers lack intrinsic intentionality. The linguistic objects that a computer operates on and produces are given meaning from the outside. They are meaningless to the computer. The symbols the computer manipulates, transforms, and produces contain no semantic information as far as the computer is concerned. Humans, on the other hand, operate on the basis of semantically meaningful mental representations.

The No Consciousness Objection

A computer might be said to possess derivative intentionality and thus be said "to know that 'p'." The intentionality is derivative in the sense that we provide the semantic interpretation for 'p'. It is inconceivable, however, that a computer could be said to be conscious, that is, to be self-aware that it "knows that 'p'." Without doubt, however, we possess the sort of self-awareness in question.

The No Point of View Objection

To be a person is to be something it is like to be that person, to possess a unique subjective point of view. Even animals possess a unique point of view; to paraphrase Thomas Nagel, "there is something it is like to be a bat."[86] There is, however, nothing it is like to be a computer.

The No Free Will Objection

Most modern naturalists solve the free-well problem by taking a soft-determinist stance. Whereas they deny that there is any sort of unconstrained metaphysical freedom of will such as Descartes described, they insist that there is something to the notion of free action. In particular, an action is free if it has as its proximate cause effort by a conscious, deliberating, reasoning agent (the fact that the modes of consciousness, reasoning, and deliberation are themselves determined is just the modern notion of freedom of will). On the other hand, an action is not free if it is the result of a short circuit, that is, if it does not involve some sort of deliberation, reasoning, planning, or the like.

The No Free Will Objection then is this: although computer scientists are forever writing programs with names like COMMANDER, DELIBERATOR, REASONER, and CHOOSER, which give the appearance that their is autonomous agency in the relevant sense going on, in reality these supernouns are merely jazzy, foot-stomping names for stupid processors.[87]

John Searle has produced the paradigm-case hollow-shell argument in a paper called "Minds, Brains, and Programs," in which he constructs his famous Chinese-speaking room. In a rendition of his argument in the *New York Review of Books*, Searle says,

> Suppose we write a computer program to simulate the understanding of Chinese so that, for example, if the computer is asked questions in Chinese the program enables it to answer questions in Chinese; if asked to summarize stories in Chinese it can give such summaries; if asked questions about the stories it has been given it will answer such questions. [N]ow suppose that I, who

understand no Chinese at all and can't even distinguish Chinese symbols from some other kind of symbols, am locked in a room with a number of cardboard boxes full of Chinese symbols. Suppose that I am given a book of rules in English that instruct me how to match these Chinese symbols with each other. The rules say such things as that the "squiggle-squiggle" sign is to be followed by the "squoggle-squoggle" sign. Suppose that people outside the room pass in more and more Chinese symbols and that following the instructions in the book I pass Chinese symbols back to them. Suppose that unknown to me the people who pass me the symbols call them "question," and the book of instructions I work from they call "the program"; the symbols I give back to them they call "answers to the questions" and me they call the computer. Suppose that after a while . . . my answers are indistinguishable from those of the native Chinese speakers. I can pass the Turing test for understanding Chinese. But all the same I still don't understand a word of Chinese and neither does any other digital computer because all the computer has is what I have: a formal program that attaches no meaning, interpretation, or content to any of the symbols. [W]hat this simple argument shows is that no formal program by itself is sufficient for understanding.[88]

Searle, as I understand him, wishes to establish several related points. First, the Chinese-speaking room formally imitates a bonafide Chinese speaker. Second, nothing in the room, including John Searle, really understands Chinese. This proves that instantiating a computer program is not sufficient for understanding. Third, people possess intrinsic intentionality, whereas computers possess intentionality only by virtue of the courtesy of human observers who assign a contentful interpretation to the formal ciphers such machines manipulate and produce. Fourth, we have every reason to believe that our particular kind of brain, our particular organic constitution, is the basis for intrinsic intentionality.

Now it should be easy to see how one might extend Searle's argument so that it articulates not only the No Intrinsic Intentionality Objection, but also the No Consciousness, the No Point of View, and the No Free Will Objections as well. In fact, the actual computer cited at the beginning and end of Searle's thought experiment, although dramatically underdescribed, is exactly the sort of device which is standardly charged with lacking self-awareness, a point of view, and the capacity for free action. So we will interpret Searle's argument as promoting all four objections.

One of the things Searle is after is what he sees as the main methodological presupposition of strong psychological AI—the so-called Turing test. In a 1950 paper called "Computing Machinery and Intelligence," Turing suggested that we operationalize the question "can machines think?" in terms of a purely behavioral test called the "imitation game."[89] If a computing machine can give responses to questions that make it impossible for a person to distinguish the computer from fellow *Homo sapiens*, then the answer to the question "Can machines think?" is yes.

Searle objects to the Turing test on grounds that the normal criteria we apply in imputing intelligence to persons are based on behavioral, biological, and phenomenological evidence. People not only behave as if they have intentionality, consciousness, a point of view, and free will, but they have the right sort of private experiences and the right sorts of bodies as well. The Turing test, in effect, is a form of reverse discrimination against humans. Computers only have to behave in the right sort of ways; we have to behave correctly, have the right bodies, and the right phenomenological states.

There have been several interesting responses to Searle. Some critics argue that the Turing test is not discriminatory because our belief that other humans possess intentionality, consciousness, a point of view, and free will rests exclusively on behavioral evidence. To this Searle can effectively respond that our inferences to these properties in others is a sophisticated theoretical inference based on a complex projection of the criteria for mentality that we have gathered from paying attention to our own case and our social interactions, onto creatures who are suitably similar biologically and behaviorally.

To this, some of Searle's critics offer the so-called "robot reply": give a computer a jazzy robotic body, and then if it displays all the right kinds of behavior, Searle should be committed to infer that it has the same kind of mental features he claims to have. Here the smart countermove is first to express doubts that a computer lodged in a mechanical body could ever behave in a remotely appropriate way over the long term, and second to claim that no matter how it does on a purely behavioral test, it does not have a suitably similar body; it does not, after all, share our protoplasm or our evolutionary history. The critics, of course, argue that this is silly chauvinism and hubris.

It's not obvious who wins these little tête-à-têtes; in part the problem is that the issues are, at present, so flagrantly a priori. Many of Searle's critics are committed to a form of functionalism that allows for the logical possibility of multiple (indeed, an infinite number of) nonhuman realizations of human intelligence. Because functionalism is a viable solution to the mind-brain problem these critics are correct that Searle's arguments do not prove the impossibility of strong psychological AI. Searle, on the other hand, is certainly correct that merely instantiating a computer program is not sufficient for the possession of our kind of mentality.

But what else is needed? Searle seems to think it is the right kind of body. Some of his critics accuse him of the silly view that brains actually secrete intentionality, consciousness, and a point of view. Sympathetically interpreted, however, Searle can be read as simply trying to make metaphysical functionalism more responsive to the rest of science. Science-fiction fantasies aside, it just seems implausible to him that our evolutionary history, genes, biochemistry, anatomy, and neurophysiology have nothing essential to do with our defining features. Of course it is logically possible that they do not, but is it remotely plausible? Would anyone ever expect an inorganic device that formally instantiated all known biochemical laws about plants to actually undergo photosynthesis?

The critic replies that none of the traditional natural and social sciences explains intentionality, consciousness, and the rest; thus the (alleged) existence of these features of mentality cannot be used to support Searle's case.

But here I think Searle's critics miss his implicit point about where the burden of proof lies. Thus far we know of only one well-defined system (in the sense that we know how to distinguish members from nonmembers), that without doubt possesses the features in question, namely, *Homo sapiens.* To be sure, it is possible that an infinite number of other systems may possess these features. And it is also possible for an entire system to have properties that all its component subsystems lack. We are, I assume, just such a system. If Searle thinks that either of these is impossible, he is simply wrong.

Nevertheless, my agreement with Searle extends this far: if a brilliant young scientist told me he wanted to spend his career trying to understand intentionality and its suite, I would tell him to spend relatively more time looking at creatures that have these features, and relatively less at the infinite number of other systems that might.

Conclusion

I can now summarize my views on the philosophical assumptions and implications of cognitive science and artificial intelligence.

(1) Cognitive science is committed to the reasonable view that the mind is a representational system, that is, an intentional system that transforms, processes, stores, and retrieves information about the world.

(2) The cognitive scientist follows Kant in viewing this representa-

tional system as consisting of a rich system of a priori structures, processors, and categories which we use to create an orderly "picture" of the world. As the "picture" is enriched and revised throughout our lives we become (we hope) continually better at anticipating reality.

(3) Any science, therefore, that fails to talk about mental events and processes will not be remotely adequate. The transformations which take place between our ears are the missing links needed to account for the regularities between stimuli and responses. The behaviorist's tactic of only attending to lawlike connections between observable events is comparable to resting satisfied with the knowledge that the Big Bang is responsible for the present state of the cosmos and not giving a hoot about what has gone on in between!

(4) The epistemological problem the cognitive scientist faces is making a case for the respectability of trying to study hidden structures, states, and processes. Fortunately cognitive science has the blessing of both the philosophy of science, which sees all scientific judgments, including judgments about so-called "observables," as underdetermined by the evidence, and subatomic physics, which has had much-heralded success in cracking deep—and in some cases, in principle unobservable—mysteries about physical processes. Cognitive scientists perform their transcendental inferences (the method is an adaptation of Kant's method of "transcendental deduction") by generating hypotheses about mental processes, gathering relevant data from human subjects in experimental settings (reaction-time experiments are the current favorite), seeing whether the data are compatible with the initial hypothesis, and thereby corroborating, refining, or rejecting the initial conjectures. Standard science.

(5) Cognitive scientists pitch their explanations at the higher functional levels of analysis (at what Dennett calls the intentional and design stances), rather than at the level of brain physiology (the physical stance). The choice of the higher level of analysis is justified in two main ways. First, the software-hardware distinction from computer science is considered the possibility proof that different levels of description can be equally illuminating, depending on one's explanatory goals. Second, metaphysical functionalism, the currently favored solution to the mind-body problem, helps legitimize the view that psychological, that is, functional, explanation, is autonomous. Metaphysical functionalism is the view that although every mental event is some physical event or another (token-physicalism), mental types are not reducible to physical types.

(6) Cognitive science has several important philosophical implications, of which three stand out. First, the data indicate that the

traditional view that humans unavoidably bear eyewitness to the goings-on of their own minds—that each individual knows first and best what is on his or her mind—is, at the very least, dramatically overstated. People often lack knowledge of underlying mental processes; we are not adept at identifying the causes of our behavior and mental states; and we are even sometimes mistaken about the contents of our minds. Second, cognitive science casts doubt on the thesis of the unity of mind—the view that a mind is a single undivided whole through which consciousness continually courses. Many psychologists and philosophers (though certainly not all) believe that the data support a more modular view of the mind, that is, a view which sees the mind as a system of many different special-purpose processors, most of which have no idea what the others are doing. Third, research in cognitive science indicates that the view that humans are intuitively, or naturally, logical and rational is mistaken. Well-educated students, scientists, and logicians are prone to a wide variety of characteristic reasoning and judgment errors.

An interesting consequence of our discussion of these three philosophical implications is that to whatever extent we are capable of achieving self-knowledge, rationality, and an accurate picture of the nature of mind as a whole, it will require much more than peering inward with our mind's eye and applying knowledge and reasoning abilities that come naturally. It will require that we internalize the best available objective information about the kind of person we are, how human minds in general work, and what the principles of rationality are.

(7) As I mentioned in (5), the program of cognitive science receives support from metaphysical functionalism, the view that while all mental events are physical, psychological kinds are best captured in an autonomous functional vocabulary. Cognitive scientists, however, need to be careful not to assume that metaphysical functionalism has been definitively established. Functionalism, identity theory, and eliminativism, or any mix of them, could still turn out to be true. This is important because it is almost as easy for the functionalist as it was for the dualist to act as if neuroscientific information is irrelevant to psychology. Legitimate claims to the autonomy of psychological explanation notwithstanding, cognitive scientists would be wise to view their functional explanations and those of neuroscience as mutually constraining.

(8) Many cognitive scientists are attracted to Artificial Intelligence. The reasons are obvious: first, computers formally capture the ideas of rule following and information processing that are used less rigorously within cognitive science; second, certain kinds of computers,

allegedly like minds, manipulate, that is, perform computations on symbolic representations; third, there is good reason to believe that computers can simulate any formal process; fourth, the state of the art in terms of intelligent behavior is mind-boggling. Finally, the recent arrival of more biologically realistic connectionist models have resulted in spirited debate within cognitive science about the proper way to conceptualize cognitive processing. PDPAI provides a rival to GOFAI and raises foundational questions about the standard picture of mind as a rule-following symbolic processor. Its advent has served to increase excitement in the field while at the same time (happily) taking attention away from the debate about strong AI.

(9) Different members of the Artificial Intelligentsia, however, have different attitudes about the relationship of AI to the science of the mind. Those working in nonpsychological AI see work in AI as having no particular relevance to human psychology. Computer scientists are writing programs that do interesting and helpful tasks with blazing speed and efficiency. To be sure, these tasks would require intelligence if done by us, but they're not. AI and cognitive science are, therefore, different kinds of research. The proponent of suprapsychological AI, on the other hand, thinks the latter view underestimates AI. On his view, AI is about every conceivable form of intelligence. Every program instantiates a form of intelligence, and AI is the project of producing ever-new forms. AI is cognitive science and beyond!

Weak psychological AI is considerably more mellow. It sees AI as methodologically relevant to cognitive science. AI programs can simulate and test the implications of different hypotheses about cognitive processes, and thereby generate new ones. AI, on this view, is a research arm of cognitive science. Strong psychological AI is the view that the appropriately programmed computer or possibly the appropriately constructed connectionist device will actually duplicate—and then, some warn, go on to beggar—human mentality.

(10) Naturally, most of the philosophical and psychological interest has focused on weak psychological AI and strong psychological AI. After looking at a variety of objections to both programs my own assessment is this: weak psychological AI is, as its proponents claim, a perfectly credible, already extraordinarily useful research addendum to cognitive science. Strong psychological AI is more problematic. Even if we are machines, as I believe, the credibility of full-blown artificial duplication of human mentality rests on metaphysical functionalism turning out to be true. That is, it rests on the view that mind not only can, but will, be realized in many different kinds of machines. It is conceivable that this will happen. Nevertheless, there is

nothing foolish about thinking that certain features of our minds, such as intentionality, consciousness, and the emotions, are in some essential way tied to the specific kind of organic machines we are. The danger of strong psychological AI is that it turns its back irrevocably on the brain sciences.

(11) Finally, there is the issue of the relationship of cognitive science and AI to the rest of the human sciences. It is worth pointing out that although cognitive science and AI are at present exceedingly fruitful and exciting research programs, they will never replace the other human sciences. To be sure, utopian cognitive science and AI, should they ever come to exist, will tell us a complete story of how we process, store, and retrieve information, as well as why we respond to various kinds of experiences in the ways we do. But utopian mind science will never be able to predict the information we will receive nor the experiences we will have. Such predictions, insofar as they will be available, will come from the other special sciences: sociology, politics, anthropology, and economics, as well as agronomy, meteorology, astronomy, medicine, and so on. Cognitive science and AI, therefore, unlike the sociobiological theories we will examine next, make no reductionist pronouncements. They claim to supplement the rest of the human sciences, not to replace them.

Suggested Readings

General Introductions to Cognitive Science and AI

Anderson, J. (1980), *Cognitive Psychology and Its Implications*.
Boden, M. (1977), *Artificial Intelligence and Natural Man*.
Johnson-Laird, P. N. (1988), *The Computer and the Mind: An Introduction to Cognitive Science*.
Osherson, D. N. (1990), *An Invitation to Cognitive Science*. Three Volumes.
Rumelhart, D. E., McClelland, J., and the PDP Research Group (1986), *Parallel Distributed Processing: Explorations in the Microstructure of Cognition*, two volumes.
Simon, H. (1974), *The Sciences of the Artificial*.
Smolensky, Paul (1988), "On the Proper Treatment of Connectionism."
Stillings, N., et al. (1987), *Cognitive Science: An Introduction*.

Philosophical Foundations

Block, N. (1980a), *Readings in Philosophy of Psychology*, two volumes.
Churchland, P. M. (1988), *Matter and Consciousness*, revised edition.
Dennett, D. (1978a), *Brainstorms*.
Fodor, J. (1981a), *Representations: Philosophical Essays on the Foundations of Cognitive Science*.
Haugeland, J. (1981a), *Mind Design*.
Haugeland, J. (1985), *Artificial Intelligence: The Very Idea*.

Hofstadter, D. (1980), *Gödel, Escher, Bach: An Eternal Golden Braid.*
Turing, A. M. (1950), "Computing Machinery and Intelligence."

Identity Theory

Smart, J. J. C. (1959), "Sensations and Brain Processes."

Functionalism

Fodor, J. (1981c), "Special Sciences."
Block, N. (1980b), "Troubles with Functionalism."

Eliminativism

Churchland, P. M. (1981), "Eliminative Materialism and the Propositional Attitudes."

Rationality and Self-Knowledge

Cherniak, C. (1986), *Minimal Rationality.*
Cohen, L. J. (1981), "Can Human Irrationality be Experimentally Demonstrated?"
Dennett, D. (1978b), "Intentional Systems."
Dennett, D. (1978e), "Toward a Cognitive Theory of Consciousness."
Goldman, A. (1986), *Epistemology and Cognition.*
Harman, G. (1986), *Change in View.*
Nisbett, R. E.,, and Ross, L. (1980), *Human Inference: Strategies and Shortcomings of Social Judgment.*
Nisbett, R. E., and Wilson, T. D. (1977), "Telling More Than We Can Know: Verbal Reports on Mental Processes."
Tversky, A., and Kahneman, D. (1974), "Judgment Under Uncertainty: Heuristics and Biases."

Unity of Mind

Anderson, J. (1983), *The Architecture of Cognition.*
Fodor, J. (1983), *The Modularity of Mind.*
Gardner, H. (1983), *Frames of Mind: The Idea of Multiple Intelligences.*
Marks, C. (1980), *Commissurotomy, Consciousness, and Unity of Mind.*

Important Attacks on AI

Dreyfus, H. (1981), "From Micro-Worlds to Knowledge Representation: AI at an Impasse."
Searle, J. (1980), "Minds, Brains, and Programs."
Searle, J. (1984), *Minds, Brains, and Science.*
Weizenbaum, J. (1976), *Computer Power and Human Reason.*

Chapter 7

Minds, Genes, and Morals: The Case of E. O. Wilson's Sociobiology

Today I learn
that they have just
discovered
the substance
that turns on the genes
telling, for instance,
the nose genes
that the nose
is about to be made
and turning off,
therefore,
the toe genes
finger genes
and the rest,
so as to preserve
the pure form
of the nose
and, as it were,
not end up
with a mess
part toe & part nose
a toe-nose, so to speak;
and I say to myself
how smart the body is:
much smarter
than the tribe
of philosophers
& the transcendence
that sings in their heads.

(Reprinted with permission from I. Menkiti, *The Jubilation of Falling Bodies* 1978.)

On Human Nature (1978) is the most accessible introduction to E. O. Wilson's thought. Also see R. Dawkins, *The Selfish Gene* (1976).

It might seem odd to discuss the views of the world's most renowned insect expert in the book devoted to the philosophy and psychology of *homo sapiens*, were it not for the fact that E. O. Wilson, the entomologist in question, has proposed extending his research program to humans. At one point or another in the past 20 years Wilson has suggested a sociobiological explanation for such human phenomena as altruism, competing systems of morality, parent-child conflict, the sexual double standard, sex differences in personality, sexual jealousy, the incest taboo, lying, ethnocentrism, the nuclear pair-bonded family, cannibalism, women's fashions, and homosexuality—to name a few. Furthermore, Wilson has argued that such traditional philosophies as behaviorism and Marxism are false because they incorrectly assume that humans are very pliable.[1] In his most polemical moments Wilson has even proposed replacing both psychology and philosophy—in fact all the social sciences and humanities—with his particular brand of evolutionary biology.

In a more recent book, *Genes, Mind, and Culture: The Coevolutionary Process* (written with Charles Lumsden) Wilson's tone has mellowed somewhat, but his fascination with large all-encompassing theory remains as strong as ever. In this book, Lumsden and Wilson propose nothing less than a framework for understanding the relation between our genetic makeup, our cognitive processing system, and culture.

The mind is pivotal in Lumsden and Wilson's most recent extension of human sociobiology in a way it was not in Wilson's earlier work. Although the construction of the human mind was a building project which took nature many thousands of years, it is now flawlessly and rapidly orchestrated by the genes we pass on through sexual intercourse. According to Lumsden and Wilson, the particular features of our perceptual, cognitive, and emotional system(s) are genetically determined and bias us to make certain cultural choices and to have certain values and interests. For example, we, but perhaps not dogs, prefer our music not to be in the ultrahigh frequency range. We, but apparently not orangutans, take pleasure in mathematics and science. And we, but certainly not birds and bees, place higher value on the happiness of fellow humans than on that of birds and bees.

According to the most recent version of the theory, if and when a set of biased cultural choices and creations lead to a higher survival and reproduction rate for some members of a culture over other members, then the set of genes which biased the individual minds to make the successful cultural choice in the first place will increase in frequency. This feedback which nature gives to the genes, by way of culture and the mind, completes what Wilson and Lumsden call the "coevolutionary circuit."

Here I want to look at sociobiological theory—literally the attempt to exploit biological knowledge in the explanation of social behavior—in both its bold and brazen early form and its later more politic version. First, I discuss some of the conceptual foundations of E. O. Wilson's sociobiology. Second, I try to elucidate Wilson's pre-1981 views on the nature of mind and the possibility of a human sociobiology. Third, I look at Lumsden's and Wilson's views as expressed in their 1981 book, *Genes, Mind, and Culture*. Finally, I use certain reductionistic pronouncements of both the early and later versions of human sociobiology regarding moral philosophy as a way of reflecting on the relationship among the different sciences and as a way of taking a firm stand against certain naive brands of reductionism.

The Conceptual Foundations of Sociobiology

Think of classical Darwinian theory, circa 1859, in the following way. Individual organisms that possess characteristics or traits which allow them to best utilize the resources of nature, survive and reproduce. In reproducing, these successful organisms pass on their traits and characteristics at a higher rate than the less reproductively successful members of the species. Evolution occurs as the characteristics of the fittest are passed on to their offspring and become more frequent in the population. Think, therefore, of an organism as fit to the degree that it survives, reproduces, and passes on its traits. Darwinian fitness, then, is a measure of an organism's reproductive success.

In an important paper, Richard Lewontin, a renowned Harvard University geneticist, claims that the indispensible core of Darwin's theory, which has inspired the modern neo-Darwinian synthesis, consists of three basic principles (here presented in slightly modified form).[2]

Phenotypic Variation
Let *phenotype* refer to the totality of the observable traits of an individual organism. This first principle then simply says that different individuals in a population have different phenotypes, that is, different shapes, physiologies, temperaments, and behaviors.

Differential Darwinian Fitness
Different phenotypes have different rates of survival and reproduction in different environments.

Hereditability of Fitness

There is a (dramatically imperfect) correlation between parents and offspring in phenotype and in the reproductive contribution of each to future generations. That is, there is a correlation between parents and offspring in overall Darwinian fitness.

I follow Lewontin here and exploit the generality of these three principles, emphasizing that they are utterly neutral with respect to the issue of *biological determinism,* the thesis that phenotypic traits are caused primarily by an organism's inherited traits. This neutrality is clear if one notices what these principles taken together do not say. First, the three principles do not specify what factors go into the production of the phenotype. Second, the three principles do not specify the degree to which the phenotype of any particular individual is the causal outcome of biological factors as opposed to nonbiological factors. Third, they do not specify the degree to which similar phenotype and similar degree of Darwinian fitness among individuals are caused by inheritance. The correlations among relatives are simply noted. A father and son may well have the same kind of walk. But the three principles tell us nothing about whether this similarity is due to a shared biology or is the result of imitation.

The three principles, therefore, do not imply or even suggest that all phenotypic traits or characteristics are determined by an organism's biology. On the other hand, it is expected that inheritance does make some significant contribution to the phenotype.

Of course it is now widely agreed that the primary mechanism of inheritance is the gene, the informationally rich coils of DNA that are carried on the chromosomes inside the nuclei of every bodily cell. Let us refer, therefore, to the entire genetic constitution of a particular individual as the individual's *genotype.*

The conviction that genes are the primary mechanism of inheritance suggests the appealing idea of looking at biological evolution in terms of changes in the frequency of genes rather than in terms of changes in the frequency of phenotypic traits or characteristics. The idea of studying biological evolution at the level of gene transmission is an important advance because the three core principles of neo-Darwinian theory do not tell us anything at all about the degree to which the phenotypes are the direct outcome of the genotypes. The fact that the gene has been identified as the primary unit of inheritance, however, suggests a research strategy for beginning to answer that question— isolate genes, study their correlations with phenotypic variations, examine the ways in which different levels of biological organization and different sorts of environmental interaction (natural and social) affect both the genotype and phenotype, and extrapolate the relative contributions all the different factors make to the organism's morphological, physiological, behavioral, and temperamental characteristics.

This is no easy task, however. First, there are logical and methodological issues that make the whole question of the relative contribution of genes as opposed to everything else seem intractable or naive. Second, there is the daunting fact that a fertilized human egg contains on the order of two hundred and fifty thousand pairs of genes. Many of these genes are *polygenic,* that is, several of them work interactively to contribute to a single characteristic, and many are *pleiotropic,* that is, they affect more than one characteristic. Add to this the ethical issues related to human experimentation and one sees that resolving the issue of degree of genotype-phenotype link in the case of humans will have to be based mostly on indirect and exceedingly slippery evidence.

In any case, looking at evolution in terms of changes in relative frequency of genes suggests a way of refining the concept of fitness. In place of Darwinian fitness we define a new concept, genetic fitness. Genetic fitness is a measure of an organism's genetic contribution to the next generation: specifically, a measure of how many copies of its genes are inherited by other organisms.

Notice that, theoretically at least, the concept of genetic fitness makes no use at all of phenotypic characteristics in assessing fitness. This is just as well, because when looking at phenotypic characteristics one is tempted to think that fitness has to do with the "goodness" of the organism, the "attractiveness" of its traits, or with whether it seems well suited to its environment. Genetic fitness is a sparser and utterly biological measure of fitness. All this is true theoretically. In practice, phenotypic traits are still the primary evidence for genotypic ones.

In any case, it turns out that looking at fitness from the genetic level suggests a solution to at least one traditional evolutionary conundrum. If organisms are fit to the degree that they contribute to the perpetuation of copies of genes they possess, then why do sterile insect castes (such as those commonly found among bees, wasps, ants, and termites), not die out? After all, the sterile insects are not reproducing and therefore not passing on copies of their genes. To make matters even more puzzling, many of these sterile insects are the colony's "professional altruists," martyrs in the cause of protecting kin. So the insects do not reproduce and even if they could they are predisposed to behavior which results in early death. What an unlikely set of traits to be allowed by natural selection!

The generally accepted answer to this puzzle rests on the idea that one can contribute to the perpetuation of copies of one's genes by contributing to the survival and reproductive success of near relatives. This process is known as "kin selection."

The sterile heroic termite who gives its life in battle protects its more fertile brothers and sisters who, by virtue of being near relations, possess copies of many of its genes (including perhaps the one(s) promoting self-sacrifice). The hero's siblings then send on copies of some of the hero's genes to its nieces and nephews. Thus by enhancing the fitness of near kin the heroic termite indirectly contributes to the perpetuation of copies of its own genes.

Cases such as these indicate that it is often useful to understand genetic fitness inclusively, that is, as the sum of an organism's direct genetic contribution to the next generation plus any contribution the organism makes to the perpetuation of copies of its genes independently of reproduction.[3]

The concept of inclusive genetic fitness as applied to the behavior of the social insects is one of the main inspirations for Wilson's brand of sociobiology. It suggests the possibility of explaining a sophisticated "social" trait, such as "fighting to the death for the sake of the larger community," in terms of genetic fitness. The underlying assumption, of course, is that there is a powerful causal connection between a termite's genes and its willingness to die for its comrades.

In its simplest and most uncontroversial form sociobiology is simply, as Ernst Mayr says, the science that "deals with the social behavior of organisms in the light of evolution."[4] Or as Wilson puts it, sociobiology is "the systematic study of the biological basis of all behavior."[5]

All this sounds relatively innocent, especially if one interprets "biological basis" in its broadest sense. Sociobiology is simply the part of evolutionary biology that studies the genetic contribution to the social behavior of all species. Described in this way sociobiology need not be viewed as involving any a priori commitment one way or another as to how much the genetic contribution will turn out to be for any particular species or for any particular trait(s) within a species.

In point of fact Wilson's sociobiology is not such a neutral research program. Wilson holds strong views on the genetic contribution to the behavior of all species, including *homo sapiens*.

Since it is human sociobiology we are ultimately interested in let us examine Wilson's views more closely. In *On Human Nature*, Wilson states that

> The heart of the genetic hypothesis is the proposition, derived in a straight line from neo-Darwinian evolutionary theory, that the traits of human nature were adaptive during the time the human species evolved and that genes consequently spread through the population which predisposed their carriers to develop those traits. . . . if an individual displayed the traits he stood a greater

chance of having his genes represented in the next generation than if he did not display the traits.[6]

There is an argument lurking here. It runs as follows:

1. Some (all, many) phenotypic traits which current humans possess were adaptive during the time we evolved.
2. These adaptive phenotypic traits were predisposed by the genotype(s).
3. The genotype(s) which predisposed us to the favorable phenotypic traits have, therefore, been selected for.
4. The genotype(s) which predisposed their owners to maladaptive phenotypic traits meanwhile have died out.
5. The widespread presence of the favorable genotype(s) is the reason why we show the favorable phenotype(s).

Suppose, for example, that the trait in question was male involvement in the rearing of their own offspring (one of the necessary conditions for the now-prevalent nuclear family). And suppose that at some time long ago only one male in a tribe of twenty males and twenty females showed this trait (and suppose it was a time of great scarcity). Suppose further that this male's behavior (say, hunting and bringing food home) enhanced the life-span of his children so that they reached reproductive maturity and in fact reproduced. Assuming that this male's behavior was due to or predisposed by his genotype, we might expect some of his male children to possess the predisposing genes. This in turn would make it more probable that they would display a similar phenotype. Meanwhile some of his daughters might be carriers and pass on the relevant genes to their sons. If the environmental conditions contributing to the adaptiveness of this behavior relative to that of domestically disinterested males continued over time, we would expect the trait of male participation in childcare to increase in frequency.[7]

Lumsden and Wilson put the overall idea very clearly in *Genes, Mind, and Culture*:

> *The central tenet of human sociobiology* is that social behaviors are shaped by natural selection. In spite of perturbations due to time lag and random effects, those behaviors conferring the highest replacement rate in successive generations are expected to prevail throughout local populations and hence ultimately to influence the statistical distribution of culture on a worldwide basis.[8]

It is essential to see that "the straight line from neo-Darwinian evolutionary theory," which Wilson claims warrants his view that prevalent features of human societies and cultures are prevalent because the genes predisposing us to them have been selected for over several thousand years, is not quite as straight as he paints it. Recall that the three core principles of neo-Darwinian theory are neutral on the issue of the nature of the fit between genotype and phenotype for any particular species, as well as for any particular trait within a species. But the only way for Wilson to get to his view that human social behaviors and culture itself are the result of selective pressures operating primarily at the level of the genotype is by establishing that there is a tight, or fairly tight, fit between genotype and phenotype.

To get a grip on the alternative view suppose that male involvement in family life began this way: the mother of the male in question told him when he was young that she wished his father had helped out. He remembered this and decided to stick around when his time for fatherhood came. He found he enjoyed participating in family life and spread the word among his male friends who happened to respect his opinions. Several of them tried family life and liked it too. Meanwhile the mothers and children favored the practice. Word spread between generations and the practice became widespread in the culture.

Nothing depends on the truth of this particular story about male involvement in family life. The point is simply to highlight two very different ways of explaining human behavior. The first story assumes a fairly tight fit between specific phenotypic traits and the genotype, and it is the sort of story Wilson normally favors. He often claims, for example, that the genes have culture on a leash.[9] (Why claim that something is on a leash if that which holds the leash isn't in control?) I call this sort of story "vertical" because the plot line always moves from the bottom to the top, from genes to behavior.

The second story assumes only that the genotype endows us with certain very open-ended capacities, such as the ability to understand the desires of others, to try novel actions suggested to us, to evaluate these actions and recommend them to others, to transmit information, and to learn. The second view requires no strange discontinuity in nature; it simply assumes that we have evolved as very flexible, epistemically powerful organisms for whom cultural evolution is Lamarckian. That is, we discover, try out, and pass around new ideas, inventions, and social practices quite in excess of the information specifically encoded in our genes.[10] I call this sort of account "horizontal" because of the assumption that an adequate explanation of human behavior must make essential reference to the rich natural, social, and historical contexts in which our lives are embedded.

Both the vertical and the horizontal stories are compatible with the claim that if some phenotypic trait has a strong genetic component (such as eye color) and if that trait differentially enhances the genetic fitness of the organism which possesses it (such as engaging in sexual intercourse), then that trait will become more frequent in the population. The proponent of the vertical story bets that most phenotypic traits are strongly determined by the genotype, whereas the proponent of the horizontal story is skeptical. The project, therefore, for the human sociobiologist is to provide reason to believe that many socially or culturally significant phenotypic traits have a strong genetic component, and thereby to make the case for the preferability of the vertical story.

Closing the Genotype-Phenotype Gap: The Opening Gambit

It is important to emphasize that the issue between the biological determinist, the person who believes in a tight genotype-phenotype fit, and his opponents does not necessarily have to do with the issue of determinism at all. For example, the position I have advocated throughout this book is a deterministic one. On my view, human behavior, is the lawlike outcome of complex interactions taking place between us—viewed as biological organisms possessing a powerful information-processing system—and the natural world. Someone sympathetic with soft determinism could object perfectly reasonably that the biological determinist has a simplistic view of things, simplistic in three ways: he doesn't understand how genes work; his view is largely monocausal and unidirectional while everything we know about complex systems indicates multicausality and multidirectional interaction; and he underestimates the importance of the human mind and the relative independence of cultural evolution from biological evolution.

Wilson's initial attempts to close the genotype-phenotype gap in *Sociobiology: The New Synthesis* and *On Human Nature* were, I think, simplistic in precisely these ways. (His more recent view in *Genes, Mind, and Culture* is more sophisticated.) In his pre-1981 writings Wilson uses three basic arguments to make a case for thinking that there is a tight fit between genotype and phenotype in humans.

Strategy 1: Deflate the Mind, Inflate the Genes. One way to close the genotype-phenotype gap is by showing that the levels normally taken to mediate and therefore transform the expression of the genotype are either inconsequential or simply feeder mechanisms for the expression of genes. This was one of Wilson's favorite early strategies. Both *Sociobiology: The New Synthesis* and *On Human Nature* are peppered with statements such as these: "the organism is only DNA's way of making more DNA"; the mind is "an epiphenomenon of the neuronal machinery of the brain"; "morality has no other demonstrable function" than to keep genetic material intact; each individual "is a unique and accidental subset of all the genes constituting the species"; "the individual organism is only their [the genes'] vehicle."

Richard Dawkins, a fellow sociobiologist, is a master at vividly painting higher levels of biological organization, the mind, the organism, or the person, as more or less incidental features of reality, as copying machines for genes. In his book, *The Selfish Gene*, Dawkins baldly announces that "We are survival machines—robot vehicles blindly programmed to preserve the selfish molecules known as genes." Elsewhere he refers to persons as "colonies of genes" and tells us that "Genes are the primary policy makers; brains are the executors."[11]

Notice the general move here: the sociobiologist anticipates that his opponent will argue (1) there are many higher levels of organization than the gene, such as cell, organ, brain, person, family, group, and so on, (2) all these different levels affect each other (as well as even higher levels, such as the natural and social environment) in both directions, (3) resulting in multiple transformations from genotype to phenotypic expression.[12]

The sociobiologist tries to head off these objections by diminishing the causal significance of the higher levels and claiming that they do not do much more than facilitate the transportation of genes from generation to generation.

But here the sociobiologist loses. First, it is simply not true that each person is a colony of genes, or just a subset of the genes constituting the species. On the contrary, it is a biological fact that the genes are a subset of each person. Second, it begs the genotype-phenotype question to assume that genes make policy that brains merely execute. Third, it is misleading, and once again begs the question, to imply epiphenomenal or inconsequential status for the higher levels of biological and psychological organization by claiming that the organism "is only DNA's way of making more DNA." Is DNA then only the Big Bang's way of continuing to make itself heard? In point of fact, human organisms do more than just make DNA. They make bridges, houses, love, war, books, noise, and history—to name a few. Fourth, nothing in evolutionary biology requires the view of the mind or the person as a mere gene-transporting device. On the contrary, one should expect an adaptation as complex as the human mind to have a significant causal impact on both lower and higher levels of organization.

The sociobiologist's opening gambit is largely a rhetorical flash-in-the-pan. Ironically, it fails to increase the plausibility of tight genotype-phenotype fit precisely because it tries to elbow out of the way the most likely candidate for creating a genotype-phenotype gap. Stephen Jay Gould puts it best:

The central feature of our biological uniqueness also provides the major reason for doubting that our behaviors are directly coded by specific genes. That feature is, of course, our large brain . . . markedly increased brain size in human evolution may have had the most profound consequences of all. The increase added enough neural connections to convert an inflexible and rigidly programmed device into a labile organ. . . . Flexibility may well be the most important determinant of human consciousness; the direct programming of behavior has probably become inadaptive.[13]

Strategy 2: Analogize.   Another tactic for closing the genotype-phenotype gap is to build a series of arguments from analogy. After all, there are many phenotypic traits which we know to be, or have good reason to suspect, are strongly determined by the genotype. No one balks, for example, at the idea that bipedality, or even being conscious, are genetic. The reason is that we treat bipedality and consciousness as species characteristics.

Analogously (call this argument from the analogy principle) if other traits are found to be (and to have been) widespread across cultures, there is prima facie evidence of a powerful genetic component to them. This case is strengthened (1) if there has been no or minimal communication between cultures or within a culture; (2) if the trait is found in other species in which we have reason to think it has genetic causes; (3) if there is evidence of high hereditability of the trait between parents and offspring; and (4) if the trait appears in very different natural and social environments.

There is nothing inherently wrong with the analogy principle as a rule of thumb for hypothesis generation; it is the sort of principle that warrants making the plausible conjecture that incest avoidance has a strong genetic component, whereas playing soccer, which is also widespread, does not. But it is important to remember that nothing is proven until the relevant genes have been identified, and to date that has almost never been done. On the other hand, the principle can easily lead to trouble.

First, there is the critical matter of identifying the widespread or universal traits. In speaking of the last chapter in Wilson's *Sociobiology: The New Synthesis*, Gould worries that universal traits may be largely in the eye of the beholder. He says, "Chapter 27 abounds with statements about supposed human universals. For example, 'Human beings are absurdly easy to indoctrinate—they *seek* it.' Or, 'Men would rather believe than know.' I can only say that my own experience does not correspond to Wilson's."[14] Second, clause (2), which warrants inferring like causes from like effects across species, is notoriously problematic.

Recall the altruistic termites. In the opening chapter of *Sociobiology: The New Synthesis*, entitled "The Morality of the Gene," Wilson indicates that he views human altruism as having the same sort of powerful genetic link as it has in the termites. Such an argument is warranted by the logic of the analogy principle. Furthermore, it does the desired job of narrowing the genotype-phenotype gap.

The argument is implausible, behavioral similarities notwithstanding. Human altruism is accompanied by too much intelligent deliberation to be viewed as on a direct link to altruistic genes. It seems perverse even to think of human and termite altruism as forms of the same phenotypic trait. Wilson eventually realizes this. In the last chapter of *Sociobiology: The New Synthesis* and again in *On Human Nature* he moves toward the position that human altruism is not hard-core and kin-exclusive like that of the termites, but soft-core and based on the expectation of reciprocation.

But notice that once one moves in this plausible direction one has a genotype-phenotype gap on one's hands again. After all, there is no longer a direct genetic link being drawn between altruistic genes and altruistic behavior, but at most a link between understanding, intelligence and the desire to maximize happiness, on the one hand, and altruistic behavior, on the other. In this case, the correct story is that our genes (with help, because genes don't do anything on their own) have endowed us with an exceedingly flexible cognitive system that allows us to engage in reciprocal altruism. The genes, however, help build the intelligent, happiness-maximizing capacity, not the altruistic behavior.[15]

This difference between genetic allowance or capacity, on the one hand, and genetic promotion or predisposition, on the other, is crucial. Especially in his first pronouncements on human sociobiology, Wilson fudged it. If all Wilson wished to claim was that genes have been selected for that allow things like incest avoidance, altruism, aggression, cooperativeness, mendacity, honesty, the nuclear family, polygamy, capitalism, communism, being illiterate, and understanding relativity physics, no one could conceivably object. After all, it is trivially true that anything an organism does is allowed by its genes.

The claim that certain behaviors are promoted by genes, however, is a considerably stronger thesis. Larry Bird, for example, can dunk a basketball through a basketball hoop. Clearly this is allowed by his genes. To say it is promoted by his genes, however, seems very odd. If basketball dunking is promoted by anything at all one would think it is by the utterly contingent fact that the odd sport of basketball exists and is valued in our culture.

Strictly speaking, it is wrong even to say that genes allow anything on their own. After all, when Larry Bird is ninety years old he will no longer be able to dunk a basketball, but, barring radiation poisoning, or whatever other poison we may have invented by that time, his genes will be the same! Stephen Jay Gould puts the point this way: "The statement that humans are animals does not imply that our specific patterns of behavior and social arrangements are in any way directly determined by our genes. *Potential* and *determination* are different concepts."[16]

This brings me to a worry about the use of clause (3) in the analogy principle, the clause that takes evidence of high hereditability between parent and offspring as evidence for a tight genotype-phenotype fit. Richard Burian puts the objection this way:

> Suppose (as I believe is approximately correct) that the hereditability of height in America and in Japan is 0.8. Does this mean that 80% of our height is determined genetically? *NO.* Transplant fifty families from America to Japan and fifty families from Japan to America and provide them with the local dietary regimens and there is a major difference—somewhere around three to six inches. . . . Because of this hidden dependence on background conditions . . . it is not clear whether a clear meaning can be given to the claim that the genes, or some complex of genes, determines—or determines $n\%$ of—a given trait.[17]

Burian's excellent example points to two intimately related concerns about some fairly standard logic regarding hereditability in particular, and genotype-phenotype fit in general. First, there is the problem that naturalistic observation of parent-child trait similarity often takes place in situations where parent and child share the same or very similar environments. But if one frames the question at hand as: how much does the environment contribute to the phenotypic traits? then one can see that absolutely no relevant evidence is being adduced by such observations. After all, the environment is the controlled context in which the observations of trait similarity take place. But finding out if something is causally significant requires it to be varied. Second, hereditability is normally taken as a measure of the genotype-phenotype fit. But what is normally measured is phenotype-phenotype match, in particular, the correlation between parent-child height, parent-child IQ, or parent-child eye color. The trouble with the standard data base is that the only thing that warrants thinking that the correlation between parent-offspring phenotypes is a measure of genotype-phenotype fit is already assuming high hereditability and therefore a context-independent match between the two!

Strategy 3: The Argument from Adaptation.   According to his Harvard colleagues Gould and Lewontin, E. O. Wilson (like many other thinkers who are influenced by Darwin's view that natural selection is unforgiving of maladaptive traits) tends to adopt a "Panglossian paradigm." The Panglossian paradigm is a sort of regulative ideal named after Dr. Pangloss, the indefatigable Leibnizian of Voltaire's *Candide* who believed that each and every thing that exists, exists for the best.[18] On Gould's and Lewontin's view, Wilson's sociobiology assumes that there are atomizable phenotypic traits which are underwritten by atomizable genotypic configurations and that therefore any phenotypic trait (that lasts) must be adaptive, and its adaptiveness must be explainable by the selection of the underlying genotype. In both *Sociobiology: The New Synthesis* and *On Human Nature*, Wilson tells one Panglossian story after another. For instance, he cites the religiously sanctioned cannibalism of the Aztecs as a cultural response to the genetically programmed need for protein.[19]

There are three major objections to this adaptationist approach. First, there is the objection to the atomizing itself. Consider the cannibalism case. The trouble here is: thinking that a complex social practice like cannibalism can be isolated from the other practices of the society; rejecting a priori the possibility that the explanation of the practice might arise more naturally from the system of other practices in which it is embedded (taking into account, of course, all relevant biological pressures); and requiring the practice to turn out to have been adaptive or functional in the first place—why not sick, sordid, and wasteful?

Second, the expectation that any phenotypic trait will turn out to be underwritten by a naturally selected complex of genes overtly begs the question of the genotype-phenotype link by assuming that the existence of the phenotypic trait, especially if it is widespread, results from the selection for an underlying adaptive genotype. The mistake here (and I think it is the sociobiologist's standard one) involves thinking of Nature as a banker dealing only in genetic coin.

Arthur Caplan sees Wilson's research program as biased in exactly this way. Caplan's complaint is this:

(a) Wilson conflates the concepts of *advantage* and *adaptation*.

(b) *Adaptation* results from the process of natural selection and therefore has a genetic basis; *advantage* can accrue in any number of ways. For example, a dark coat on a rodent might lead to enhanced genetic fitness whether it came about from natural selection *or* from frolicking in the mud.

(c) It is the tendency to see all *advantages* as *adaptations* which results in Wilson's tendency to look for a genetic basis for advantageous (as well as adaptive) human characteristics.[20]

Let me give a human example to make clear Caplan's important point. Suppose we somehow decided, in a fit of rationality, that all nuclear weapons should be dismantled and did so. Such a policy I trust would be advantageous. It would certainly enhance our genetic fitness more than the alternative scenario of blowing ourselves up. But it would be very peculiar to think that this wise, advantageous decision was the result of an evolutionary adaptation.

The third worrisome feature of the adaptationist approach is that for any particular trait there are often many equally plausible Panglossian stories to tell. Cannibalism, for example, might be seen as a response to the need for protein or as a response to overpopulation. I have recently heard female infanticide, of the sort being reported in the People's Republic of China, described as a double-edged biological strategy for controlling population whereby the overall death rate is increased and the pool of potential future mothers simultaneously decreased. The rival non-Panglossian story, of course, is that the strict Chinese government policy regarding birth control plus patriarchal attitudes with long prerevolutionary histories are significant factors behind the female infanticide.

The trouble with evolutionary Panglossianism is that the intuitive satisfaction, fascination, or appeal of the story is often taken as sufficient to prove that it is more than an entertaining fable. This is especially problematic given the fact that in the human case one possible story is that the trait in question, suppose it to be a widely shared social characteristic, was discovered by someone who found it an excellent idea and then passed it around. Or alternatively, as in the infanticide case, the trait is a bad idea that is unfortunately deeply embedded in a complex holistic system of cultural beliefs and practices. But this story is usually exactly the one the sociobiologist does not want, since the intervention of mentality loosens the genotype-phenotype fit.

Let me summarize: The task of human sociobiology, as I framed it, is to provide reason for thinking that there is a fairly tight fit between genotype and phenotype. Showing a tight fit is a necessary condition for thinking that there is a significant causal connection between complex social and cultural processes and the genotype. However, the three main strategies Wilson deploys in *Sociobiology: the New Synthesis* and *On Human Nature* are all deficient.

Wilson's arguments fail for several related reasons. First, he underestimates the transformational power of mind, its ability to mediate between higher and lower levels of organization. Other than the impoverished conception of persons as copying machines for genes, Wilson offers virtually no psychology or philosophy of mind in his early work.[21] Second, Wilson tends to assume what he needs to show, namely that in the human case there is a tight genotype-phenotype fit. Third, he tends to think of both genotypic and phenotypic traits as isolatable, relatively insulated, context-independent entities. Fourth, he tends to conflate the concepts of advantage and adaptation, and assume that all advantages, all functional traits, are adaptations underwritten by genes.

Closing the Genotype-Phenotype Gap: The New Argument

The publication in 1981 of *Genes, Mind, and Culture: The Coevolutionary Process* was an important event in the sociobiology debate. In this book, Charles Lumsden and E. O. Wilson, rather than climbing off the socio-biological high horse, claim finally to be in possession of the *"grail of a unifying theory of biology and the social sciences."*[22]

Besides containing the "grail," the book is meant to answer two valid objections to the earlier theory: (1) that no adequate theory of the mind was provided; (2) that no adequate explanation for the remarkable diversity of cultures was provided.[23]

The new theory is especially interesting from the point of view of philosophy and psychology because Lumsden and Wilson now propose to close the genotype-phenotype gap by way of the mind. In particular, they propose to explain social behavior by way of a circuit in which the genes build the rules by which the mind functions; these rules bias their owners to make certain social and cultural choices over others; these choices lead to differential genetic fitness of the choosers which in turn lead to increased frequency of the genotype that built the rule system of the persons making the most adaptive choices. The overall argument, as I understand it, runs as follows:

1. Human culture is the interactive result of all the artifacts, behavior, institutions, and ideas mentally or physically deployed by some population.

2. The "perceivable features" of the integrated cultural system are called *culturgens*. For example, telephones, calculus, seventeenth-century English literature, Judaism, marriage, divorce, professional wrestling, international espionage, and the space program are all culturgens.

3. During socialization the culturgens are processed by what are "loosely labeled the *epigenetic rules.*"

4. These epigenetic rules are "the genetically determined procedures which direct the assembly of mind."[24]

5. The epigenetic rules bias their owners to choose certain culturgens over others.

6. Collective choices in behavior and cognition "create the culture and social fabric."

7. "Genetic variation exists in the epigenetic rules, contributing to at least part of the variance of cognitive and behavioral traits within a population."[25]

8. Individuals whose choices enhance their inclusive genetic fitness transmit more genes to future generations, "and as a consequence the population as a whole tends to shift toward the epigenetic rules and the forms of cognition and behavior favored by the rules. The coevolutionary circuit is thus completed."[26]

The crucial premises here are 3, 4, 5, and 7. Together they support the view that the mind is comprised of a set of genetically determined rules that favor certain interpretations of the physical world and certain social and cultural choices over others. It is this view of the mind which leads Lumsden and Wilson to the view that although *"Homo sapiens* is the most complex species on earth by a spectacular margin, it is probably far less complex and difficult to understand than contemporary social theory leads one to believe."[27]

Lumsden and Wilson see four sorts of evidence as needed to even put their coevolutionary theory in the running. First, biased epigenetic rules must be shown to exist. Second, epigenetic rules must be shown to have a hereditable component. Third, a link between specific culturgens and genetic fitness must be established. Fourth, molecular and cellular mechanisms must be discovered "that directly link genes to cognitive development."

Is the theory in the running? In terms of the four necessary conditions of theory acceptance the answer is yes. First, some biased epigenetic rules exist. For example, some people are color-blind, others not. Clearly, a color-blind person will not be disposed to make the same sorts of selections for a bright and flashy wardrobe as a person with normal color vision. Second, some epigenetic rules have an unquestionable hereditary component. Linguistic ability, for example, is clearly hereditable. Third, some social choices undoubtedly affect genetic fitness. For example, mainlining narcotics, being celibate, or making a living as a professional mercenary normally decrease overall genetic fitness. Fourth, there is evidence linking the genes to cognition by way of intermediate levels of biological organization, for example, via neurotransmitters. Almost everyone, in fact, believes that messages written in DNA are instrumental in the building of the central nervous system.

So the coevolutionary version of human sociobiology could be true, but is it plausible? There are reasons to be wary. Unfortunately, a good deal rests on the issue of how exactly to interpret the revised theory. In spite of a wealth of mathematics which gives the overall appearance of great theoretical precision, Lumsden and Wilson are often very unclear regarding exactly what is being claimed. The general tone, emphasis, and rhetoric of the book, however, displays, I think, some of the naivete and simplistic biological determinism of the earlier theory. Let me focus on the newest component in the theory, the epigenetic rules, in order to make the nature of my reservations clear.

My general complaint about the coevolutionary version of sociobiology is that it rests on a vertical fallacy, the fallacy of explaining human behavior in exclusively bottom-to-top and top-to-bottom terms. The fallacy arises from failing to pay attention to the way human behavior is also embedded horizontally, in complex social and historical contexts.

Lumsden and Wilson's epigenetic rules are simply what we normally think of as the psychological laws in accordance with which an individual mind processes information. Lumsden and Wilson devote the first three chapters of *Genes, Mind, and Culture* to reviewing a wide array of psychological experiments that they think establish the existence of epigenetic rules which "are modulated by culture" and which bias their owners to make certain choices over others. Their overall strategy is to appropriate work being done in cognitive science and claim for it exactly the status many cognitive scientists wish, namely, describing the innate program, the functional structure of mind.

According to Lumsden and Wilson, the entire system of epigenetic rules consists of two different types, primary and secondary rules. Primary epigenetic rules are "the more automatic processes that lead from sensory filtering to perception. Their consequences are the least subject to variation due to learning." The secondary epigenetic rules meanwhile act on all "information displayed in the perceptual fields. They include the evaluation of perception through the process of memory, emotional response, and decision making through which individuals are predisposed to use certain culturgens instead of others."[28]

Innate color classification is an example of a primary epigenetic rule. Although all humans can perceive variance in light along a continuum, at an age as early as four months we divide colors into categories: blue, green, yellow, red being primary. In general, the primary epigenetic rules involve the five sensory modalities. We can hear tones only within a certain range, smell and taste things with a certain chemistry, see objects of nonmicroscopic size, and feel stimuli over a certain tactile-kinaesthetic threshold.

The primary epigenetic rules are similar to Kant's forms of sensibility; they are the ways we necessarily construct the sensible world. Furthermore, they constrain us as much as they liberate us. For example, if visitors from outer space arrived and asked us to appreciate their ultraviolet outfits and their ultrasonic music, we could never honestly comply because we could not see their outfits as ultraviolet or hear their music as ultrasonic. We're simply wired wrong!

The mainstay of the secondary epigenetic rule system is higher-level information processing: feature detection, long- and short-term memory, recall, interpretation, and computation. Other secondary epigenetic rules include things as various as the manner of gripping objects, emotional biases, and incest avoidance.

The basic picture is this. The primary epigenetic rules structure sensory experience and deliver their output to the secondary rules. The secondary rules work their transformations, deliver their interpretations, and compute utility and preference weightings. These transformations result in some particular cognitive or behavioral choice.

There are four strands to my argument that Lumsden and Wilson tend to commit the vertical fallacy.

1. Lumsden and Wilson continually state that the epigenetic rules are "genetically determined." This is misleading. First, the new theory claims to be sophisticated in its recognition of the fact that nothing is genetically determined *simpliciter*. Insofar as there exists a genetic program to write certain epigenetic rules into some individual nervous system, the theory succeeds only if the general biochemical (nutritional, viral, bacterial) environment cooperates. Second, and this follows from the first, the epigenetic rules are phenotypic traits. The existence of an epigenetic rule is always inferred from observed behavior. This means that, contrary to Lumsden and Wilson's assumption, it is a priori an open question to what degree the epigenetic rules are even strongly constrained by the genotype, as opposed to the environment in which the entire organism is embedded.

2. Let us allow, however, that many epigenetic rules such as those comprising short-term and long-term memory, linguistic ability, and general intelligence (widely shared species characteristics) are strongly determined by the genotype. (After all, the opponent of biological determinism never intends to deny that our mental ability is largely due to our genotype, he merely wants to deny that specific beliefs and behaviors are.) But is it remotely plausible to think that all epigenetic rules are strongly linked to the genotype? I find it implausible. Imagine the average professional mathematician or logician—thanks to a combination of natural ability and lots of education and practice such an individual will become proficient at processing information in novel and highly idiosyncratic ways. For example, the logician might become expert at simultaneously comprehending the meaning of a passage in a philosophy paper and testing for logical soundness and validity. Are the logician's internalized abilities part of his epigenetic rule system?

They certainly fit the bill of involving information processing, computation, interpretation, and so on.

My guess is that Lumsden and Wilson would argue that the transformational rules the logician applies are products of the epigenetic rules, not part of the rule system itself. But as far as I can tell, given their characterization of epigenetic rules, the only warrant for not counting the logician's way of thinking as part of the epigenetic rule system is that it is not genetically determined.

Whereas it is often useful to distinguish between information-processing rules that are innate and those that are acquired, it is important to understand that acquired rules can enter the cognitive processing system. These will include intentional objects as abstract as the rules used by logicians and mathematicians, rules of thumb as specific as "*i* before *e* except after *c*" or "three strikes and you're out," and deeply internalized emotional dispositions such as the disposition to distrust people in the military.

Lumsden and Wilson tend to speak as if all that proceeds from the innate epigenetic system are specific beliefs and behaviors. My point is, however, that the information-processing system itself can be dramatically enriched by the acquisition of new rules and knowledge. This point is important because it indicates that the road from the genotype to a specific belief or behavior may be much longer than Lumsden and Wilson typically map it to be. The reason is that information is normally transformed by an epigenetic rule system of fantastically greater complexity than the one we are born with.

3. Lumsden and Wilson mention, here and there and almost incidentally, that humans are highly prone to imitate other humans. They treat the disposition to imitate as a constraint on the epigenetic rule system rather than as an epigenetic rule itself. A strong case could be made, I believe, that some such general disposition is part of the initial rule system. But whether or not one treats the propensity to imitate as an epigenetic rule or as a constraint on the epigenetic rules, it follows that, given this propensity, much of what any human does or knows is determined horizontally, by what other members of his social world are doing and thinking. The recognition of the horizontal influence of social context on individuals renders simplistic the metaphor, which continues to appear in this book, "genes holding culture on a leash." I maintain that most culturgens, from the rules for Parcheesi to our current understanding of the physical universe, must be explained in large part horizontally. There is simply no remotely sufficient vertical story to tell.

Actually, that is a bit too harsh. There is the interesting issue of how our fantastic information-processing capacity is built and how exactly it is realized in the nervous system. Notice, though, that even this story, once completed, will not be a story about the genesis of specific beliefs or behaviors, only about the genesis of our original information-processing program(s).

4. The coevolutionary circuit for which Lumsden and Wilson argue is openly vertical: genes build the epigenetic rules that bias their owners toward making certain behavioral choices at the societal level; if these choices increase (or decrease) the organism's overall fitness the organism's genes become more (or less) prevalent.

The hypothetical nature of the coevolutionary circuit is worth emphasizing. The vertical coevolutionary circuit only operates when the phenotypic behavior increases or decreases genetic fitness; and when the phenotype is underwritten by the genotype.

This means that for any trait that neither helps nor hinders genetic fitness there will be no selection pressure from above. I would expect that teaching philosophy, eating cereal for breakfast, owning a telephone, and going to college belong to this enormous class of traits which (within our society) neither help nor hinder genetic fitness. Furthermore, this implies that if a particular phenotypic trait does in fact help (or hinder) fitness, the underlying genotype will be selected for (or against). Smoking a pack of cigarettes a day, driving a car, hang gliding, and being a kamikaze pilot are reasonable candidates for decreasing fitness, while exercise, living in a nonpolluted area, and eating a balanced diet probably increase fitness. It would be odd, however, to think that there was some specific gene or set of genes that underwrote car driving, and which, therefore, was decreasing in frequency because 50,000 American's with the gene(s) died in automobile accidents every year.

The trouble is that there are many candidate genotypes that could underwrite the same phenotype. In the human case a genotype that promotes the open-ended disposition to imitate others, to do what is required, valued, and supported in one's social context, and to learn from one's own and others' mistakes, is all the genetic underwriting any of these traits require. There is simply no explanatory need for the implausible assumption of a specific set of genes that promote car driving, smoking, hang gliding, or being a kamikaze pilot.

Lumsden and Wilson might charge me with being unfair, since surely they would never want to claim that there was a perfectly tight fit between genes and a behavior like car driving. After all, on their view the epigenetic rules mediate all phenotypic behavior. In my defense, Lumsden and Wilson's book claims to explain the remarkable diversity of cultures in terms of the vertical coevolutionary circuit. The crucial premise in Lumsden and Wilson's overall argument is that genetic "variation exists in the epigenetic rules, contributing to at least part of the variance of cognitive and behavioral traits within a population."

At one level their point is obvious but perhaps worth reminding any old-fashioned *tabula rasa* theorists still around. An individual with a low IQ is unlikely to choose a career as a particle physicist; a deaf person will not make a good musician, nor a blind person a good visual artist. It is important to Lumsden and Wilson's case for the coevolutionary circuit, however, that such individual differences often lead to increased or decreased genetic fitness, and thereby to frequency changes in the genotypes of human populations. But Lumsden and Wilson give almost no evidence of phenotypic characteristics which are strongly predisposed by genotypic differences and which, in contemporary cultures, significantly affect genetic fitness.

All this weakens Lumsden and Wilson's program. In many cases there is no vertically selective coevolutionary circuit in operation. In those cases where there is selective pressure from above, it is most plausible to think of the underlying genotype as supporting a species-specific information-processing system, but not specific beliefs or behaviors. Actually, the evolution of a plastic information-processing system as opposed to rigidly canalized behaviors is predictable on general evolutionary grounds. Imagine a situation "in which genes favoring general intellect are competing with genes favoring some cultural trait that is adaptive in a particular environment. Whenever the environment changes (as it always does) the genes for intellect would gain."[29]

To the degree that the genotype favors general intellect we will need to explain specific individual and cultural traits by embedding them horizontally, by weaving tales involving social, historical, and cultural concepts; the vertical coevolutionary story will simply not be illuminating. Robert Van Gulick puts it well:

> Given the diversity of rapid and sophisticated self-correcting mechanisms that characterize the modern enterprise of acquiring knowledge, there seems little role to be played by the slow information-collecting mechanism of genetic selection that originally set the whole self-propelling process in motion. [T]hus, in the cognitive sphere, claims of cultural autonomy come to more than mere humanistic resistance to seeing human activity brought within the scope of natural science. Natural selection has freed the mind by giving it methods to acquire knowledge more powerful than its own. So provident a parent surely would not begrudge us our autonomy, and we would be ungrateful to deny the openness of our possibilities."[30]

This emphasis on the autonomy of cultural evolution with respect to biological evolution is not mere wishful thinking. As Gould points out, "We have no evidence for biological change in brain size or structure since *Homo sapiens* appeared in the fossil record some fifty thousand years ago. . . . All that we have done since then—the greatest transformation in the shortest time that our planet has experienced since its crust solidified nearly four billion years ago—is the product of cultural evolution."[31]

Sociobiology and Morality

Finally, I want to focus on the specific relation of human sociobiology to ethics. This will help us to understand better the relationship among the various disciplines: sociobiology, psychology, and philosophy in particular. I want to suggest that sociobiology does have a contribution to make to both moral psychology and moral philosophy, but that the contribution is not nearly as great as Wilson says it is. Early sociobiological claims to explain ethics and ethicists "at all depths" were implausible, simply because they underestimated extragenetic influences on human behavior. On the other hand it is equally wrong, if not downright pernicious, to deny the importance of biology for moral philosophy.

Think of ethics in the broadest possible sense, as consisting first of the actual practical activities to which we assign moral concepts (this, of course, will vary from individual to individual and more dramatically from society to society, culture to culture, and time to time); second, as consisting of the intrapsychic characteristics of such activities, of the fact, for example, that to be in a bind like Euripides' Medea where "I know what crimes I am about to commit, but my anger is stronger" is to be in a uniquely ethical predicament which exacts its pound of psychic flesh regardless of actual outcomes; third, as consisting of the modes of moral evaluation we use in resolving conflicting practical moral dilemmas. These might range from applying a utilitarian rule for maximizing pleasure, to applying Kant's categorical imperative and treating everyone as an inherently precious end in himself, to consulting the Koran or the Bible. Fourth, think of ethics as consisting of three different kinds of theories: genealogical theories that try to explain how moral beliefs develop; metaethical theories that try to explain the meaning and function of ethical discourse, and that try, therefore, to get at the epistemological and metaphysical presuppositions of our ethical idioms; and normative ethical theories, like Kant's or Mill's that try to justify a particular mode of moral evaluation and action.

Wilson believes that sociobiology can make a significant contribution in all these areas; his confidence is motivated by the historical fact that the central insight behind sociobiology came from the explanation of the altruistic behavior of sterile insects in terms of genetic fitness. It was the temptation to generalize the insights about insect altruism that led Wilson to announce that sociobiology would one day reduce ethics.[32] Consider the following four theses about the connection between sociobiology and ethics. These theses are possible ways of understanding what Wilson might intend by his reductionist views about the relationship between sociobiology and morals.

1. Sociobiology can explain the genesis of our moral capacities.
2. Sociobiology can explain the genesis of particular moral beliefs.
3. Sociobiology can explain the nature and function of morality, and thereby reveal the true content of ethical discourse.
4. Sociobiology provides a way of getting us from 'is' to 'ought.' That is, certain normative principles follow from sociobiological premises.

Theses 1 and 2 are about the genealogical portion of ethics; 3 is a metaethical thesis, 4 a normative one. Let us look at each thesis in turn.

Thesis 1: Sociobiology can explain the genesis of our moral capacities. Wilson is undoubtedly right that sociobiology can shed light on the genealogical portion of ethics, on the question of how our species-wide moral capacities developed in the first place. The sociobiological answer to the question of how we got to a place where we constituted ourselves morally is simple and certainly correct, given the prior acceptance of a general evolutionary framework. We have the capacity for morality because of the way we have evolved. From the convergence of factors involving our cerebral development, our sociality, our dependency, and natural necessity, has emerged the capacity to speak, think, and act in moral terms. Furthermore, the moral nature of our species is, thus far, compatible with the genetic fitness of our species.[33] There are, after all, more humans on earth this minute than existed over the entire first fifty thousand years of our species' history.

At the species level, therefore, there is no question that natural selection figures essentially in the explanation of the origin of our moral capacities. In fact every prominent feature of morality rests on some biological feature of our species. A necessary condition of articulating a moral code is having linguistic ability; a necessary condition of giving that moral code meaningful semantic content is having intelligence; the widespread nature of moral codes makes sense only on the assumption that we are a social species also afflicted by a certain amount of selfishness; and the specific content of certain widespread moral precepts, such as those prohibiting murder and assault, presuppose a natural fear of death and bodily harm.

Wilson specifically singles out the origin of our species-wide capacity for altruism among nonrelatives as involving a biological component. Wilson's view, which he appropriates from Robert Trivers, is this:

(1) Termite altruism is unilateral. The martyr termite has no expectation of reciprocation; this indicates that termite altruism is the hard-wired result of kin selection. That is, termite altruism is the genetically determined result of selection pressures operating on individual members of a small, closely related group. This explains why termites never behave altruistically to nonrelatives.

(2) Human altruism, on the other hand, is bilateral and often takes place between nonrelatives. It (frequently) involves the expectation of reciprocation, negotiation, implicit or explicit bargaining, promising, and contracting. In this sense human altruism is context-sensitive. This indicates that human altruism, is not hard-wired in.

(3) However, since all human societies, no matter how varied the environment, show signs of altruism between strangers, it is reasonable to think that altruism has been an important factor in the recent evolution of our species and therefore that the underlying emotional dispositions predisposing us to altruistic behavior have important genetic components.

There is nothing, as far as I can see, particularly tendentious about this argument, so long as we interpret (3) carefully. It makes sense to think that human altruism is accompanied by intelligence and affect, and that both the intelligent ability (for example to calculate the probability of personal gain relative to loss) as well as the emotional dispositions (for example, to feel positively toward those who have been most kind and helpful to oneself, or who resemble those who have been most kind and helpful to oneself in the past) have "important genetic components." Nor is the idea here particularly new. Hume, for example, believed that humans are naturally self-interested, equipped with fellow feeling (or "sympathy," as his fellow Scots called it), and naturally disposed to deploy a sophisticated inductive logic to figure out ways to maximize the "greatest happiness altogether."

The evolutionary explanation of the origin of our altruistic moral capacity does preempt the supernaturalist alternative that holds that our moral capacities exist because God gave us souls and free will. In this way the sociobiologist's account is superior to Hume's otherwise similar story since, thanks to Darwin, it says more about the genealogy of our moral abilities.

But notice again that sociobiological first principles do not in any way require that there be genes for "reciprocal altruism" as many sociobiologists like to insinuate. All evolutionary theory requires is that the genotype equips us with certain needs, certain emotional dispositions, and powerful inductive abilities. On this parsimonious interpretation, one can conceive of altruistic behavior as the result of computations of our intelligent information-processing system that take into account our innate and acquired needs, our innate and acquired emotional biases, and local conditions.

Therefore, a sociobiological explanation of our capacity to engage in moral talk and construct moral codes, our complementary abilities to control behavior with altruistic moral principles and to fall prey to selfish temptations we would prefer to avoid, and our tendency to emblazon morality with powerful affect, should not make us overconfident that we have thereby explained ethics "at all its depths." This in-depth account, when and if it ever exists, will require citation of multifarious horizontal influences on morality. We must be careful not to make the logical mistake of thinking that because we possess an understanding of the phylogenesis of our moral capacity we have explained something substantive and specific about morality.[34] It is trivially true that everything we in fact do is allowed by our genes.

Thesis 2: Sociobiology can explain the genesis of particular moral beliefs. The sociobiologist, however, has faith that he can contribute in more specific detail to the genealogical portion of ethical theory. The reason for confidence that sociobiology can explain the origin of particular moral tenets comes from the sociobiologist's conviction that the particular ethical beliefs that (well-adapted) *groups* hold will tend to be those which have enhanced genetic fitness in the past.

Take the belief that murder is wrong. This seems a perfect example of a widely shared principle with a potential genetic fitness rationale. Or take the principle prohibiting adultery. One can make a plausible argument that this principle, rather than being written on high by God, is a principle (supported by powerful emotional predispositions to feel sexual jealousy) that enhances the stability of the nuclear family, an institution that tends to enhance the inclusive genetic fitness of its practitioners.

Or take the widely shared attitude that one's moral responsibilities decrease in accordance with the expanding circle model. This model pictures (and therefore describes rather than recommends) one's moral responsibilities to others as diminishing in accordance with the degree of relatedness between self and others. That is, one has greatest responsibility to protect the welfare of one's immediate family over one's social group, and a responsibility to the social group over the larger society, and to that over one's nation, and to one's nation over other nations, and so on.[35]

Prima facie the behavioral regularity depicted by the expanding circle model is a natural candidate for a sociobiological explanation, since one's degree of genetic relation falls off rapidly in ratios that would make the expanding circle principle roughly predictable. Parents share approximately 50 percent of their genes with their own parents, their siblings, and their children, 25 percent with their aunts and uncles, nieces and nephews, 12.5 percent with first cousins, and so on. Such facts indicate why it is tempting to explain the powerful protectiveness and unconditional altruism of human parents for their children in terms of kin selection, while reserving a less biologically based explanation in terms of reciprocal altruism for the conditional, negotiated forms of moral consideration in which we engage with lesser relations.

In general the sociobiologist, or any evolutionary biologist for that matter, is committed to the view that persisting moral beliefs should contribute to, or at least not obstruct, the genetic fitness of the group that adheres to them.

This strikes me as plausible. The basic idea is very close in spirit to the plausible commonsensical view that the purpose of morality is to help us live happy, productive, and safe personal and interpersonal lives. Living such a life of course will, on the average, enhance genetic fitness.

But it is essential to notice that the sociobiological first principle that requires persisting moral principles to have enhanced or at least not obstructed the genetic fitness of the population that practices them does not imply that the content of a group's morality has genetic causes. There is an important distinction between a cultural practice which is advantageous in the sense that it enhances genetic fitness, for example pollution control laws, and a biological adaptation which does the same. Believing that polluting is wrong is advantageous to our genes, but there is no overwhelming reason, as I see it, to think that the belief that polluting is wrong is itself the result of a biological adaptation.

Furthermore, the answer to the question of how best to protect or enhance one's genetic fitness will depend on local conditions, on the ecological, geographical, historical, meteorological, agricultural, and social environment one is born into. Identical twins, if put in radically different cultural and ecological niches, will have different moral perspectives. This means that the specific content of a group's moral code will depend heavily on the horizontal features of its particular natural and social environment.

Facts such as these are consistent with sociobiological principles, properly understood. But they weigh decisively against advocacy of genetic determinism, as well as against the thesis that sociobiology can reduce ethics. The horizontal concepts which will figure in the full explanation of a moral code will come from disciplines other than sociobiology—from anthropology, history, economics, political science, psychology, and sociology. If sociobiology has any hope for reducing the genealogical portion of ethics it will need the help of all the human sciences. But then we do not have a sociobiological account of the origin of moral codes. And we certainly do not have a sociobiological reduction of morality. We have an incredibly rich multidisciplinary account![36]

Thesis 3: Sociobiology can explain the nature and function of morality and thereby clarify the *true* meaning of ethical discourse. I italicize the word "true" to emphasize the view shared by sociobiologists as well as many others that morality does not transparently disclose what it is about. Freud, Marx, and Nietzsche, to name three prominent non-sociobiologists, also doubted that the way morality represents itself (or better: the way we represent ourselves in moral discourse) reveals the true function and purpose of a moral code. Their suggestion was that the standard honorific and ennobling vision of morality, typically theologically embedded, conceals the degree to which morality is a compromise, a way of minimizing losses, controlling our seamy side, and dulling the pain of it all.

Wilson, as I understand him, sees sociobiology as having two major metaethical implications. First, morality viewed as a general capacity evolved as a genetic fitness strategy and continues to function as such. Second, moral judgments typically express subjective feelings rather than objective or rational facts.

The first point, as we have seen, follows directly from evolutionary first principles. The best bet for any universal species-specific trait is that it has been naturally selected for, that is, it has contributed to the genetic fitness of organisms that possessed the trait in the past. Metaethically this thesis does serious damage to several traditional views regarding the origin and content of ethics.

Take, for example, the Christian view on the human predicament. The idea is that God made us in His image and endowed us with free will and reason so that we could autonomously and intelligently follow His divine commands. Our success or failure in following His commandments will bring everlasting happiness or damnation. In either eventuality we as individual souls will live for all eternity.

On this view, morality originates with God and thus the content of a (correct) moral code is divine principles. Statements such as "murder is wrong" or "adultery is immoral" mean "murder and adultery are prohibited by God" (with, we presume, good, but inscrutable, reason).

Wilson denies that morality has any other-worldly origin, ground, or function. We exist as individuals only until our bodily death. The only immortality we possess is metaphorical. It will come by leaving remnants, copies of our genes, in the gene pool available to future humans. Wilson says, "no species, ours included, possesses a purpose beyond the imperatives created by its genetic history . . . we have no particular place to go. The species lacks any goal external to its own biological nature."[37]

Wilson argues that because morality originated via natural selection the content of a moral code is a set of imperatives that enhance human genetic fitness relative to that of other species in a particular ecological niche. As usual one has to be careful of Wilson's rhetoric here as he swiftly concludes that morality has no other function than to keep human genetic material intact.

Even if one is sympathetic, as I am, with Wilson's rejection of supernaturalistic views on the origin and content of morality, it does not follow that the function of a moral code is to enhance genetic fitness *simpliciter*, nor that the content of a moral code consists merely of strategies our genes have for self-replication. In fact this is where the metaphorical talk of "selfish genes" really gets in the way.

The logic of Wilson's argument for the thesis that the content of morality consists of self-replication strategies of genes runs as follows:

1. Morality evolved because it enhanced our genetic fitness.
2. Therefore, moral statements are (disguised) statements about genetic fitness strategies.

To get a grip on the nature of the fallacy here, consider this parallel argument:

1. Our arithmetic and scientific abilities evolved because they enhanced our genetic fitness.
2. Therefore, arithmetic and scientific statements are (disguised) statements about genetic fitness strategies.

Needless to say, the conclusion of this second argument is preposterous even though the premise is presumably true. What has gone wrong? The answer is that both arguments go astray by committing a variety of genetic fallacy in which the original cause of a mental capacity and its content are conflated.

It is utterly consistent to maintain that our moral, arithmetic, and scientific capacities evolved because they contributed to the fitness of our species; that they continue (thus far) to do so; and that morality is about how best to live happy and productive social lives, arithmetic is about numbers, and science is about nature.

Wilson, however, has the second metaethical consequence of sociobiology standing by to spoil my analogy between morality on the one hand and arithmetic and science on the other. This is his thesis that moral judgments normally express subjective emotions which in turn express genetic fitness strategies. On Wilson's view, it might have been the case that the content of ethics was like the content of arithmetic or science, that is, not self-referential. But as a matter of fact ethics turns out to take its content from the subjective states of individuals, while arithmetic and science happen to have objectivity.

To get a grip on Wilson's view we can draw a rough distinction among three different metaethical positions: intuitionism, emotivism, and naturalism. Intuitionism is the view that moral knowledge comes by way of some sort of direct rational insight, the same sort of self-evident insight, say, whereby one knows a mathematical axiom. The intuitionist believes that moral statements express unprovable, but nonetheless indubitable, rational truths. Emotivism is the view that moral statements express (more or less exclusively) deep-seated emotional feelings of the person making the statement. Naturalism is the view that moral statements express beliefs or judgments about how best to live our individual and collective lives based on facts about human nature (including our emotional natures) and facts about the external world.

Wilson reads most moral philosophy as supported by an intuitionistic moral epistemology, thus he centers his criticism of mainstream moral philosophy on intuitionism. In *Sociobiology: The New Synthesis*, he claims that the "Achilles heel of the intuitionist position is that it relies on the emotive judgement of the brain."[38] In *On Human Nature* he says,

> innate censors and motivators exist in the brain that deeply and unconsciously affect our ethical premises . . . . science may soon be in a position to investigate the very origin and meaning of human values, from which all ethical pronouncements and much of political practice flow. . . . Like everyone else, philosophers measure their personal emotional responses to various alternatives as though consulting a hidden oracle. [T]he oracle resides in the deep emotional centers of the brain, most probably within the limbic system, a complex array of neurons and hormone-secreting cells located just beneath the "thinking" portion of the cerebral cortex. Human emotional responses and the more general ethical practices based on them have been programmed to a substantial degree by natural selection over thousands of generations.[39]

Wilson's basic strategy is to undermine intuitionism with an argument for emotivism. Ethical pronouncements flow from the "hormone-secreting cells located just beneath the 'thinking' portion of the cerebral cortex." For this reason they lack the logical or factual objectivity of which the cerebral cortex is capable. The powerful confidence people have about their ethical judgments is explained in terms of properties of the hormones. No one, of course, has ever suggested that truth or objectivity are among these properties! On the sociobiological view, therefore, ethics might not have taken our feelings as its content, but in fact it does.

One of the attractions of the emotivist position is that it helps account for two widely noticed facts: first, that moral debate often seems irresolvable, and second, that moral debate is more passionate than scientific debate is.[40] Wilson even claims to be able to explain sex and age differences in morality via his brand of emotivism. Genetically programmed hormonal differences between the sexes and among different age groups account for moral differences. These hormonal differences explain for example why males care less about intimacy than women do and why old people are more disposed toward altruism than young ones are. Wilson argues that these genetically determined hormonal differences cause various emotional biases resulting in "an innate moral pluralism," and he insists that it should be clear "that no single set of moral standards can be applied to all human populations, let alone all sex-age classes within each population."[41]

I agree that emotional preferences figure essentially in morality and that in some cases moral statements have only subjective content. But overall emotivism is simplistic. Reflect on what Wilson says about the moral philosophies of John Rawls, the liberal, and Robert Nozick, the laissez-faire libertarian. Wilson claims that although Rawls and Nozick write long books filled with seemingly rational argument they, like everyone else, get their moral views from private consultations with their hormone-secreting cells. Although moral philosophers like Rawls and Nozick give the appearance of offering rational arguments, they are really only writing about how they feel.

Wilson's argument, however, does not work. Even if we accept that moral philosophers, like everyone else, feel strongly about their moral points of view and even if we allow that these feelings have a biochemical basis (brought on by innate characteristics, life histories, or both), it does not follow that philosophers like Rawls and Nozick are not also giving us good reasons for their theories, nor does it follow that the content of Rawls's and Nozick's moral theories consists merely of idiosyncratic feelings and moods orchestrated by their hormones. In fact we have every reason to believe they are using their cerebral cortex, the seat of reason, when they engage in moral philosophizing since only the cerebral cortex has linguistic capacity.

Robert Simon and Stephen Zegura make it clear why the sociobiologist cannot maintain his extreme emotivism regarding ethics. They write, if sociobiology shows that we are genetically wired to reach certain conclusions *regardless* of the evidence, we could not have any rational evidence for accepting sociobiology or anything else for that matter. On the other hand, if the claim is that reasoning *tends* to be constrained by nonrational biological predilections, no reason has been given for thinking the tendency is harder to overcome in ethics than in biology.[42]

In general, and this is the naturalist's view, there is nothing logically implausible about both believing powerfully in some theory and presenting good reasons, good arguments, for the theory. For example, an argument to the effect that given what we know about human needs, desires, and abilities, and given what we know about the way the world is, we ought to behave less militaristically. Furthermore, and this is the other side of the same coin, it is obvious that being moral sometimes requires overcoming powerful inclinations with principles. But we have overwhelming evidence that people overcome temptation all the time. The observation that morality often consists of the conquest of emotion and inclination is the starting point of Kant's moral philosophy.

The upshot is this: although Wilson is undoubtedly right to question the implausible intuitionist view that morality is a species of purely rational insight, and although his emphasis on the powerful emotions which color morality is important, he tends to underestimate the degree to which moral philosophizing also focuses on nonemotional, nonsubjective features of reality (for example, the needs of others, economic factors, political agreements), and thereby has nonsubjective content. Insofar as morality has such content, it cannot be exhaustively analyzed in sociobiological terms—any more than the content of science can. By looking at some of Wilson's own pronouncements on normative philosophy I can show that he himself is unable to maintain a consistent emotivist position.

Thesis 4: Sociobiology provides a way of getting from "is" to "ought." That is, certain normative principles are derivable from sociobiological premises. After Wilson describes the largely emotive character of ethics he reflects and worries.

> Which of the censors and motivators should be obeyed and which ones might better be curtailed or sublimated? . . . we must consciously choose among the alternative emotional guides we have inherited. To chart our destiny means *we must shift from automatic control based on our biological properties to precise steering based on biological knowledge.*[43]

The first and most important thing to notice is that Wilson's suggestion that "we must shift from automatic control" to a more knowledge-based and consciously controlled moral mode presupposes that the emotive preferences of our limbic system can be overcome. The ethical naturalist, of course, claims that humans consciously control their behavior all the time. This fact is the basis for the naturalist's claim that morality typically involves more than the mere articulation or display of individual emotional preferences. Wilson's recommendation that we take conscious control of our moral lives implies, at the very least, that it is not necessarily the case that moral judgments only bespeak emotional preferences. Therefore Wilson logically cannot be committed to the universal truth of emotivism as a view about the content of ethics. The second thing to notice about the quotation above is that Wilson is suggesting that the sociobiologist can assist in the project of normative philosophy. That is, in addition to assisting in figuring out how we in fact behave or are biologically predisposed to behave, he can assist in the project of figuring out how we ought to behave. Third, notice how Wilson thinks sociobiology will assist in normative philosophy. It will help us "steer" ourselves by utilizing "biological knowledge." What might this mean?

One thing Wilson might have in mind is this. The sociobiologist can tell us about certain deep-seated biological tendencies, such as aggression, which were adaptive when we evolved but which have to be watched closely today. Given the availability of nuclear weapons our belligerent side contains the seeds of our own species' destruction. This sort of use of biological information in normative thinking strikes me as utterly relevant and immensely useful. On the naturalist view that I advocate, any and all (true) information is important in ethical reasoning.

Ironically, just as Wilson makes this sort of optimistic suggestion for a sociobiological contribution to ethics, he displays another, more pessimistic, side regarding the relevance of biological knowledge to normative ethics. In discussing Rawls's view that a just society is a morally good society, Wilson says,

> While few will disagree that justice as fairness is an ideal state for disembodied spirits, the conception is in no way explanatory or predictive with reference to human beings. Consequently, it does not consider the ultimate ecological or genetic consequences of the rigorous prosecution of its conclusions . . . the human genotype and the ecosystem in which it evolved were fashioned out of extreme unfairness.[44]

There is a spectacular non sequitur here. Rawls's theory of justice is a normative theory. It does not claim to be explanatory or predictive of how people in fact behave (although if everyone became convinced by Rawls and began to act more justly, we could then easily explain and predict human behavior in terms of the widespread acceptance of Rawls's theory). Furthermore, it does not follow that Rawls is insensitive to the "ultimate ecological or genetic consequences" of his theory just because he makes no mention of the unfair conditions under which our species evolved. The fact that the human genotype was fashioned in conditions of extreme unfairness is about the past. It is only relevant to normative philosophizing about what ought to be if our evolutionary past so tightly constrains us that widespread fairness is impossible. But if that is the case then biological knowledge cannot really contribute to normative moral philosophy. Rather it dashes all hope of its possibility. On such an interpretation, all of Wilson's talk about taking conscious control of our moral lives is fatuous. What ought to be just is!

On the other hand, if normative philosophy is possible, and if it is possible because our cognitive apparatus equips us with the abilities to know, plan, and overcome powerful inclinations, then in addition to how people in fact behave it is not unreasonable or unrealistic to worry and wonder about how they ought to behave. So, for example, if we assume that Wilson is sincere when he talks about conscious steering, then his thesis that there is "an innate moral pluralism" (because different ages and sexes have different hormonal flows that powerfully affect their behavioral dispositions) is relevant to moral philosophy. But it does not imply that anatomy determines moral destiny—not at least if people can learn that it is advisable to intelligently overcome their powerful hormonal dispositions.

Wilson therefore seems fairly confused about the consequences of sociobiology for normative ethics, sometimes allowing his nativism and emotivism to raise doubts about whether normative ethics is even possible. Wilson's basic problem arises from underestimating the degree to which the mind receives and processes information, rather than merely carrying out the orders of the genes.

In *On Human Nature*, Wilson is explicit about three normative principles which he thinks follow from sociobiological premises. I close this section with a discussion of these three cardinal values.

The Principle of Concern for the Future of the Gene Pool
Wilson argues that,

> 1. An individual is an "evanescent combination of genes drawn from the pool, one whose hereditary material will be dissolved back into it."[45]

2. Therefore, we ought to concern ourselves with the continued survival of human genes in a common pool. There is "the cardinal value of the survival of human genes in the form of a common pool over generations."[46]

Many philosophers will jump at the chance to gleefully and dismissively point out that this argument commits the naturalistic fallacy, the fallacy of trying to derive "ought" from "is."

Let me simply say that on the naturalistic view I espouse, moving from statements describing factual states of affairs to statements recommending norms or actions is perfectly legal. Moral reasoning is simply a variety of inductive reasoning, science's handmaiden. In inductive arguments the conclusion is always underdetermined by the evidence.[47] On my view, therefore, the only way to commit a naturalistic fallacy is to make the foolish mistake of claiming that a normative conclusion follows necessarily from a set of descriptive premises. There is no fallacy so long as one admits that any normative conclusion could be wrong or could be revised depending on new or additional information.

There is, however, always the question of whether a normative moral argument is inductively strong. What about the inductive warrant for Wilson's argument for the Principle of Concern for the Future of the Gene Pool?

The first thing to notice is that in practical terms this principle comes to the same result as the widely shared principle of concern for future generations, the principle that says that we ought to care about the long-run consequences of our actions for future persons. For example, in mapping military strategy and in planning our industrial futures we should concern ourselves with the kind of world we will leave to future human individuals. Acting on such a principle will, of course, contribute to the continuation of the gene pool. But if that is true we don't need a principle of concern for future genes in addition to a principle of concern for future persons. Thus, it is not clear what the sociobiologist is recommending that we do not already have.

Nevertheless, there is still the question of why we should care about future generations of genes or individuals anyway. The mere fact that a person is "an evanescent combination of genes drawn from the gene pool" who will dissolve back into the pool does not provide any inductive support for the normative conclusion that we should care about future generations.

Clearly we need to make explicit the assumption that lurks implicitly: namely, that humans naturally seem to care about the future of *homo sapiens*. Why is that the case? Here the sociobiologist has, I think, as illuminating a (naturalistic) answer as has ever been offered. Humans value their species' future because past persons naturally disposed to value future persons had higher replacement rates than those not similarly disposed. The cause of the higher replacement rate was simply that such individuals cared more than others about leaving and protecting progeny and therefore did so. The natural predisposition to care about succeeding generations, therefore, is now widespread.

The traditional answer to the question of why humans naturally care about future generations is of the "they just do" variety. Classical utilitarians, for example, simply contend that it is naturally pleasing to think of the species happily surviving even if we understand that we as individuals will not.

The sociobiologist's explanation for our concern for future generations is better because it subsumes the utilitarians' answer, "it's just one of those things that give us pleasure." According to the sociobiologist, showing concern for future generations is naturally pleasure-producing because past persons who found it pleasure-producing were more genetically fit than those who were not so disposed. Thanks to the differential genetic fitness of the two groups the value has become widespread in the population.

As I see it, the sociobiological contribution is double-edged with regard to the principle of concern for the future of our species. First, the sociobiologist precludes any nonnaturalistic justification of the principle, such as a justification in terms of God's will. Second, the sociobiologist shows that, at least in the case of this principle, the underlying rationale is fundamentally emotive: it comes from a powerful species-wide inclination.

On the other hand, the claim of a significant sociobiological contribution to normative philosophy seems overblown when one realizes that in the case of the principle of concern for the future of the species we have (a) a case of a noncontroversial principle in which (b) duty and inclination naturally coincide. Furthermore, any particular view on how in practice we ought to show our concern for the future of the species will need to go beyond the simple emotivism of the general underlying principle and enter the realm of more objective, natural facts. For example, at one time it might be important to dramatically lower the birthrate in order to protect future generations, at another time to increase it. One set of historical, economic, or sociological conditions might require new technological innovations, another set might require less technology, and so on. This means that substantive normative policies will require looking at nonsociobiological evidence and employing nonsociobiological concepts. Even with regard to this uncontroversial, biologically grounded principle, sociobiology alone is not remotely equipped to provide the data necessary to make moral policy.

The Principle of Genetic Diversity
According to Wilson,

> (1) Variation "in mental and athletic ability is influenced to a moderate degree by heredity. . . . Truly exceptional individuals, weak or strong, are, by definition, to be found at the extreme of the statistical curves."
> (2) Variation sufficient to produce exceptional individuals is desirable.
> (3) Therefore, "correct application of evolutionary theory . . . favors diversity in the gene pool as a cardinal value."[48]

Unlike Wilson's derivation of the previous principle, which tells us that we ought to have a concern we are already strongly predisposed to have, the thrust here is "prohibitive." Wilson is suggesting that we ought not to engage in eugenic practices, such as cloning, which would substantially decrease the diversity of the gene pool.

Once again the conclusion seems relatively uncontroversial. But it is important to notice that the support for (2), the crucial premise, is not and indeed cannot be only sociobiological. To see this consider how one would defend the premise that variation sufficient to produce exceptional individuals is desirable. Presumably one would make a case that exceptional individuals, such as geniuses, have on the whole contributed positively to human culture in the past. Such a case, however, would be made, insofar as it can be made, on the basis of historical evidence. Thus Wilson's conclusion should read "a correct understanding of evolutionary theory" together with historical evidence about the contributions of exceptional individuals "favors diversity in the gene pool." Once again this takes the wind out of the sails of Wilson's confident proclamation that sociobiology can explain ethics "at all depths."

One might try the tactic of attempting to produce an entirely sociobiological warrant for the principle of genetic diversity along the following lines. The principle of concern for the future of the species implies the principle of genetic diversity since genetic diversity is an excellent hedge against species extinction if the environment changes.

This is a good argument. But one crucial premise has to do with the possibility of the environment changing. Much of the argument's inductive support rests on the likelihood of that possibility. Where does evidence that the environment might change come from? The answer,

of course, is meteorology, astronomy, physics, geology, history, ar-
chaeology, and anthropology, as well as sociobiology.

The Principle of Universal Human Rights
Wilson argues that,

> (1) "Our societies are based on the mammalian plan: the indi-
> vidual strives for personal reproductive success foremost and that
> of immediate kin secondarily; further grudging cooperation rep-
> resents a compromise struck in order to enjoy the benefits of group
> membership."
>
> (2) Because "power is too fluid in advanced technological societies
> . . . the long-term consequences of inequity will always be visibly
> dangerous to its temporary beneficiaries."
>
> (3) Therefore, given our basic human nature and given the way
> the modern world is it is rational to "accede to universal human
> rights," to this "invention of recent European-American civiliza-
> tion." "Universal human rights might properly be regarded as a
> third primary value."[49]

This is an interesting argument. But once again the conclusion follows
only when we conjoin sociobiological principles about the nature and
evolution of human altruism with certain alleged facts about the way
the modern world is. In particular, "because power is too fluid in
advanced technological societies . . . the long-term consequences of inequity will always be visibly dangerous to its temporary beneficiaries."
Insofar as the claims about the fluidity of power in the modern world
and the dangers of social inequity are credible, they are the sorts of
knowledge I would expect political scientists and economists to have.
There are as far as I can tell no sociobiological principles from which
the existence of our particular kind of "advanced technological" world
could have been predicted or in any other way known. Thus, to the
extent that this argument provides an (inductive) warrant for the belief
in universal rights it does so by conjoining a broadly sociobiological
premise (1) with a political premise (2). All of which is fine: the more
evidence we have for a particular moral principle the stronger are our
epistemological foundations. But once again the fact that the argument
is a sociobiological *cum* political-economic one means that sociobiology
alone cannot provide the evidence necessary for normative ethics.

In sum, the overall relation of sociobiology to ethics looks like this.
Sociobiology can contribute to the understanding of the evolution of
our moral capacities and to a lesser extent to the understanding of
certain widespread moral beliefs and practices, such as those involving
the prohibition and punishment of murder and incest. However, insofar

as the sociobiologist is committed to an emotivist account of the meaning of ethical statements, he fails to provide an adequate metaethical theory. Furthermore, although all (true) biological information is relevant to normative ethics, the sociobiologist is in absolutely no privileged position to tell us what ought to be done. This is not because normative ethical knowledge requires some kind of special insight which only philosophers or saints have, it is because in most cases nothing normative follows from sociobiological premises taken by themselves.

Conclusion

I can now summarize my overall evaluation of E. O. Wilson's theory.

(1) Wilson's brand of sociobiology rests on the assumption that there is a tight fit between the human genotype and phenotype. This assumption, which Wilson claims follows from general Darwinian principles, warrants his confidence that better understanding of the process of genetic fitness in general, and the human genotype in particular, will make for revolutionary progress in psychology and the rest of the human sciences. In addition, Wilson argues that acknowledgment of the degree to which all higher-level human activities are controlled by genes will require complete renovation of standard philosophical views on the nature of persons and the meaning of life. This core assumption about the tightness of genotype-phenotype fit, however, is problematic. First, Darwinian principles do not imply a tight genotype-phenotype fit in the human case, or for that matter in any other case. We need an argument for thinking that there is a tight fit for each phenotypic characteristic of each species. Second, in both *Sociobiology: The New Synthesis* and *On Human Nature*, Wilson tends to play down the very best reason we have for thinking that direct genetic programming is an unlikely evolutionary outcome in the human case. Namely, that the emergence of the human mind has freed us from the vertical, bottom-to-top, control characteristic of lower organisms and has provided us with the cognitive processing equipment capable of responding flexibly and sensitively to the novel contexts in which we find ourselves.

(2) In their 1981 book, *Genes, Mind, and Culture*, Lumsden and Wilson tried to enrich Wilson's earlier impoverished sociobiological picture of mind, the view of mind as a mere gene-transporting device, a sort of copying machine for genes. The basic strategy in *Genes, Mind, and Culture* was to appropriate mainstream work in cognitive science and claim that the characteristics of our information-processing system are as they are because these characteristics contributed to the genetic fitness of past members of the species. (This seems perfectly reasonable.) Then Lumsden and Wilson make the following interesting move. They

claim that the characteristics of the information-processing system (what they call the epigenetic rules) bias individuals to make certain cultural choices over others. When these choices increase the fitness of organisms who are biased to make them, the biased rules increase in frequency, thereby increasing the frequency of the particular cultural choice. Lumsden and Wilson call the hypothesized feedback circuit going from genes to mind to culture back to genes, the coevolutionary circuit. The circuit is openly vertical: it operates bottom-to-top and top-to-bottom.

The picture of the mind here is much improved from Wilson's pre-1981 work but the overall program continues to display an unreasonable bias against horizontal explanations of human behavior. By horizontal explanation I simply mean an explanation of human behavior which locates many causally relevant factors in the particular social and historical contexts in which human organisms find themselves. The trouble with Wilson's bias is that to the extent that the conception of mind as a plastic, self-updating representational system is correct it follows that intentional explanations framed in terms of the concepts and categories of the traditional human sciences will continue to be extraordinarily illuminating.

William C. Wimsatt, a philosopher of biology, has done some important work on the way subtle biases of a scientific research program can produce fantastically misleading explanations. Wimsatt says, "I conjecture that *any heuristic, once we understand how it works, can be made to fail.* That is, given this knowledge of the heuristic procedure, we can construct classes of problems for which it will always fail to produce an answer, or for which it will always produce a *wrong* answer. This property of systematic production of wrong answers will be called the *bias*(es) of the heuristic."[50] The biases of sociobiology as I see them generally produce wrong or radically incomplete answers in cases where information about the sociocultural environment is required.

(3) Finally there is the question of the sociobiological contribution to ethics. Sociobiology is part of a growing consensus (growing especially since the mid-nineteenth century) that morality lacks a supernatural foundation. Like everything else moral codes are natural phenomena and have natural causes. Unfortunately this widely held, broadly naturalistic point of view makes Wilson overconfident about the possibility of a sociobiological reduction of ethics. Although sociobiological information is relevant to both the descriptive and normative sides of ethics, it is not even remotely sufficient. An adequate explanation of the origin of a particular moral conception, say the development of Judeo-Christian morality, will need to make use of an enormous number of nonsociobiological concepts, such as historical and psychological ones. (See Nietzsche's *The Genealogy of Morals* in this regard.) An ad-

equate argument for a particular normative ethical principle, for example, the principle that persons should never be used as means (say, for gaining medical knowledge) but ought always to be treated as ends, could not possibly be justified, on purely sociobiological grounds. The sort of narrative required to justify such a principle, if indeed it can be justified, will be an incredibly complex story involving the concepts and categories of all the human sciences, as well as, perhaps, literature.

We are, as Wilson rightly insists, biological organisms, living out our lives in a natural world filled with other biological organisms. But one consequence, and it is a consequence of overwhelming importance, of our particular kind of biological equipment is that we possess consciousness. We are self-conscious creatures who can remember, wonder, plan, hope, and transmit knowledge. We can reflect on where we have been as individuals and as a species and where we might go in the future, and we can wonder and worry about the meaning of our individual and collective lives. Biological evolution and fifty thousand years of human history have conferred on us enormous complexity and plasticity. Thanks to this complexity and plasticity neither our nature nor our future is fixed. What will become of us from here on out is very much up to us.

Suggested Readings

Conceptual Foundations

Dawkins, R. (1976), *The Selfish Gene*.
Hamilton, W. D. (1964), "The Genetical Theory of Social Behavior I & II."
Lumsden, C. and Wilson, E. O. (1981), *Genes, Mind, and Culture: The Coevolutionary Process*.
Trivers, R. (1971), "The Evolution of Reciprocal Altruism."
Wilson, E. O. (1971), *Insect Societies*.
Wilson, E. O. (1975), *Sociobiology: The New Synthesis*.
Wilson, E. O. (1978), *On Human Nature*.

Important Philosophical Criticisms and Commentaries

Burian, R. (1981–82), "Human Sociobiology and Genetic Determinism."
Caplan, A. L. ed. (1978), *The Sociobiology Debate*.
Caplan, A. L. (1981–82), "Say It Just Ain't So: Adaptational Stories and Sociobiological Explanations of Social Behavior."
Gould, S. J. (1978), "Biological Potential vs. Biological Determinism."
Gould, S. J. and Lewontin, R. (1979), "The Spandrels of San Marco and the Panglossian Paradigm: A Critique of the Adaptationist Programme."
Kitcher, P. (1985), *Vaulting Ambition: Sociobiology and the Quest for Human Nature*.
Ruse, M. (1979), *Sociobiology: Sense or Nonsense?*
Singer, P. (1981), *The Expanding Circle: Ethics and Sociobiology*.
Wimsatt, W. (1980), "Reductionist Research Strategies and Their Biases in the Units of Selection Controversy."

Chapter 8

Consciousness

Three of the greatest perplexities are these. First, why is there something rather than nothing? How is it possible that there is anything at all? Second, how is it possible that among the stuff that exists there is life? Third, how is it possible that some living things are conscious? Alongside and intimately related to the questions of how these things are possible in the first place are questions about the nature of these things: what is the nature of what there is (the stuff comprising the universe), of life, and of consciousness?

Here I take on the third perplexity and sketch a naturalistic theory of consciousness. The aim is to say something illuminating about the nature, function, and possibility conditions of consciousness. The theory proposed is a *neurophilosophical* one.[1] Subjectivity has emerged so far only in certain biological systems. It makes sense, therefore, to seek a theory of consciousness with the guidance of the neo-Darwinian theory of evolution and the best current brain science.

Cognitivism and Consciousness

Behaviorism, positivism's close kin and psychology's prude, fell from power during the 1960s, and psychologists renewed the study of mind with great energy and freedom. The new regime was cognitivism.[2] For every action there is an equal reaction in the opposite direction.[3] The irony is that the return of mind to psychology attending the demise of behaviorism and the rise of cognitivism did not mark the return of consciousness to the science of the mind. Mind without consciousness? How is that possible?

In the first place, the rejection of behaviorism did not take place with complete methodological abandon. A certain appropriate positivistic reserve remained. It was one thing to draw inferences about the decay rates of visual images after brief exposures and about the structure of short-term memory and its relations to long-term memory by way of sensitive tachistoscopic experiments, reaction-time tests, and retention experiments. It was a wholly different thing to try to make scientific pronouncements about consciousness. Consciousness, after all, had press of this sort:

> O, what a world of unseen visions and heard silences, this insubstantial country of mind! What ineffable essences, these touchless rememberings and unshowable reveries! And the privacy of it all! A speechless theatre of speechless monologue and prevenient counsel, an invisible mansion of moods, musings, and mysteries, an infinite resort of disappointments and discoveries. A whole kingdom where each of us reigns reclusively alone, questioning what we will, commanding what we can. A hidden hermitage where we may study out the troubled book of what we have done and yet may do. An introcosm that is more myself than anything I can find in the mirror. This consciousness that is my self of selves, that is everything, and yet nothing at all.[4]

Now *this* seemed like a good thing for a psychologist interested in gaining a reputation not to study. Whereof one cannot speak one should be silent. What is essentially private, if indeed anything is, is something about which science should offer no opinion. "Invisible mansions of moods, musings, and mysteries," as appealing as they might be to mushy-minded mystics, hold no interest to the scientist of the mind.

In the second place, it seemed that one could map the mind, could provide, as it were, a theory of intelligent mental life without committing oneself to any general view about the nature, function, or role of consciousness. To be sure, much work assumed that a certain amount of conscious mental activity was taking place in the domain under study. For example, research on imagistic rotation accepted that most people in fact experience themselves rotating picturelike mental objects. But the study of imagistic rotation was designed in part to test the accuracy of these conscious experiential reports. These experiences were not considered closed off to verbalization, nor did the verbalizations stand as the last word on the underlying processes. Furthermore, the study of specific cognitive domains characterized in part by conscious experiences in those domains did not require any general commitment to the nature of the alleged "hidden hermitage," to the "introcosm that is more myself than anything I can find in the mirror." Indeed, such work could and did proceed in a spirit of skepticism about the whole idea of inner theaters, introcosms, and realms that are in principle inaccessible.

For many, the hope was that the rhapsodic received view, with its ghostly resonances, would eventually come undone. A picture of conscious mental life would eventually emerge. But it would emerge in a piecemeal fashion, associated with deepened understanding of specific cognitive domains and alongside rejection of the idea that there exists a specific faculty of consciousness. But this would take time, and in the meantime no respectable, or at least no respected, psychologist was trying to provide a general theory of consciousness. The general attitude during the rebirth of cognitive psychology is aptly described by Daniel Dennett: "Consciousness appears to be the last bastion of occult properties, epiphenomena, immeasurable subjective states—in short, the one area of mind best left to the philosophers who are welcome to it. Let them make fools of themselves trying to corral the 'quicksilver of phenomenology' into respectable theory."[5]

There was a third and in some ways philosophically more interesting reason why the renewed excitement about the science of the mind was not accompanied by the reemergence of a theory of consciousness. It was widely noticed in many domains that the project of mapping out the complex information flows, catches, and networks constituting mind, be that done at the brain level or the level of cognition, could be done without bringing consciousness into the story. Linguistic acquisition and semantic processing, facial recognition, and the like seemed to proceed largely unconsciously. Furthermore, the dominant philosophical theory of mind, *computational functionalism* was (and still is) committed to the view of *conscious inessentialism*. This is the view that for any mental activity M performed in any cognitive domain D, even if *we* do M with conscious accompaniments, M can in principle be done without these conscious accompaniments.

Whereas most skeptics of strong artificial intelligence press worries that machines cannot be given consciousness, computational functionalism can be read as making this objection irrelevant. Mind does not require consciousness. All the input-output relations between stimuli and responses could be preserved in a system that passed the toughest conceivable Turing test. To be sure, such a system might totally lack experience. But that simply proves the point: consciousness is not essential to intelligent mentality.

One can see how commitment to conscious inessentialism makes respectable the idea of a science of the mind that pays no significant attention to consciousness. It also explains why AI workers, be they members of aboriginal von Neumann tribes or young connectionist upstarts, are not obsessed with finding the right wiring diagrams to make consciousness emerge. Most everyone has abandoned the old illusion that consciousness is definitive of the mental, that each and every mental event is a conscious one. AI workers think that a certain kind of species chauvinism has made us hang on to yet a second illusion. We think that consciousness, even if not involved in all mental activity, is essentially involved in being intelligent and purposeful in the ways in which we are. But it is not, because, the argument goes, any set of input-output relations can be subserved by an endless multiplicity of internal connections and thus the toughest conceivable Turing test can be passed by systems totally lacking consciousness.

I want to defend the view that being intelligent and purposeful in the ways in which we are essentially involves consciousness, from those who claim that this is an illusion or based on one. Consciousness *is* essentially involved in being intelligent and purposeful in the ways in which we are. Computational functionalism, in part because it involves commitment to conscious inessentialism, is the wrong sort of functionalism for the philosopher of psychology to be committed to. It would not be the wrong sort of view if *the* question was, What sorts of systems can preserve the input-output relations that we take to be (partly definitive) of intelligence and purposefulness? It would not be the wrong answer to that question, because the answer to that question is simply the long disjunctive list of possible mechanical and biological models that could realize the proper input-output relations—some of the models mindful, some of them mindless. But computational functionalism is the wrong sort of view for the philosopher of mind to be committed to if he or she takes one of the central facts to be explained to be the existence of conscious output and if he or she sees the project as continuous with that of explaining how intelligent, purposeful life occurs in humans and other earthly creatures.

I take these questions as fundamental, and this is why I favor *Darwinian* or *teleological functionalism*. Darwinian functionalism requires an analysis of input-output relations that preserves the psychological character (including the qualitative character) and the neurobiological character of the processes that mediate and subserve them in the normal biological cases, not in any possible cases whatsoever. It also involves a commitment to the biological adaptiveness of many (but not all) of our conscious capacities.[6]

There is a fourth reason, partly related and partially independent of the previous reasons, why the reemergence of mind did not result in consciousness returning to its former pride of place. Call it the *epiphenomenalist suspicion*. It was noticed in many domains in which there were in fact conscious accompaniments of the mental activity under study, that those conscious accompaniments did not play any obvious or important causal role. First-person, autophenomenological reports of the way things seem provided interesting data about experiences of imagery, short-term memory in matching tests, and so on. But the reports of conscious experience often seemed, following Dennett's wonderful analogy, to be like the press releases of the government spokesman who is typically out of the decision-making loop himself. The spokesman is one of the last persons inside the government to know what is going on. His role is quite unlike that of a truly important government functionary, the Secretary of Defense or State, for example, who exerts a firm hand in what is going on at each crucial choice point. Indeed, the press agent may, unbeknownst to himself, be engaged in massive dissembling—strategically misrepresenting the facts at the behest of those in the know. At other times he may misspeak not so much because he is being called upon to play the role of misspeaker but because he is too many communicative links away from the original action, like the fourth or fifth player in a game of "telephone."

The emergence of cognitive science has been accompanied by the surprising reappearance of the sort of epiphenomenalism that had been found attractive a century before, during the birth of the science of the mind. Recall Huxley's brazen pronouncement that the "soul stands to the body as the bell of a clock to the works, and consciousness answers to the sound which the bell gives out when it is struck. . . . We are conscious automata."[7] Consciousness stands to the mind-body as the president's press agent stands to the workings of the Oval Office, the Departments of State and Defense, the National Security Council, and the Office of Management and Budget. The fact that the press agent's speech acts occur *after* the important causal activity and decision making have taken place suggests the possibility that consciousness may play an analogous role in the governance of our individual lives.

One might resist the analogy by insisting that consciousness simply is not like the president's press agent. It is like the president himself. But this is precisely the unquestioned assumption being challenged. Furthermore, even if we accept that consciousness has a presidential role, it is important to remember that we have in the very recent past had a president who, by almost everyone's admission, was not in control of the government. He was a puppet, the entertaining and eloquent spokesperson for a cadre of smart and hardworking powers (actually layers of powers), some known to outsiders, some unknown. To the best of my knowledge, Ronald and Nancy Reagan are the only people who think that this is not a reasonable description of the Great Communicator's role, first as governor of California and eventually as president. The point is that one can feel presidential, indeed, one can even *be* the president, and still be less in control than it seems.

Conscious Shyness and the "New Mysterians"

So far I have isolated four reasons why the reemergence of the study of mind associated with the rise of cognitivism did not result in the simultaneous reemergence of grand theorizing about consciousness. First, there was a certain methodological scrupulousness, a vestige of the draconian restrictions of behaviorism on the study of the "inner" and the "unobservable." Second, there was the view that one could analyze various aspects of mentality with a background commitment to the existence of conscious experience in the domain under study but without commitment to any general theory of the nature and function of consciousness. Third, there was the belief, inspired by computational functionalism, that consciousness was not in fact metaphysically essential. The thesis of conscious inessentialism says that there are possible worlds in which creatures who are Turing-identical to us at the level of input-output relations do not possess consciousness. Fourth, there is the epiphenomenalist suspicion, the suspicion that the role of consciousness may be far more limited in our case than we consciously (not surprisingly) think it is, and thus that the study of consciousness is of less importance in the overall project of understanding the mind than we ordinarily think.

I will call an approach "conscious shy" if it sidesteps or tries to finesse the study of consciousness for any of the above reasons. Conscious shyness has, as it were, four causes. A scientist of the mind can be conscious shy because she is methodologically modest, practicing a sort of enlightened neopositivism. Alternatively, she might believe in the reality of consciousness but think that it names such a vague or, what is different, such a heterogeneous set of phenomena that it is not the sort of thing for which a general theory can be developed (at least not yet). Different still, she might be attracted to the brand of functionalism that holds that the aim is to explain intelligent mentality in its most abstract form, that is, in terms of the metaphysically essential properties required for the explanation of intelligence in any possible world that contains it, not in terms of the contingent properties that might be associated with just our kind of minds, and which might, not surprisingly, be especially dear to our hearts. Finally, she might simply think that we should postpone any general theorizing about the role and function of consciousness until the evidence gives further indication of the extent to which consciousness is involved in the causal fray, until, that is, there is evidence that it does play a significant role in the overall economy of mind. Even if consciousness plays a presidential role in mind, there is still the question of whether it is presidential in the way Reagan was or in the way FDR was.

Besides the conscious-shy types there is another type that eschews the scientific study of consciousness. I call this second type the "new mysterians," after a forgettable 1960s pop group called Question Mark and the Mysterians. The new mysterians think that consciousness will *never* be understood. Whether its causal role is significant or not, it will not be understood. The old mysterians were dualists who thought that consciousness could not be understood because it operates according to nonnatural principles and has nonnatural properties. The new mysterians are naturalists. They believe that mind and consciousness exist and that they operate in accordance with natural principles and are comprised of natural properties. But the new mysterians are a postmodern group, naturalists with a kinky twist. They are trying to drive a railroad spike through the heart of scientism, the view that science will eventually explain whatever is natural. Thomas Nagel was the founder of this group.[8] In his famous paper "What Is It like to Be a Bat?" Nagel argued that there can be no remotely plausible naturalistic account of consciousness, that something essential will always be left out of even our very best theory. Nagel writes, "Consciousness is what makes the mind-body problem really intractable. . . . Without consciousness the mind-body problem would be much less interesting. With consciousness it seems hopeless."[9] In his book *The View from Nowhere*, a work that Nagel describes as "deliberately reactionary," Nagel develops his argument. He insists that "we have at present no conception of how a single event or thing could have both physical and phenomenological aspects, or how if it did they might be related."[10]

More recently Colin McGinn has declared the new mysterians alive and well.[11] McGinn writes, "We have been trying for a long time to solve the mind-body problem. It has stubbornly resisted our best efforts. The mystery persists. I think the time has come to admit candidly that we cannot resolve the mystery."[12] McGinn thinks that "we know that brains are the *de facto* causal basis of consciousness." But "we are cut off by our very cognitive constitution from achieving a conception of that natural property of the brain (or of consciousness) that accounts for the psychophysical link."[13] McGinn, like the other new mysterians, thinks that there is some natural property or set of properties, *P*, that accounts for consciousness. Consciousness comes with our kind of brain. Psychological properties supervene on certain physical properties of our nervous systems in the way in which water supervenes on collections of H_2O molecules.[14] McGinn simply thinks that it is in principle impossible for us to comprehend P.[15] Whatever natural property, P, causes certain neural events to be consciously experienced by realizing these very conscious states is closed to us. If an omniscient God exists, then God knows all about P and how it gives rise to consciousness. But both P and the intelligible connection between P and consciousness is closed to us, its owners, as it were.

Although the doctrine is reactionary and extremely mischievous, coming from a naturalist, it is a coherent position. Limitative results in physics and mathematics—for example, Heisenberg's Uncertainty Principle and Gödel's Incompleteness Theorem—tell us of certain in-principle impossibilities faced by the physicist or mathematician. Just as we cannot know the position and momentum of an electron at one and the same time or just as we can know that a certain sentence in arithmetic is true while it is in principle impossible for us to prove it within arithmetic, it is conceivable that we can know that consciousness is a natural phenomenon while at the same time it is in principle closed to us what sort of natural phenomenon it is.[16]

As a result of some recent work in neuropsychology, cognitive science, and philosophy we have, I think, the beginnings of a unified theory of consciousness, and we can therefore start to mount a response to both groups, the conscious shy and the new mysterians. The best response to both the conscious-shy folks and the new mysterians will be to show that a coherent theory sketch can be given. After all, what is actual is possible.

Mind, Brain, and Experience

Let us start at the beginning. The main problem is this: how can a physical device give rise to conscious experience? We can simplify the question by dropping the word "conscious." For the question is really, first and foremost, how experience or sentience of any sort is possible. The first problem is that there are kinds of sensitivity that we are not sure involve experience in even the lowest-level sense of the term. For example, there is the light sensitivity of unicellular organisms like paramecia. A short distance up the phylogenic scale there are the chemical sensors of the scallop that cause it to move when an unfamiliar object intrudes in its space. Information is being received and living creatures are responding to this information, but there is no reason at this point in time to think that paramecia or scallops can feel or experience anything at all. This gives us a first approximation of what, at the very lowest level, needs to be explained. What is it about some physical devices that makes systems

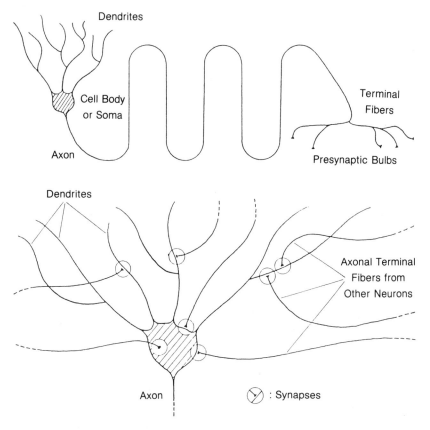

Figure 8.1
Typical neurons. (Reprinted with permission from P. M. Churchland 1988, pp. 131, 132.)

who possess the properties they possess *subjects of experience*, creatures that feel something?

Consider the brain. According to the best recent estimates the brain consists of roughly 100 billion (10^{11}) neurons.[17] This means that there are about the same number of neurons in each brain as there are stars in the Milky Way galaxy. There are three main types of neurons, differentiated by their involvement in various kinds of activity: sensory neurons, motor neurons, and interneurons (the ones involved in everything else: message transfers between the sensory and motor neurons, memory, higher-level thought, and so on).

Typical neurons are shown in figure 8.1. When a depolarization pulse (an "action potential" or "spike") runs down an axon, it causes release at the bulbs of its characteristic neurotransmitter, for example, acetylcholine, dopamine, serotonin, noradrenalin. Depending on the neurotransmitter released and those on the other end, this pulse will serve to excite or inhibit the synapse by creating a positive or negative charge. Neuronal cells are almost always jittering. A spike is simply a very powerful jitter, a jolt. A second determinant of neural behavior other than depolarization itself is the frequency of depolarization. If 3,000 inhibitory synapses are active only once per second and 300 excitatory synapses are active thirty times per second, then excitation dominates, and (all else being equal) the neuron will fire.[18] Neurons jitter in ensembles, in populations comprising on the order of 5 to 50 layers (possibly as many as 100 layers in certain cases). The jitters of these neuronal groups (comprised of 50 to 10,000 neurons each) are determined not only by activation occurring at the sensory periphery but also from projections from next-door neighbors (horizontal projections) and from above (descending axonal projections) especially the more we as individuals know. The brain is a "recurrent network" with constant "reentrant mapping" among sectors activated in parallel.[19]

A recurrent network with reentrant signaling is one in which functionally segregated brain areas respond in parallel to various aspects of some stimulus and pass the information they compute back and forth to other regions involved in perception and cognition. For example, the visual cortex of a monkey contains on the order of 20 functionally segregated areas dedicated to visual processing. Visual detection occurs by these areas' passing information back and forth at blazing speed. Perceiving is not the result of a set of serial computations that eventually reach the "perception center." It is the result of coordination among the system of functionally distributed processors vertically and horizontally communicating back and forth. Recurrent patterns of activation and rapid reentry of signals yields a unified perception without the involvement of any perception center.[20]

The neuronal network retains representations, but not in permanently coded files. It retains representations as dispositions to reactivate distributed activation patterns selected during previous experience. Once a particular distributed activation pattern has reached an equilibrial state such that it is activated by a certain type of stimulus pattern, it frames novel occurrent stimulation with that activation pattern (see the discussion of connectionism in chapter 6). This leads to quick and easy identification of the stimulation and, depending on its connections to other neuronal groups, to the right motor response. The neuronal groups are selected to detect certain constellations of features. The groups are extremely sensitive but not overly fussy. This explains why we are so quick to identify degraded stimuli, for example, letters written in new and obscure handwriting. The right pattern of activation is turned on by any stimulus that possesses some sufficient number, or some adequately patterned configuration, of the relevant features. The stimuli need not be exactly the same as the stimuli the neuronal group was trained up on. Indeed, a system that could only recognize duplicates of previous stimuli would be of no use at all in our fluid ecological surround.

If one harbors doubts that a system of dopey neurons could remotely begin to account for the range of thought and the plasticity of cognition, consider this: A typical neuron has synaptic connections emanating from on the order of 3,000 other neurons (this is an average; some neurons have as many as 10,000 synaptic inputs, others as many as 100,000, and some only a few). That would make for on the order of 10^{14} distinct possible synaptic connections (10^{11} neurons times 10^3 synaptic connections). If we assume that each of these 10^{14} connections is capable of one of only 10 possible weights at any given time (this is a conservative estimate), the total number of distinct neural states is $10^{10^{14}}$ or $10^{100,000,000,000,000}$. Paul Churchland puts these numbers in perspective. "To get some idea of the size of this number, recall that the total number of elementary particles in the universe is generally estimated to be about 10^{87}."[21]

Even if we assume that 99 percent of these states don't add up to anything cognitively worthwhile, that still leaves .01 ($= 10^{-2}$) $\times$ $10^{100,000,000,000,000} = 10^{99,999,999,999,998}$ states capable of doing worthwhile cognitive labor. And if we reduce the estimate to 99.9 percent nonfunctional states and only .1 percent functional (10^{-3}), that still leaves $10^{99,999,999,999,997}$ functional states. Suppose that 99.9 percent of these states subserve functional but nonconscious states. That still leaves on the order of $10^{99,999,999,999,994}$ states for *conscious* mental life!

One causal feature of the brain that can't be emphasized enough and that differentiates the brain from every computer has to do with the neurotransmitters and the family of other neurochemicals permeating nervous tissue. Neurotransmitters don't just function to turn neurons on or off. They are also involved in how things feel qualitatively. Neurotransmitter levels are becoming increasingly implicated in diseases like parkinsonism and schizophrenia, in anxiety disorders, and in dreaming. Some extremely effective new antidepressants (for example, Prozac) work by inhibiting the reabsorption of serotonin by the neurons releasing it. It is not that serotonin reabsorption causes depression or that serotonin levels alone are responsible for depression. But serotonin seems to be implicated in the complex causal etiology of at least certain forms of depression.

I will shortly return to the specific issue of qualitative feel, of qualia. But first I need to say a little more about brain function and the evolution of consciousness. I hope that the picture drawn so far of the brain as a supremely well-connected system of processors capable of more distinct states than any system ever known by several orders of magnitude provides reassurance that the brain is complex enough to be our *res cogitans,* our thinking thing.

The Evolution of Darwin Machines

The picture of mind sketched so far is one in which the mind is the brain and the brain is what William Calvin calls a "Darwin Machine."[22] The brain is a biological device in which pressures to achieve adaptive coordination between the organism and the external world operate to select populations of neurons from predisposed groups to recognize certain patterns in the external world, as well as within the body itself, and to activate certain appropriate motor routines in response to the patterns recognized.

Higher-level thought, planning with foresight and problem solving, also involve processes analogous to those involved in natural selection. We select approaches to problems that have worked in similar situations in the past. In utterly novel situations we spin out novel problem-solving strategies by mixing previous solution strategies, creating "idea mutations," as it were. We try some of these, and if they get the job done, there is selection in their favor in the future.[23] As George Mandler puts it, the general rule is, "When current conscious constructions do not account for the state of the world, then a new conscious state will be initiated."[24]

Actually, the picture of the brain as a massively parallel Darwin machine suggests a particular gloss on Mandler's point that the system works by creating new ideas when old ones fail. If current conscious constructions do not account for the state of the world, new conscious constructions will be generated. But these new conscious constructions need not, indeed they typically will not, be generated consciously themselves. In the mid 1940s Kenneth Craik proposed the hypothesis that the nervous system is capable of modeling both the external world and itself and of simulating possible worlds and possible actions based on past experience. Craik realized that such anticipatory modeling would need to operate largely unconsciously to be maximally efficient. In a very efficient cognitive system a new conscious state would be initiated only when the nervous system was finished unconsciously weighing, in parallel, various possible scenarios and action plans. William Calvin explains how the brain conceived as a massively parallel Darwin machine could do the job Craik thought it in fact did.[25]

> A Darwin machine now provides a framework for thinking about thought, indeed one that may be a reasonable first approximation to the actual brain machinery underlying thought. An intracerebral Darwin Machine need not try out one sequence at a time against memory; it may be able to try out dozens, if not hundreds, simultaneously, shape up new generations in milliseconds, and thus initiate insightful actions without *overt* trial and error. This massively parallel selection among stochastic sequences is more analogous to the ways of darwinian biology than to the "von Neumann" serial computer. Which is why I call it a Darwin Machine instead; it shapes up thoughts in milliseconds rather than millennia, and uses innocuous remembered environments rather than noxious real-life ones. It may well create the uniquely human aspect of our consciousness.[26]

The capacities to think ahead, to recognize novel situations as harbingers of good or ill, and to speedily and imaginatively solve problems are among our most valuable capacities. They were almost certainly keys to the survival and proliferation of our species. Dennett writes that the "key to control is the ability to *track* or even *anticipate* the important features of the environment, so all brains are, in essence, *anticipation-machines.*"[27] Overall, our brain is the most powerful anticipation machine ever built. But other systems are more sensitive to, and thus better anticipators of, certain classes of events, especially those relevant to their survival, than we are. Snakes, for example, are reliable detectors of impending earthquakes, more reliable, some say, than scientific instruments sunk far deeper in the ground.

What function might sensory or perceptual consciousness serve? Such consciousness could enable an organism to be sensitive to stimulus saliencies relevant to its survival and to coordinate its goals with these saliencies. Informational sensitivity without experiential sensitivity could conceivably serve the same function. Indeed, it often does. But the special vivacity of perceptual experience might enable quicker response times and more reliable and functional responses than a less robustly phenomenological system and thus might have resulted in small selection pressures in favor of becoming a subject of experience. At least this is one possible explanation for why Mother Nature would have selected a mind with capacities for robust phenomenological feel in the sensory modalities. It is good that reptiles are sensitive detectors of earthquakes. It enables them to get above ground before disaster hits. It is good that we feel pain. It keeps us from being burned, cut, and maimed. Persons who are bad pain detectors are in a great danger of these sorts of harms.

The story of exactly how consciousness evolved is underdetermined by the available information. For reasons just mentioned, direct selection for sensitivity to pleasant and painful stimuli seems likely. Evidence that there are six universal basic emotions distinguished by their qualitative feel, movements of the facial musculature, and their underlying biology suggests that there was also selection at the species level for a phenomenologically robust "emotive economy."[28]

Experiential sensitivity to pleasant and painful stimuli and powerful emotional dispositions seem to be enough sensitivity to gain fairly robust biological fitness. Any system equipped with a "conative economy" (the phrase is Dennett's) should do well when it comes to the activities—fleeing, fighting, food gathering, and sex—necessary for biological fitness. Why, then, did we evolve to possess the higher-order mental and linguistic capacities capable of creating culture, art, history, science, and schemes of self-comprehension? The answer is contained in what was already said about selection for anticipation machines. What capacities a particular type of organism needs to have depends essentially on what kind of organism it is, what dangers lurk in its ecological niche, what it needs to do to live long enough to reproduce, and so on. Creatures of our size (we used to be smaller) would not have been given great odds for survival in some primeval betting pool. Ancestral humans were not nearly as fast or as strong as the predators that existed alongside them and savored the taste of their flesh. In addition, human young need constant care for terms longer than any other mammal. Furthermore, even when humans were hairier, we were still not nearly as well suited to contend with the vagaries of global weather as other animals. So how did we survive?

The short answer is that someone had the bright idea to use tools and the rest of us caught on. Hunting, gathering, and clothing became possible once tool making was invented. But food sources could quickly become scarce, so we moved a lot. Nomads need to be quick students of new niches. Nomads need to learn what in the new locale is useful, what is harmful, and they need to anticipate in advance when the next move is advisable. Creatures who are relatively weak and who move a lot would be rational to want to have sophisticated capacities of thought, attention, anticipation, and plasticity of response. Mother Nature, of course, doesn't give creatures what they want or need unless they themselves produce a few mutations with the capacities that would enhance the reproductive fitness of these mutants relative to their normal fellows. Selection follows upon differential reproductive success.

Since we possess the relevant higher-order capacities, the inference to the best explanation for this fact is that once upon a time such mutants appeared among our ancestors. Mutants capable of higher-order conscious thought might seem to require that the miracle of consciousness needed to occur not just once when it arose for pleasure and pain, sensation, and the emotions but also a second time when it arose for conscious thought, planning, self-consciousness, and so on. The simplest assumption, however, is that the mutants' higher-order conscious capacities piggybacked on the first, not as free riders, but as further developments of the first set of conscious capacities. Roughly, the idea is that conscious sensitivity to pleasure, pain, and the sensory environment, as well as phenomenologically robust propensities to fight, flee, or engage the affections of a compatriot at the appropriate times already confer a certain fitness. The higher-order conscious capacities do not so much supply us with new fitness-conferring equipment as they enhance and improve upon the initial equipment. Conscious recognition of regularities in nature and the capacity to plan ahead for such regularities as seasonal changes, for example, dramatically increase our ability to arrange the world so that we are the beneficiaries of more pleasure than pain. The sort of mutations that would be most likely to be selected for (and probably also to have emerged in the first place) would be ones in which the higher-order capacities linked up to the lower-order capacities that they were, so-to-speak, designed to serve.[29]

In any case, it seems likely that one or two mutant nervous systems with the capacities for higher-order conscious thought would have proliferated like crazy. Imagine that there were two populations of thoughtful mutants (the paleontological evidence indicates that there were several species of hominids existing alongside *Homo sapiens*). The first group did all its anticipating consciously and tried out all possible action options under the full light of consciousness. The second group computed many options simultaneously in parallel networks and passed on for conscious reflection only things worth worrying about and options worth considering. Assuming that both systems were equally smart and would reach the same conclusions under the same circumstances, one might think that neither group would be favored over the other. But if speed of processing mattered, and it almost certainly did and does, then the second group would have been favored. A hungry sabertooth demands one's attention, but one had better not spend too much time reflecting on how to respond to its presence unless one doesn't mind being lunch. So the second group would have displaced the first. All else being equal, Darwin-machine mutants will always win in a head to head battle with von Neumann–machine mutants.

Higher-level consciousness did not need to come into being. This is true for two reasons. First, we did not need to exist. Had it not been for those mutants, our ancestral accidents, we would not have evolved, survived, and proliferated. Second, it is conceivable that creatures as capable as us and more or less behaviorally indistinguishable from us might have evolved in such a way as to get by on pure informational sensitivity and unconscious higher-level problem solving (for example, the way a computer plays chess) without ever experiencing a thing. We, however, did not evolve that way, and therefore consciousness possesses a natural history. The nature of brain tissue guarantees us that there will be no fossils of consciousness. The project of recounting the causal origins of consciousness as we know it involves us in what Dennett aptly describes as "software archeology."[30] We need to reconstruct a credible tale from present brain structure and function and the tangible evidence of what our nonhuman and hominid ancestors lived like. The true and complete story may eternally elude us, and it undoubtedly involves not only majestic feats of engineering but also all manner of quirky contingency, free riders, and emergent properties that would not have been in the plans of an omniscient designer.

The sketchiness of the story of the emergence of consciousness is analogous to the sketchiness of the story of the emergence of life. It was not until the mid 1950s that a remotely credible theory of how life might have emerged was put forward and tested. Experiments showed that adding electricity to an environment of hydrogen, ammonia, and methane started some amino-acid-building activity. Amino acids are the building blocks for proteins, which are necessary but not sufficient for DNA. But no one is sure that this is exactly how life evolved. This is because we are not certain what the primeval inorganic materials were or in what amounts they subsisted, whether the consummating action took place in the seas or in marshes, and what form of life was the very first to arise. Furthermore, even if someone actually got a unicellular life form to emerge in an experiment like that just described, this would not prove that life on earth in fact evolved that way. It would only show that we had come upon one of the ways in which it might have evolved. The natural history of life and mind are intimately bound together. We know that DNA is the basis for life and that the brain is the basis for mind. But we do not possess a full explanation of how DNA or the human nervous system evolved. Because of the very nature of natural history, it is unlikely that any story in either domain will force a clear-cut choice among several viable alternative scenarios.

Neural Darwinism

The brain, I have suggested, is a Darwin machine, a device governed by principles of massively parallel processing and neuronal group selection. Gerald M. Edelman, a Nobel prize winner, is the major proponent of the theory of "neural Darwinism."[31] Five main ideas of the theory stand out. First, it is mathematically inconceivable that the human genome specifies the entire wiring diagram of the brain. The genome, powerful as it is, contains too few instructions by several orders of magnitude to build a fully functional brain. The synaptic connections that evolve in a brain over time are the complex causal outcome of genotypic instructions, endogenous biochemical processes, and vast amounts of individually unique organism-environment interactions.[32] It follows that talk of the brain as hard-wired is misleading. To be sure, the overall structure of the brain is fixed by our genes and certain neuronal paths, and certain specific areas are designed to serve certain dedicated functions. But the "wires" in the brain, even the ones built during fetal development and those serving specific functions, are soft. Furthermore, all the wires are capable of being drawn into novel and complex connections with indefinitely many other segments of the neural network. The key to our magnificent abilities as "anticipation machines" involved fixing gross architecture while leaving the development of the connections at the level of microstructure undedicated and adaptable.

Second and relatedly, individual brains are extraordinarily diverse in terms of structure and connectivity. Identity theory has some real credibility in the domain of sensory experience. Certain characteristic neural patterns subserve similar cross-personal sensory experiences. But by and large, most mental states seem not to involve type identity between mental and neural state types. Thus one and the same conscious mental state, for example, believing that a speeding fire engine is coming from behind, may be subserved by compositionally distinct neural states in all the different drivers who have that thought. Once massive connectivity is added in, it is no surprise that this thought kicks off different series of other thoughts for each of us. One person worries about the victims and their property, and another that he will be delayed. A third is thrown into a Proustian reminiscence of summer nights in his childhood spent with grandfather, the fire chief, at the station. He feels the humid summer breeze on his face as he rides to a fire and the smells of burning embers and pictures of lonely stone chimneys well up in him. Neural connectivity is the mother of "meaning holism" and of the "drift of thought." We are good at keeping attention focused, but certain events send thought reeling to unanticipated places, some welcome, others not. Neural connectivity explains why this happens so easily.

Third, neuronal ensembles projecting through many levels are *selected* during experience to map and thereby represent certain saliencies. Which ensembles represent what is determined jointly by the genetically specified receptivities of different neural locations (so visual processing takes place in areas dedicated to vision and not to audition) and by the neuronal groups available for selection and strengthening at the time a stimulus is presented.

Fourth, because recognition and recall do not involve permanent storage and thus lost storage space each time a particular pattern becomes recognizable, neuronal groups play multiple roles. My detectors for red are activated whenever red is before me. But when red things are not before me, my red detectors are available for other recognitional labor, purple and orange detection, for example.

Fifth, a neuronal system functioning according to principles of ontogenic, life-span selection, as opposed to phylogenic, species-level selection, is fluid in several respects. (1) It can gain, retain, revise, and abandon all sorts of thoughts, ideas, desires, and intentions in the course of a life. (2) The system can lose certain neurons to death or in a labor dispute to some other function without any loss in functional capacity. If the capacity to recognize a banana as edible is subserved by parallel activity in numerous recurrent layers of neuronal groups, then all manner of degradation and loss of members is compatible with continuous high performance. Neuronal destruction can, of course, reach a point in which the amount of neuronal degradation is great enough to lead to functional incapacitation in certain domains, as it does, for example, in Alzheimer's patients. (3) Neuronal dedication to a task is not fixed for all time once the neuronal group subserving the recognitional or motor task in question is well honed. For example, the neuronal group responsible for pressure detection on two adjacent fingers will "segregate into groups that *at any one time* are nonoverlapping and have sharp boundaries."[33] But these dedicated groups can shift boundaries over time because of differential experience and possibly even randomly. Imagine the boundary between the United States and Canada shifting several miles one way or another each day along its entire expanse.[34]

Self and Nonself

One of the most important things a well-designed system will need to be sensitive to is the distinction between self and nonself, between me and not me, between inner and outer. A crucial piece of evidence in favor of the neural Darwinist model is the existence of a neural basis of the distinction between self and nonself. Self, in the relevant sense, is not the self of narrative awareness, the thick self constitutive of personal and social identity (more about that self later). It is in the first instance the subject of interoceptive signals that alert the organism to its own homeostatic state: to its autonomic, neuroendocrinological, and hedonic condition. According to the theory of neural Darwinism, perceptual consciousness arose in part because of selection pressures favoring coordination of "the two kinds of nervous organization," and favoring in particular the selection of neuronal groups capable of retaining information about the relations between certain outer things and events and internal homeostasis and well-being.[35] Edelman writes,

> I shall use the term "self" and "nonself" in a strict biological sense, not in the personal or psychological sense of "self-awareness," or in the social or philosophical sense of "personhood." In richly endowed nervous systems, these portions must be organized differently but also be in communication. While neural parts of the first kind (e.g., the hypothalamus, pituitary, various portions of the brain stem, amygdala, hippocampus, and limbic system) operate within developmentally given parameters, those of the second kind (e.g., cerebral cortex, thalamus, and cerebellum) operate largely through ongoing exteroceptive sensory interactions with the world, that is, through experience and behavior.[36]

Consciousness is the result of the interaction of "the two kinds of nervous organization." Consciousness emerged with the development of segregated neural equipment subserving, on the one hand, internal hedonic regulation and, on the other hand, information processing about the state of the external world. The full blown Jamesian "stream of consciousness" came into being with the evolution of a memory system capable of continuously projecting past matches of hedonic value or disvalue onto novel (possibly even future) states of affairs and then on the basis of new outcomes updating the models and hypotheses it contains.[37]

The story is credible. Dennett has pointed out that some sort of sensitivity to the boundaries of the self is a necessary condition for survival: "the origin of complex life forms on this planet was also the birth of the most primitive sort of self, whatever sort of self is implied by the self-regard that prevents the lobster when hungry, from eating itself."[38] Lobsters, I suspect, are dim experiencers. But the important point is that designing systems that make the self-nonself distinction is one of the very first design problems Mother Nature faces. Either Mother Nature makes us experientially sensitive to the self-nonself distinction, or she makes us informationally sensitive to it. But she has no choice except to make us sensitive to the distinction. Otherwise, predation will start with the nearest tasty morsel—possibly oneself! The good thing for the neural-Darwinist story about the evolution of the self-nonself distinction is that it does not depend on a design solution uniquely arrived at in the human case. Something like the distinction is ubiquitous among organic systems that have made it this far. If one is a mere photosynthesizer and ground-nutrient absorber, the self-nonself distinction might not be one that the system needs to be sensitive to. But if one depends on eating for survival, one will need the requisite sensitivity.

Sensory Qualia and Neural Vectors

With this bare-bones sketch of the structure, function, and evolution of our partly conscious, massively parallel brain before us, we can reformulate our initial question in this way: How can a system of 100 billion well-connected neurons set in a soupy mixture of neurochemicals in which the only things that happen are activations of sets of neurons at different rates, together with changes in the composition of the soup, give rise to conscious experience? This question, like the original question, might be asking us to dispel *all* mystery, or it might be asking merely for some relief from mystery. Minimally, we want a plausible picture of how this rambunctious bundle of nervous activity set in its complex biochemical environment can ever add up to experiences that are clearly individuated by the subjects who experience them, as are, for example, the taste of lemonade, the smell of a rose, the feeling of sadness or elation, and so on.

For us, the lowest level of conscious experience involves sensory qualia, the so-called "raw feels" of taste, touch, sight, and the like. If we can beat back the mystery surrounding sensory qualia even a little, we will have gained some ground, for it is here that many think the intractability problem begins.[39] Here is one answer sketched by Paul Churchland for sensory qualia.[40] The basic idea is that different sensory qualia are produced by a certain subset of the vast number of patterned distributions of neural activity. Different qualia are produced by distinct characteristic spiking patterns of the sensory pathways that project through the brain to the cortex according to mathematically tractable transformations. One can easily see how this basic story might be generalized to certain emotional qualia and possibly to other kinds of experiences as well.

This hypothesis is simply the inference to the best explanation for sensory qualia. The evidence in favor of this analysis comes mainly from two different directions. First, there are the autophenomeno-logical and behavioral data indicating that there are sensory experiences and that they have some cross-personal regularity. Persons across cultures pick out the same chip as focal red, persons across cultures claim to see images in which horizontal or vertical lines come to the fore or recede to the ground in predictable patterns depending on the stimuli presented. Second, there is information about the nervous system. The story of spiking frequency has the virtue of fitting the two sets of data together in a coherent manner. It predicts, for example, that sighted and non-color-blind people will report seeing red only if there is neural activity of a certain sort going on. To be more precise, the story for color, taste, and olfaction runs as follows.

With respect to color there appear to be three distinct kinds of cells (cones) in our retinas that are sensitive to short, medium, and long wavelengths of light. Color perception is caused by different levels of activity in the three kinds of cones. In particular, each experience of a particular color or shade is subserved by a unique ratio of activity in the three cone types. This hypothesis was put forward by Hermann von Helmholtz in 1860, and twentieth century brain science shows it to be almost certainly true.[41]

With respect to taste, there are four distinct kinds of receptor cells on the tongue. For olfaction, there are six or seven distinct sensory receptors. In general, for each domain there is a small set of sensory receptor cells that exhausts the location of inputs subserving the relevant types of sensory experience: experiences of taste, color, and smell.

Now the story so far may look hopelessly thin and inept. Three or four receptor cells to explain the seemingly endless multiplicity of tastes and colors. So much for the naturalists' story! But here we have to be careful. The receptor cells, as we have seen in the case of color, are not each responsible for one and only one taste or color. If that were so, your capacity to see any particular color would evaporate upon the death of the neuron (or neuron type) responsible for it. The essential feature of the receptor cells is that they can vary across a fine-grained continuum in their degree of activation.

It is the relative activity of the receptor cells along their idiosyncratic continua that determine what is experienced. The involvement of ensembles of cells explain how death or inactivity of individual neurons can have no significant effect on the experience or information pickup.

It is best to think of each sensory cell in each domain as a variable that can take on different numerical values, each representing a different level of stimulation. So for taste we have a set of variables $\{S_{t1}, S_{t2}, S_{t3}, S_{t4}\}$. We then define a sensory-coding vector as any determinate list of numerical values representing the level of stimulation assigned to the four variables. The proposal, then, is simply this: for each and every human taste, there is a unique sensory-coding vector. The extraordinary range of sensory experience in the taste modality is explained by the extraordinary, but not infinite, set of values that can be taken by each receptor cell and the vast combinatorial possibilities available among the four cells. The same story goes for olfaction, color, and so on. If we suppose that there are 10 distinct discriminable states each receptor cell can give rise to (this is almost certainly an underestimation for each modality), then we can distinguish 10^3 colors, 10^4 tastes, 10^6 or 10^7 odors, and so on. A bloodhound capable of distinguishing every person on the planet could do so with the same number of odor receptors that we have so long as these were about 3 times as sensitive as ours. If each receptor state could give rise to 30 discriminable states along its axis, then 30^7 (22 billion) unique odor discriminations would be possible. Alternatively, a system with 10 odor receptors capable of 10 distinct states would also do the job, since it would be capable of 10 billion unique discriminations (it is estimated that there will be 6.3 billion humans on earth by the turn of the century).

Certain philosophers have argued that qualia are inherently mysterious and that nothing, at least nothing scientific, can be said about them. But Paul Churchland rightly points out that

> this approach to understanding sensory qualia is both theoretically and empirically motivated. . . . it suggests an effective means of expressing the allegedly inexpressible. The "ineffable" pink of one's current visual sensation may be richly and precisely expressed as a 95Hz/80Hz/80Hz "chord" in the relevant triune cortical system. The "unconveyable" taste sensation produced by the fabled Australian health tonic Vegamite might be poignantly conveyed as a 85/80/90/15 "chord" in one's four channeled gustatory system. . . . And the "indescribable" olfactory sensation produced by a newly opened rose might be quite accurately described as a 95/35/10/80/60/55 "chord" in some six-dimensional space within one's olfactory bulb.[42]

Sensory qualia, according to the proposal being offered, are just the characteristic spiking frequencies or activation patterns (these include, I emphasize, the changes in the biochemical environment produced in the creation of the activity pattern) in the relevant sensory pathways. There are locations, really spaces, in the continua of values which each set of pathways can take that correspond to what psychologists call "just noticeable differences" (jnd's). If for me Pepsi and Coke taste differently, this is because the activation ranges in the relevant pathways are distinct *and* because I am sensitive to their distinctness. According to the theory, similarity judgments are based upon actual proximity of position or degree of overlap in the relevant state space (see the discussion of connectionism in chapter 6).

The sensory-coding-vector story may generalize beyond qualia associated with the five familiar sensory modalities. Take facial recognition. Persons with prosopagnosia cannot recognize faces, but normal persons take for granted their abilities to *re*-cognize faces. I emphasize the "re" because the crucial thing is that once we see a face, we experience it as seen before, and this is true even if we can't associate a name to the face. It is possible that facial recognition works according to the vector-coding strategy.[43] There are several good reasons for thinking that the neural network contains a sector built for facial coding. First, there is decisive evidence that certain sorts of right-hemisphere damage to the parietal lobe causes prosopagnosia. Second, thanks to the work of Hubel and Wiesel and others, we know that receptor cells in the eye are very sensitive to the different orientations of lines, and we know from work on coordination between the visual and motor systems that we are good at judging distances (from our body to a cup we want to grasp, for example). Third, there are good evolutionary reasons to think that there would have been selection pressures to build networks capable of quickly and effortlessly recognizing the faces of conspecifics. A system that quickly recognizes its mate, fellow travellers, and enemies will do better than a system that does not.

We consciously recognize faces, but we are not conscious of how we recognize faces. The most plausible hypothesis is that the facial-coding sector operates as an unconscious geometrician. It detects some of the main facial aspects: the shape of the eyes, the distance between the eyes, mouth width, nose length and width, distances between (and among) eyes and nose, nose and jaw, ear to ear, jaw and hairline, and so on. If there are, let us suppose, 10 or 12 saliencies such as these to which we are sensitive and as few as 10 values (this is probably a serious underestimation) that can be encoded for each, this would allow for unique vector assignments for between 10 billion (10^{10}) and 1 trillion (10^{12}) faces. More than enough!

Experiential Sensitivity versus Informational Sensitivity

Our informational sensitivities exceed by far our conscious sensitivities. If the sensory-vector story is true for sensory qualia, it is true in the following sort of way. For any qualitative experience q, q has the qualitative character it has because q is both a token of a type of neural activation in the relevant sensory pathway and at the same time a token of the relevant experiential state type. The thesis is not that for each different vector there is a distinct sensory quale. The Pepsi-Coke case shows why. Coke and Pepsi almost definitely differ in the activation vector they cause. Not all persons are *experientially sensitive* to all significant differences in the sensory vectors. To some people Pepsi and Coke taste the same. Now a person might be experientially *in*sensitive to the difference between two stimuli while at the same time he or she is *informationally sensitive* to the difference. If the person who honestly claims to experience no taste difference between Pepsi and Coke reliably chooses Pepsi in blind forced-choice situations, then we must infer that some complex calculation of information differences, in interaction with a complex economy of desire, is taking place. For the vector-activation story to be credible, there will have to be some underlying difference in the Pepsi and Coke vectors subserving the eventual behavioral difference. All distinct sensory experiences are subserved by distinct vectors. But not all distinct vectors subserve distinct experiences. This is why the hypothesis is that a sensory experience occurs only if there is the relevant sort of nervous activity in the sensory pathways. The hypothesis says "only if" rather than "if and only if" for two reasons. First, the relevant sensory vector is necessary, but perhaps not invariably sufficient, for the relevant sensory experience. Neural activity quickly spreads from the sensory periphery up and outward throughout the brain. More neural activity than the right sensory-coding vector may be needed to experience "red." Second, the sensory vector that unambiguously differentiates Pepsi from Coke might be active without the whole system experiencing the difference. The activated vector may nonetheless play an important role in our overall psychological economy.

The distinction between experiential sensitivity and informational sensitivity is useful across a wide array of domains.[44] But it is hardly pure. First, there is a grey area of what Freudians call preconscious experience, where some stimulation to which we display clear informational sensitivity is not in awareness but can be brought into awareness. Our capacity to become sensitive to what it is about the taste of Pepsi that makes us prefer it even when we are initially unaware of any experience that could subserve such a preference suggests that there are attentional mechanisms that can be brought into play to bring to experience what is initially only a neural difference that makes an informational difference. Second, in the Coke-Pepsi case both tastes are experienced. It is the difference in taste that is not experienced. There are other kinds of cases in which there is informational sensitivity but no experiential sensitivity at all. Indeed, the literature on subliminal perception indicates that for each sensory modality there is a level of stimulation below which experience fails to occur but in which information about stimuli is received and processed. For example, emotionally threatening words presented below the experiential visual threshold cause changes in auditory sensitivity and vice versa.[45] On my view, we respond to such stimuli, but they are not objects of experience. Third and correlatively, dreams are experienced and thus conscious. We are notoriously bad at remembering our dreams when awake, but they involve phenomenologically robust experience.[46] All things considered, the distinction between experiential sensitivity and informational sensitivity has a credible basis, as does the identification of conscious mental life with experience simpliciter.

Identity Theory to a First Approximation?

To a first and rough approximation, identity theory seems true for (the type identity) of sensory qualia within persons and—if we allow for differences in individual brains—possibly within the species. One advantage of this story is its compatibility with evolutionary theory. A certain uniformity in receptor-cell sensitivity and in mappings from the sensory periphery to the cortex could easily have been selected for in view of the overwhelming survival importance to ancestral humans of getting the basic features of the external world right. For example, the discovery that distinct receptor cells in the hand subserve detection of pain, temperature, vibration, and pressure comes as no great surprise in light of the great importance of the hands in the evolution of *Homo sapiens*. Patricia Churchland writes,

> Neurons carrying information from the sensory periphery terminate at selected areas of the thalamus, where they are arranged in a somatotopic representation of the body. These thalamic areas in turn project to selected areas of the cortex, all in very orderly fashion and with substantial reciprocal projection from the cortex. In the cortex, neurons are again mapped in such a way as to preserve neighborhood relations of body parts, though there are some interesting discontinuities. Accordingly, neurons responsive to stimuli on the index finger are between neurons responsive to stimuli on the thumb and those for the middle finger, but distant from those on the big toe or the scalp.[47]

Strictly, the system subserving sensory perception of touch, deep pressure, limb position, vibration, and conscious proprioception in general, the lemniscal system, projects fairly precisely through the spinal system, to the thalamus, and onto the cortex. The spinothalamic system that detects pain, temperature, and some kinds of touch projects onto the cortex via spinal and thalamic routes in a somewhat coarser manner than the lemniscal system does. Specialized detector cells working in parallel, along with the iteration of their findings through many layers of neuron ensembles, explains how a complex experience of a hot, painful pressure on one's finger can happen with such rapidity.

The reason I said that identity theory is only approximately true for sensory qualia should now be clear. Despite the fact that the maps for certain sensory qualia project relatively neatly through the network hierarchy, not all the mappings are so tidy. There are precise mappings for certain sensation types (for example, color, taste, touch, and vibration), but the mappings are coarser for other sensation types (for example, pain and temperature). Furthermore, there is the evidence mentioned above about the changing boundaries and the *intra*individual variation of neural maps. The mappings from the sensory receptors to the cortex are remarkably fluid within a certain range. William Calvin writes,

> In the 1980's, we were all shocked to hear (from Michael Merzenich, Jon Kaas, Randy Nelson, and their colleagues) that somatosensory cortical maps were a day-to-day affair, changing size if the hand was exercised more; if a particular fingertip was regularly rubbed on something . . . , more cells in the somatosensory cortex would come to specialize in that finger. And conversely, the size of the receptor-field center for a cell specializing in that finger would become stronger. . . . [U]sually when this happened, the new forefinger cells would come from cells that formerly specialized in adjacent fingers—but sometimes from cells that formerly specialized in the face! The face's connections to such versatile cells were turned down to nothing, while the forefinger's connections were enhanced—and so a "retrained worker"! . . . [B]ut they also noticed that some changes in cortical boundaries seemed to occur spontaneously from week to week, even though the monkey wasn't being trained and was just moving about his cage. For example, the boundary between face and hand cells in the cortex moved from week to week, back and forth—some weeks the cells near the boundary were face specialists, other weeks the very same cells were thumb specialists. To neurophysiologists, this was approximately as if you had told us that the state line between California and Oregon was moving a few miles back and forth from week to week for no apparent reason.[48]

Even if we accept this story of iterated distributed mappings through neuronal layers with somewhat fluid boundaries for sensory perception, we still need an explanation for the fact that we are experientially sensitive to certain saliencies but informationally sensitive to these plus some. The explanation according to neural-network models will once again simply have to do with characteristic patterns of activation and connection within the nervous system, perhaps even within the system as a whole. However, this explanation does not simply posit the divide between experiential sensitivity and informational sensitivity as an inexplicable surd. As I have insisted, consciousness did not need to evolve at all. But since it did, there are resulting design constraints. An optimally designed system with finite powers better not be conscious of everything. Any efficiently designed finite cognitive system will be sensitive to far more than it is conscious of.

One mistake to stay away from is positing a center of consciousness—a specific faculty devoted to consciousness—that receives some but not all messages causally relevant in human activity.[49] Some patterns of neural activity result in phenomenological experience; other patterns do not. The story bottoms out there. It bottoms out in the way the explanation of complex life bottoms out in the microstructure of the double helix.

The analogy to the genetic code indicates that the story's bottoming out does not mean that dead silence ensues or that we can say nothing more that illuminates the way in which some kinds of somatosensory activity subserve different kinds of experience and others do not. We know, for example, that informational sensitivity to fine-hair movement in the ears is very important to the maintenance of balance, and we can say something about the patterns of neuronal activation involved. But almost no one experiences the position of the hairs in his or her ears. In fact, most people don't even know that there are fine hairs in their ears. And it is not clear that all the effort in the world could overcome the phenomenological impenetrability of the existence and movement of our ear hairs! Furthermore, the account implies—and there is already considerable confirmation for the hypothesis—that phenomenological distinctions in conscious experience—differences in color, speech, shape, musical perception, and so on—are subserved by differences in patterns of neural activation.[50]

Paul Smolensky, a leading connectionist, has suggested that the experiential-informational distinction might be grounded in something like the size or spread of activation: the higher, wider, and deeper the spread of activation, the greater the experiential feel.

Since consciousness seems to be a quite high-level description of mental activity, it is reasonable to suspect that it reflects the very coarse structure of the cognitive dynamical system. This suggests the following hypothesis: The contents of consciousness reflect only the large-scale structure of activity patterns: subpatterns of activity that are extended over spatially large regions of the network and that are stable for relatively long periods of time.[51]

Radiality, a high degree of horizontal and vertical spread, may well be the right sort of account of what is involved in the phenomenology of the ongoing stream of consciousness. But it is implausible that what distinguishes Coke-versus-Pepsi experience from Coke-versus-Pepsi information sensitivity (in someone who does not taste the difference) is radiality. The person who chooses Pepsi over Coke but tastes no difference detects the distinctiveness of Coke from Pepsi. This information is passed on from receptor cells on the sensory periphery to cortical cells, and it makes contact with the overall economy of desire.

Information about Coke "taste" and Pepsi "taste" radiates wide and far in both tasters and nontasters. This suggests that radiality may not be the most reliable indicator of when neural activity gives rise to experience. Furthermore, we know that there are stimulations of relatively limited spread that are experienced. For example, chemicals released by cells at the tips of the toes are both localized and vastly important in the painful experience of a stubbed toe. To be sure, stubbed toes are experienced only if stubbed-toe messages are received upstairs. The point is that this vivid and compelling experience of pain might well involve a straight ballistic shot upwards rather than radial transmission upward and outward. Furthermore, it is not inconceivable that subliminal perceptions spread as wide and deep as experienced perceptions. They activate different sectors of the neural network, not necessarily more of it.

Indeed, there exist blind-sighted persons who do not experience themselves as seeing but who display clear evidence that they process visual stimuli. The visual information blind-sighted persons process radiates far and wide throughout the visual cortex. The difference between people who "see" things in the sense that they receive information about these things and people who see the same thing in the standard sense involving information detection plus phenomenological feel has to do primarily with a breakdown in orderly connectivity in visual area V1 of the striate cortex. In addition to projections to the striate cortex, the retina also projects to six or seven areas in the occipital and parietal lobes. Blind sight occurs in cases where processing in V2 through V6 or V7 is functional but lesions cause breakdowns of orderly processing in V1. Degree of spread is not the main issue; correct connectivity is.[52]

Smolensky suggests that radiality is necessary but not sufficient for conscious experience. But if it is true that certain experiences, certain pains, for example, have relatively restricted spreads, then radiality is not even necessary. Overall, the sort of consciousness associated with sensory qualia may involve less spread and less radiality than higher-order self-consciousness or awareness of the Jamesian stream of consciousness. Indeed, the fact that some refined version of traditional identity theory may be true for sensory qualia should not be taken to have any implications for the relative locality or spread of the neural activity subserving other kinds of consciousness. The heterogeneity of types of consciousness is almost certainly subserved by neural activity that differs greatly in the degree of localism or spread, in neurochemical involvement, in the degree to which it is subserved by bottom-up or top-down processes, and so on.

The New Mysterians' Response

Conscious mental life includes much more than sensory qualia. It also includes moods, emotions, dreams, many kinds of intentional states, various kinds of self-consciousness, conscious attention, and self-control. We will eventually need a complete *neurophilosophical* theory of these kinds of consciousness. The new mysterians do not simply think that these other, more exotic kinds of consciousness will remain eternally inexplicable. They think that no convincing naturalistic account of sensory consciousness can be given. The inexplicability begins, as it were, at the beginning, at the very lowest levels of conscious mental life. Forget about self-reflection, self-control, conscious life planning, and moral self-scrutiny. We cannot even provide a theory about consciousness at the lowest levels, at the level shared by us with most other animals. For this reason it makes sense to join the battle at the level of sensation, since my side says that the problems of sensory consciousness are tractable in roughly the way just sketched and the new mysterians think that in principle intractability begins with sensory qualia.

The first question is whether the sensory-vector story about sensory qualia, with the suitable caveats in place, is true. I think that something like it is true. It is the best explanation available. Is the story certain? Of course not. One could remain skeptical in a variety of ways. One could simply deny that anything physical could cause anything mental, or one could, and this is the new mysterians' favored tactic, claim that it is very hard to be convinced that the relevant sensory vectors confer sensory consciousness. After all, one doesn't see consciousness in the brain or in the theoretically derived vectors. "A point whose significance it would be hard to overstress . . . is this: the property of consciousness itself (or specific conscious states) is not an observable or perceptible property of the brain."[53] On the assumption that consciousness is a property of the brain, this shows that "there *are* properties of the brain that are necessarily closed to perception of the brain."[54]

The smart move for those of us who favor the proposed analysis of sensory qualia is to claim that it is not based on direct observation. Rather, it is an inference to the best explanation. Inference to the best explanation, also called abduction, proceeds as follows. One has a set of observations, a set of background assumptions (observational and theoretical), and the inference drawn best explains the total set of reasonable commitments.

McGinn thinks that "no form of *inference* from what is perceived can lead us to *P*," where *P* is the property or set of properties that naturalistically explains consciousness. McGinn's position is puzzling because he is, as I have said, a naturalist. He is also a metaphysical realist. He believes in a mind-independent reality and thinks that whether or not we know what *P* is and whether or not we come to understand how *P* renders consciousness intelligible, *P* does exist, and it renders consciousness intelligible. This is why McGinn says that there "is no *metaphysical* problem."[55] It will be useful to set out McGinn's general argument as perspicuously as possible. This is how it goes:

1. Introspection will not reveal what *P* is, where *P* is the brain property that subserves or renders consciousness intelligible.
2. Examination of the brain won't reveal what *P* is either. This is because for any candidate *P*, we won't be able to *see* how *P* could explain or render consciousness intelligible.
3. Since perceptual closure does not entail cognitive closure (we can think about things that we have never perceived, e.g., transcendental numbers), one might think that there is some form of inference to the best explanation that will work to make the link between consciousness and brain states intelligible.
4. But there is no form of inference to the best explanation that could draw an intelligible link between any set of brain properties and consciousness. This is due to the *homogeneity constraint* on concept introduction: psychological concepts should not be introduced to explain physical phenomena nor physical concepts to explain the psychological unless we are forced to do so. "Inference to the best explanation of purely physical data will never take us outside the realm of the physical, *forcing us* to introduce concepts of consciousness. Everything physical has a purely

physical explanation. So the property of consciousness is cognitively closed with respect to the introduction of concepts by means of inference to the best explanation of perceptual data about the brain."[56]

Explanation of (4): The basic idea behind (4) is that perception of brain facts will never ground an inference to the best explanation of the form "*P* is what renders consciousness intelligible," because to explain brain facts, we only need to appeal to other brain facts. Since consciousness is not perceived by looking at the brain and is therefore not a phenomenon to be explained, we do not need to introduce any theoretical concept *P* (referring to some complex set of neural facts) to explain consciousness. McGinn writes, "To explain the observed physical data we need only such theoretical properties as bear upon these data, not the property that explains consciousness, which does not occur in the data. Since we do not need consciousness to explain these data, we do not need the property that explains consciousness."[57] Conversely, if we set our sights on explaining consciousness as it appears to conscious subjects, nothing will force us to introduce physical concepts to explain its existence.

5. The impossibility of uncovering an intelligible link between brain processes and consciousness is not merely epistemic. That is, the epistemological diagnosis fails that sees the cause of the problem in differences in how we come to understand or be acquainted with consciousness, as opposed to brain facts (including facts about our own brains), in "the peculiarity of the epistemological situation."[58]

6. The best diagnosis is that even though there is some natural property *P* that explains consciousness from "the God's eye point of view," this property is cognitively closed to us.[59]

A Critique of the New Mysterians' Argument

McGinn's argument is inductive rather than deductive. We can't render the link between consciousness and the brain intelligible from the point of view of consciousness, and we can't render the link intelligible by observing the brain. So we cannot render the link intelligible at all. Like any argument, this one depends on the plausibility of its premises, so let us take his argument one step at a time. Premise (1) seems to me uncontroversially right. Consciousness reveals nothing about my brain, not even that I have one!

Premise (2) is uncontroversially true on one interpretation and patently problematic on another interpretation. The uncontroversially true interpretation is the one according to which we will not literally "see" how P explains or renders consciousness "intelligible" by looking at the brain alone. It is hard to see why this should worry us.[60] In complex scientific contexts we invariably need to bring a theory to some set of observational data to draw that data into a web of intelligibility. But McGinn has some funny ideas about the rules governing inference in a scientific context. The patently problematic interpretation of (2) is that the "unobservability" of the link between P and consciousness prevents us from inferring that P is, in fact, where the link resides. This interpretation comes from reading back into (2) what he goes on to say at (3) and (4).

Evidence that McGinn holds absurdly high standards of intelligibility and at the same time that he abides overly restrictive methodological principles emerges in steps (3) and (4). Strictly speaking, step (3) is unproblematic, but it sets a trap that (4) is designed to catch us in. The trap set in (3) involves thinking that there might be some acceptable form of inference from some set of brain facts P to the conclusion that P subserves consciousness, that P causes consciousness, or that consciousness supervenes on P.

But in (4) McGinn sets out some rules on concept introduction and inference that are designed to stop us from thinking that there is any such acceptable inference pattern. One reason is that "a certain *homogeneity* operates in our introduction of theoretical concepts on the basis of observation."[61] He clarifies what he has in mind by the homogeneity constraint on concept introduction when he quotes Nagel to the effect that "it will never be legitimate to infer, as a theoretical explanation of physical phenomena alone, a property that includes or implies the consciousness of its subject."[62] Consciousness is a different kind of property from the perceptible properties of the brain (it is heterogeneous, not homogeneous), so the homogeneity constraint prohibits its introduction.

McGinn's misstep comes from forgetting that consciousness has already been introduced. We are not looking for an explanation of "physical phenomena alone," at least not physical phenomena narrowly understood. There is a prior commitment to the existence of consciousness. Thus both facts about the brain and facts about consciousness are on the table to be explained. We then infer that the constellation of a certain set of autophenomenological reports of restricted range ("tastes sweet") correlate with certain sorts of brain activity (activation in the relevant pathways), and we infer, because of an overall commitment to naturalism, that the latter explain the former. McGinn's argument involves a relatively flat-footed trick. When looking at the brain, you are only allowed to draw links among brain states, and when introspecting, you are only permitted commentary on how things seem, on what reveals itself in the conscious stream. Since neither way of looking at things will (by itself) get you to the other, the link between the two is closed, a mystery.

To see that something has gone awry here, that the "homogeneity constraint" is overly restrictive, consider the case of the ubiquitous electron. If we assume a commitment to standard contemporary physics, it is the inference to the best explanation that certain observable processes in a cloud chamber are the traces of unobservable electrons. We never see the electrons directly while observing the process in a cloud chamber, nor for that matter do we see them anywhere else. Electrons are a theoretical construct whose postulation best explains certain observable data and whose postulation is in turn supported by certain (predicted) observations.

The same is true in the case of consciousness. We do not *see* consciousness when we look into the brain. Our access to consciousness is not mediated by our senses. It is first-personal. But because of our prior commitment to the existence of consciousness and a naturalistic view of the world, certain observations of brain properties, especially if these are reliably linked to certain kinds of first-person reports and behavior, can easily warrant claims linking brain processes and different kinds of sensory awareness.

The relevant sort of inference pattern occurs in the cases of blind sight. What are the facts in such cases? There are patients who say they do not see anything on, say, their right side but who, if asked to reach in that direction or guess what is there, move their fingers and hands in the right preparatory movements to pick up the object that is there and guess with considerable accuracy. Such individuals typically have some sort of lesion in area V1 of the visual cortex but possess unimpaired function in the other distinct areas that the retinal image projects to. Contrary to what McGinn says, this data set seems precisely the kind that warrants, as an inference to the best explanation, the invocation "of consciousness [or the lack thereof] to explain [the] data." Conversely, we need to invoke certain neural properties to explain why visual consciousness is present in the normal case and lacking in the blind-sight cases. There are lesions in the striate region of the visual cortex in the latter but not in the former. McGinn writes that to "explain the observed physical data we need only such theoretical properties as bear upon those data, not the property that explains consciousness, which does not occur in the data. Since we do not need consciousness to explain those data, we do not need the property that explains consciousness."[63]

But my point is that to explain the observable data about the differences between sighted and blind-sighted people, for example, differences in verbal behavior, we need to invoke the property of visual consciousness (or the lack thereof). Since we need to invoke the concept, we also need to invoke the brain properties, an intact versus a lesioned V1 area, that explain the different kinds of consciousness in the two cases.

For reasons such as these, premise (4), which espouses the "homogeneity constraint," is untenable if it is intended to render it impermissible to draw explanatory links between some set of events or processes unless all these events or processes are simultaneously observable in the domain under study. Such a restriction is totally unwarranted. It would lead us back into the dark ages in science.

McGinn demands that we be shown an "intelligible connection" between P and consciousness, and he claims at every turn that this cannot be done. But if one is in the proper Humean mood, one will wonder why any naturalist would set the absurdly high standard on intelligibility that McGinn sets. To be sure, we think that water *is* H_2O, and we think that it is a necessary a posteriori truth that this is so. But we also think that it is an utterly contingent fact about the course of the universe that there turned out to be any water at all, and that it turned out to possess the molecular structure it in fact possesses. Furthermore, the necessity ascribed is provisional. "Water is H_2O" is necessary *if* true. The truth is vulnerable to displacement, or so we think, in a way in which the truths of arithmetic or logic are not. But if there is room for skeptical doubt about well-established and allegedly necessary a posteriori truths, then it is hard to see how any scientific theory could render any connections "intelligible," except in some standard fallibilistic sense. If the standards of necessity or intelligibility are those operative in logic or arithmetic, then *no* scientific statements will satisfy the standard, and we can be said to know nothing about the world. So this hardly seems like the right set of standards for explanation.

In one place McGinn compares the case of consciousness with the case of the emergence of life. "We cannot take the arrival of life as a primitive brute fact, nor can we accept that life arose by some form of miraculous emergence. . . . [W]e rightly insist that it must be in virtue of some natural property of (organized) matter that parcels of it get to be alive."[64] He goes on to insist that the necessary connections that led to the emergence of life may eternally elude us.[65] I think he is right in this. But earlier I pointed out that we possess some plausible sketches for how life emerged and that we have deep knowledge of certain connections between life as it did emerge, in the form of the double helix, and phenotypic features of many different kinds of living things. Unless we hold absurdly high standards of intelligibility, the story of the emergence and subsequent natural history of life is becoming increasingly intelligible to us. The "genome project" currently underway, the project of mapping the structure and function of every kind of human gene, will undoubtedly increase our understanding by several orders of magnitude.

McGinn, I think, causes himself the problem of irremedial mystery that he is so awed by. The problem is caused by placing draconian restrictions on the inferential context and, in particular, by prohibiting the introduction of the property of consciousness in scientific contexts unless it can be shown to be needed to play some explanatory role relative to perceptible properties of the brain. But this is an unnecessarily positivistic sort of constraint. Introspective, autophenomenological data should be sufficient to convince us that consciousness exists. Functional deficits, such as profound amnesia, prosopagnosia, and blind sight as reported in the writings of Luria, Sacks, and Weiskrantz, involve defects of consciousness. Consciousness is needed to explain what has gone wrong, and certain neurological facts are needed to explain why consciousness is missing or deficient. Facts about consciousness, facts about the brain, and questions about the links between the two are all on the explanatory platter at once.

In the end, I think that the correct diagnosis of why the air of mystery can never be dispelled is the epistemological diagnosis that McGinn rejects in (5). Indeed, McGinn's trick turns on making mischievous use of our epistemic situation. We are never allowed, according to the homogeneity constraint, to move from the subjective to the objective or from the objective to the subjective. We are inferentially locked on whichever side of the subjective-objective equation we start.

To see that the epistemological diagnosis is correct and that the new mysterians in fact depend on its correctness, consider Thomas Nagel's argument for the new mysterians' favored conclusion in *The View from Nowhere*. Nagel emphasizes the impossibility of capturing the subjective point of view in any completely objective analysis. Nagel is right that no description cast in the language of neuroscience can *capture* what it is like to be me. The question is what follows from this concession? Nagel suggests the viability of a dual-aspect theory.[66] On the one hand, he thinks that mental processes are identical with physical processes.[67] But on the other hand, he is attracted to "the view that one thing can have two sets of mutually irreducible essential properties, mental and physical."[68] Now in view of Nagel's concession to the supervenience of the mental on the physical, it is hard to imagine that Nagel thinks that the irreducibility is metaphysical.

If mental processes are identical to physical processes, how can it be that the true story of how my brain works will not *capture* what it is like to be me? The answer is simple and far from mysterious. The objective story of my brain life does not capture what it is like to be me because it is a description. Imagine a third party, an omniscient neuroscientist, watching my brain operate in real time. What I experience, because of how I am hooked up to myself, and what the omniscient neuroscientist experiences are utterly different. The omniscient neuroscientist sees certain patterns of neural activity and says such things as "There he goes experiencing red again." But I experience red, not him. Actually, I see no in-principle impossibility to a third party hooking into my brain and having my perceptual experiences. This possibility notwithstanding, there is no temptation to think that my conscious states, indescribable as they are from the omniscient neuroscientist's point of view, are not realized in the very hookups he observes. Nor is there any temptation to infer from the fact that my subjective point of view gives me no clue about the nature of the processes that subserve these states, that my subjective mental life is not, in fact, realized in my brain states. Cartesians are notoriously prone to make this inferential error. A better inference is that I am simply not in touch with the "braininess" of my conscious states first-personally. The situation is somewhat analogous to the perceptual case: I see light but perceptually know nothing about its nature. I see light as light. But the nature of the mechanisms that subserve my perception of light tell me nothing at all about whether light involves waves or particles, about whether it has a speed, let alone what its speed is, and so on.

The point is that the epistemological diagnosis seems just right in this case. Dual-aspect theory is true if it is understood epistemically. So understood, it is metaphysically unproblematic. Consider the analogy with gestalt illusions, for example, the image that produces the vase-face illusion or a Necker-cube reversal (see figure 8.2). Strictly speaking, there is just one physical configuration before one's eyes, but it can be seen in either of two ways, as a vase or as a pair of faces in the one case and as a cube with reversed foreground and background in the other case. Gestalt illusions such as these show the possibility that something metaphysically unproblematic (the Necker cube is just a bunch of lines) may be seen, known, or described in two different ways. Gestalt illusions have a further important property: when one is seeing the image in one way, one cannot at the same time see it in the other way. But remember, gestalt illu-

Figure 8.2
Face-vase illusion and Necker cube.

sions *are* illusions. There is just one thing there. It has two aspects epistemically irreducible to each other, but not irreducible to the whole they comprise, not irreducible in some hoary metaphysical sense.

The alleged mystery of consciousness has its source in biological facts that underwrite the different kinds of epistemic access we have to brain facts, on the one hand, and what it is like to be each one of us, on the other hand. We grasp facts about the brain through our sensory organs, typically with the help of sensory prostheses: magnetic resonance devices, CAT and PET scanners. On the other hand, we are acquainted with consciousness by way of direct, internal reflexive biological hookups to our own nervous systems. To this point in human history all such hookups are first-personal. The nature of our access to what we are made of and to how we function as complex biological systems is different in kind and provides different information than does our first-person on-line hookup to our selves. The biological fact that we possess a direct first-person, reflexive hookup to one and only one body explains how the most complete explanation from the physical point of view does not *capture* what it is like to be me. Only I can capture that. Only I am hooked up to myself in the right sort of way. As John Dewey wrote, "Given that consciousness exists at all, there is no mystery in its being connected with what it is connected with."[69]

The important point is that we possess a good naturalistic explanation of our inability to capture the phenomenology of what it is like to be each one of us from the objective point of view. The hookups, the epistemic access relations, are essentially different in the first-person and third-person cases. The fact that we possess this explanation of the dual-aspect phenomenon means that there is no reason to infer that the failure to capture the relevant first-person phenomenology third-personally, undermines the naturalist's hope of isolating the specific properties that subserve first-person experience.

Conscious Inessentialism, Absent Qualia, and the Epiphenomenalist Suspicion

So far I have provided a bare-bones sketch of a naturalistic theory of consciousness, and I have tried to show how the new mysterians' argument that no such theory is possible goes wrong. Even if it is true that consciousness can be naturalistically analyzed, there is still the question of what function or functions consciousness serves.

Consciousness did not have to evolve. It is conceivable that evolutionary processes could have worked to build creatures as efficient and intelligent as we are, even more efficient and intelligent, without those creatures being subjects of experience. Conscious inessentialism is true in that sense. But systems that do everything we do absent qualia, absent semantically transparent thought, absent the emotions, and so on, would not be duplicates of us. They would lack consciousness. Consciousness is essential to our natures. So conscious inessentialism is false in that sense. The upshot is that conscious inessentialism is true in one sense, the deep metaphysical sense involving possible beings in possible worlds, and it is false in another sense: it misdescribes the nature of human beings in the actual world. This means that there need not be heated disagreement, indeed, there need be no disagreement at all, between, on the one hand, those philosophers and AI workers interested in possible worlds populated by Turing duplicates who lack inner lives and, on the other, those of us committed to providing a philosophical analysis that captures human nature as it exists in the actual world. We are interested in different things.

The thesis of conscious inessentialism is not the only source of trouble and confusion. There is also the epiphenomenalist suspicion, the suspicion that although consciousness exists, it plays a relatively inconsequential role in mental life, akin to the earlier described government functionary who is ineffectual, often misled, and ever late to the real action.

I take the epiphenomenalist suspicion seriously. Consciousness might be essential to our natures without being centrally involved in the causal fray. It is possible, even on the neo-Darwinian picture I have recommended, that consciousness does little work, or at least that it does less work than we standardly give it credit for. To be sure, our species would not have survived if we had not been quick to respond to harmful stimuli. The natural temptation, therefore, is to think that conscious sensitivity to painful and dangerous things was directly selected for. The trouble with this sort of facile adaptationism is that there are species that have survived much longer than we have, that detect when danger lurks, but that are conscious of nothing. Scallops, for example, get out of the way of potential predators without experiencing them as such, and when they fail to do so, they get eaten alive without (quite possibly) experiencing pain.

It is possible that we survived as a species because our ancestors were unconsciously responsive (informationally sensitive) to harmful and useful stimuli, for example, the appearance of a predator or a mate. And it is possible that the capacities to *experience* fear and lust, pleasure and pain, simply came on board as free riders at some later time and play no important psychological role even now, save whatever role is played by letting ourselves and others know how we feel. The standard view is this:

(1)   hot stimulus on hand ⟶ feeling of pain ⟶ withdrawal of hand

The epiphenomenalist suggests that the real picture is this:

(2)   hot stimulus on hand ⟶ feeling of pain / withdrawal of hand

I will not try to allay all the fears that motivate the epiphenomenalist suspicion. In part, this is because I think there is something right about the suspicion. The suspicion, even if crazy paranoia in its extreme form, is a useful corrective to views that overstate the role of consciousness in mental life. Only in the last century has the idea that consciousness is definitive of the mental yielded. Even if we no longer believe that consciousness is involved in all mental activity, we tend to think that when it is involved, it is centrally involved. Consciousness itself impels us to overestimate its causal role in mental life.

That said, the epiphenomenalist suspicion is often overstated or misplaced.[70] Consider this widely discussed experiment of Benjamin Libet.[71] Libet's experiment has been thought by some to prove dualism and by others to secure the case for materialism. I am interested in it only as it relates to the epiphenomenalism issue. The experiment works as follows: First, subjects are hooked up to electroencephalographs, which measure "the readiness potential" (RP) in the cortical area thought to subserve hand movement, and to electromyographs, which measure onset of activity in the hand muscles. Second, subjects are told to spontaneously flex their right hand whenever they feel like it. They are also told "to pay close introspective attention to the instant of the onset of the urge, desire, or decision to perform each such act and to the correlated position of a revolving spot on a clock face (indicating 'clock time'). The subject is also instructed to allow such acts to arise 'spontaneously,' without deliberately planning or paying attention to the 'prospect' of acting in advance."[72]

The findings were these: First, in cases where subjects experience no preplanning, the consciousness of an intention to flex occurs about 350 milliseconds after the onset of RP and about 200 milliseconds before muscle activation. Second, in cases where the subjects reported a feeling of preplanning, of getting ready to spontaneously flex a few seconds before they flexed, the subjects still were able to distinguish this preplanning stage from the immediately preceding urge to flex, and the finding that RP precedes conscious intention or urge, which precedes muscle movement, was confirmed. Libet writes, "Onsets of RP regularly begin at least several hundred ms before reported times for awareness of any intention to act in the case of acts performed ad lib. It would appear, therefore, that some neuronal activity associated with the eventual performance of the act occurs before any (recallable) conscious initiation or intervention. . . . This leads to the conclusion that cerebral initiation of the kind studied . . . can and does usually begin *unconsciously*."[73] Libet asks, "If the brain can initiate a voluntary act before the appearance of conscious intention, that is, if the initiation of the specific performance of the act is by unconscious processes, is there any role for conscious function?" He answers that "conscious control can be exerted before the final motor outflow to select or control volitional outcome. The volitional process, initiated unconsciously, can either be consciously permitted to proceed to consummation in the motor act or be consciously 'vetoed.'"[74]

This experiment is very interesting, but one wonders why it generates such surprise and why it is taken by many to be so deflationary. In the first place, the strong evidence that subjects can veto flexion in the 200 milliseconds between the experience of the urge or intention to flex and the response indicates that consciousness can play an important functional role in this particular motor routine. So consciousness is hardly shown to be epiphenomenal by this experiment. Second, it is hard to see what causes the surprise that brain processes precede conscious experience, unless it is, as I suspect, a lurking Cartesian intuition that in voluntary action our conscious intentions are prime movers themselves unmoved (except possibly by prior intentions). From a naturalistic perspective, this intuition, familiar as it is, gives rise to a set of deep illusions that are to be avoided at all costs. According to the naturalist, only some neural activity is conscious. All conscious processes occur in complex causal networks in which they both supervene on certain neural processes and are caused by and cause other mental processes (also supervenient on the neural), some of which are conscious but most of which are not. It would be amazing and completely unexpected if all the causal antecedents of conscious mental processes were themselves conscious.

Conscious mental processes emerge out of the neural processes that give rise to them. It would be absurd to expect these emergent conscious neural processes to precede the neural processes they arise from.

Frozen water supervenes on collections of water molecules whose mean molecular kinetic energy has slowed to 32 degrees Fahrenheit. Freezing is caused by water reaching that temperature. But getting to that temperature involves a process of cooling, and it would be absurd to expect the frozen water to antedate the process that brings it about.

In addition to misunderstanding the nature of emergent properties, the picture of the mind as conscious of all that goes on in it falls prey to a further difficulty. It involves a very inefficient design. The "buzzing confusion" that, James though (probably incorrectly), constituted the experiential world of the infant would be our lot for life if we were aware of everything happening in our nervous system!

Third, there is a problem with the interpretation of the experiment. The experiment and most of the discussion about it ask us to picture the experiment this way:

(1) RP (500 ms) ——→ conscious awareness of urge to flex (200 ms) ——→ flexion

The trouble with this way of conceptualizing things is that it leaves out the fact that the subjects are first asked *to make a conscious effort* to let flexion occur spontaneously. To do what they are asked to do, the subjects have to load from conscious awareness an instruction to perform a certain complex task. Perhaps the instruction could be given subliminally to comatose patients or to normal persons in deep sleep. The fact is that in the actual experiment the instructions are given to fully conscious individuals who agree to comply with the experimental instructions and who try to do so. How we load such instructions and get ourselves to do such things is completely closed off to introspection (to my introspection anyway).[75] But it seems of the utmost importance that this is how the experiment begins. The right picture, then, is this:

(2) conscious awareness of instructions ——→ conscious self-instruction to comply (minutes later) ——→ RP (500 ms) ——→ conscious awareness of urge to flex (200 ms) ——→ flexion

The upshot is this. Conscious processes are not epiphenomenal even on (1), the narrow description of the experimental situation. They serve as the middle link in a three-term causal chain, and they have the power to inhibit (or veto) the motor response being readied if the agent so desires. On (2), the wide description, conscious processes appear at two different stages: first when instructions are given and the effort to comply is made and second when the instructions loaded at the first step are actually being carried out.[76]

I conclude that Libet's results, far from offering solace to the suspicious epiphenomenalist, are precisely the sort of results one would expect if one believes that conscious processes are subserved by nonconscious neural activity and that conscious processes play variable but significant causal roles at various points in different cognitive domains.

Teleological Functionalism

Teleological or Darwinian functionalism conceives of most mental capacities, both conscious and unconscious, as typically playing some adaptive role for the systems that have them.[77] There is evidence from individuals with certain defects of consciousness that this hypotheses that consciousness has a function, that it generally serves a purpose, is true.

A computational system that passes the Turing test behaves just like us but lacks an inner life altogether. It is a duplicate if all we focus on are the observable input-output relations. It is not a duplicate if we require that these inputs are linked to the outputs in the characteristic ways in which they are in our case and if we allow for unobservable inputs and outputs. The neurological cases I now consider differ from Turing duplicates in that they have inner lives. But their inner lives differ from those of normal persons in a variety of ways. These differences in conscious mental life cause certain functional deficits and permit certain inferences about the role of consciousness in normal persons. Consider the following cases:[78]

First, there are the blind-sighted persons I have mentioned several times. Blind-sighted persons have damage to the striate cortex (area V1) and therefore claim not to see objects in certain portions of the visual field, usually on one side. The evidence indicates that although such individuals are consciously insensitive to stimuli in their blind fields, they are informationally sensitive to these stimuli. This shows up in a variety of ways. If patients hear an ambiguous word, for example, "BANK" or "PALM," and have been primed in the blind field with another word relevant to the interpretation of the heard word ("MONEY"/"RIVER") or ("HAND"/"TREE"), they favor the interpretation tied to the word shown in the blind field. Blind-sighted persons do far less well at this task than sighted people. But their responses are far better than at the chance level one would expect with the truly blind.

Furthermore, if a blind-sighted individual is asked to say what object is on her blind side, she says she does not know. But if told to reach for what is there, "preparatory adjustments of the wrist, fingers, and arm are suited much better than chance to the shape, orientation, size, location, and distance of the objects."[79]

The evidence of semantic disambiguation and preparatory hand movements indicates that blind-sighted persons are informationally sensitive to things they are not conscious of. Their being in certain unconscious intentional states—unconsciously knowing that there is a glass of water rather than a ball to their right or that "MONEY" was flashed in the blind field—best explains their better-than-chance performance.

The fact remains that blind-sighted persons claim to know nothing about the goings-on in their blind fields. They are wrong in this. But we have to press them to get them to show what they know. The case is altogether different with normal persons, and this difference is crucial from a functional point of view. Conscious awareness of a word that favors a particular interpretation, e.g., river *bank* over money *bank*, leads to better performance on disambiguation tasks than does mere informational sensitivity to the helpful clue. Conscious awareness of a water fountain to my right will lead me to drink from it if I am thirsty. But the thirsty blind-sighted person will make no move toward the fountain unless pressed to do so. The inference to the best explanation is that conscious awareness of the environment facilitates semantic comprehension and adaptive motor actions in creatures like us.

Persons with memory deficits provide a different sort of example. Sadly, amnesiacs are commonplace. There are people with a good grasp of their lives before some time but who lack the capacity to remember new things. There are people, victims of Korsakoff's syndrome, advanced Alzheimer patients, and persons who have suffered certain kinds of traumatic brain injury, who cannot remember anything from one second to the next. Often people who can't remember what has happened to them or what they did in the near or distant past still comprehend language, can speak, and have no trouble with routinized motor tasks, such as walking, reaching for things, cooking a meal, and using bathroom facilities.

Amnesiacs are functionally impaired in different ways that depend on the nature and extent of the amnesia. One well-studied amnesiac, H. M., knows how to work the Tower of Hanoi puzzle. However, H. M. is not aware that he knows how to work the puzzle. Each time the puzzle is brought to him, he claims never to have seen it before. But his performance has improved over the years from that of a normal beginner to that of a fairly proficient player. Each time H. M. works on the puzzle, his performance starts close to the level he previously reached. He does not begin at the point of someone like H. M. of many years ago who truly did not know how to do the puzzle. With respect to the Tower of Hanoi puzzle, H. M. is epistemically impaired. He is less epistemically impaired than would be a patient who not only said he never saw the puzzle before but also always returned to a beginner's performance level. Such a patient would be both experientially insensitive and informationally insensitive. He might work on the Tower of Hanoi puzzle but the information about how to do it would not sink in or would not stick. In H. M.'s case the knowledge sinks in and sticks. But he believes certain falsehoods, namely, that he has never seen the puzzle before and that he has no idea how to do it. H. M.'s epistemic impairment is caused by his inability to consciously remember certain things.

H. M.'s problems are more than epistemic, of course. He belongs to a class of persons who have identity disorders. There are identity disorders (such as multiple-personality disorder or MPD) that have nothing directly to do with neurologically based deficits. But I will concentrate here on identity disorders linked to neurologically based amnesia. Cases of severe loss of autobiographical memory involve incapacities to constitute and reconstitute one's sense of identity, of who one is, of where one is coming from and where on is going. It was John Locke who, in the second edition of his *Essay Concerning Human Understanding*, published in 1694, most famously linked the first-person sense of identity with conscious memory: "[A]s far as this consciousness can be extended backwards to any past action or thought, so far reaches the identity of that person." From a subjective point of view, I am who I remember myself being.

In *The Man with the Shattered World: The History of a Brain Wound*, A. R. Luria, the great Russian neuropsychologist, tells the story of Zazetsky,a soldier who suffered massive damage to the left occipito-parietal region of his brain.[80] After being shot Zazetsky lived in a visually chaotic world: the right side of both his body and the external world were not there for him. He suffered profound incapacities to understand and produce language, and he had lost his memory. Most of his past was a blank.

What I want to emphasize about Zazetsky's case is that he (eventually) showed clear evidence of possessing an enormous amount of information about his own past. His first problem was getting this information out. He had to figure out a way to express the information he had inside himself so that he himself could see it again. His second problem was to consciously reappropriate this information, to get it back for himself as the right description of his self and his life. Zazetsky succeeded in many respects at solving the first problem. But the second remained in large measure intractable.

There are cases in which the loss of self-consciousness, of autobiographical memory, involves the complete destruction or erasure of all the relevant information. There is nothing there—no permanent file, no well-honed set of distributed neural activity—to gain access to or to reactivate. The memories constitutive of one's past self and deeds are gone, never to return. Zazetsky's case, like H. M.'s on the Tower of Hanoi puzzle, was not like this. The information was still in there, and Zazetsky tried each day for almost three decades to get it out and to regain thereby his identity.

How did he do this? Well, especially in the early stages conscious effort was to no avail. The breakthrough came when Zazetsky made a fortuitous discovery. Luria writes, "[A] discovery he made one day proved to be the turning point: writing could be very simple. At first he proceeded just as little children do when they first learn to write— he had tried to visualize each letter in order to form it. Yet he had been writing for almost twenty years and as such did not need to employ the same methods as a child, to think about each letter and consider what strokes to use. For adults, writing is an automatic skill, a series of built-in movements, which I call 'kinetic melodies.'"[81] The next step was to convince Zazetsky to let his writing flow automatically, to let the "kinetic melodies" emerge without worrying about what he was writing or whether it made sense. In fact, it did make sense, and gradually over the course of twenty-five years Zazetsky produced what Luria called an "archeological study of his memory."

Once the wound had healed, Zazetsky was able to remember his childhood fairly well. But the years after that were not there for him. As Zazetsky wrote automatically but with extreme difficulty, a life began to appear on paper. Zazetsky was able to recognize certain things he wrote as true of him, and he was able with extreme effort to order the narrative into something approximating its right temporal sequence. The saddest irony is that although each piece of Zazetsky's autobiography was consciously reappropriate by him each time he hit upon a veridical memory in writing, he himself was never able fully to reappropriate, to keep in clear and continuous view and live with the self he reconstructed in the three thousand pages he wrote. His memory impairment was deep and abiding. Furthermore, many grammatical constructions, including many of those he himself was able to produce on paper, were exceedingly hard for him to decipher and even harder for him to keep in mind over time. Tragically, Zazetsky was kept, to some significant degree, from regaining himself and from reconstituting himself in the first-personal way that Locke thought is necessary if one is to have an identity.

The Self as the Center of Narrative Gravity

Cases like Zazetsky's provide further evidence for functional deficits that are caused by deficits of consciousness, which are caused in turn by underlying neurological problems. Zazetsky is at loose ends, he feels aimless, and his life lacks meaning. He cannot find his self. Much of the information about his self is inside Zazetsky. Indeed, he has externalized many of the most salient parts of his self in his monumental autobiography. He is simply unable to consciously reappropriate the whole story and own it. He has problems of identity and meaning, and these are rooted in problems of self-consciousness.

Two kinds of self-consciousness might be distinguished. First, there is the low-level sort of awareness that comes from the primitive self-nonself distinction discussed earlier. Most animals and all humans are aware of the distinction between inner and outer experience. Even creatures who are not *aware* of the boundary between "me" and "not me," our lowly scallop, for example, are destined to be informationally sensitive in ways that lead them to abide and be responsive to the relevant boundaries, to act *as if* they are aware of the self-nonself boundary. Otherwise, they do not survive.

With respect to both inner and outer experience we are aware that "something is happening here." This is Nagel's ubiquitous "subjective point of view." We are also typically aware of whether a particular stimulation—"a something happening here"—originates inside us or in the external world. The self-consciousness involved in the ever present "something is happening here" phenomenology may be what James had in mind when he wrote, "Whatever I may be thinking of, I am always at the same time more or less aware of myself, of my personal existence."[82] This low level sense of "meness," of "something happening here," does seem to underlie all conscious experience. All conscious experiences are, in addition to being experienced, experienced as attached to the subject of those very experiences.[83]

James presumably did not mean, because if he had meant it it would be false, that we bring some sort of rich narrative conception of our self to each and every experience. What is true, however, is that humans in all cultures come to cast their own identity in some sort of narrative form. We are inveterate story tellers. Zazetsky's quest to reconstruct and reappropriate his self, to locate an identity constituted by a particular history, a direction, and a set of identity-conferring likes, dislikes, roles, commitments, and the like, is a universal one.

With selves, the basic principle is "one to a customer."[84] Zazetsky has been cheated; he has been robbed of his fair share. Some other kinds of identity disorders, cases of MPD, involve having too many selves. This is no fun either.

The sort of self that Zazetsky has too little of and MPD patients have too many of is what Dennett calls "the self as the center of narrative gravity."[85] We start at one end of the continuum with the dim and inchoate self-nonself distinction, the awareness of what is me and what is not me. Such awareness requires virtually nothing in the way of knowledge or awareness of my nature: lobsters and dogs are aware of the self-nonself distinction but are very unclued into their natures across most every dimension. At the other end of the continuum we reach the weighty self of narrative gravity. This is the self that we present to ourselves for planning, self-scrutiny, and a sense of the whole of our lives and to others for their recognition and approval of who we are.

The construction of a self begins in earliest childhood as parents try to shape the emerging character of the charges they love. Since we abide the "one self per customer" principle, we try to assist the child in building an integrated self that comprehends basic social norms and is equipped with a system of beliefs, desires, and values that will help it to live successfully and well. The "one self to a customer" principle is not just an arbitrary social construction. The Darwin machine itself favors minimal cognitive dissonance and maximal integration. Indeed, the brain is designed to fully cooperate in the construction of one and only one self, although it is capable in extreme situations of cooperating in the construction of multiple selves.[86]

So the process of self-construction starts in the hands of the elders, and it begins well before the child uses language. The parents provide models for self-construction in what they do and say and in how they express their own formed being. Rarely does a parent try to construct a child's self through direct linguistic instruction (and when they do try, they are almost always unsuccessful at getting what they want). Increasingly, as time proceeds, the child engages her parents with her own emerging self and modifies their attempts to shape her. With the onset of the ability to speak, she will be able to say things about herself and to articulate appeals about her own desires in a form that could formerly only be expressed through resistance or tears, on the one hand, and happy compliance, on the other hand. There comes that day when the parents learn that it is not the individual food items on the plate that Kate dislikes, it is the fact that these items are touching. "I hate when the spaghetti touches the lettuce, Mommy!"

With language, time, maturity, autonomy, and elaborate and multifarious interactions with others, the self emerges. The construction of the self involves many players. Our selves are multiply authored. Lest this sound too deflationary, it is fair to say that normally we are one of the main authors of our identity.

The self "bubbles up" in development (as Dennett likes to say). And once formed, it bubbles up each day. Let me give a personal example. I identify deeply with my role as father to my children. But I do not wake up each day and put on my father self. I am a self who is partly constituted by being a father. Furthermore, I did not self-consciously choose to be the kind of father I am or to be so gripped by the self-constituting role of father. Nor, of course, did I have any choice whatsoever in the particular children I am father to. Like most parents, I sometimes need to reflect on and make adjustments to the kind of father I am being. But that mainly involves tuning the fatherly personality I already have. I am fine-tuning who I am, not creating a new father in me from scratch.

I sometimes reflect on the fact that I see my parenting, I suspect as my own parents did, as preparation for my children to be good parents themselves someday. But I don't have very much to say about good parenting that can be expressed in the form of rules or algorithms. I doubt that such algorithms exist. But even if they do, I doubt that direct instruction in them would be an effective way to help children become good parents. One equips children to be good parents not by talking about how it is done but by showing them as best one can how it is done, warts and all.

Despite my lack of explicit knowledge of any algorithms for good parenting, much of what I think about and say to others and how I am identified by others involves reference to a narrative essentially involving my family. I see myself as uniquely related as husband and father to three other unique selves, and I am known by all my friends as a character essentially embedded in that familial narrative. I know about this self, and I talk about it, as I am doing here. Did I consciously create this self? Do I consciously call up this self as needed? The best answer to both questions, it seems to me, is no.

> [W]e (unlike *professional* human storytellers) do not consciously and deliberately figure out what narratives to tell and how to tell them; like spider webs, our tales are *spun* by us; our human consciousness, and our narrative selfhood, is their *product*, not their *source*. [T]hese strings or streams of narrative issue forth *as if*

from a single source—not just in the obvious physical sense of flowing from just one mouth, or one pencil or pen, but in a more subtle sense: their effect on any audience or readers is to encourage them to (try to) posit a unified agent whose words they are: in short to posit what I call a *center of narrative gravity*.[87]

To some extent my familial self and my philosopher self are played for different audiences. Different audiences see who I am differently. Neither self is a self that I have the slightest sense of having labored alone to create. My two selves bubble up to the surface in different interpersonal ecological niches. Displaying either self and getting my audience (or myself) to posit one or the other as my center of narrative gravity is, in a sense, to produce a sort of illusion, since to me, first-personally, these two selves are part of an integrated and unified narrative that contains as proper parts both of these selves that I sometimes display in isolation.

Dennett insists that the self that is the center of narrative gravity is a fiction, a useful fiction, but a fiction nonetheless. What might this mean? If our highest-order self, the self in whose embrace we find identity and meaning is a fiction, then the epiphenomenalist suspicion seems secure at least as regards the *self*. This inference, however, would be a mistake. The idea that the self is a fiction is compatible with its being real and its playing a functional role in an individual's psychological economy and social life.

The idea that the self is a fiction is in part a way of expressing the fact that it is, for the reasons given, a construction. Mother Nature does not give us a robust self. She starts us off caring about homeostasis, and she equips us with the equipment to distinguish "me" from "not me." But she hardly wires in a personality or an identity. Identity is the joint production of many sources, including one's own evolving self. Michael Gazzaniga has suggested that evidence from split-brain patients indicates that the narration of this fictional self emanates from the left cerebral hemisphere in most people. The left brain loves to tell stories about the system of which it is a part, and it will spin fantastic tales if need be. So the self is a fiction in the sense that it is constructed and because it unfolds like a story that is not yet completed.

The idea that the self is a fiction also captures a second feature of identity. The self that I am is subject to constant revision. This is true in two senses. Not only do new things I do change the ongoing story, but sometimes the past is reconstructed or filled out from the point of view of hindsight. Sometimes these reconstructions are self-serving ("I never really loved her anyway"). Other times they involve rendering various indeterminacies determinate and answering questions that arise now but hadn't arisen before. One wonders in one's thirties, for example, why one cares so deeply about a certain worthless thing, and one reconstructs some story of one's distant past to explain to oneself, and possibly to others, why things are as they are. Most such reconstructions are uncorroborated; some are uncorroboratable.

So the self is fictional because it is a construction and because it involves all manner of revisitation to past indeterminacies and of reconstruction post facto. Dennett has us imagine John Updike's making the Rabbit trilogy into a quartet not by writing about a still older Rabbit Angstrom (as he has in fact done) but by creating the story of a very young Rabbit Angstrom. The original trilogy constrains what Updike can say about the Rabbit who existed before the Rabbit of *Rabbit Run*. But the indeterminacy of Rabbit's former life is vast, and thus there are numerous credible ways in which the story of the earlier years could be told. For certain parts of our lives we have similar degrees of freedom in how we tell the story of our selves.

There is a third way in which the picture of the self as fictional is appropriate. A piece of fiction starts off from some narrative hook, or set of hooks, and pins a character and his story on those hooks. In the case of pure fiction, the author has complete freedom in choosing what hooks to pin a character on. But if she wants to sell copies, she had better make sure that there is something compelling about her characters and their story(ies). The same principles apply in the first-person case. A life is satisfying from the inside and respected from the outside when its central themes are built around worthy aims and values. But what is compelling to one's readership, or worth respecting, is temporally, culturally, and subculturally variable. Different kinds of narratives fly at different times and in different places. The book-buying and interpersonal markets create selection pressures favoring certain kinds of narratives and disfavoring others in given contexts. We see these pressures at work in everyday life when one presents oneself primarily as a concerned parent in one context and as a professional philosopher in another. In each context there is almost a gestalt effect. The features of one's identity that are dominant in one form of presentation recede in the other.

This brings me to a fourth way in which the self trades in fiction rather than fact. The self that is the center of narrative gravity is not only constructed out of real-life materials, out of things that really have happened to me; it is also constructed in such a way that it holds, abides, and strives to maintain certain ideals that are not yet realized. The narrative is in many cases organized around a set of aims, ideals, and aspirations that the self has. But since these have not yet been realized, they are fictions, albeit useful and necessary ones.

To conceive of the self as a fiction seems right for these four reasons: it is an open-ended construction; it is filled with vast indeterminate spaces that can be filled out post facto; it is pinned on culturally relative narrative hooks; and it expresses ideals of what one wishes to be but is not yet.

But there are two important respects in which the analogy of the self with a piece of fiction can be misleading. First, there is the issue of constraints. The author of a true piece of fiction has many more degrees of freedom in creating her characters than we have in spinning the tales of our selves. Despite the indeterminacies operative in the case of self-construction and despite the fact that different narrative emphases will be reinforced in different communities, there are more firm and visible epistemic constraints in the case of self-construction than in the case of ordinary fictional construction. There are, after all, the things we have done and the characteristic dispositions we reveal in social life. Third parties will catch us if we take our story too far afield. We may also catch ourselves. There are selection pressures to keep the story that one reveals to one's self and to others in some sort of harmony with the way one is living one's life.

Some people, of course, are massively self-deceived. Self-deception makes sense only if selves are not totally fictive, that is, only if there are some facts constraining what is permitted to go into our self narrative. Self-deceived individuals sequester certain facts from view, possibly totally unconsciously. In this way they keep these facts from entering the narrative. Some alcoholics know that they have a problem but try to keep their drinking a secret from others. They deceive others, but not themselves. Other alcoholics display their alcoholism publicly but develop immunities to comprehending social feedback intended to challenge their self-conception that they have no drinking problem. They deceive themselves, but not others.

So real selves are fictional. But they are less fictional than fictional selves because they are more answerable to the facts. The second way in which the idea of our higher-order self as a fiction can be misleading is if it leads one to think that the self plays no functional role in mental life. In fact, it plays several crucial roles. In briefest terms, it plays the role of giving organization and meaning to a life that will last on average three quarters of a century. In what sense, you ask, can a fiction organize or guide anything? And how can a fiction give *real* meaning to a life?

The answer, in broad strokes, is that one's higher-order self is one of the many models contained in one's brain. There are also the multifarious models of the external natural world, of other selves, of social norms, of various motor routines, and so on. Whether one's model of one's self is grandly self-deceived or well grounded in the way one lives and whether one's self aims at worthy or unworthy ideals, it is, once acquired and in operation, part of the recurrent brain network that is causally responsible for the life one lives and how one thinks and feels.

Now it is tempting to think that the mind *must* have a control center and that the narrative self must be *the* control center in the mind. During the heyday of "functional flowchartology," i.e., over the course of the last twenty years, almost every picture of mind contained a box named "control" (see, for example, figure 8.3, reprinted from Dennett 1978e). One reason for thinking that the mind must have a single central control device is that an efficient design will involve a "high level processor that monitors and controls the overall goals of lower-level processors, which in turn monitor and control the processors at a still lower level, and so on in a hierarchy of parallel processors, which at the lowest level govern sensory and motor interactions with the external world."[88] The phenomenology of the stream of consciousness together with this sort of reasoning has lead many philosophers and cognitive scientists to posit consciousness as the operating system of mind. It is implemented as a serial von Neumann device laid over the system of massively parallel processors.

The basic idea has considerable appeal. Consciousness is serial. It has a heavily representational character. We typically do what we consciously intend, and so on. Johnson-Laird suggests a possible evolutionary scenario in which a serial conscious control mechanism might have emerged: "A primal form of consciousness may originally have emerged from the web of parallel processors as a way of overriding deadlocks and other pathological interactions."[89]

An alternative and underestimated possibility is that there is in fact no center of control, no von Neumann device laid over the system of parallel processors. What there is instead is the Darwin machine all the way down (more akin to a connectionist PDP device). The idea that there is a single serial control device might be a "user illusion," to use Dennett's phrase. According to this centerless view, conscious experience emerges seriatim because the recurrent network of parallel processors declares one winner at a time in the competition among all its tracks. (Imagine the tracks as a multitude of students in a lecture hall who are raising their hands to gain the floor but who can do so only one at a time.) When there are lots of events worthy of one's attention, the brain queues them up in an orderly fashion. The winner of the competition for attention is the joint production of the over-

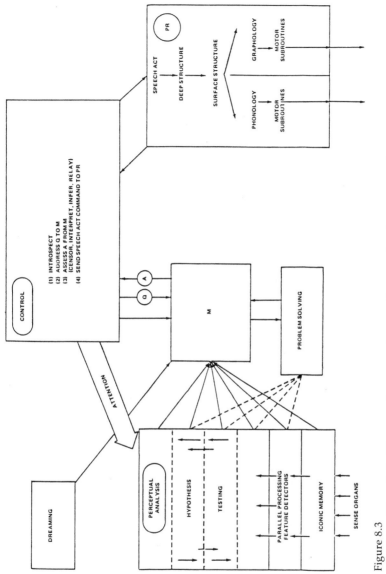

Figure 8.3
A picture of the mind with a conscious control center. (Reprinted with permission from Dennett 1978e, p. 155.)

all state of the nervous system due to certain wired-in weightings (pain gets attention) and to the coordinated system of weighted models of the world and the self. (It is thus less arbitrary in its method of selection than most teachers are in the manner in which they call on questioners from a sea of enthusiastic flailing arms.) In this model we no longer need a box marked "control," although there may be something like a serial buffer (or many serial buffers only one of which can be operative at a time: if the pain buffer is on and registering excruciating pain, then the theorem-proving buffer cannot also be on). The idea that the brain is a Darwin machine with many modular parallel processors working at once helps us to understand both how consciousness can emerge without reaching any single central and unified consciousness faculty and how control can emerge without any single model (the self) or any single processor directing the entire show.

Apparently, many bird flocks operate according to this basic theme. It has now been established that certain flocks maintain cohesion without depending on any single leader or even on a small cadre of leaders. Flocks paint the skies with the most amazing aesthetic patterns and with many different birds moving to the flock's leading edge at different times. "Birds of a feather are chaotic together."[90]

William Calvin compares the process whereby we come to display a particular personality, and to experience ourselves as unified, as akin to the situation of a choir. "The population evolves, as the scattered group of novel individuals start coalescing into a synchronous chorus. The dominant version now becomes the one that won out in the competition, not the one written down on some preordained sheet of music."[91] The synchronous chorus is in one sense not really a serial processor. It might seem like one to the chorus and to the audience as it listens to the music produced. It is *virtually* serial, but strictly speaking, the choral performance is the straightforward emergent product of a system of parallel processors (the singers and players) working in synchrony.

> [T]he narrator of our conscious experience arises from the current winner of a multitrack Darwin Machine competition. It isn't an explanation for everything that goes on in our head, but it is an explanation for that *virtual* executive that directs our attention, sometimes outward toward a real house, sometimes inward toward a remembered house or imagined doll's house, sometimes free-running to create our stream of consciousness. Directing sensory attention may seem unlike making movement plans, but the neural circuits seem analogous, all parts of that frontal lobe circuitry used in making preparations for action.[92]

Either way, whether consciousness is implemented in an *actual* serial brain processor or a *virtual* one, the higher-order model of the self plays an important causal role in our overall psychological economy. Although the self may not be *the* control center, in setting out plans, aspirations, ideals, and so on, it does give the rest of the cognitive system information about what subplans to implement when, and what parts of the natural and social world to focus on in the effort to stay on course. But just as other conscious and unconscious models contained in the brain are responsive to the higher-order model of the self, so the higher-order model of the self is responsive to new experiences. The self of narrative construction changes, sometimes radically, over the course of a life.

The self changes, evolves, and grows. It displays a certain continuity, and its home is the brain. The fact that my higher-order conception of my self is a model housed in my brain explains the first-person feel I have for my self (but not for your self), and it explains my special concern that the story go as I plan. If things go awry, if my plans don't materialize, if great pain befalls me, it will happen to this subject of experience, to the individual wrapped in this particular narrative. It is not surprising that I care so deeply that the story go the way I intend. It is "me" we are talking about after all.

A Unified Theory of Consciousness?

Some naturalists think that there cannot be a theory of consciousness. This is not because they are new mysterians. It is because they think that consciousness names a heterogeneous hodgepodge and because they do not believe that one can develop a theory for a hodgepodge. Consciousness includes sensations, perceptions, moods, emotions, propositional-attitude states, and large narrative structures. Dreams are experienced, as are other altered states of consciousness, many psychotic states, and so on. At a fine-grained level we will want to individuate types within these larger types, so that, for example, there will be a different experiential type for each sensory modality (touch, olfaction, vision, and so on). And one can easily imagine the need to divide these subtypes into finer-grained types, for example, seeing red versus seeing blue.

I think the claim that consciousness names a heterogeneous set of phenomena is absolutely right. But I don't share the conviction that this implies that the search for a theory of consciousness is an idle fantasy.

First, there is the *shared property*. Despite the truth of the heterogeneity thesis, all conscious mental events share a property. This is the property of being in awareness or being experienced. Another candidate shared property, according to James and possibly Kant, is this: a mental event is conscious if and only if accompanying the awareness of whatever it is one is aware of is a representation of self or "me" or "I" or, degeneratively and less controversially, a representation that "something is happening here."

The shared property raises the possibility that at least at one level of analysis, conscious mental life is a natural kind. Something is a natural kind only if (1) all the tokens of the type or kind share a property and (2) the shared property allows the type to play some explanatory role in our science, e.g., to figure in scientific causal explanation, to be projectable in counterfactual generalizations, and so on. The properties of being soluble, a fish, a mammal, an electron, and so on, constitute natural kinds in this sense, whereas being born on the fourth of July does not. Notice that being governed by natural law is not sufficient to make something a natural kind, since everything fits that bill.

In any case, conscious mental life satisfies condition (1). It is possible that it also satisfies condition (2). For example, suppose that there is some underlying physical property P that is necessary and sufficient for all experiences. If this is so, then just as water is H_2O, so too experience = being in state P, and therefore, it is a truth of nature that if some organism is in state P, it is consciously aware of something. The new mysterians actually frame things in this way, that is, as if there is from God's point of view some such property P (which they insist we will never discover) that subserves all experience. Actually, I am skeptical of the idea that there is any single brain property P that plays the role for all experiences that the virus plays in subserving a variety of conditions, differing widely in severity and symptomatology, that we call the common cold. It seems more likely that there is a large set of neural connections capable of subserving different kinds of conscious experience. But no one yet knows one way or the other. But if there exists some single property P that subserves all consciousness or, alternatively, some disparate set of brain properties (the second possibility is surely true even if the first is not), then there are lawlike links between brain property P and experience or between the set of relevant brain properties and experience.

Another approach to meeting condition (2) would involve showing that consciousness plays an essential role in explanation and prediction. Evidence discussed above indicates that this is so. There are important functional differences between people with phenomenal awareness in certain domains and those without. Suitably motivated individuals with normal sight naturally carry out voluntary actions toward seen things. When thirsty, we step over to the water fountain we see to our right. However, blind-sighted individuals who are identically motivated and who process information about the very same things in their visual fields do not naturally or efficiently carry out the suitable actions toward the "seen" things. There are also the differential abilities of amnesiacs to form integrated self concepts and to create and abide a consistent narratively constructed self model. Persons incapable of experiencing certain qualia, for example, color-blind people, show all sorts of functional differences from non-color-blind people.

This evidence suggests that there are true counterfactual generalizations in the domain of consciousness. Some of these generalizations will relate psychological phenomena. For example, persons with qualia of kind q do x in circumstances c, but persons without qualia q (but who are otherwise identical) fail to do x in c. Other generalizations will link psychological processes with brain processes. Here are three from a multitude of possible examples. (1) Persons with damage to the speech centers and in particular to the left brain interpreter will have trouble generating the narratively constructed self. (2) Persons with certain kinds of frontal-lobe damage will have trouble formulating plans and intentions; other kinds of frontal-lobe damage will obstruct links between consciously formulated action plans and actually carrying out the intention. (3) Rats, cats, and humans all possess four types of taste receptors. In rats the pathway subserving bitter tastes "shows a narrower range of evocable activity (it is less discriminating) than it does in humans. In cats, it shows a wider range of activity (it is more discriminating)."[93] This explains why rats eat anything and cats are finicky eaters. It also gives us, as Paul Churchland says, some insight into what it is like to be a rat (or a cat).

Since these sorts of generalizations already exist and have been corroborated, it follows that there are laws that conscious mental life answers to. To be sure, the laws are pitched to the heterogeneous multiplicity of events and processes that possess the *shared property*. But taken together, I see no reason to say that they are not part of an emerging theory of consciousness, one basic insight of which is that consciousness is heterogeneous. Physics deals with an extraordinary variety of heterogeneous entities and processes, many of which remain unknown. But no one is tempted to think that there cannot be a physical theory. We do not infer the impossibility of a unified field theory from the heterogeneity of the known physical forces. We do not think celestial mechanics is suspect because of the heterogeneity of the compositions, sizes, and gravitational forces of bodies in our solar system. Nor do we think that the astronomical variety of sub-atomic particles, within the three main classes, forecloses the possibility of quantum theory. A theory of consciousness will in the end be part of a unified theory of the mind. This is compatible with the theory's making generalizations suited to whatever deep local idiosyncrasies exist. Physics tells us that bodies at extremely far distances from each other travelling close to the speed of light are subject to regularities very different from objects moving around our little spherelike home. It would be no more surprising and no more damaging to the success of the science of the mind if it tells us that visual consciousness obeys very different laws and is subserved by different neural mechanisms than is conscious reflection on one's love life. In fact, this is exactly what we expect.

Parity of reasoning suggests that we put aside our skeptical doubts and get on with the hard work of providing the right fine-grained analysis of conscious mental life. It will be our proudest achievement if we can demystify consciousness. Consciousness exists. It would be a mistake to eliminate talk of it because its semantic past is so bound up with ghostly fairy tales or because it names such a multiplicity of things. The right attitude, it seems to me, is to deliver the concept from its ghostly past and provide it with a credible naturalistic analysis. I have tried to say a bit about how this might be done, indeed, about how it is already being done.

Conclusion

Here in summary form are my proposals for how we ought to think about the problem of consciousness.

(1) The theory I have sketched pictures consciousness as a name for a heterogeneous set of events and processes that share the property of being experienced. The theory is Jamesian in that consciousness is taken to name a set of processes, not a thing or a mental faculty. The theory is neo-Darwinian in that it is committed to the view that the capacity to experience things evolved via the processes responsible for the development of our nervous system: natural selection, genetic drift, and free riding. The theory is neurophilosophical in that it tries to mesh a naturalistic metaphysic of mind with our still sketchy but maturing understanding of how the brain works. The most plausible hypothesis is that the brain is a Darwin machine, a massively well-connected system of parallel processors interacting with each other from above and below and every which way besides. It is no wonder that meaning holism is true, that we somehow solve the frame problem, and that my belief that snow is white is realized

in a somewhat different way in my brain than the same belief is realized in yours. Finally, the theory is neo-Spinozistic in that it claims to provide an explanation of the gap between the first-personal way in which conscious mental life reveals itself and the objective point of view. Mind and brain are one and the same thing seen from two different perspectives.

(2) Conscious inessentialism is a doctrine that can be set to one side when the task is, as I have framed it, to sketch a naturalistic theory of consciousness consistent with our natures as biological creatures with nervous systems of a certain kind. There are possible creatures that are Turing-identical to us at the level of observable input-output relations but that have no inner lives. We are not like this. Consciousness is essential to human nature.

(3) The epiphenomenalist suspicion should be taken seriously, but it should not overwhelm us. Some conscious processes are akin to the ineffectual functionary who is always the last to know. But other conscious processes and models, including the self as the center of narrative gravity, figure crucially in cognition and in the overall conduct of our lives.

(4) The new mysterians are mischievous reactionaries who argue that although consciousness is part of the natural order, it will never be understood as such. The new mysterians' main trick involves setting impossibly high standards on explanation and intelligibility. The trouble is that keeping to their standards would mean that we know nothing about any interesting natural processes, for example, about the origin and nature of life, the existence of the subatomic world, and so on. If we operate with more sensible standards of intelligibility, there are several credible stories that can already be told and that explain how such things as sensory qualia supervene on certain patterns of neural activity. Just as water *is* H_2O and is *caused* by its being H_2O, so too experiences of colors, tastes, and smells are identical to and caused by activity patterns in certain brain pathways. Higher-level sorts of consciousness also supervene on brain processes. But it is unlikely that they do so by satisfying even roughly hewn type-identity conditions.

(5) Despite its extraordinary difficulty, the problem of consciousness is beginning to yield. One will not see the entry points if one declares the whole thing beyond us and, like the proverbial ostrich, puts one's head in the sand. But if one looks to naturalistically informed work in the philosophy of mind, to neuroscience and neuropsychology, and to certain segments of cognitive science, then one will see the sort of work I have tried to describe here, and one will be less reticent about undertaking the project of making conscious-

ness reveal its secrets. Understanding consciousness with consciousness is a wonderful, giddy idea and yet at the same time a genuine possibility. So let the fun begin.

Suggested Readings

The Best Recent Collection of Work on Consciousness

Marcel, A. J., and Bisiach, E., eds. (1988), *Consciousness in Contemporary Science.*

The Phenomenology of Altered Consciousness

Hobson, J. Allan (1988), *The Dreaming Brain.*
Luria, A. R. (1972), *The Man with the Shattered World.*
Sacks, Oliver (1985), *The Man Who Mistook His Wife for a Hat and Other Clinical Tales.*

Functionalist-Computational Theories of Consciousness

Dennett, D. (1969), *Content and Consciousness.*
Dennet, D. (1978e), "Toward a Cognitive Theory of Consciousness."
Jackendoff, R. (1987), *Consciousness and the Computational Mind.*
Johnson-Laird, P. N. (1988), *The Computer and the Mind: An Introduction to Cognitive Science.*
Lycan, W. G. (1987), *Consciousness.*

Neurophilosophical Theories of Consciousness

Calvin, W. H. (1990), *The Cerebral Symphony: Seashore Reflections on the Structure of Consciousness.*
Churchland, P. M. (1988), *Matter and Consciousness.*
Churchland, P. M. (1989), *A Neurocomputational Perspective: The Nature of Mind and the Structure of Science.*
Churchland, P. S. (1986b), *Neurophilosophy.*
Edelman, G. M. (1987), *Neural Darwinism.*
Edelman, G. M. (1989), *The Remembered Present: A Biological Theory of Consciousness.*

The Self, Self-Consciousness, and Multiple Selves

Dennett, D. (1988a), "Why Everyone Is a Novelist."
Humphrey, N., and Dennett, D. (1989), "Speaking for Ourselves."
James, W. (1892), "The Stream of Consciousness," in *Psychology: The Briefer Course.*
James, W. (1892), "The Self," in *Psychology: The Briefer Course.*

The New Mysterians

McGinn, C. (1989), "Can We Solve the Mind-Body Problem?"
Nagel, T. (1979d), "What Is It like to Be a Bat?"
Nagel, T. (1986), *The View from Nowhere.*

Notes

Chapter 1

1. Descartes (1634), p 130.
2. Descartes located the place in the brain that released the "animal spirits" in the pineal gland. The high status Descartes gave to the pineal gland—he came to call it the "seat of the soul" (but not the soul itself)—was based on thoroughly epistemological considerations. He said, "I reflect that the other parts of the brain are all of them double . . . ; and inasmuch as we have but one solitary and simple thought of one particular thing at one and the same moment, it must necessarily be the case that there must somewhere be a place where the two images which come to us by the two eyes . . . can unite . . . but there is no other place in the body where they can be thus united unless they are so in this gland." Descartes (1649), p. 346. If contemporary research is correct, Descartes was wrong in assuming that the mind is a simple unity. From a modern perspective, Descartes had this sort of problem again and again, because he relied too heavily on conscious introspection. See chapter 6 for a discussion of the thesis of the unity of mind.
3. The one-for-one stimulus-response pairings required by such a model are exceedingly unwieldy, especially if we conceive of the reflex arc routes along the lines of the hydraulically controlled robots in the Royal Gardens. Any very complicated robot made up of tubes with water coursing through them would have to be of enormous physical dimensions, perhaps the size of an entire continent. At one level, therefore, modern computer engineering with its microprocessing and miniaturization lends credibility to the reflex arc model by providing models of very small systems that do many complicated things. On the other hand, modern computer science also suggests reasons for thinking that the reflex arc account would simply not have been a parsimonious way for nature to have wired us. See chapters 2, 4, and 6 for further discussion of reflex analyses of human action.
4. Descartes (1649), p. 350.
5. Ibid., p. 398.
6. A couple of caveats are in order here. First, it is logically possible, though rare, to be a mechanist and not be a metaphysical materialist. For example, many scholars read Leibniz as thinking that matter is epiphenomenal, a secondary side effect of the way mental stuff is organized. Leibniz, nevertheless, seemed to think that the organization of the universe, of mental stuff, obeyed mechanical—broadly Newtonian—principles. Also some people, in particular the biographer Ernest Jones, read Freud as a mechanist who is not a materialist (I am, however, skeptical of this interpretation. See chapter 3). Second, I knowingly use "mechanism" in a very broad sense, to refer to any, roughly deterministic, causal analysis. Thus each specific kind of mechanism discussed here and elsewhere in the text has a prefix, such as *reflex* mechanism or

information-processing mechanism. Some philosophers think of mechanism more narrowly, for example, as a thesis about systems that operate just like a reflex system in terms of pushes and pulls, springs and motors, and hard-wired circuits.

7. One might want to argue that although these examples show that the specific information I have about my body is inferential, the simple knowledge that I have a body is noninferential. I doubt that such an argument could work.

8. Descartes (1641), p. 153.

9. It is hard to tell how much this self which is known first and best is meant to encompass for Descartes. He might merely mean that each person can know one very general thing about himself, namely, that he has a mind. Or he might mean that humans can know their personality better than they can know anything else. The latter claim is more interesting and controversial from the perspective of modern psychological science, but I think it is probably best to read Descartes as almost exclusively concerned with the self as such, with the pure ego, as opposed to the personality. Nevertheless, one can see how the belief that the self or mind as such is known first and best is quite compatible with the view—commonly attributed to Descartes—that self-knowledge, in the sense of knowledge of all the contents of consciousness as well as of one's personality, is also epistemically privileged. See chapters 2,3,4, and 6 for more on the issue of privileged access.

10. Descartes (1637), p. 101.

11. This is a useful place to call attention to the distinction between deductive and inductive logic. An argument is "deductively valid" just in case whenever the premises are true, then the conclusion is necessarily true. So, the argument (i) All zebras speak French (ii) Oscar is a zebra (iii) Therefore, Oscar speaks French, is deductively valid because if the premises were true the conclusion would necessarily be true. Deductive validity has, therefore, to do with the purely logical structure of an argument. A deductive argument is "sound" just in case its premises are, in fact, true. So, the argument (i) All zebras are mammals (ii) Oscar is a zebra (iii) Therefore, Oscar is a mammal, is valid and sound. All arguments that are not deductively valid are inductive. (The idea that deductive and inductive arguments can be distinguished more straightforwardly in terms of one going from the general to the particular and the other from the particular to the general is wrong.) And all inductive arguments yield probabilistic conclusions. A good inductive argument strongly supports, but does not necessarily imply, its conclusion. So, the argument (i) The Boston Celtics are a good basketball team (ii) Good teams usually win more games than they lose (iii) Therefore, the Celtics are likely to have a winning season, is a strong inductive argument. The distinction between inductive and deductive arguments is messier than meets the eye, because often, if not usually, in evaluating a premise of a deductive argument for soundness (for example, all zebras are mammals), one is assessing the inductive warrant behind the premise. In any case, whenever I say something like "the conclusion does not follow from the premises" I normally mean it does not deductively follow, that is, it does not necessarily follow. And whenever I worry about the truth of a particular premise or the truth of some implicit assumption behind an argument I am almost always worried about its inductive warrant, that is, I am worried about whether or not there is an inductively strong argument to back it up. With respect to Descartes' arguments for dualism it is important to remember that an argument which is put forward as a deductive argument and fails can still be a strong inductive argument.

12. Descartes (1641), p. 190.

13. There is a deep philosophical issue regarding the so-called essential properties. Some philosophers, Descartes among them, view the essential properties as isolating some

crucial feature in the things themselves. Other philosophers, following the later Wittgenstein, view a property as essential only relative to some description. The first kind of essential properties are *de re*—they originate in the things themselves; the second kind are *de dicto*—they originate in the ways we talk. Obviously in order to establish a genuine metaphysical dualism one needs to show that mind and body have different essential properties *de re*, and not merely different essential properties relative to our shared linguistic framework.

14. Descartes (1641), p. 196.
15. The phrase "modularity of mind" is Jerry Fodor's. See chapter 6.
16. This argument obviously depends on a distinction between one's mind as such, one's "pure ego," and one's personality, because no one would deny that loss of an arm or a leg would affect one's personality.
17. Someone like B. F. Skinner would maintain that all the practical sense of doling out rewards and punishments and speaking in moral terms could be maintained even if we gave up our shared theory that human nature is free. We would simply be using rewards and punishments to shape, control, and maintain sets of behaviors that we (as individuals, small groups, or whole societies) find pleasing. See chapter 4.
18. Descartes (1641), p. 192.
19. See, for example, Margaret A. Boden (1981c) in Boden, 1981a.
20. This point is very tricky. One might argue that we actually have all sorts of evidence that there are nonphysical things: for example, the logical relations among the sentences in this paragraph, the number *pi*, the set of all real numbers, and so on. Surely these are all real things, but they are not physical objects; they occupy no space and have no molecular structure. There are two standard ways for the materialist to respond to this sort of argument. Call the first way *nominalism* and the second way *conceptualism*. The *nominalist* argues that numbers are not real things. To speak of numbers is to adopt a way of speaking that is useful in talking about nature, it is to adopt a way of speaking that has heuristic value, but it entails no ontological commitment to numbers as such. The *conceptualist* argues that, indeed, numbers are real; they are real mental concepts. And because all mental concepts are physical, numbers and the like are just physical things—mental representations—in human brains. A different sort of evidence for nonphysical things might be thought to come from physics itself. Electrons are described as point particles with no extension and even lacking a determinate location. However, it would be wrong to take this way of conceptualizing electrons as evidence of nonphysical things. Electrons are still considered bits of matter. What the world of the subatomic and the world of collapsed stars and their like show is not so much that physics itself countenances the nonphysical as that its conception of the physical is not fully commensurate with the common-sense conception of the physical.
21. As with all things philosophical, conservation principles are sometimes thrown into doubt. The *New York Times* (29 March 1983) reported that: "nature seems to have a way of 'cheating,' rapidly creating matter, then making it disappear. . . . If, as many now suspect, the conservation laws can be violated . . . it becomes very plausible that our observed universe emerged from nothing or from almost nothing." Needless to say, if true this would hurt my objection to dualism from the principle of conservation of energy. On the other hand, even if conservation principles are sometimes violated we would need to know a lot more to have reason to think they are violated by our minds.
22. One could argue against this model of science that even physics operates with talk of nonphysical things. Causation itself, as David Hume pointed out, is not obviously

physical: we don't see the causality operating between events, we just observe "constant conjunctions" between events. Furthermore, even if mental states are not links in the normal mechanical scheme of things, we might still be able to make lawful generalizations linking mental states and actions, for example, "when people have a strong desire and have a simple means at their disposal to meet the desire, they will use the means to achieve the desired end." The only difference would be that psycho-physical laws would consist of two-term chains, and two terms only, while strictly scientific laws might go back ad infinitum.

Chapter 2

1. The existence of a discipline of scientific psychology separate from philosophy is generally agreed to date from 1879 when Wilhelm Wundt founded his laboratory in Leipzig. James differed from earlier thinkers interested in philosophy and psychology, such as Locke, Hume, and Kant, in that he held academic appointments in both fields. James began his career as an instructor of anatomy at Harvard Medical School. He was then made professor of philosophy while he was writing *The Principles of Psychology*. In 1889, a year before the publication of the *Principles*, he was named professor of psychology. By this time his commitment had become so self-consciously philosophical that he had his title changed back to professor of philosophy. Philosophers attracted by his combining the dry epistemic notion of truth with the exciting realities of social practice, usefulness, and human interest, considered him and Charles S. Pierce to be the founders of philosophical pragmatism. Psychologists who welcomed his importation of the biological conception of humans as organisms trying to find an adaptive fit with the environment saw James as instrumental in the founding of psychological functionalism.

2. I want to make it clear that naturalism is a variety of materialism or physicalism. The reason for using the term naturalism, however, is to avoid certain unfortunate but historically understandable connotations of materialism. In particular, materialism is usually associated with the world view that emerged from the physical sciences in the seventeenth and eighteenth centuries, and is thought of, correctly or incorrectly, as a static and reductionistic view of inert matter. Naturalism, as I see it, is the world view inspired by the growth of the biological sciences in the nineteenth century; it stresses interaction among living biological systems which it views holistically. For the best history of the development of biological naturalism which also makes clear its differences from the materialism of physical science, see Ernst Mayr's excellent *Growth of Biological Thought* (1982), especially chapter 2.

3. One might argue that this involves an important adjustment to the prevailing view that philosophy must lay down foundations for psychology, not the other way around. James would not be at all concerned about "contaminating" his philosophy with psychology or vice versa. James was committed to a form of naturalism that saw all disciplines, all forms of inquiry, as mutually illuminating. James, in fact, set the stage for the eventual rejection in American philosophy of the view of philosophy as foundational, as the discipline which sets the a priori conditions for knowledge in all other disciplines. W. V. Quine, probably the most influential American philosopher in the last quarter century, is the champion of the view James anticipates. Quine sees philosophy as continuous with science, not as providing the foundation for science. See, for example, Quine's 1969 essay.

4. James, *Principles* (1890), p. 15

5. Ibid., p. 185.

6. See Lackner and Garrett (1973). Dennett (1978e); (1982) is a major opponent of introspectionism.

7. James, *Principles* (1890), p. 191.

8. James is so temperamentally disposed to think of mental life in terms of conscious life that he might well respond to the argument that conscious mental life is only the tip of the iceberg by asserting that the tip of the iceberg is pretty much all that interests him. (He dismisses worries about the unconscious by baldly asserting that to the extent we come to know about unconscious mental life it will only be because it has become conscious!) When James does give a nod to experimental and comparative animal techniques as ancillary methods for psychology, his whole tone indicates that he views these techniques as supplementary to introspection, as methods for further refining introspective data. And James cannot keep his true mood from surfacing when he says of the meticulous experimental work of the great German psychologists, Weber, Fechner, and Wundt, "This method taxes the patience to the utmost and could hardly have arisen in a country whose natives could be *bored*." *Principles* (1890), p. 192. Although James was temperamentally disposed to overemphasize the role and extent of consciousness, he does emphasize the importance of unconscious habits in the *Principles*. Furthermore, he was greatly impressed by Freud's ideas when Freud visited Clark University in Worcester, Massachusetts, in 1909, the year before his own death.

9. Dennett (1978e), p. 149.

10. James, *Principles* (1890), p. 21.

11. Ibid., p. 23.

12. There have been lots of silly worries about the status of teleological explanations over the years, worries of the form: how can my making spaghetti sauce explain my current behavior of chopping garlic since the spaghetti sauce will not exist until after I have chopped the garlic? After all, a future event cannot cause a present one! The solution, *mirabile dictu*, comes from the fact that whereas the spaghetti sauce will not exist until I chop the garlic, my intention to make spaghetti sauce certainly exists before the chopping of the garlic.

13. Brentano thought that mental phenomena were doubly intentional. First, every mental act has its "primary" content, that is, the object that fills in the bracketed blank in "I believe that [_____]," or "I desire that [_____]." Second, every mental act has a "secondary" content, which is the "self-consciousness" of oneself as the believer or desirer. This secondary content, Brentano thought, was represented, known, and felt in every mental act. For more on Brentano see Antos Rancurello's excellent short study (1968). Many philosophers and psychologists doubt that all mental events are intentional. Whereas it seems plausible that "my belief that I am in pain" is intentional, it seems less plausible that "my pain" itself is intentional. What, after all, is the content of my pain, what is the object my pain takes, and what is my pain about? For an excellent work on the development of the concept of intentionality after Brentano that also pays attention to the centrality of the notion for cognitive science, see Hubert L. Dreyfus, ed. (1982).

14. James, *Principles* (1890), p. 214. Elsewhere he says, "*Human thought appears to deal with objects independent of itself; that is, it is cognitive, or possesses the function of knowing*." p. 262

15. Consciousness, of course, is a weaker criterion of mentality than self-consciousness. A self-conscious creature knows that it knows; it stands in a second-order epistemic relation to its first-order awareness. James, like Brentano, usually has self-consciousness in mind when he speaks of human consciousness. Notice, however, that requiring only consciousness, as opposed to self-consciousness, allows for a science of the mental life of animals as well as humans. Actually it is possible to make a fairly persuasive argument for the thesis that a concept of consciousness is not needed in

addition to a concept of intentionality in order to mark off mental phenomena from nonmental phenomena. The argument would run as follows: books, thermostats, computers, rain clouds and the like are not really intentional, because part of the essence of an intentional state is that it be a sentient state. Therefore, an exhaustive list of all the types of intentional states (beliefs, hopes, purposes, loves, hates, and the like) would be able to do all the work supposedly done by consciousness since all these states are (in their own intentional way) already essentially sentient.

16. James, *Principles* (1890), pp. 220–221. James is actually careful to say that "thought *tends* to personal form" because of the facts of "sub-conscious personality."

17. See Thomas Nagel (1979a), especially the essays (1979c and 1979d). James (1890), p. 278, captures the universality of taking a point of view when he says "One great splitting of the universe into two halves is made by each of us; and for each of us almost all of the interest attaches to one of the halves. When I say that we all call the two halves by the same names, and that those names are '*me*' and '*not-me*' respectively, it will at once be seen what I mean."

18. John Dewey (1922), p. 62.

19. Ralph Barton Perry (1938), p. 81.

20. See Derek Parfit (1979) for the best recent article against the all-or-none view on personal identity. Also see Robert Nozick's discussion of the problem in chapter 1 of his *Philosophical Explanations* (1981).

21. James, *Principles* (1890), p. 220.

22. Ibid., p. 724.

23. John Dewey (1929), p. 208.

24. John Dewey (1896) in J. Ratner, ed., 1963, p. 100. Kant, of course, was an early proponent of the view that we *anticipate* the world. Many phenomenologists, Husserl and Heidegger being the most prominent, developed the idea that we bring an enormously complex set of schema or expectations to experience. Surprisingly, the problem of describing with any precision the cognitive structures with which we anticipate experience is now one of the deepest problems in cognitive science and artificial intelligence, and is officially known as "the frame problem." See chapter 6 for more on the frame problem.

25. James anticipates a wide modern philosophical consensus unhappy with realism and representationalism. See, for example, Nelson Goodman (1978); Richard Rorty (1979) and (1982a); Hilary Putnam (1981a); Robert Nozick (1981).

26. Israel Scheffler (1974), p. 109.

27. James, *Principles* (1890), p. 135.

28. Ibid., p. 141.

29. Ibid., p. 140.

30. Ibid., p. 142.

31. Ibid., p. 135.

32. Ibid., pp. 136–137.

33. Ibid., p. 164.

34. Ibid., p. 162. See John Searle (1980) for a similar argument.

35. James, *Principles* (1890), pp. 160–161.

36. Dennett, for one, is optimistic that Artificial Intelligence will provide a convincing and sufficiently complicated model of a self-understanding system without requiring an "exempt agent." On Dennett's view, the solution to "Hume's problem" will involve, among other things, much more interaction between components of the system than the mind-stuff theory allows. Actually, as I shall show later, James heads in Dennett's direction by construing CML as a functional property of the brain.

37. James, *Principles* (1890), p. 179. The picture suggested here is the sort that is attractive

to many contemporary thinkers who view the mind as made up not so much of individually conscious neurons, but of active systems engaged in information processing and information exchange. Compare, for example, the role of what James calls the "pontifical cell" with the "control unit" in Dennett's theory of consciousness in (1978e).

38. James, *Principles* (1890), p. 180.

39. Ibid., p. 181. This mood about causality does not pervade the *Principles*. James usually emphasizes that he views CML as causally efficacious. Furthermore, he makes clear in his evolutionary discussions that we should expect the causal relations within the natural world to be between members of the same metaphysical kind.

40. Ibid., p. 151. Admittedly James expresses some doubts that this can be done for consciousness since it would seem to require that consciousness existed in some primordial form—so-called mind-dust—before its full-blown emergence in us. James eventually put this worry aside and came around to the view that, one way or another, consciousness must have emerged naturally.

41. James (1904), p. 4.

42. Ibid.

43. Perhaps an even better analogy than breathing or walking would be to think of the function a carburetor serves in a car. A carburetor is causally efficacious in keeping a car going because it performs the function of aerating the gas in order for it to burn. But in no coherent sense is the aeration of the gas the same thing as the carburetor. Aerating the gas, on the other hand, is something that really happens and without which the car will not run.

44. James, *Principles* (1890), p. 164, my italics. I should emphasize that the functionalist position on the mind-body problem is not so much a solution as the bet that a naturalistic solution exists. To really solve the problem we would need a story in overwhelming detail as to how exactly CML is realized. The analogies with breathing and walking and the aeration of gas are designed as possibility proofs for the coherence of the functionalist position, but they do not prove it is true.

45. Dewey (1922), p. 14.

46. James, *Principles* (1890), p. 1177.

47. James (1892), p. 328: See also James (1884).

48. Contemporary advocates of the soft determinist view among philosophers of mind include Daniel Dennett and Margaret Boden. See Dennett (1978c) and Boden (1981c) in Boden, 1981a.

49. Dewey (1894) in J. Ratner, ed., 1963, p. 205.

50. Dewey (1922), pp. 18–19. Overall Dewey takes James's psychology in a more explicitly social direction. Although it is implicit in all of James's writings that interactions with other humans figure importantly in psychological development, Dewey makes sure to emphasize that our character is molded in a social environment by the responses of other people to our behavior. Dewey's motto was that humans learn by doing. We acquire our character and habits by responding within systems of reward and punishment provided by the natural and social environment. In this way, Dewey can be viewed as an early promoter of the "law of effect," which says that behavior is shaped by its consequences. Ironically, the "law of effect" was to become the primary explanatory principle of behavioristic psychology, a psychology with which Dewey had little patience. See chapter 4 for more on the "law of effect."

With regard to the social emphasis of Dewey's philosophy of mind, some recent promoters of a purely cognitive psychology have argued that if psychology has to take account of external physical, as well as social, economic, and interpersonal phenomena it stands no chance of being scientific. See Jerry Fodor (1981b) for an argument to this effect. There may be something to this objection, but I doubt that it establishes any more than if Dewey and James are right about the need to explain mentality in terms of an expanding circle of external relations, psychology may not be able to be rigorous in the way, say, physics or chemistry are. Indeed, there may have to be a trade-off within the human sciences of rigor and precision for enhanced understanding or explanatory comprehensiveness. Fodor's objection, however, suggests a way of analyzing why the sciences seem to get softer as they get more social!

51. Dewey (1922), p. 303.

Chapter 3

1. Walter Kaufmann (1980) makes a case for Freud's admiration of and debt to Nietzsche. Freud is reported by Jones (1953) to have said of Nietzsche that he had greater self-knowledge than any man who ever lived or probably ever will live.

2. B. Russell (1927), pp. 32–33. See O. Flanagan (1981) for more on the issue of the ways nonempirical concerns enter into the construction of psychological theory.

3. Adolf Grünbaum (1980), p. 317.

4. I. P. Pavlov (1927).

5. Freud (1953–1974), vol. 1, p. 295, my italics.

6. See Hilary Putnam (1981b).

7. See Jerry Fodor (1981c) for a sophisticated argument for token-physicalism without reductionism. Also see chapter 6.

8. Freud (1917), pp. 20–21.

9. Ibid., p. 21.

10. Ernest Jones (1953), vol. 1, p. 368, my italics.

11. See Frank Sulloway (1979) for an extensive discussion of Freud's debt to the materialistic thinking of evolutionary biology. Erich Fromm (1980) also argues for Freud's materialism. But Fromm links Freud with the Helmholzian thinking he met in medical school, and less with evolutionary thinking per se.

12. Calling this view Cartesianism is slightly misleading. Even though the idea follows neatly from Descartes' views on the nature of mind and philosophical method, many empiricists, both classical empiricists like Locke and logical positivists like Carnap, also promote the idea of privileged access.

13. In what follows I am staying close to the first fifteen lectures of Freud (1917). These lectures contain, in distilled form, the central points from the turn-of-the-century books on dreams, jokes, and *parapraxes*.

14. Alasdair MacIntyre (1958) criticizes Freud for having conceived of the unconscious as an entity. Daniel Dennett calls this "Freud's Crutch" in Hofstadter and Dennett (1981). MacIntyre and Dennett are certainly correct that Freud conceived of the unconscious this way. Nonetheless Freudian theory can be kept intact without such an assumption by, for example, conceiving of the unconscious as referring to the set of all unconscious memories, wishes, and so forth, but not as referring to an entity that contains these memories and wishes.

15. Freud (1953–1974), vol. 5, p. 608; vol. 4, p. xxxii.

16. Freud, like Jung, believed that there were certain symbols that have culturally "fixed" meaning. Both Freud and Jung (the latter more extremely) thought that this fixity had an evolutionary basis in some sort of Lamarckian memory. See Sulloway (1979), and Freud's lecture on "Symbolism" in (1917), especially p. 165, for more evidence of Freud's Lamarckianism.

17. A Cartesian might argue that introspective testimony is only highly reliable when it is about mental contents, period. Testimony about the causes of the contents is much more problematic. This strikes me as a plausible—albeit still hard to defend—move

to make, especially since much recent literature casts serious doubt on our ability to get relatively obvious causes of our mental states right. See R. E. Nisbett and T. D. Wilson (1977) and chapter 6.

18. Grünbaum (1980) attributes precisely such a view to Freud. Grünbaum says, "the conception of freedom of action is clearly part of an essentially *deterministic* conception. . . . It makes the freedom of an act contingent *not* on *whether* it is causally determined but only on the *particular character* of its causal determinants.", p. 317. Grünbaum reads Freud as taking the sort of soft-determinist stance on the problem of free will that I defended in chapter 2.

   In her delightful semifictional account of psychoanalysis, Janet Malcolm (1981) has her chief character Aaron Green describe the psychoanalytic conception of freedom this way: "Analysis isn't intellectual. It isn't moral. It isn't educational. It's an operation. It rearranges things inside the mind the way surgery rearranges things inside the body. . . . It's that impersonal and that radical. And the changes achieved are very small. We live our lives according to the repetition compulsion, and analysis can go only so far in freeing us from it. Analysis leaves the patient with more freedom of choice than he had before—but how much more? This much: instead of going straight down the meridian, he will go five degrees, ten degrees—maybe fifteen degrees if you push very hard—to the left or to the right, but no more than that." (p. 108).

19. Scientific theories are, to use Quine's metaphor, incredibly complex webs of belief. The multifarious logical relations within a scientific theory make it naive to expect that each and every sentence of a theory will entail some potentially falsifying prediction. Furthermore, there is an important social dimension to science that bears crucially on how a particular theorist sees a potential falsifier. To a proponent of a theory a falsifier is a problem, perhaps a mistaken observation; to an opponent it is a refutation. Thus when I use the word "refute" throughout this section it should be taken weakly because, strictly speaking, a theory can no more be proved absolutely wrong than it can be proved absolutely right. See Putnam (1979). Two important recent papers on Freud and the problem of falsification are Barbara Von Eckardt (1983), and Adolf Grünbaum (1979).

20. Popper (1968), pp. 34–35.
21. See Freud (1917), p. 50.
22. Quoted in Von Eckardt (1983), p. 158.
23. Von Eckardt (1983), pp. 156–158.

Chapter 4

1. B. F. Skinner (1976), p. 3.
2. Skinner (1972c), p. vii.
3. Skinner (1970). For the classical discussion of operationism see Percy Bridgman (1927).
4. Skinner (1979), p. 117. In Flanagan (1980b), I discuss the shift in Skinner's position on private events. By 1964 Skinner was calling his brand of behaviorism "radical" precisely because he saw himself as taking the problem of privacy seriously! See Skinner (1964) in 1972a. The section "The Theoretician's Dilemma" in this chapter involves a change from my thesis in the 1980 paper. There I argued that Skinner's behaviorism was more metaphysically than epistemologically inspired. I now think that I seriously underestimated the epistemological side of Skinner's behaviorism.
5. Skinner (1972f), p. 384.
6. The concept of the "intentional stance" is developed in a series of papers in Dennett (1978a).
7. Skinner (1964), p. 227.

8. Ibid., p. 228.

9. Skinner (1972f), p. 383.

10. It is worth pointing out that it is inconceivable that all private events should turn out to be private behavior, although Skinner sometimes talks as if they will. For example, whereas "thinking" might be usefully analyzed as a kind of behavior, something like "being happy" seems much more usefully analyzed as an internal state, perhaps purely physiological, but a state nonetheless.

11. Skinner (1972b), p. 243.

12. In (1972b) Skinner puts it this way: An explanation is a "theory" if "it appeals to events taking place somewhere else, at some other level of observation, described in different terms, and measured, if at all, in different dimensions." (p. 69).

13. Skinner (1953), p. 35. Carl Hempel's famous paper (1958) in Hempel, 1965, takes its theme from this passage in Skinner.

14. The logical peculiarities of intentional idioms are threefold. First, all sentences of the form "John believes that p"—where "believes that" can be replaced by any other intentional verb, for example, "thinks that," "recognizes that," "wants to," "desires that"—are logically contingent. Thus whereas the sentence "all triangles have internal angles equivalent to 180 degrees" is logically necessary, the sentence "John believes that all triangles have internal angles of 180 degrees" is contingent. Second, the principle of inference called existential generalization works peculiarly for intentional verbs. Whereas it logically follows from "Unicorns have beautiful manes" that "There is something which has a beautiful mane," it does not follow from "John thinks that unicorns have beautiful manes" that "There is something whose mane John thinks is beautiful." Third, the principle of substitutivity of identicals works abnormally for intentional verbs. Whereas it follows from "The president is a Republican" and "Bush is the president" that "Bush is a Republican," it does not follow from "John believes that the president is a Republican" and "Bush is the president" that "John believes that Bush is a Republican." John, after all, might not know that Bush is the president. The fact that substitution of identicals does not preserve truth value for sentences with intentional verbs provides strong support for the view that sentences with intentional verbs cannot be translated into sentences without them. This is very important, first, because it means that Brentano was right that intentionality is the ineliminable mark of the mental, and second, because it means that all attempts to translate intentional mentalistic vocabulary into nonintentional physicalistic vocabulary, such as those proposed by operationists, logical positivists, and most behaviorists, are doomed to failure. If humans truly possess intentional states then any psychology that eschews talking about them is destined to be incomplete.

    Some philosophers of mind who accept the impossibility of translating intentional descriptions into nonintentional descriptions recommend, like Skinner, that intentional descriptions ought to be avoided if psychology is ever to rest on epistemological terra firma. For example, Quine (1960) says, "One may accept Brentano's thesis either as showing the indispensibility of intentional idioms and the importance of an autonomous science of intention, or as showing the baselessness of intentional idioms and the emptiness of a science of intention. My attitude, unlike Brentano's, is the second" (p. 221).

15. Dennett (1978b), p. 15. Also see Dennett (1978d).

16. I want to forestall an obvious objection, namely, that there are clear examples of nonlinguistic knowledge, for example, knowing how to throw a frisbee, or knowing how to eat with chopsticks. The distinction I want to call upon, without asking it to bear too much weight, is the distinction between *knowing how* and *knowing that*. In

this section I am talking about the *knowing that* kind, and not practical knowledge, the *knowing how* kind.

17. Skinner (1957), p. 130.
18. Ibid., p. 135, my italics.
19. Ibid., p. 134.
20. Ibid., p. 140.
21. Ibid., p. 137.
22. Not being a Wittgenstein expert, I do not dare to attribute this view to Wittgenstein. But see Harold Morick, ed. (1967) for several essays that do.
23. Popular wisdom, thanks to Noam Chomsky's famous review (1959) is that Skinner's views on language learning are seriously deficient. However, even if Chomsky is profoundly correct about the extent to which language acquisition rests on preprogrammed brain structures, even if he is right that the syntactic structure of language is innate, it does not seem too incredible to think that the specific semantic properties, that is, the meaning and reference a word has, are learned or at least fixed (for novices, anyway) in something like the manner Skinner describes.
24. S-R psychology is often used to refer to two logically distinct kinds of psychology. Sometimes it is used as I am using it here, to refer to the substantive position that all behavior consists of unconditioned and conditioned reflexes. Other times S-R psychology is used to refer to the methodological view that psychology should not talk about what is going on inside the organism (O). On this second view, S-R psychology is to be contrasted with S-O-R psychology.
25. Charles Taylor in his important book (1964) says that the difference between mechanistic and teleological explanation is that teleological explanation involves "reference to goals" and mechanistic explanation does not. Taylor, however, makes the mistake of thinking that Skinner is an S-R theorist who is limited to mechanistic explanation.
26. The S-R theorist might try the plausible tactic of putting the purpose or goal inside the person, so that, for example, it is John's purpose to get fit and trim by jogging even if he doesn't succeed. But in order to make this help, the S-R theorist will have to maintain the utterly implausible thesis that a jogger's purpose is just an internal chain of unconditioned responses or conditioned responses closely related to some innately available set of covert responses.
27. See Skinner (1981).
28. In his 1959 review of Skinner's *Verbal Behavior*, Noam Chomsky argues that the concept of reinforcement is vacuous and tautological because a reinforcer is always specified *after* we see a response increase in frequency. But here Chomsky is surely wrong. The class of reinforcing stimuli cannot be known a priori. Thus there is no other way to initially identify them than after the fact. However, once we thus identify a reinforcing stimulus there are all sorts of predictive tests which can be run to test the accuracy of our identification.
29. Skinner (1972c), p. 7. Notice: operants are defined *functionally*, that is, in terms of their relational properties, not in terms of their physical properties. The same physical movement, say raising my left arm, can be a number of different operants. It can be a right-turn signal, a way of resting my arm, a neurotic habit, and so on.
30. Skinner (1981), p. 501.
31. It is important to clarify the intended sense of "explain" in this argument. One must distinguish between explaining how novelty is possible in the ultimate philosophical sense, and explaining how it develops and increases in quantity once you have some novelty to begin with. Both the operant and the evolutionary models provide analyses which, I think, can be said to explain novelty in the second sense, but not in the first sense. The problem of novelty in the first sense is a deep dark mystery, the

solution of which is inconceivable to me. For more on this problem see the discussions of Piaget's constructivism in chapter 5.

32. N. Block (1971).

33. Skinner (1976), p. 55.

34. Skinner (1948); (1971). In 1982 I asked Skinner what his favorite of his own books was. He told me *Walden Two*.

35. See Skinner (1972e), p. 11.

36. One might argue that surely prediction is one of the requirements of the hypothetico-deductive method. Skinner's assumption, and the assumption I am objecting to, is that prediction (along with control) is an end in itself.

37. Skinner (1981), p. 503.

38. See Robert Nozick (1974), pp. 160–63 for an argument that proves—to my mind—that even if we all agreed at time T_1 that x, y, z are the right ends, that inevitably at some time T_2 someone will disagree. At this point we can either adjust our ends by letting this person do his own thing, or we can force him to get back in line. If we do the first we give up our vision, and if we do the second we are not using positive reinforcement.

39. See Alasdair MacIntyre (1981) for a lucid discussion of moral diversity and for an argument to the effect that disagreements over moral and political ends are ultimately not rationally or scientifically tractable precisely because every moral position presupposes its own self-justifying standard of rationality.

Chapter 5

1. Jean Piaget (1932).

2. Skinner can be seen as standing in this tradition. The laws of operant conditioning and the laws of classical conditioning exhaust the ways we are wired to learn. Skinner frequently expresses confidence that these laws plus experiential input can account for all our behavior. See chapter 4.

3. The concept of "cognitive structure" will do a lot of work in this chapter but I don't intend to worry much about giving it a precise definition. I do want a "cognitive structure" to be understood as an active sort of thing, as a sort of mental processor. Cognitive structures will consist both of abstract logical principles like *modus tollens* (if $p \longrightarrow q$ & $\sim q \longrightarrow \sim p$) and empirically rich rules or concepts. ("This situation is a lot like that situation so what's going on is probably such and such.") In Piaget (1980b), Piaget calls his structuralist theory a "dynamic Kantianism" (p. 150). See chapter 6 for more on Kant.

4. Actually there are ways for a Humean empiricist to introduce talk about mental structures. The laws of association constitute the innate structure or program of the mind. These laws take sensory experience as input and give two kinds of output: specific beliefs like, "that's a gaggle of geese in the sky," and structural beliefs or principles like the principles of the probability calculus. The bet of the cognitivists, of course, is that three laws of association will never generate enough structures to account for human mentality. The initial program is just too weak.

5. As noted earlier, the "intentional stance" is Dennett's (1978a) way of describing an approach to psychological explanation that deploys intentional idioms in roughly Brentano's sense.

6. Someone might object that only physical things can causally explain other things and that because mental structures, like conservation principles, are almost always functionally described, not physically described, they cannot be taken to causally explain behavior. The way around this objection is by taking the standard functionalist

line that although a human is no doubt a physical system, the functionalist (intentional) way of describing mental phenomena is the most illuminating way in which to talk about psychologically real phenomena like conservation transformations. See chapters 2, 3, 4, and 6 for more on functionalism.

7. Piaget prefers to use the word "schema" when speaking of the more primitive and disorganized rules of the young child, and reserves "structure" for the well-organized operational rules of the adolescent and adult.

8. Margaret A. Boden (1981b) in Boden, 1981a, p. 237. Also see Boden (1979).

9. In what is probably the fullest statement of the state of his theory, Piaget (1971) cites only three stages of cognitive development. There he collapses the preoperational and the concrete operational stage into one stage. Nevertheless, he continues to think that each of these stages is made up of many substages. See pp. 17–18.

10. This is a functionalist line of defense. The functionalist tries to avoid excessive worries about the radical underdetermination of theory, the infinite number of logically equivalent descriptions, and the like, by resting satisfied with a workable abstract functional description of a mental process. Although I do not directly discuss Piaget's position on the mind-body problem in this chapter, he, like most psychologists, is best viewed as a philosophical functionalist: although a human is a biological system (see the section "Assimilation, Accommodation, and Autoregulation") the most illuminating analysis of human intelligence will be framed in a functional, intentional vocabulary rather than in an exclusively physical one. As will become especially clear later, Piaget also blends elements of the older and more biological functionalism (see chapter 2) of James and Dewey. He emphasizes the importance of activity in the development of intelligence, and he emphasizes the natural tendency of all biological systems to seek an adaptive fit with the environment. See note 6.

11. See Jonathan E. Adler (1984).

12. Rochel Gelman (1978) is an excellent review of these experiments, many of which come out of her laboratory at the University of Pennsylvania. Also see Margaret Donaldson (1978). John Macnamara (1982) musters some very interesting empirical and conceptual arguments about name learning to argue, against Piaget, for the structural equivalence of the child's and adult's minds. Also see Susan Carey (1983). Carey persuasively argues that all the differences between adults' and children's minds reduce to children knowing less, literally having less domain-specific information at their disposal than adults. Carey argues against the view that the child deploys a different logic from adults, or differs in terms of representational capacity.

13. See Charles J. Brainerd (1978) for an interesting discussion of this charge. Also see John H. Flavell (1963) for an early discussion of the description versus explanation issue. This question of whether Piaget's stage theory is descriptive as opposed to explanatory is sometimes conflated with the question I discuss in the next section, namely: how deep do the explanatory powers of Piaget's theory go, that is, can he explain stage change itself?

14. I use the term "stage" throughout as a name for a collection of "structures."

15. This is where I disagree with Brainerd's critique of Piaget. Brainerd (1978), promotes three conditions that govern the introduction of cognitive stages as explanatory constructs. The main condition he thinks Piaget cannot satisfy is the one which requires that "procedures whereby the antecedent variables can be measured *independently* of behavioral changes must also be specified." (p. 174) Brainerd gives Coghill's biological stage theory as an example of theory which meets this condition. Coghill's theory explains changes in the motor development of *Amblystoma* embryos in terms of neurological stages. Since the neurological stages are measurable independently of the changes in motor behavior they are legitimate explanatory stages. Piaget, on

the other hand, specifies no neural correlates of his stages, although he no doubt expects that such exist, and therefore has no way of measuring mental stages independently of behavior.

But Brainerd's condition is simply too strong. In physics there are many explanatory constructs, electrons for example, which cannot be measured independently of the observable situations in which they figure explanatorily. What vindicates the explanatory use of such constructs is the fact that, given everything else we know about nature, electrons best explain the observable processes in a wide array of experimental tests, and lead to successful predictions. I think that exactly the same defense could be made of Piagetian mental structures and stages: they are simply, given everything else we know, the best explanation of the (age-variant) regularities in the ways humans transform experiential input.

16. R. S. Peters (1966), p. 229.

17. J. H. Flavell and J. F. Wohlwill (1969), p. 86.

18. Recent data show that Piaget is wrong that virtually everyone in all cultures reaches a stage of formal logical operations. And the data are equally strong that even people who reach a stage of formal logical operations do not think that way all the time. See Jonathan St.B. Evans (1982) for a good review of this literature.

19. Brainerd (1978), p. 176. There is a young man in his early twenties who is a chess master and plays all comers for money in Harvard Square. I recently watched him play a one-and-a-half-hour game of blindfold chess. When I asked him how he kept track of the location of every piece, he said it was hard to explain exactly, but it was partly pictorial and partly something else, "sort of mathematical"; but whatever it was he had been able to keep a chess game totally in his head since he was five or six. It seems likely to me that there are people like this chess genius, or musical geniuses like Mozart, who may well have possessed "reversible operations" with logical or musical objects well before they possessed "reversible operations" with, say, clay, or who might have possessed certain formal-operations skills even before they had achieved sensory-motor maturity. Assuming that such exceptions exist, it follows that Piaget's stages cannot depict only logical truths, otherwise such genius would be logically impossible.

20. Boden (1979), p. 82. For a series of illuminating examples of situations in which content and context affect the ability to deploy abstract logical principles see Jonathan Adler (1984), Daniel N. Osherson (1974), P. C. Wason (1977).

21. Piaget (1980b), p. 164, my italics.

22. Piaget (1971), p. 26.

23. Inhelder and Piaget (1958) claim that the essential principle governing autoregulating systems is the principle of equilibrium.

24. Piaget (1971), p. 28. Both Boden (1979) and Papert (1980) emphasize the cybernetic roots of Piaget's theory.

25. Piaget (1980b) in Piattelli-Palmarini, ed., 1980, p. 33.

26. Ibid., p. 31.

27. See Piaget (1971), pp. 10–13; and Piaget (1980a), p. 25.

28. Piaget (1977b), p. 840, my italics.

29. Piaget (1977a), p. 17, my italics.

30. See especially Piaget (1978). In this book Piaget claims that his theory of cognitive development is vindicated by allying the biological theories of C. H. Waddington and Paul Weiss. Waddington provides biological support for the principle of equilibrium and Weiss for the additional principle of equilibration. Sophie Haroutunian (1983) contains a good critical discussion of the biological models appropriated by Piaget.

31. See, for example, the responses of some of the biologists at the Royaumont Conference of 1975 in Piattelli-Palmarini, ed. (1980).

32. Piaget (1971) says, "abstraction consists first of taking cognizance of the existence of one of these actions or operations, that is to say, noting its possible interest, having neglected it so far. . . . Second, the action noticed has to be 'reflected' (in the physical sense of the term) by being projected onto another plane—for example, the plane of thought as opposed to practical action, or the plane of abstract systemization as opposed to that of concrete thought (say, algebra as opposed to arithmetic). . . . The name I propose to give this process of reconstruction with new combinations, which allows for any operational structure at any previous level to be integrated into a richer structure at a higher level, is 'reflective abstraction (abstraction reflechissante)' " (p. 320).
33. See John Macnamara (1976) and (1978) for a clever and in-depth argument on the circularity problem.
34. This, by the way, is the tactic the Piagetian should use if he wants to avoid the charge of circularity. If the "equilibration drive" is viewed not (merely) as being instantiated in conscious thought, but as being primarily a feature of the neuronal program of the brain operating in the dumb language of neuron firings, then we are not guilty of explaining intelligence by intelligence when we cite the equilibration principle. Our *explanans* and our *explanandum* are now at different levels within the system. When we locate the equilibration drive in the brain's program we are—to paraphrase Dennett—coming upon homunculi so dumb that we do not need to worry that we are any longer explaining intelligence in terms of intelligence. On the other hand, it is not clear that we can make these neural processes dumb enough to allay all our fears. After all, it would seem that the brain will still need to be intentional in Brentano's sense. That is, it will have to be capable of semantic expression, of representing meaningful states of affairs. See Fodor (1981a), pp. 20–24 for a persuasive argument to this effect.
35. J. A. Fodor (1980) in Piattelli-Palmarini, ed., 1980, p. 148.
36. Hypothesis formation and confirmation is a process of selection by consequences. This would no doubt lead a behaviorist to argue that it is only a special case of operant conditioning.
37. See Fodor (1979), especially chapter 2. Fodor says, "learning does not increase the *expressive power* of one's system of concepts (construed as the state of affairs that one can represent) though, of course, it can and often does increase one's information about what states of affairs actually obtain." (p. 93).
38. Fodor (1980) insists that "a theory of the conceptual plasticity of organisms must be a theory of how the environment selects among the innately specified concepts. *It is not a theory of how you acquire concepts, but a theory of how the environment determines which parts of the conceptual mechanism in principle available to you are in fact exploited*" (p. 151).
39. See Fodor (1979), p. 93. Fodor says, "But what *couldn't* happen, however, is that the device uses the available conceptual system to *learn* the more powerful one. That is, it couldn't happen that it gets from stage one to stage two by anything we would recognize as a *computational* procedure. In short, trauma might do it; so might maturation. Learning won't." This way of putting the constructivist's fallacy results in part, I think, on relying too heavily on computational metaphors. Biochemical systems, unlike mechanical systems, often develop properties as a result of nontraumatic interaction with the environment (see chapter 7). Furthermore, there is a long, respected tradition in philosophy which requires that to count as "knowledge" a hypothesis must minimally be a justified belief. Beliefs, however, are only justified when they are corroborated. Thus there is a very important sense in which a hypothesis formation and confirmation system of the type Piaget proposes is a theory of learning. If I know which mental structures to deploy in confronting the world because one of my con-

jectures has been confirmed by experience, then the interplay between my conjectures and the world results in learning an exceedingly useful piece of information. Fodor claims that there is no learning, only belief fixation. But if experiential feedback is what causes the cognitive system to fix on a small number from among an infinite number of logically possible structures, I would say the system is learning something!

40. Someone might object that if the cognitive system's representational resources are all preformed and if it is also environmentally sensitive, then the ways in which it is sensitive must also be programmed in from the start, and thus such a system will really be preformed. However, it does not necessarily follow that the program for environmental sensitivity need be in place at birth (although much of it undoubtedly is). Some of the program might emerge maturationally, or through environmental interaction. It is still an open question. But even if all the representational resources as well as the program for environmental sensitivity are in place at birth we need not be too concerned, because it is really only environmentally insensitive cognitive systems which constructivists and sophisticated empiricists need object to.

41. See Harry Bleilin (1971), especially p. 90, for an argument to the effect that Piaget holds a "preformationist" or "maturationist" philosophy of mind. Hilary Putnam (1980) reads Piaget in much the same way.

42. Piaget's model rests on the assumption that *when* a child develops or constructs a mental structure—a cognitive *competence*—she then uses it to organize experience; she *performs* with it. Many antidevelopmentalist followers of Chomsky and Fodor argue that (many) underlying cognitive competencies, particularly linguistic ones, are present at birth, awaiting only the feedback from experience, after which performance will catch up (more or less) with competence.

43. See Piaget (1970) for an extended discussion of the adequacy thesis.

44. Piaget is only committed to the claim that the highest stage of cognitive development is the epistemologically most advanced of the stages normal humans go through relative to the equipment they have and the way the world is. Thus for example, he could allow that Reimannian geometry, Einsteinian physics, and modern quantificational logic are epistemically superior to Euclidean geometry, Aristotelian or Newtonian physics, and traditional logic, but maintain that we do just fine in this world of slow-moving objects with these more primitive theories.

45. When a developmental theorist claims that one stage is more integrated than an earlier stage, he usually means that the stage absorbs all the competencies of the previous stage and enlists new ones. This is sometimes expressed by referring to a stage as more "integrated" and "differentiated" than its predecessor.

46. See Plato (1960); Immanuel Kant (1785); John Rawls (1971).

47. For a more complete description of the six stages see the appendix to L. Kohlberg (1981a).

48. See H. Hartshorne and M. A. May (1928).

49. See R. E. Nisbett and T. D. Wilson (1977); and R. E. Nisbett and L. Ross (1980).

50. L. Kohlberg (1981b), p. 185.

51. Ibid., p. 189.

52. Ibid., p. 183.

53. See Carol Gilligan (1977); (1979); (1982); O. J. Flanagan (1982c), (1982d); and O. J. Flanagan and J. E. Adler (1983) for further discussions of the problems facing Kohlberg's theory as it tries to account for women's moral conceptions. In response to critics like Carol Gilligan and Owen Flanagan, Kohlberg has become aware of this shortcoming and acknowledged that there may be two parts to moral theory: a theory of justice and a theory of the good life. I take it that he would now only claim that his developmental theory is about how the conception of justice develops. See Kohlberg (1982), pp. 515–18.

54. Kohlberg (1982), p. 514, claims that the choice of hypothetical third-party dilemmas was made on the presumption that this would isolate judgments of "should" from judgments of "would." But I do not see that he justifies this presumption anywhere. I cannot help but think that judgments of the "what I would do if I were Heinz" sort must contaminate the response data.
55. Kohlberg (1982), p. 518.
56. Ibid., p. 517.
57. Ibid.
58. See Rest (1979).
59. Kohlberg (1982), p. 516.
60. C. Gilligan and J. M. Murphy (1979), p. 90. Also see C. P. Edwards (1975) and E. L. Simpson (1974) for critiques of Kohlberg's claims of universality, invariance of sequence, and irreversibility.
61. Kohlberg (1982), p. 523.
62. Kohlberg (1981b), p. 165.
63. Ibid., p. 164.
64. Kohlberg (1982), p. 525.
65. Ibid., p. 523.
66. One mistake I think I made in my (1982c) and (1982d) papers was interpreting Kohlberg as thinking that he could prove the adequacy thesis. This led me to speak as if by raising some skeptical doubts about each strand in his argument I was disproving it. I now think that the sorts of problems I raised in those papers, and the ones I raise here, show only that it will be very hard for Kohlberg to secure an adequacy thesis.
67. Kohlberg (1981c), p. 211.
68. B. Puka (1982), p. 470.
69. Kohlberg (1973), p. 633.
70. Ibid.
71. Kohlberg and C. Power (1981d), p. 345.
72. Kohlberg (1981c), p. 211, my italics.
73. Ibid., p. 199.
74. Many German soldiers used the harmonious fit between their behavior and Nazi values to argue for their innocence at the Nuremberg trials.
75. R. M. Hare (1981), for example, claims to be a utilitarian, while Kant rejects utilitarianism. Of course, now that Kohlberg has collapsed stages 5 and 6 this might be less of a problem since Hare's utilitarianism has Kantian features such as universalizability.
76. Alasdair MacIntyre (1981) and Bernard Williams (1982) are two distinguished philosophers who argue against both utilitarianism and Kantianism. MacIntyre has told me explicitly that he rejects Kohlberg's argument for the adequacy thesis because he rejects the moral philosophy it mimics.
77. Shweder (1982) describes Kohlberg as thinking this way. "For Kohlberg the history of the world, and the history of childhood in all societies is the story of the progressive discovery of the principles of the American Revolution" (p. 421).
78. In my "Moral Structures?" (1982a), I critically compare Kohlberg's theory and social-learning approaches to morality. John Macnamara has pointed out to me that Kohlberg might defend himself against my argument that there is no one social world relative to which his highest stage is the most adequate, by arguing that his theory is more like a mathematical theory, and thus that the lack of an actual physical or social model for his moral theory is no more worrisome than the lack of a physical model for arithmetic. I cannot see how Kohlberg can use this imaginative tactic. First, he often talks as if his stages either are, or are not, in equilibrium relative to the way

some social world is. Second, the claim for the adequacy of his highest stage carries none of the epistemological certainty that arithmetic theorems carry.

79. Puka (1982), p. 471.

80. The first example is adapted from Andrew Oldenquist (1982), the second is mine. Lawrence Blum (1980) also argues that ethical theories aligned with Kantianism have trouble making room for friendship, loyalties, and special responsibilities.

81. I have actually done an informal survey with the canoe counterexamples among my students and colleagues, sampling fifty or sixty people. The first *Gedanken* experiment produced fairly unanimous support for the view that the mother should save her own child. The second produced majority agreement but some people are clearly consistent utilitarians who thought the numbers mattered. I would like to see some psychologist get better data with a larger sample on the canoe cases. Kohlberg might try to respond to the canoe counterexamples by arguing that since the highest stage, 5-6, incorporates the loyalty stage (stage 3), that a stage 5-6 mother could use loyalty considerations to justify saving her child. This will not work, though, because the stage 5-6 principles are supposed to override the lower-stage principles when the two sets of principles are in conflict, as they are in the canoe cases. A better strategy for Kohlberg would be to argue that the response rates I got are easily explained by the fact that almost no one is a true Kantian and very few people are consistent utilitarians. Against this I would simply assert that however the highest stage is described it must imply that one should save one's own child (at least in the first case). To do so is just a clear-cut matter of (Aristotelian) practical reason.

Chapter 6

1. G. A. Miller, E. Galanter, K. H. Pribram (1960), p. 8.
2. E. C. Tolman (1948).
3. John Haugeland (1981b), p. 243.
4. Ulric Neisser (1966), p. 4.
5. John R. Anderson (1980), p. 3.
6. See Dennett's classic essay (1978b), p. 6.
7. See Robert Cummins (1980) and Barbara Von Eckardt (1978).
8. See Patricia Smith Churchland (1986b) for a completely convincing defense of this coevolutionary research ideology against the alternative view that functional explanation can remain oblivious to theories of brain function.
9. Immanuel Kant (1781), pp. 22–23. Kant takes his own Copernican stance when in the next passage he announces that the mind "has rules which I must presuppose as being in me prior to objects being given to me and therefore as being a priori. They [the rules] find expression in a priori concepts to which all objects of experience necessarily conform." Kant (1783), p. 67, puts his view this way: *"The understanding does not derive its laws (a priori) from, but prescribes them to, nature."*
10. The fact that we contribute to our own knowledge is not cause for skepticism or for fear that our subjective a priori concepts will lead to delusions. In fact, if we append the theory of evolution to Kant's theory we can better understand why a system of a priori mental structures would have been a reasonable outcome of evolution. After all, selection pressures will tend to favor those members of a species who are good at anticipating the world. An a priori cognitive system is precisely such an anticipatory system.

  One surprising result of Kant's Copernican revolution is that the kind of "metaphysics which will be able to come forward as a science" is not going to have much in common with traditional speculative metaphysics. Metaphysics as a science, like traditional metaphysics, will still try to get behind and beyond physics, but it will do so by taking the unusual tactic of trying to penetrate our subjectivity, rather than of trying to penetrate the outer limits of nature and get at ultimate truths. Kant's scientific metaphysics therefore is the harbinger of modern cognitive science. It openly psychologizes a major portion of philosophy.

11. For example, another famous transcendental deduction occurs in the "Transcendental Aesthetic" of 1781, where Kant offers roughly the following argument:

1. Geometry exists and consists of necessary truths.
2. Since geometry exists, it is possible.
3. How is it possible?
4. Sense experience is insufficient to explain the existence of geometrical truths, because sense experience does not contain ideal geometrical objects nor does sense experience ever give certainty.
5. The best explanation for the existence of geometry therefore is that our minds are structured a priori to see the world in terms of (something like) the principles of Euclidean geometry. The mind, in effect, comes wired to organize sense experience in Euclidean terms. Only this assumption accounts for the certainty and intuitiveness we attach to the truths of geometry.

12. Saul Sternberg (1966).

13. Ibid., p. 653. Sternberg addresses the point about nonoptimality. He says, "One can, however, conceive of systems in which a self-terminating search would be inefficient. For example, if the determination of whether or not a match had occurred were a slow operation that could not occur concurrently with scanning, self-termination would result in a long interruption in the scan after each comparison." My point is that even if we are such a system in which an exhaustive search procedure is optimal it is only optimal relative to the sort of preexisting design constraints discussed in the quotation.

14. On the other hand, when an individual is in fact experiencing the real thing, it is not clear that he or she is experiencing something we would want to call an auditory, tactile, visual, gustatory, or olfactory image either. Take visual perception. The last bona fide image that occurs in vision is retinal. Information about the retinal image is transformed into some other medium as it ascends the optic nerve. It is information processed in this secondary medium that is the proximate cause of our seeing. Thus the only credible version of the six-code theory claims that the modes in which mental representation occur are analogous to the five modes of sensation/perception and the one mode of natural language representation. According to this refined version of the six-code theory, when you imagine your mother's face you are doing something very similar to what you are doing when you look directly at her. In neither case is there an actual picture in your brain. When you imagine the smell of a skunk you are doing something similar to actually smelling one. In neither case is there an odor in your brain. Georges Rey (1981), p. 123, calls this "the hypothesis of *quasi-perception:* the processes that underlie image-experiences are significantly like the processes that underlie actual perceptual experiences." Steve Kosslyn's recent work supports the six-code hypothesis for visual imaging. He tells me that many of the brain areas implicated in vision are, in fact, also implicated in visual imaging.

15. See N. Block, ed. (1981), pp. 2–3. This volume contains many of the important papers on the imagery debate.

16. Anderson (1980), chapter 4.

17. Many arguments—some having to do with the nature of brain processes, others claiming that what is introspected is not really imagistic at all—have been put forward for the unified-code theory. One of the more interesting arguments from an epistemological point of view is this. The six-code theory is committed to a view that thinking and remembering can occur in terms of the representational resources of any one of the six autonomous codes. Thus it is compatible with the six-code theory that I remember that my deceased grandmother had blue eyes, either by consulting a sentence in the linguistic code—"grandmother had blue eyes"—or by looking at a private picture (in color) of grandmother constructed in the visual code.

The unified-code theorist objects that although the story about remembering solely in terms of quasi-linguistic representations can be made to work, the one about doing so solely in terms of pictures cannot. The difficulty is that images, odors, tastes, and spatial arrays cannot interpret themselves. With specific reference to the problem of getting pictures to self-interpret, Kosslyn et al. (1981), staunch advocates of mental imagery, admit that "an image cannot represent an object or scene uniquely without some interpretive function that picks out certain characteristics of the image as being important and others as being incidental. That is, an image of John sitting could represent John, John's head, bent knees, and so forth, depending on what one pays attention to in the image. And the 'stage directions' indicating what is important in an image cannot *themselves* be images—if they were, the problem would only be pushed back a step. This class of objections is to the point: images cannot be the *sole* form of internal representation that exists in human memory" (p. 131).

The unified-code theorist can argue that his view has parsimony on its side. If higher-level mental processes, such as thinking and remembering, occur in images, we will still need quasi-linguistic "stage directions" in order to interpret them and pick out salient features, for example, to get us to grandmother's blue eyes as opposed to her grey hair or short stature. A unified system of quasi-linguistic representations, however, will need no other mode to assist it in the job of representation; it can be self-interpreting in the sense that it can simply fetch the uniquely encoded quasi proposition that states that "grandmother had blue eyes," without also fetching all the other information about her, as a picture would. It makes sense, therefore, that the cognitive system encodes information from all the sensory modalities in a unified quasi-linguistic code. If God or evolution engineered us optimally a unified code would surely be the way to go.

This is an interesting argument, but it is by no means decisive. First, there may well be ways in which a system with several different modes of mental representation is more efficient and more adaptive from an evolutionary point of view than a unified one. Second, even if multiple code systems are less efficient, this does not mean that nature did not wire us that way. There is always the possibility that the mind is a "kludge."

18. R. N. Shepard and J. Metzler (1971).

19. This alternative transcendental deduction would still have some explaining to do about the reaction times. Presumably, it would need to postulate that the number of quasi-linguistic propositions abstracted from the figures increase linearly with the degree of rotation, and are ordered in such a way that computation time over them increases linearly. The point for now is that this scenario is possible; the unified-code theory is not ruled out by the Shepard and Metzler data.

20. See Dennett (1982). Dennett (1978e) contains an earlier argument against introspection.

21. See Thomas Nagel (1979c).
22. Cognitive science allows the logical possibility of being a Process Cartesian about self-knowledge without being a Cartesian on the mind-body problem. Recall that part of Descartes' rationale for believing in mind-body dualism was based on the fact that his introspections yielded no evidence whatsoever that his mind was physical. We might express his point this way nowadays: even the most committed materialist does not experience his mental processes as if they are neural events. The cognitivist's way out of the "introspective trap" here comes from the analogy of the mind to a computational system. Computational systems can be described at different levels of grain, for example, at the level of hardware, at the level of symbolic manipulations in machine language, and at the level of higher-level symbolic manipulations in programming languages such as BASIC or Fortran. A computer, of course, is a physical system and everything it does at every level is a physical process or event. Nevertheless, descriptions of a computational system, as we move from bottom to top, become increasingly abstract and increasingly removed from implementation. (See Hofstadter, 1980.) Descartes' mistake was to think that because he only had access to his mind at the higher functional levels of organization, this was evidence that his mind was nonphysical. The corresponding mistake with a computational system would be to take a description of an abstract computer program running on some computer as a description of a disembodied process. In any case, a physicalist of the computer functionalist persuasion conceivably could advocate Process Cartesianism in the following way: although we have no special access to the neural implementation of our mental processes, we have privileged access to mental processes at the functional level.
23. Perhaps you could divide yourself in two and play both questioner and answerer in the assenting-test, but this too would weaken the underlying idea that your mind is one unified whole with privileged access to its contents.
24. J. Lackner and M. Garrett (1973).
25. Richard E. Nisbett and Timothy D. Wilson (1977). With respect to what I call Content Cartesianism, Nisbett and Wilson make the interesting suggestion that one reason we often mistake our confidence in our autophenomenological reports for their accuracy has to do with the fact that "Disconfirmations of hypotheses about the workings of our minds is hard to come by" (p. 256).
26. R. E. Nisbett and L. Ross (1980).
27. Ibid., p. 195.
28. This thesis has recently been advocated by one of the foremost cognitive psychologists, John R. Anderson. In his most recent book (1983) Anderson announces, "The most deeply rooted preconception guiding my theorizing is a belief in the unity of human cognition, that is, that all the higher cognitive processes, such as memory, language, problem solving, imagery, deduction, and induction, are manifestations of the same underlying system. This is not to deny that there are many powerful, special-purpose 'peripheral' systems for processing perceptual information and coordinating motor performance. However, behind these lies a common cognitive system for higher-level processing" (p. 1). Anderson claims to have a theory, (actually it is a computer model), ACT*, which "if given one set of experiences develops a linguistic facility, if given another set of experiences develops a geometry facility, if given another set of experiences develops a programming facility. Therefore, ACT* is very much a unitary theory of mind" (p. 3).
29. Noam Chomsky (1980), p. 3. Caveat: Chomsky's talk of "mental organs" is somewhat misleading. Nothing in the modularity idea depends on the existence

of precise brain locations for each "mental organ" in his sense of the term. Modular systems can differ functionally without clear-cut anatomical differences.

30. Jerry Fodor (1983). Fodor is less interested in arguing for Chomsky's language module, his number module, and so on, than he is in extending the modularity thesis to new domains.

31. Ibid., p. 21.

32. Ibid., p. 42.

33. Ibid., p. 47.

34. Ibid., p. 51.

35. Ibid., p. 61.

36. Ibid., p. 64. See Zenon Pylyshyn (1980).

37. Howard Gardner (1983).

38. R. Puccetti (1973).

39. T. Nagel (1979b).

40. The discourses on new methodologies in science and philosophy which began to appear with frequency in the seventeenth century in the writings of thinkers like Descartes, Spinoza, and Bacon constituted the beginnings of a literary genre devoted to the search and defense of the proper rational procedures.

41. See J. E. Adler (1984), and O. J. Flanagan and J. E. Adler (1983) for more on some of the tensions among logic, rationality, and moral concerns.

42. See P. C. Wason and P. N. Johnson-Laird (1972).

43. See Amos Tversky and Daniel Kahneman (1974), reprinted in Kahneman, Slovic, and Tversky, 1982. Page numbers refer to the reprinted version.

44. Ibid., p. 5.

45. Ibid., p. 11.

46. Ibid., p. 12. Many cognitive psychologists and philosophers have thrown up their hands and declared the *Enlightenment Competence Theory* a case of wishful thinking. L. Jonathan Cohen (1981), an Oxford philosopher, however, resists this move, and boldly declares that "nothing in the existing literature on cognitive reasoning, nor in any possible future results of human experimental enquiry, could have bleak implications for human rationality, in the sense of implications that establish a faulty competence." I think Cohen is onto something, although he puts his point too strongly.

47. Three important books published recently on the relation of findings in cognitive science, epistemology, and logic are C. Cherniak (1986), Alvin Goldman (1986), G. Harman (1986).

48. Jerry Fodor (1981c), p. 133.

49. The example was suggested by Jerry Samet. See David Lewis (1980) for a similar thought experiment. Also see Ned Block's fine introduction to the "Functionalism" section of Block, ed. (1980) for more on the debate about possible realizations of functional states, and on the qualia objections to functionalism.

50. Paul Churchland (1981) p. 76. See also Patricia Smith Churchland (1980).

51. Paul Churchland (1984).

52. See Stephen Stich (1983).

53. Marvin Minsky (1980), p. 439.

54. Turkle (1984), p. 313.

55. Haugeland (1985), p. 113.

56. Fodor (1979), pp. 65–66, 116. The postulation of a rock-bottom "language of thought" in whose terms all concepts must be formulated is the source of Fodor's radical concept nativism (see chapter 5).

57. Haugeland (1985), p. 106.

58. A. M. Turing (1937).

59. John Haugeland (1981c), p. 31.
60. Long ago F. Rosenblatt (1962) invented a simple class of connectionist networks called "perceptrons." Connectionism might, therefore, be thought of as the vindication of his vision. I am grateful for the help of Chuck Rosenberg, an MIT student, for his careful reading of this new section and his valuable comments.
61. Paul M. Churchland (1988), p. 121.
62. Ibid.
63. Paul M. Churchland (1989), p. 132.
64. See Daniel W. Hillis (1985).
65. See Paul M. Churchland (1989).
66. Gorman and Sejnowski (1988a, 1988b).
67. Paul M. Churchland (1988).
68. Terry Sejnowski and Charles Rosenberg (1986, 1987).
69. The example is from Dan Lloyd (1989). Lloyd's book, especially chapter 4, contains an excellent discussion of connectionism and of the debate over whether, and if so in what way, "representations" figure in connectionist systems.
70. See Paul M. Churchland (1989), chapter 10, for a discussion of some of the important biological differences between connectionist systems and actual brains. Also see the articles by J. T. Schwartz, by J. D. Cowan and D. H. Sharp and by G. N. Reeke, Jr., and G. M. Edelman in the special issue of *Daedalus* on Artificial Intelligence in the winter 1988 issue, vol. 117.
71. John Searle (1980), p. 417.
72. Turkle (1985), p. 240.
73. Charniak and McDermott (1985), p. 7.
74. Allen Newell (1973). Also see Zenon Pylyshyn (1981) for a staunch and articulate defense of weak psychological AI along the lines suggested.
75. Two of the most respected and successful researchers in the field, Roger Schank of Yale University and John R. Anderson of Carnegie-Mellon, do just such model building. See Anderson (1983), and Schank (1982). Anderson, as I mentioned earlier, is a critic of the modularity thesis. One way of reading Anderson is as believing that the piecemeal, example-driven nature of most experimental cognitive psychology gives the illusion that the mind is modular. Anderson sees three sorts of evidence favoring the unitary approach. "One is the short evolutionary history of many of the higher human intellectual functions, such as those concerned with mathematical problem solving. The second is that humans display great plasticity in acquiring functions for which there was no possibility of evolutionary anticipation. The third is that the various cognitive activities have many features in common" (p. 5).
76. Actually there may be natural systems that cannot be treated as formal systems. For example, it is not clear what formal algorithms a quantum-physical system can be said to obey.
77. Douglas Hofstadter (1980), p. 301.
78. Hilary Putnam (1981b), p. 218.
79. Paul Churchland (1984), points out that, "Inevitably neurons are likened to the logic gates in the CPU of a digital computer. But the differences are as intriguing as the similarities. A single logic gate receives input from no more than two distinct sources; a neuron receives input from well in excess of a thousand. A logic gate emits outputs at a metronomic frequency, 10 to the 6th hz, for example; a neuron varies freely between 0 and 10 to the 2nd hz. Logic gate output is and must be coordinated with all other gates; neuronal output is not. . . . [A]nd the functional properties of a logic gate are fixed; those of a neuron are decidedly plastic, since the growth of new synaptic connections and the pruning of old

ones can change the input/output function of the cell. The dendritic branches can grow tiny spines in a matter of minutes, to effect new synaptic connections, and these changes are themselves induced, in part, by prior neuronal activity." See Paul Churchland (1989), chapter 10, for similar illuminating points about the biological realism of connectionist devices.

80. Hubert Dreyfus (1981), especially pp. 179-191.

81. See Marvin Minsky (1981), Roger Schank and Robert P. Abelson (1977), and Schank (1982).

82. One of the main criticisms of the functionalist, broadly computational theory of mind, has to do with objections about its inability to deal with qualia. The basic problem is this: functionalism is good with relational features of mind, but qualia are nonrelational; they are raw and stand alone. See N. Block (1980b).

83. Keith Gunderson (1971).

84. Georges Rey (1980), p. 192.

85. John Haugeland (1981c), p. 32.

86. See Thomas Nagel (1979d).

87. The notion of supernouns comes from Eric Hughes.

88. John Searle (1982), pp. 4–5; Searle (1984).

89. A. M. Turing (1950).

Chapter 7

1. See E. O. Wilson (1978), pp. 64–65, 190, 207. Wilson claims that this book is the last of an unplanned triology. First was *Insect Societies* in 1971, whose concluding chapter was entitled "The Prospect for a Unified Sociobiology." Next came *Sociobiology: The New Synthesis* in 1975, whose concluding chapter was entitled "Man: From Sociobiology to Sociology." And finally there was *On Human Nature*. In 1981 Wilson collaborated with physicist Charles J. Lumsden to produce *Genes, Mind, and Culture: The Coevolutionary Process*.

2. Richard Lewontin (1970), p. 1.

3. See Charles Darwin (1859), pp. 237–238, and W. D. Hamilton (1964) for some background on the concepts of inclusive genetic fitness and kin selection. Most sociobiologists follow G. C. Williams (1966) in thinking that almost all examples of adaptations which look good for the group and bad for the individual can be explained in terms of direct selection of individuals or in terms of kin selection. I want to make it clear, however, following Lewontin and others, that this does not mean that all selection pressures operate directly on the individual organism. Selection pressures are mediated at both lower, such as RNA and cellular levels, and higher levels, such as group, population, species.

4. Ernst Mayr (1982), p. 598.

5. E. O. Wilson (1975), p. 4.

6. E. O. Wilson (1978), p. 32.

7. There are biological differences, beyond the obvious ones, on the basis of which sociobiology predicts cognitive and behavioral sex differences. Consider this: human males release on the order of one hundred million sperm in each ejaculation. Supposing that the average male ejaculates several thousand times in a lifetime, the average male releases hundreds of billions of sperm. In theory, a male could father a child with each and every ejaculation so long as he had intercourse with many different females. Human females, on the other hand, produce approximately four hundred eggs in a lifetime. Of these an absolute maximum of, say, twenty-five can result in children. E. O. Wilson claims that the "consequences of this gametic dimorphism ramify through the biology and psychology of human sex."

8. C. Lumsden and E. O. Wilson (1981), p. 99, my italics.

9. Admittedly, E. O. Wilson sometimes talks as if the genes have given up their sovereignty in the human case. But no one familiar with his work can fail to read such comments as ambivalence rather than his considered position. My favorite piece of evidence for my reading of Wilson as a biological determinist is his claim that the great geneticist Theodosius Dobzhansky was an "extreme orthodox environmentalist" for having said "Culture is not inherited through genes, it is acquired by learning from other humans." Need I say more? Actually what is most puzzling about Wilson's predilection for genetic determinism is that he and Lumsden (1981) claim to provide a proof that, given what is known about the informational capacity of DNA and given what is known about the underlying competence of a normal language user, it is inconceivable that language could be explained genetically. It would require 10^{16} kilograms of DNA to contain the information sufficient for a 10,000 word vocabulary utilized in sentences of up to ten words. And that amount of DNA is far in excess of the weight of all four billion humans put together! See Lumsden and Wilson (1981), pp. 334–37.

10. In *On Human Nature* (1978), pp. 78–79, Wilson actually refers to cultural evolution as Lamarckian. But his work taken as a whole makes it clear that he never means this to imply the sort of openness to new information and the plasticity of cognition I have in mind.

11. Richard Dawkins (1976), pp. ix, 49, 64.

12. See R. Levins and R. C. Lewontin (1980), W. C. Wimsatt (1980), and E. Sober (1980) for three excellent discussions of the effects of many different levels of biological organization.

13. Stephen Jay Gould (1978), pp. 348–349.

14. Ibid., p. 346.

15. See R. L. Trivers (1971). It is unclear to me whether Trivers is claiming that we have a genetic capacity for reciprocal altruism or whether he is claiming that we have a genetic predisposition for reciprocal altruism, or something stronger still. Since it is trivially true that anything any organism does it has the capacity to do, one would think that Trivers is making one of these stronger claims, since it is hard to see why everyone would get so excited by the trivial claim. But I could be wrong. People may be excited by the fact that they incorrectly read Trivers as providing evidence for some stronger thesis. I do not see the evidence.

16. S. J. Gould (1978).

17. R. M. Burian (1981–1982), pp. 50–51.

18. See S. J. Gould and R. C. Lewontin (1979).

19. E. O. Wilson (1978), p. 94.

20. A. L. Caplan (1981–1982).

21. The little Wilson does offer in this regard (1978, pp. 74–77) anticipates somewhat the theory of mind that he and Lumsden deploy in (1981).

22. Lumsden and Wilson (1981), p. ix, my italics.

23. Wilson is quoted by Roger Lewin (1981), p. 908, as viewing Lumsden and Wilson (1981) as an attempt to respond to these two objections.

24. Lumsden and Wilson (1981), p. 7.

25. Lumsden and Wilson (1982), p. 2. This is an excellent summary of the book, plus commentary by twenty-odd friends and foes.

26. Ibid.

27. Lumsden and Wilson (1981), p. 350.

28. Ibid., p. 36.

29. H. E. Gruber (1982), p. 12.

30. R. Van Gulick (1982), p. 28.

31. S. J. Gould (1981), p. 324.

32. Wilson proposed in (1975), pp. 3–7, that "ethics . . . be removed temporarily from the hands of the philosophers and biologized." He proclaimed that "we must explain ethics and ethical philosophers if not epistemology and epistemologists at all depths."

33. I do not mean to suggest by referring to our "moral nature" that we are good as opposed to bad, but merely to refer to the fact that all people in all cultures characterize actions and agents in moral and immoral terms.

34. It is important to keep in mind the difference between general genetically determined moral capacities on the one hand and specific moral beliefs or behaviors on the other. As I emphasized earlier, it is trivially true that anything an organism does it has the capacity to do. But neither the citation of a capacity nor the explanation of its origin (even if it is a capacity we are powerfully predisposed to use) necessarily explains or illuminates anything about any present action or function, even if the action or function requires the capacity. For example, the most elaborate explanation of my cerebral cortex, citing both the history of the species and my own genetic history, will explain absolutely nothing about what I have just said, or why I have said it. Nevertheless, my cerebral cortex is a necessary condition for my having said anything at all.

35. See Peter Singer (1981).

36. Whereas sociobiology can shed light on the development of our moral capacities and possibly on the genesis of certain widely shared moral principles at the group level, the general theoretical orientation of sociobiology makes it implausible to think that the sociobiologist can give an adequate account of the genesis of moral views at the individual level. See O. J. Flanagan (1981–1982).

37. E. O. Wilson (1978), pp. 2–3.

38. E. O. Wilson (1975), p. 562.

39. E. O. Wilson (1978), pp. 5–6.

40. As we have learned from people like T. S. Kuhn, it is something of a fiction that science is dispassionate. But it is interesting to notice that many of the most passionate moments in the history of science have had to do with moments in which some scientific theory was thought to have implications for the image of persons. I am thinking of course of Galileo, Newton, Darwin, Freud, Skinner, and Wilson himself.

41. E. O. Wilson (1975), p. 564.

42. See R. Simon and S. Zegura (1979), p. 777, and Flanagan (1981–1982) for further discussion of the rationality issue.

43. E. O. Wilson (1978), p. 6, my italics.

44. E. O. Wilson (1975), p. 562.

45. Ibid., p. 197. Although I do not intend to press the point here it is simply not a fact that an individual "is an evanescent combination of genes." What is true is that an individual contains an "evanescent combination of genes."

46. Ibid., pp. 196–197.

47. I have developed this naturalistic view of ethical reasoning further in Flanagan (1982b) and in (1991).

48. E. O. Wilson (1978), p. 198.

49. Ibid., pp. 198–199.

50. See Wimsatt (1980), p. 162, and also Flanagan (1980a).

Chapter 8

1. The concept of "neurophilosophy" was coined by Patricia S. Churchland in her important book by that name (1986b).

2. See Howard Gardner (1985) for an excellent history of the emergence of cognitivism.

3. See Flanagan (1981) for an argument to the effect that psychology is especially prone to theoretical reaction formation.

4. J. Jaynes (1976), p. 1.

5. Dennett (1978e)., p. 149. A few years later Dennett wrote, "Consciousness is making a comeback in psychology, but there is still residual skepticism, anxiety, and confusion about how to approach this perilous phenomenon scientifically" (1982, p. 159).

6. For reasons discussed in the last chapter, one can believe that a general capacity is adaptive (or unadaptive) and at the same time believe that it is an open question whether any particular exercise of that capacity is adaptive (or unadaptive).

7. James (1890), p. 180.

8. Donald Davidson's (1970) argument for the autonomy of the mental provided some early inspiration for the new mysterians.

9. Nagel (1979d), pp. 165–166.

10. Nagel (1986), p. 47.

11. Colin McGinn (1989).

12. Ibid., p. 349.

13. Ibid., p. 350.

14. Supervenience means "comes along with" or "comes on top of." The idea that mental events supervene on neural events and that conscious mental events supervene on a subclass of neural events simply means that they come along with these events. But they don't simply come along incidentally, for a ride, as it were. Whenever neural activity of a certain sort occurs, it is essential that conscious mental states are realized. Thinking of supervenience in this way allows us to bring the notions of identity, realization, and being caused by together in a unified way. Conscious mental events are realized by suitably configured neural states. Indeed, they just are (identical to) these states. Furthermore, a conscious mental event is caused by a certain set of neural events giving rise to another set of neural events upon which the conscious state supervenes, in which it is realized, and to which it is identical.

15. McGinn is somewhat unclear whether it is P that we cannot understand or how P accounts for consciousness or makes the existence of consciousness "intelligible."

16. Some naturalists believe in irreducibly nonnatural properties, e.g., numbers. But it is hard to see how one could justify a homogeneity constraint on the introduction of concepts if all the concepts under consideration are thought to refer to natural properties. Since McGinn writes that P, the property that explains or instantiates consciousness, is a natural property, it is hard to see why the homogeneity constraint would prohibit the introduction of the concept of consciousness, since it is *not* a nonnatural property on his view.

17. P. S. Churchland (1986b), p. 36, gives an estimate of 10^{12}, possibly as high as 10^{14}. A common conservative estimate that one sees is 100 billion (10^{11}), and I will stick with it throughout, although it may be low by several orders of magnitude.

18. P. M. Churchland (1988).

19. See P. M. Churchland (1989) and G. M. Edelman (1989).

20. Edelman (1989), pp. 64–90. Presumably, the same sort of story is involved in higher-level cognition. At the level of cognition the recurrent and reentrant properties of the brain involve continual updating of our knowledge of the world and the bringing to bear of previously acquired knowledge to current

experience. There is no faculty of thought, no "thought center." What there is instead is massive parallel processing involving coordination of disparate neural areas.

21. P. M. Churchland (1989), p. 132.
22. William H. Calvin (1990).
23. See B. F. Skinner (1981) and D. C. Dennett (1978g) for two important essays explaining why Darwinian processes can be expected to operate in the shaping of individual behavior and thought.
24. Mandler (1985), chapter 3.
25. Kenneth Craik (1943).
26. William Calvin (1990), pp. 261–262.
27. Dennett (1988b), p. 6.
28. See Ekman, Levinson, and Freisen (1985). This important work vindicates Darwin's hypothesis that certain emotions are basic and occur across cultures. These emotions have associated with them characteristic movements of the facial musculature and physiological responses. It seems perfectly plausible also that they each have associated with them a characteristic qualitative feel. The six core emotions are fear, anger, surprise, disgust, happiness, and sadness.
29. There is, of course, nothing like perfect coordination among the parts of the brain. Structurally, the human brain is triune, with an old mammalian brain on top of a reptilian brain, all covered by our large neomammalian brain. Emotional life appears to originate in the lower parts, and it displays a certain amount of impenetrability to control from above.
30. D. Dennett (1986).
31. G. M. Edelman (1987, 1989).
32. Edelman (1989), p. 30.
33. Ibid., p. 52.
34. The wonderful analogy of shifting geographical boundaries comes from William Calvin (1990), p. 175.
35. See G. M. Edelman (1989) for a much more complete story.
36. G. M. Edelman (1989), p. 94.
37. There is strong evidence that the dorsal parietal region of the cortex is essential to concern for the well-being of the self. Lesions in these areas result in a loss of self-concern. Conversely, lesions in ventral (temporal) regions of the cortex diminish attention to and awareness of the external world. See Gardner (1983), p. 266.
38. Dennett (1989), p. 9.
39. Absent and inverted qualia give functionalism lots of trouble. See P. M. Churchland (1988) for an excellent discussion.
40. P. M. Churchland (1988, 1989).
41. William Calvin (1990), pp. 144–145.
42. P. M. Churchland (1989), p. 106.
43. P. M. Churchland (1988), p. 150.
44. The distinction is related to Dennett's (1969) distinction between awareness$_1$ and awareness$_2$. I prefer my distinction because Dennett's informational sensitivity, awareness$_2$, seems to me (often) not to involve awareness. The same is true for Robert Van Gulick's conception of "opaquely embedded consciousness" in his important (1988) paper—it need not involve experience or awareness. On the other hand, Van Gulick's "transparent consciousness" is experienced.
45. See N. F. Dixon (1987).
46. In thinking that dreams should be classified as experiences, I am agreeing with J. Allan Hobson (1988), who writes, "Consciousness is the continuous, subjec-

tive awareness of the activity of billions of cells firing at many times a second, communicating instantaneously with tens of thousands of their neighbors. And the organization of this symphony of activity is such that it is sometimes externally oriented (during waking), sometimes oblivious to the outside world (during sleep), and sometimes so remarkably aware of itself (during dreams) that it recreates the external world in its own image" (p. 133). Dennett (1978f) is skeptical that dreams should be classified as experiences. In part, this is because experience for him depends more than it does for me on guiding behavior, on being able to say what one is experiencing, and on recall.

47. P. S. Churchland (1986b), p. 108.

48. William Calvin (1990), p. 175.

49. One problem with Dennett's awareness$_1$ is that it characterizes conscious awareness as information that is in, or capable of being outputed by, the speech center. Besides possibly tying conscious experience too closely to language, this way of thinking tempts us to think that all conscious experience is routed to or through some center. Dennett himself is now leading the charge to abandon the idea of a center of consciousness.

50. See Jackendoff (1987) for a computational account compatible with this sort of neural account.

51. Smolensky (1988), p. 12.

52. See Weiskrantz (1988).

53. McGinn (1989), pp. 356–357.

54. Ibid., p. 357.

55. Ibid., p. 363.

56. Ibid., p. 358, my italics.

57. Ibid., p. 359.

58. Ibid., pp. 359–360.

59. If there is no God, the story of consciousness is presumably "absolutely" closed. Even creatures much smarter than us (highly evolved aliens, for example) couldn't understand our conscious minds, since even if they were staring right at the neural processes upon which our consciousness supervenes, they would not be able to make the link from these brain states to our consciousness intelligible if their consciousness had a different qualitative character from ours. The reason is Nagel's reason: they would not be able to *capture* what it is like to be us. See Nagel (1979d) and McGinn (1989), pp. 355–356.

60. In (1989), p. 357, McGinn writes that P "is closed to perception." This is false if P is understood to refer to just those observable features of the brain upon which consciousness supervenes. It is true if P must be seen under the description that captures its phenomenal, qualitative properties. But I have already explained why P can't be seen in that way (without guidance from some theory, which McGinn does not allow), even though conscious mental life supervenes on P.

61. McGinn (1989), pp. 357–358.

62. Nagel (1979a), p. 183.

63. McGinn (1989), p. 359.

64. Ibid., p. 353.

65. Ibid., p. 353.

66. Nagel (1986), p. 49, admits that his dual-aspect theory involves a certain amount of "hand waving," is exceedingly elusive, and perhaps not "perfectly intelligible." I think he is right, and so I offer no apologies for not making his version perfectly intelligible.

67. Nagel (1986), p. 46.

68. Nagel, (1986), p. 31.

69. John Dewey (1922), p. 62.
70. The epiphenomenalist suspicion can be extraordinarily hard to dispel. Take the case of pain. The usual hypothesis is that the experience of pain plays a functional role in mediating responses to potentially harmful stimuli. The epiphenomenalist hypothesis is that the experience of pain is just a very noticeable added attraction of the causal fray, all sparkle, glitter, and noise, that in fact does no useful work. One might think that the first hypothesis easily defeats the second, since individuals who are otherwise normal but who lack pain receptors on their skin are in constant danger of being scalded, of hemorrhaging, of losing fingers, limbs, and life. The trouble is that it can be argued that these people are disfunctional not because they do not experience pain but because they lack the receptors that, besides getting people to remove their hands, etc., from harmful objects, also typically give rise to feelings of a certain sort.
71. B. Libet (1985).
72. Ibid., p. 530.
73. Ibid., p. 536.
74. Ibid., p. 536–537. Libet points out that so long as there is veto power, a trigger would be redundant. That is, consciousness allows the action to proceed to consummation unless it has reason to stop it. So long as it can stop a motor movement before it occurs, it does not need to actively trigger it.
75. The power of intentions to be carried out come what may is made vivid in cases where individuals suffer petit mal seizures while driving to some destination and who then unconsciously complete the drive to that destination. Once they have reached the destination, they just stop, unless they come out of the seizure-induced sleeplike state!
76. See the responses of Charles Wood (1985) and Robert Van Gulick (1985) to Libet's target article (1985) for related points. These responses are published as "Peer Commentary" with Libet's article.
77. The word "typically" is important. It is fairly easy to tell a story about the emergence of the emotions that gives them a role in enhancing fitness. This is compatible with certain emotional displays being less functional now than they were originally. The biological function of objectless moods, especially bad ones, is fairly obscure. Further, much of what we are conscious of is culturally transmitted. The capacities to learn that subserve the acquisition of knowledge are clearly adaptive. But the details of what we learn and how we use the information we acquire, e.g., about how to make weapons, may or may not be functional in the short or long run.
78. I am depending here especially on Anthony J. Marcel (1988) and Van Gulick (1990).
79. Marcel (1988), p. 136.
80. A. R. Luria (1972).
81. Luria (1972), p. 72.
82. William James (1892), p. 43. On one interpretation, Kant's view that the representation "I think" accompanies all my thoughts is similar. See David Rosenthal (1986) for an analysis of conscious thoughts as involving "higher order thoughts." According to Rosenthal, "a mental state is conscious if it is accompanied by a suitable higher order thought" (p. 336).
83. There may actually be exceptions to this generalization about the ubiquity of this low-level sense that "this is my experience." For example, autistics and persons suffering from severe dissociative psychoses of certain sorts may lack the relevant connections to their "own" experiences.
84. The principle was coined by Dennett (1989).

85. Dennett (1988a).
86. See N. Humphrey and D. Dennett (1989) for a gripping account of MPD. Almost all MPD patients were sexually or otherwise physically abused as children. They create additional selves to fend off the pain of the abuse. Often the abuser helps in the process of construction, presumably to reduce his own dissonance at being so awful, by offering alters to the child as they play "Daddy games." Why there is such a proliferation of alters once the process starts is unclear, but why a child would want not to be the self who was abused and would not want to see one or more of her caretakers as an abuser is easy to understand.
87. Dennett (1989), p. 15.
88. P. N. Johnson-Laird (1983), p. 463. See also Johnson-Laird (1988), pp. 353–368.
89. Johnson-Laird (1983), p. 464 and also p. 477.
90. R. Weiss (1990), p. 172. Actually, Ken Winkler tells me, many birds that migrate long distances, Canadian geese, for example, depend on a cadre of leaders trading the leader's role to avoid exhaustion. They work like a team of cyclists who trade the lead and tuck in behind the ever changing beacon to catch the vacuum he creates. The fact remains that neither in the case of swarming starling or sparrow flocks nor in the case of flocks of geese or ducks does any single leader run the whole show.
91. William Calvin (1990), p. 269.
92. Ibid., p. 270, my italics.
93. P. M. Churchland (1989), p. 105.

Bibliography

Adler, J. E. 1984. "Abstraction Is Uncooperative." *Journal for the Theory of Social Behavior.* 14:165–181.

Anderson, A. 1964. *Minds and Machines.* Englewood Cliffs, N.J.: Prentice-Hall.

Anderson, J. 1980. *Cognitive Psychology and Its Implications.* San Francisco: Freeman.

Anderson, J. 1983. *The Architecture of Cognition.* Cambridge: Harvard University Press.

Bleilin, H. 1971. "The Development of Physical Concepts." In Mischel 1971.

Block, N. 1971. "Are Mechanistic and Teleological Explanations of Behavior Incompatible?" *Philosophical Quarterly* 10:109–117.

Block, N. 1980a. *Readings in Philosophy of Psychology.* 2 vols. Cambridge: Harvard University Press.

Block, N. 1980b. "Troubles with Functionalism." In Block 1980a.

Block, N., ed. 1981. *Imagery.* Cambridge: MIT Press.

Boden, M. 1977. *Artificial Intelligence and Natural Man.* New York: Basic Books.

Boden, M. 1979. *Jean Piaget.* New York: Viking.

Boden, M. 1981a. *Minds and Mechanisms: Philosophical Psychology and Computational Models.* Ithaca: Cornell University Pres.

Boden, M. 1981b. "Artificial Intelligence and Piagetian Theory." In Boden 1981a.

Boden, M. 1981c. "Human Values in a Mechanistic Universe." In Boden 1981a.

Blum, L. 1980. *Friendship, Altruism, and Morality.* London: Routledge & Kegan Paul.

Brainerd, C. J. 1978. "The Stage Question in Cognitive-Developmental Theory." *Behavioral and Brain Sciences* 2:173–213.

Bridgman, P. 1927. *The Logic of Modern Physics.* New York: Macmillan.

Burian, R. 1981–1982. "Human Sociobiology and Genetic Determinism." *Philosophical Forum* 13 (2–3): 43–66.

Calvin, W. H. 1990. *The Cerebral Symphony: Seashore Reflections on the Structure of Consciousness.* New York: Bantam.

Caplan, A. L., ed. 1978. *The Sociobiology Debate.* New York: Harper & Row.

Caplan, A. L. 1981–1982. "Say It Just Ain't So: Adaptational Stories and Sociobiological Explanations of Social Behavior." *Philosophical Forum* 13 (2–3): 144–160.

Carey, S. 1983. "Are Children Fundamentally Different Thinkers and Learners than Adults?" In Chipman, Segal, and Glaser 1983.

Charniak, E., and McDermott, D. 1985. *Introduction to Artificial Intelligence.* Reading, Mass.: Addison-Wesley.

Chase, W., ed. 1973. *Visual Information Processing.* New York: Academic Press.

Cherniak, C. 1986. *Minimal Rationality.* Cambridge: MIT Press.

Chipman, S., Segal, J., and Glaser, R., eds. 1983. *Thinking and Learning Skills,* vol. 2 Hillsdale, N.J.: Erlbaum Associates.

Chomsky, N. 1959. "Review of Skinner's *Verbal Behavior.*" In Jakobovits and Miron 1967.

Chomsky, N. 1980. "Rules and Representations." *Behavioral and Brain Sciences* 3:1–61.

Churchland, P. M. 1981. "Eliminative Materialism and the Propositional Attitudes." *Journal of Philosophy* 78:67–90.

Churchland, P. M. 1984. *Matter and Consciousness*. Cambridge: MIT Press.

Churchland, P. M. 1988. *Matter and Consciousness*. Rev. ed. Cambridge: MIT Press.

Churchland, P. M. 1989. *A Neurocomputational Perspective: The Nature of Mind and the Structure of Science*. Cambridge: MIT Press.

Churchland, P. S. 1980. "A Perspective on Mind-Brain Research." *Journal of Philosophy* 77:185–207.

Churchland, P. S. 1983. "Consciousness: The Transmutation of a Concept." *Pacific Philosophical Quarterly* 64:80–95.

Churchland, P. S. 1986b. *Neurophilosophy*. Cambridge: MIT Press.

Cohen, L. J. 1981. "Can Human Irrationality Be Experimentally Demonstrated?" *The Behavioral and Brain Sciences* 4:317–333.

Cowan, J. D., and Sharp, D. H. 1988. "Neural Nets and Artificial Intelligence." *Daedalus* 117:85–121.

Craik, K. 1943. *the Nature of Explanation*. Cambridge: Cambridge University Press.

Cummins, R. 1980. "Functional Analysis." In Block 1980a.

Cummins, R. 1983. *Psychological Explanation*. Cambridge: MIT Press.

Darwin, C. 1859. *Origin of Species*. Ed. Ernst Mayr, 1964. Cambridge: Harvard University Press.

Davidson, D. 1970. "Mental Events." Reprinted in D. Davidson, *Essays on Actions and Events*. New York: Oxford University Press, 1980.

Dawkins, R. 1976. *The Selfish Gene*. Oxford: Oxford University Press.

Dennett, D. 1969. *Content and Consciousness*. London: Routledge & Kegan Paul.

Dennett, D. 1978a. *Brainstorms: Philosophical Essays on Mind and Psychology*. Montgomery, Vt.: Bradford Books.

Dennett, D. 1978b. "Intentional Systems." In Dennett 1978a.

Dennett, D. 1978c. "Free Will and Personhood." In Dennett 1978a.

Dennett, D. 1978d. "Skinner Skinned." In Dennett 1978a.

Dennett, D. 1978e. "Toward a Cognitive Theory of Consciousness." In Dennett 1978a.

Dennett, D. 1978f. "Are Dreams Experiences?" In Dennett 1978a.

Dennett, D. 1978g. "Why the Law of Effect Will Not Go Away." In Dennett 1978a.

Dennett, D. 1982. "How to Study Consciousness Empirically or Nothing Comes to Mind." *Synthese* 53 (2): 159–180.

Dennett, D. 1984. *Elbow Room: The Varieties of Free Will Worth Wanting*. Cambridge: MIT Press.

Dennett, D. 1986. "Julian Jaynes's Software Archeology." *Canadian Psychology* 27 (2): 149–154.

Dennett, D., and Haugeland, J. 1987. "Intentionality." In Gregory 1987. *Oxford Companion to the Mind*. Oxford: Oxford University Press.

Dennett, D. 1988a. "Why Everyone Is a Novelist." *Times Literary Supplement*, September 16–22, 4, 459.

Dennett, D. 1988b. "The Evolution of Consciousness." CCM-88-1, Center for Cognitive Studies, Tufts University.

Dennett, D. 1989. "The Origins of Selves." Center for Cognitive Studies, Tufts University.

Descartes, R. 1634. *Traite de l'Homme*, vol. 11 of *Oeuvres de Descartes* (1897–1910). Paris: Charles Adam & Paul Tannery.

Descartes, R. 1637. *Discourse on Method*. In Haldane and Ross 1968.

Descartes, R. 1641. *Meditations*. In Haldane and Ross 1968.

Descartes, R. 1649. *Passions of the Soul*. In Haldane and Ross 1968.

Dewey, J. 1894. "The Ego as a Cause." In Ratner 1963.

Dewey, J. 1896. "The Reflex Arc Concept in Psychology." In Ratner 1963.

Dewey, J. 1922. *Human Nature and Conduct: An Introduction to Social Psychology*. New York: Modern Library, 1957.

Dewey, J. 1929. *Experience and Nature*. New York: Dover, 1958.

Dews, P., ed. 1970. *Festschrift for B. F. Skinner*. New York: Appleton-Century-Crofts.

Dixon, N. F. 1987. "Subliminal Perception." In Gregory 1987.

Donaldson, M. 1978. *Children's Minds*. New York: Norton.

Dreyfus, H. 1981. "From Micro-Worlds to Knowledge Representation: AI at an Impasse." In Haugeland 1981a.

Dreyfus, H., ed. 1982. *Husserl, Intentionality, and Cognitive Science*. Cambridge: MIT Press.

Dreyfus, H., and Dreyfus, S. E. 1988. "Making a Mind versus Modeling the Brain: Artificial Intelligence Back at a Branchpoint." *Daedalus* 117:15–43.

Edelman, G. M. 1987. *Neural Darwinism*. New York: Basic Books.

Edelman, G. M. 1989. *The Remembered Present: A Biological Theory of Consciousness*. New York: Basic Books.

Edwards, C. P. 1975. "Societal Complexity and Moral Development: A Kenyan Study." *Ethos* 3:505–527.

Ekman, P., Levinson, R. W., and Freisen, W. V. 1985. "Autonomic Nervous-System Activity Distinguishes among Emotions." *Science* 221: 1208–1210.

Elkind, D., and Flavell, J. 1969. *Studies in Cognitive Development*. New York: Oxford University Press.

Evans, Jonathan St. B. 1982. *The Psychology of Deductive Reasoning*. London: Routledge & Kegan Paul.

Flanagan, O. J. 1980a. "Explanation and Reduction." *American Psychologist* 35:974–975.

Flanagan, O. J. 1980b. "Skinnerian Metaphysics and the Problem of Operationism." *Behaviorism* (Spring): 1–13.

Flanagan, O. J. 1981. "Psychology, Progress, and the Problem of Reflexivity." *Journal of the History of the Behavioral Sciences* 17:375–386.

Flanagan, O. J. 1981–1982. "Is Morality Epiphenomenal?: The Failure of the Sociobiological Reduction of Ethics." *Philosophical Forum* 13 (2–3): 207–225.

Flanagan, O. J. 1982a. "Moral Structures?" *Philosophy of the Social Sciences* 12:255–270.

Flanagan, O. J. 1982b. "Quinean Ethics." *Ethics* 93:56–74.

Flanagan, O. J. 1982c. "Reply to Lawrence Kohlberg." *Ethics* 92:529–532.

Flanagan, O. J. 1982d. "Virtue, Sex, and Gender: Some Philosophical Reflections on the Moral Psychology Debate." *Ethics* 12:499–512.

Flanagan, O. J. 1991. *Varieties of Moral Personality: Ethics and Psychological Realism*. Cambridge: Harvard University Press.

Flanagan, O. J., and Adler, J. E. 1983. "Impartiality and Particularity." *Social Research* 50 (3): 576–596.

Flavell, J. H. 1963. *The Developmental Psychology of Jean Piaget*. Princeton, N.J.: Van Nostrand.

Flavell, J. H., and Wohlwill, J. F. 1969. "Formal and Functional Aspects of Cognitive Development." In Elkind and Flavell 1969.

Flower, E. and Murphy, M. 1977. *A History of Philosophy in America.* 2 vols. New York: Putnam.

Fodor, J. 1979. *The Language of Thought.* Cambridge: Harvard University Press. (First published by Crowell, London, 1975.)

Fodor, J. 1980. "On the Impossibility of Acquiring 'More Powerful' Structures." In M. Piattelli-Palmarini 1980.

Fodor, J. 1981a. *Representations: Philosophical Essays on the Foundations of Cognitive Science.* Cambridge: MIT Press.

Fodor, J. 1981b. "Methodological Solipsism." In Fodor 1981a.

Fodor, J. 1981c. "Special Sciences." In Fodor 1981a.

Fodor, J. 1983. *The Modularity of Mind.* Cambridge: MIT Press.

Ford, M. 1982. *William James's Philosophy: A New Perspective.* Amherst: University of Massachusetts Press.

Fromm, E. 1980. *Greatness and Limitations of Freud's Thought.* New York: Harper & Row.

Freud, S. 1917. *Introductory Lectures on Psychoanalysis.* New York: Norton.

Freud, S. 1933. *New Introductory Lectures on Psychoanalysis.* New York: Norton.

Freud, S. 1953–1974. *The Standard Edition of the Complete Psychological Works of Sigmund Freud.* Ed. J. Strachey. London: Hogarth.

Gardner, H. 1973. *The Quest for Mind: Piaget, Lévi-Strauss, and the Structuralist Tradition.* New York: Knopf.

Gardner, H. 1983. *Frames of Mind: The Idea of Multiple Intelligences.* New York: Basic Books.

Gardner, H. 1985. *The Mind's New Science: A History of the Cognitive Revolution.* New York: Basic Books.

Gay, P. 1988. *Freud: A Life for Our Time.* New York: Norton.

Geber, B., ed. 1977. *Piaget and Knowing: Studies in Genetic Epistemology.* London: Routledge & Kegan Paul.

Gelman, R. 1978. "Cognitive Development." *Annual Review of Psychology* 29:297–332.

Gilligan, C. 1977. "In a Different Voice: Women's Conceptions of Self and of Morality." *Harvard Educational Review* 47:481–517.

Gilligan, C. 1979. "Woman's Place in Man's Life Cycle." *Harvard Educational Review* 59:431–446.

Gilligan, C. 1982. *In a Different Voice.* Cambridge: Harvard University Press.

Gilligan, C., and Murphy, J. M. 1979. "Development from Adolescence to Adulthood: The Philosopher and the Dilemma of the Fact." In Kuhn 1979.

Gilman, S., ed. 1983. *Introducing Psychoanalytic Theory.* New York: Bruner/Mazel.

Ginsburg, H., and Opper, S. 1969. *Piaget's Theory of Intellectual Development: An Introduction.* Englewood Cliffs, N.J.: Prentice-Hall.

Goldman, A. 1986. *Epistemology and Cognition.* Cambridge: Harvard University Press.

Goodman, N. 1978. *Ways of Worldmaking.* Indianapolis: Hackett.

Gorman, R. P., and Sejnowski, T. J. 1988a. "Learned Classification of Sonar Targets Using a Massively-Parallel Network." *IEEE Transactions: Acoustics, Speech, and Signal Processing.*

Gorman, R. P., and Sejnowski, T. J. 1988b. "Analysis of Hidden Units in a Layered Network Trained to Classify Sonar Targets." *Neural Networks* 1:75–89.

Gould, S. J. 1978. "Biological Potential versus Biological Determinism." In Caplan 1978.

Gould, S. J. 1981. *The Mismeasure of Man.* New York: Norton.

Gould, S. J., and Lewontin, R. 1979. "The Spandrels of San Marco and the Panglossian Paradigm: A Critique of the Adaptationist Programme." *Proceedings of the Royal Society of London*, B, 205.

Gregory, R., ed. 1987. *The Oxford Companion to the Mind*. Oxford: Oxford University Press.

Gruber, H. 1982. "Genes for General Intellect Rather than for Particular Culture." *Behavioral and Brain Sciences* 5 (2): 11–12.

Gruber, H., and Voneche, J., eds. 1977. *The Essential Piaget*. New York: Basic Books.

Grünbaum, A. 1979. "Is Freudian Psychoanalytic Theory Pseudo-Scientific by Karl Popper's Criterion of Demarcation?" *American Philosophical Quarterly* 16 (2): 131–141.

Grünbaum, A. 1980. "Epistemological Liabilities of the Clinical Appraisal of Psychoanalytic Theory." *Nous* 14 (3): 307–385.

Grünbaum, A. 1984. *The Foundations of Psychoanalysis: A Philosophical Critique*. Berkeley: University of California Press.

Grünbaum, A. 1986. "Précis of *The Foundations of Psychoanalysis* with Peer Commentary." *Behavioral and Brain Sciences* 9 (2): 217–284.

Gunderson, K. 1971. *Mentality and Machines*. New York: Doubleday.

Haldane, E., and Ross, G., eds. 1968. *The Philosophical Works of Descartes*, vols. 1 and 2. Cambridge: Cambridge University Press.

Hamilton, W. D. 1964. "The Genetical Theory of Social Behavior I & II." *Journal of Theoretical Biology* 7:1–52.

Hare, R. M. 1981. *Moral Thinking: Its Levels, Method, and Point*. New York: Oxford University Press.

Harman, G. 1986. *Change in View*. Cambridge: MIT Press.

Haroutunian, S. 1983. *Equilibrium in the Balance: A Study of Psychological Explanation*. New York: Springer-Verlag.

Hartshorne, H., and May, M. A. 1928. *Studies in the Nature of Character*. Vol. 1, *Studies in Deceit*. New York: Macmillan.

Haugeland, J., ed. 1981a. *Mind Design*. Cambridge: MIT Press.

Haugeland, J. 1981b. "The Nature and Plausibility of Cognitivism." In Haugeland 1981a.

Haugeland, J. 1981c. "Semantic Engines: An Introduction to Mind Design." In Haugeland 1981a.

Haugeland, J. 1985. *Artificial Intelligence: The Very Idea*. Cambridge: MIT Press.

Hempel, C. 1958. "The Theoretician's Dilemma: A Study in the Logic of Theory Construction." In *Aspects of Scientific Explanation*. New York: Free Press, 1965.

Hillis, D. W. 1985. *The Connection Machine*. Cambridge: MIT Press.

Hobson, J. 1988. *The Dreaming Brain*. New York: Basic Books.

Hofstadter, D. 1980. *Gödel, Escher, Bach: An Eternal Golden Braid*. New York: Vintage.

Hofstadter, D., and Dennett, D. 1981. *The Mind's I*. New York: Basic Books.

Honderich, T., and Burnyeat, M., eds. 1979. *Philosophy As It Is*. New York: Penguin.

Humphrey, N., and Dennett, D. 1989. "Speaking for Ourselves." *Raritan: A Quarterly Review*, pp. 69–98.

Hunt, M. 1982. *The Universe Within: A New Science Explores the Human Mind*. New York: Simon & Schuster.

Inhelder, B., and Piaget, J. 1958. *The Growth of Logical Thinking from Childhood to Adolescence*. Trans. A. Parsons and S. Milgram. New York: Basic Books.

Jackendoff, R. 1987. *Consciousness and the Computational Mind*. Cambridge: MIT Press.

Jakobovits, L., and Miron, M., eds. 1967. *Readings in the Philosophy of Language*. Englewood Cliffs, N.J.: Prentice-Hall.

James, W. 1884. "The Dilemma of Determinism." Reprinted in W. James, *The Will to Believe and Other Essays in Popular Philosophy*. New York: Dover, 1956.

James W. 1890. *The Principles of Psychology*. 3 vols. Cambridge: Harvard University Press, 1976.

James, W. 1892. *Psychology: The Briefer Course*. New York: Harper & Row, 1961.

James, W. 1904. "Does Consciousness Exist?" Reprinted in *Essays in Radical Empiricism*. Cambridge: Harvard University Press, 1976.

Jaynes, J. 1976. *The Origin of Consciousness in the Breakdown of the Bicameral Mind*. Boston: Houghton Mifflin.

Johnson-Laird, P. N. 1983. *Mental Models*. Cambridge: Harvard University Press.

Johnson-Laird, P. N. 1988. *The Computer and the Mind: An Invitation to Cognitive Science*. Cambridge: Harvard University Press.

Jones, E. 1953. *The Life and Work of Sigmund Freud*, vols. 1 and 2. New York: H. Wolff.

Kahneman, D., Slovic, P., and Tversky, A. 1982. *Judgment under Uncertainty: Heuristics and Biases*. Cambridge: Cambridge University Press.

Kant, I. 1781. *Critique of Pure Reason*. Trans. N. Kemp Smith. London: Macmillan, 1929.

Kant, I. 1783. *Prolegomena to Any Future Metaphysics Which Will Be Able to Come Forward as a Science*. New York: Bobbs-Merrill, 1950.

Kant, I. 1785. *Foundations of the Metaphysics of Morals*. Trans. L. W. Beck. Indianapolis: Bobbs-Merrill, 1959.

Kaufmann, W. 1980. *Discoverying the Mind*, Vol. 2. New York: McGraw-Hill.

Kenny, A. 1968. *Descartes: A Study of His Philosophy*. New York: Random House.

Kitcher, P. 1985. *Vaulting Ambition: Sociobiology and the Quest for Human Nature*. Cambridge: MIT Press.

Kohlberg, L. 1973. "The Claim to Moral Adequacy of the Highest Stage of Moral Judgment." *Journal of Philosophy* 70:630–645.

Kohlberg, L. 1981a. *Essays on Moral Development*. Vol. 1, *The Philosophy of Moral Development*. San Francisco: Harper & Row.

Kohlberg, L. 1981b. "From 'Is' to 'Ought': How to Commit the Naturalistic Fallacy and Get Away with It in the Study of Moral Development." In Kohlberg 1981a.

Kohlberg, L. 1981c. "Justice and Reversibility." In Kohlberg 1981a.

Kohlberg, L. 1982. "A Reply to Owen Flanagan and Some Comments on the Puka-Goodpaster Debate." *Ethics* 92:513–528.

Kohlberg, L. 1984. *Essays on Moral Development*. Vol. 2, *The Psychology of Moral Development*. San Francisco: Harper & Row.

Kohlberg, L., and Power, C. 1981d. "Moral Development, Religious Thinking and the Question of the Seventh Stage." In Kohlberg 1981a.

Kuhn, D. ed. 1979. *Intellectual Development Beyond Childhood*. San Francisco: Jossey-Bass.

Kosslyn, S., Pinker, S., Smith, G., and Shwartz, S. 1981. "On the Demystification of Mental Imagery." In Block 1981.

Lackner, J., and Garrett, M. 1973. "Resolving Ambiguity: Effects of Biasing Context in the Unattended Ear." *Cognition* 1:359–372.

Levins, R., and Lewontin, R. C. 1980. "Dialectics and Reductionism in Ecology." In Saarinen 1980.

Lewin, R. 1981. "Cultural Differences Tied to Genetic Differences." *Science* 212:908–910.

Lewis, D. 1980. "Mad Pain and Martian Pain." In Block 1980a.

Lewontin, R. C. 1970. "Units of Selection." *Annual Review of Ecology and Semantics* 1:1–13.

Libet, B. 1985. "Unconscious Cerebral Initiative and the Role of Conscious Will in Voluntary Action," with peer commentary. *Behavioral and Brain Sciences* 8:529–566.

Lloyd, D. 1989. *Simple Minds.* Cambridge: MIT Press.

Lumsden, C., and Wilson, E. O. 1981. *Genes, Mind and Culture: The Coevolutionary Process.* Cambridge: Harvard University Press.

Lumsden, C., and Wilson, E. O. 1982. "Precis of *Genes, Mind, and Culture.*" *The Behavioral and Brain Sciences* 5 (2): 1–7.

Luria, A. R. 1972. *The Man with the Shattered World.* Cambridge: Harvard University Press, 1987.

Lycan, W. G. 1981. "Form, Function, and Feel." *Journal of Philosophy* 78:23–49.

Lycan, W. G. 1987. *Consciousness.* Cambridge: MIT Press.

Lyons, W. 1986. *The Disappearance of Introspection.* Cambridge: MIT Press.

McGinn, C. 1989. "Can We Solve the Mind-Body Problem?" *Mind* 98:349–366.

MacIntyre, A. 1958. *The Unconscious.* London: Routledge & Kegan Paul.

MacIntyre, A. 1981. *After Virtue: A Study in Moral Theory.* London: Duckworth.

Macnamara, J. 1976. "Stomachs Assimilate and Accommodate, Don't They?" *Canadian Psychological Review* 17:167–173.

Macnamara, J. 1978. "Another Unaccommodating Look at Piaget." *Canadian Psychological Review* 19:781–788.

Macnamara, J. 1982. *Names for Things: A Study of Human Learning.* Cambridge: MIT Press.

Malcolm, J. 1981. *Psychoanalysis: The Impossible Profession.* New York: Knopf.

Mandler, G. 1985. *Cognitive Psychology: An Essay in Cognitive Science.* New York: Erlbaum.

Marcel, A. J. 1988. "Phenomenal Experience and Functionalism." In Marcel and Bisiach 1988.

Marcel, A. J., and Bisiach, E., eds. 1988. *Consciousness in Contemporary Science.* Oxford: Oxford University Press.

Marks, C. 1980. *Commissurotomy, Consciousness, and Unity of Mind.* Cambridge: MIT Press.

Martindale, C. 1981. *Cognition and Consciousness.* Homewood, Ill.: The Dorsey Press.

Mayr, E. 1982. *The Growth of Biological Thought: Diversity, Evolution, and Inheritance.* Cambridge: Harvard University Press.

Menkiti, I. 1978. *The Jubilation of Falling Bodies.* North Cambridge, Mass.: Pomegranite Press.

Miller, G. A., Galanter, E., and Pribram, K. H. 1960. *Plans and the Structure of Behavior.* New York: Holt.

Minsky, M. 1980. "Decentralized Minds." *The Behavioral and Brain Sciences* 3:439–440.

Minsky, M. 1981. "A Framework for Representing Knowledge." In Haugeland 1981a.

Mischel, T., ed. 1971. *Cognitive Development and Epistemology.* New York: Academic Press.

Morick, H., ed. 1967. *Wittgenstein and the Problem of Other Minds.* New York: McGraw-Hill.

Myers, G. E. 1986. *William James: His Life and Thought.* New Haven: Yale University Press.

Nagel, T. 1979a. *Mortal Questions.* London: Cambridge University Press.

Nagel, T. 1979b. "Brain Bisection and the Unity of Consciousness." In Nagel 1979a.

Nagel, T. 1979c. "Subjective and Objective." In Nagel 1979a.

Nagel, T. 1979d. "What Is It Like to Be A Bat?" In Nagel 1979a.

Nagel, T. 1986. *The View from Nowhere.* New York: Oxford University Press.

Neisser, U. 1966. *Cognitive Psychology.* New York: Appleton-Century-Crofts.

Newell, A. 1973. "You Can't Play 20 Questions with Nature and Win." In Chase 1973.

Nisbett, R. E., and Wilson, T. D. 1977. "Telling More than We Can Know: Verbal Reports on Mental Processes." *Psychological Review* 84:231–259.

Nisbett, R. E., and Ross, L. 1980. *Human Inference: Strategies and Shortcomings of Social Judgment.* Englewood Cliffs, N.J.: Prentice-Hall.

Nozick, R. 1974. *Anarchy, State, and Utopia.* New York: Basic Books.

Nozick, R. 1981. *Philosophical Explanations.* Cambridge: Harvard University Press.

Oldenquist, A. 1982. "Loyalties." *Journal of Philosophy* 79:173–193.

Osherson, D. N. 1974. *Logical Abilities in Children.* Hillsdale, N.J.: Erlbaum.

Osherson, D. N. 1990. *An Invitation to Cognitive Science.* 3 vols. Cambridge: MIT Press.

Papert, S. 1980. *Mindstorms: Children, Computers, and Powerful Ideas.* New York: Basic Books.

Parfit, D. 1979. "Personal Identity." In Honderich and Burnyeat 1979.

Pavlov, I. P. 1927. *Conditioned Reflexes: An Investigation of the Physiological Activity of the Cortex.* Trans. and ed. G. Anrep. London: Oxford University Press.

Perry, R. B. 1938. *In the Spirit of William James.* New Haven: Yale University Press.

Peters, R. S. 1966. *Ethics and Education.* London: Allen & Unwin.

Piaget, J. 1932. *The Moral Judgment of the Child.* New York: Harcourt, Brace.

Piaget, J. 1970. *Genetic Epistemology.* New York: Columbia University Press.

Piaget, J. 1971. *Biology and Knowledge: An Essay on the Relations Between Organic Regulations and Cognitive Processes.* Chicago: University of Chicago Press.

Piaget, J. 1977a. *The Development of Thought: Equilibration of Cognitive Structures.* New York: Viking.

Piaget, J. 1977b. "Problems of Equilibration." In Gruber and Voneche 1977.

Piaget, J. 1978. *Behavior and Evolution.* Trans. D. Nicholson-Smith. New York: Pantheon.

Piaget, J. 1980a. *Adaptation and Intelligence: Organic Selection and Phenocopy.* Trans. S. Eames. Chicago: University of Chicago Press.

Piaget, J. 1980b. "Schemes of Action and Language Learning." In Piattelli-Palmarini 1980.

Piattelli-Palmarini, M., ed. 1980. *Language and Learning: The Debate between Jean Piaget and Noam Chomsky.* Cambridge: Harvard University Press.

Plato. *The Republic.* In E. Hamilton and H. Cairns, eds., *The Collected Dialogues.* New York: Pantheon, 1960.

Popper, K. 1968. *Conjectures and Refutations: The Growth of Scientific Knowledge.* New York: Harper & Row.

Popper, K., and Eccles, J. 1977. *The Self and Its Brain.* New York: Springer-Verlag.

Puccetti, R. 1973. "Brain Bisection and Personal Identity." *British Journal for the Philosophy of Science* 24:339–355.

Puka, B. 1982. "An Interdisciplinary Treatment of Kohlberg." *Ethics* 92:468–490.

Putnam, H. 1979. "The 'Corroboration' of Theories." In Honderich and Burnyeat 1979.

Putnam, H. 1980. "What is Innate and Why." In Piattelli-Palmarini 1980.

Putnam, H. 1981a. *Reason, Truth, and History.* London: Cambridge University Press.

Putnam, H. 1981b. "Reductionism and the Nature of Psychology." In Haugeland 1981a.

Pylyshyn, Z. 1980. "Computation and Cognition: Issues in the Foundations of Cognitive Science." *The Behavioral and Brain Sciences* 3:111–132.

Pylyshyn, Z. 1981. "Complexity and the Study of Artificial and Human Intelligence." In Haugeland 1981a.

Quine, W. V. 1960. *Word and Object.* Cambridge: MIT Press.

Quine, W. V. 1969. "Epistemology Naturalized." In Quine, *Ontological Relativity and Other Essays.* New York: Columbia University Press.

Rancurello, A. 1968. *A Study of Franz Brentano: His Psychological Standpoint and His Significance in the History of Psychology.* New York: Academic Press.

Ratner, J., ed. 1963. *Philosophy, Psychology, and Social Practice.* New York: Capricorn.

Rawls, J. 1971. *A Theory of Justice.* Cambridge: Harvard University Press.

Reeke, G. N., Jr., and Edelman, G. M. 1988. "Real Brains and Artificial Intelligence." *Daedalus* 117:143–173.

Rest, J. 1979. *Developments in Judging Moral Issues.* Minneapolis: University of Minnesota Press.

Rey, G. 1980. "Functionalism and the Emotions." In Rorty 1980.

Rey, G. 1981. "What Are Mental Images?" In Block 1981.

Rorty, A., ed. 1980. *Explaining Emotions.* Berkeley: University of California Press.

Rorty, R. 1979. Philosophy and the Mirror of Nature. Princeton: Princeton University Press.

Rorty, R. 1982a. *Consequences of Pragmatism.* Minneapolis: University of Minnesota Press.

Rorty, R. 1982b. "Contemporary Philosophy of Mind." *Synthese* 53 (2): 323–348.

Rosenblatt, F. 1962. *Principles of Neurodynamics.* New York: Spartan.

Rosenthal, D. 1986. "Two Concepts of Consciousness." *Philosophical Studies* 49:329–359.

Rumelhart, D., and McClelland, J., and the PDP Research Group. 1986. *Parallel Distributed Processing: Explorations in the Microstructure of Cognition.* 2 vols. Cambridge: MIT Press.

Ruse, M. 1979. *Sociobiology: Sense or Nonsense?* Boston: D. Reidel.

Russell, B. 1927. *An Outline of Philosophy.* New York: Meridian.

Ryle, G. 1949. *The Concept of Mind.* London: Hutchinson.

Saarinen, E., ed. 1980. *Conceptual Issues in Ecology.* Boston: D. Reidel.

Sacks, O. 1985. *The Man Who Mistook His Wife for a Hat and Other Clinical Tales.* New York: Summit.

Schank, R. 1982. *Dynamic Memory.* Cambridge: Cambridge University Press.

Schank, R., and Abelson, R. 1977. *Scripts, Plans, Goals, and Understanding.* Hillsdale, N.J.: Erlbaum.

Scheffler, I. 1974. *Four Pragmatists: A Critical Introduction to Pierce, James, Mead, and Dewey.* New York: Humanities Press.

Schwartz, J. T. 1988. "The New Connectionism: Developing Relationships between Neuroscience and Artificial Intelligence." *Daedalus* 117:123–141.

Searle, J. 1980. "Minds, Brains, and Programs." *The Behavioral and Brain Sciences* 3:417–457. Reprinted in Haugeland 1981a.

Searle, J. 1982. "The Myth of the Computer." *New York Review of Books,* April 29, 3–6.

Searle, J. 1984. *Minds, Brains, and Science.* Cambridge: Harvard University Press.

Sejnowski, T., and Rosenberg, C. 1987. "NETtalk: A Parallel Network That Learns to Read Aloud." Electrical Engineering and Computer Science Technical Report JHU/EECS-86/01, Johns Hopkins University.

Sejnowski, T., and Rosenberg, C. 1987. "Parallel Networks That Learn to Pronounce English Text." *Complex Systems* 1:145–168.

Shepard, R. N., and Metzler, J. 1971. "Mental Rotation of Three-Dimensional Objects." *Science* 171:701–703.

Shweder, R. 1982. "Liberalism as Destiny." *Contemporary Psychologist* 27:421–424.

Simon, H. 1974. *The Sciences of the Artificial*. Cambridge: MIT Press.

Simon, R., and Zegura, S. 1979. "Sociobiology and Morality." *Social Research* 46 (4): 766–786.

Simpson, E. L. 1974. "Moral Development Research: A Case Study of Scientific Cultural Bias." *Human Development* 17:81–106.

Singer, P. 1981. *The Expanding Circle: Ethics and Sociobiology*. New York: Farrar, Straus & Giroux.

Skinner, B. F. 1948. *Walden Two*. New York: Macmillan.

Skinner, B. F. 1953. *Science and Human Behavior*. New York: Macmillan.

Skinner, B. F. 1957. *Verbal Behavior*. New York: Appleton-Century-Crofts.

Skinner, B. F. 1964. "Behaviorism at 50." In Skinner 1972a.

Skinner, B. F. 1970. "Sketch for an Autobiography." In Dews 1970.

Skinner, B. F. 1971. *Beyond Freedom and Dignity*. New York: Knopf.

Skinner, B. F. 1972a. *Cumulative Record: A Selection of Papers*. New York: Appleton-Century-Crofts.

Skinner, B. F. 1972b. "Are Theories of Learning Necessary?" In Skinner 1972a.

Skinner, B. F. 1972c. *Contingencies of Reinforcement: A Theoretical Analysis*. New York: Appleton-Century-Crofts.

Skinner, B. F. 1972d. "A Critique of Psychoanalytic Theories and Concepts." In Skinner 1972a.

Skinner, B. F. 1972e. "Freedom and Control of Men." In Skinner 1972a.

Skinner, B. F. 1972f. "The Operational Analysis of Psychological Terms." In Skinner 1972a.

Skinner, B. F. 1976. *About Behaviorism*. New York: Knopf.

Skinner, B. F. 1979. *The Shaping of a Behaviorist*. New York: Knopf.

Skinner, B. F. 1981. "Selection by Consequences." *Science* 213: 501–504.

Smart, J. J. C. 1959. "Sensations and Brain Processes." *Philosophical Review* 68:141–156.

Smith, L. D. 1986. *Behaviorism and Logical Positivism*. Stanford: Stanford University Press.

Smolensky, P. 1988. "On the Proper Treatment of Connectionism." *Behavioral and Brain Sciences* 11:1–23.

Sober, E. 1980. "Holism, Individualism and the Units of Selection." In *Proceedings of the Philosophy of Science Association* 2:93–121.

Sternberg, S. 1966. "High-Speed Scanning in Human Memory." *Science* 153:652–654.

Stich, S. 1983. *Folk Psychology and Cognitive Science: The Case against Belief*. Cambridge: MIT Press.

Stillings, N., et al. 1987. *Cognitive Science: An Introduction*. Cambridge: MIT Press.

Sulloway, F. 1979. *Freud: The Biologist of the Mind*. New York: Basic Books.

Taylor, C. 1964. *The Explanation of Behaviour,* London: Routledge & Kegan Paul.

Tolman, E. C. 1948. "Cognitive Maps in Rats and Men." *Psychological Review* 55:189–208.

Trivers, R. L. 1971. "The Evolution of Reciprocal Altruism." *Quarterly Review of Biology* 46:35–57.

Turing, A. M. 1937. "On Computable Numbers, with an Application to the *Entscheidungsproblem*." In *Proceedings of the London Mathematical Society* 42:230–265.

Turing, A. M. 1950. "Computing Machinery and Intelligence." Reprinted in Anderson 1964.

Turkle, S. 1984. *Computers and the Second Self: Computers and the Human Spirit*. New York: Simon & Schuster.

Tversky, A., and Kahneman, D. 1974. "Judgment under Uncertainty: Heuristics and Biases." *Science* 185:1124–1131. Reprinted in Kahneman, Slovic, and Tversky 1982.

Van Gulick, R. 1988. "A Functionalist Plea for Self-Consciousness." *Phiosophical Review* 97 (2): 149–181

Van Gulick, R. 1990. "What Difference Does Consciousness Make?" *Philosophical Topics* 17 (1): 211–230.

Van Gulick, R. 1982. "Information Feedback and Transparency." *The Behavioral and Brain Sciences* 5 (2): 27–29.

Von Eckardt, B. 1978. "Inferring Functional Localization from Neurological Evidence." In Walker 1978.

Von Eckardt, B. 1983. "The Scientific Status of Psychoanalysis." In S. Gilman 1983.

Walker, E., ed. 1978. *Explorations in the Biology of Language.* Cambridge: MIT Press.

Wason, P. C. 1977. "The Theory of Formal Operations: A Critique." In Geber 1977.

Wason, P. C., and Johnson-Laird, P. 1972. *The Psychology of Reasoning.* London: Batsford.

Weiskrantz, L. 1988. "Some Contributions of Neuropsychology of Vision and Memory to the Problem of Consciousness." In Marcel and Bisiach 1988.

Weiss, R. 1990. "A Flight of Fancy Mathematics: Chaos Brings Harmony to a Birder's Puzzle." *Science News* 137:172.

Weizenbaum, J. 1976. *Computer Power and Human Reason.* San Francisco: Freeman.

Williams, B. 1973. *Problems of the Self.* Cambridge: Cambridge University Press.

Williams, B. 1978. *Descartes: The Project of Pure Enquiry.* Atlantic Highlands, N.J.: Humanities Press.

Williams, B. 1982. *Moral Luck.* Cambridge: Cambridge University Press.

Williams, G. C. 1966. *Adaptation and Natural Selection.* Princeton: Princeton University Press.

Wilson, E. O. 1971. *Insect Societies.* Cambridge: Harvard University Press.

Wilson, E. O. 1975. *Sociobiology: The New Synthesis.* Cambridge: Harvard University Press.

Wilson, E. O. 1978. *On Human Nature.* Cambridge: Harvard University Press.

Wilson, M. 1978. *Descartes.* London: Routledge & Kegan Paul.

Wimsatt, W. C. 1980. "Reductionistic Research Strategies and Their Biases in the Units of Selection Controversy." In Saarinen 1980.

Wollheim, R. 1974. *Freud: A Collection of Critical Essays.* Garden City, N.Y.: Anchor.

Wollheim, R., and Hopkins, J. 1982. *Philosophical Essays on Freud.* Cambridge: Cambridge University Press.

Name Index

Subject Index

Phenotype. *See* Genotype-phenotype
Phronesis, 252
Physicalism. *See* Materialism; Token physicalism; Type physicalism
Physical stance, 180–181. *See also* Design stance; Intentional stance
Physics, 131, 149
Piaget's adequacy thesis, 144–149
Pineal gland, 5, 367 n. 2
Pleasure principle, 56, 70, 135
Pragmatism, 18, 37
Prediction, 94–95, 113
 and computers, 246–248
Preformation. *See* Nativism
Principle of conservation of energy, 20–21, 64, 369 n. 21
Private events (covert events), 85, 87, 89, 90, 97, 100–102
Productions (conditional rules), 231
Propositional attitudes. *See* Belief; Intentionality
Prosopagnosia. *See* Face recognition
Psychoanalysis, 55–82. *See also* Unconscious
 dreams, 67–70, 77–79
 paranoia, 77–81
 parapraxes, 67–69
 relation of theory and therapy, 76
 scientific status of, 74–81
 self-analysis, 76
Psychokinesis, 7
Purpose(fulness), 27–28, 30–31, 36, 52, 84–85
 problem of, 104, 106, 108, 110–112

Qualia, 314–318, 394 n. 39
 absent qualia, 344–348
 experiential sensitivity v. informational sensitivity, 329–331
 and identity theory, 323, 326–329, 331–335

Radiality, 334–335
Rationality, 208–216, 260
Reality principle, 70, 135
Reductionism, 88, 259–260
 and bridge laws, 61, 217–218
 and functionalism, 218–221
 and identity theory, 217–218
 and materialism, 58–66
 and sociobiology, 267, 287–305
Reflex, 1
 conditional reflexes, 4, 105 (*see also*

Classical conditioning)
reflex arc, 3–5, 11, 34
reflex mechanism, 4–6, 8, 9, 23, 24
unconditioned reflexes, 105
Representational theory of mind, 30, 50, 52, 149, 178, 225, 259, 304
Representations, mental, 28, 29, 61, 125, 148. *See also* Intentionality
 emergent representational powers, 140
 imagistic v. propositional, 188–193
 six-code theory of mental representation, 188–193, 386 n. 17
 unified-code theory of mental representation, 188–193, 386 n. 17
Representativeness, 211–212. *See also* Rationality
Res cogitans, 4, 9, 11, 64, 87, 91, 113. *See also* Mind-body dualism
Res extensa, 4, 9, 11, 64. *See also* Mind-body dualism

Santayana's sin, xii
Selection by consequences, 104, 109, 111
Self as center of narrative gravity, 353–361
Self-knowledge, 13, 96, 116, 152–153, 156, 184. *See also* Cartesianism on self-knowledge; Consciousness; Introspection
 and cognitive science, 193–200, 259–260
 Descartes, 66–67
 and language learning, 98–104
 and psychoanalysis, 66–74, 81
 and psychological health, 66
 Skinner, 98–104
Semantics and computers, 227–229, 255–258
Social learning theory, 9, 165
Sociobiology, 265–305
 and altruism, 276, 289
 and argument from adaptation, 278–279
 and argument from analogy principle, 275–277
 and culture, 266, 267, 271, 275, 280–287
 and culturgens, 280, 281
 epigenetic rules, 280–287
 and horizontal influences, 272–273, 282, 290–291
 and meaning of life, 293